Seeking Solutions

Seeking Solutions

Framework and Cases
for
Small Enterprise
Development Programs

edited by
Charles K. Mann
Merilee S. Grindle
Parker Shipton
Harvard Institute for
International Development

KUMARIAN PRESS

AskARIES is a trademark of the President and Fellows of Harvard College.

This book was written, edited and designed on Apple® Macintosh™ computers
using Microsoft Word® 3.02 and Aldus Pagemaker® 3.0. Pages were proofed on
an Apple® LaserWriter® II NT and final pages were printed on a Linotype®
Linotronic™ 300P.

Edited by Barbara A. Conover

Cover design by Marilyn Penrod

Printed in the United States of America

Library of Congress Cataloging in Publication Data
Mann, Charles K. (Charles Kellogg), 1934–
    Seeking solutions.

    (Library of management for development) (Kumarian
Press case studies series)
    Bibliography: p.
    Includes index.
    1. Small business—Government policy—Developing
countries. 2. Small business—Government policy—
Developing countries—Case studies. I. Grindle,
Merilee Serrill. II. Shipton, Parker MacDonald.
III. Title. IV. Series. V. Series: Kumarian Press
case studies series.
HD2346.5.M36 1989   338.6′42′091724   89-2568
ISBN 0-931816-77-7

Contents

Part III   The *AskARIES Knowledgebase*
Charles K. Mann

Tables

Part I

Part II

Part III

Preface

During the past decade, numerous studies have drawn attention to the important role of small-scale and micro-enterprises in the development process. In addition to many individuals, a number of institutions have helped to generate important insights into how such enterprises contribute to production, employment, investment, and human resource development. In particular, work sponsored by the Agency for International Development, the World Bank, Michigan State University, the Cranfield Institute of Technology, and the International Labor Organization has enriched the understanding of the role of small enterprise in developing countries' social and economic structures.

Much of this research indicated that small and micro-enterprises could be assisted through: (1) focusing more attention on improving the policy environment, particularly as it affects small enterprise; and (2) strengthening the intermediary resource institutions that promote and assist small and micro-enterprises. This book addresses the second need. It deals centrally with the issues faced by the resource institutions as they attempt to design, implement, monitor, and evaluate assistance programs for small and micro-enterprises. Its purpose is to provide guidance about how institutions and their programs can become more efficient, effective, and sustainable. To this end, we draw extensively on the literature about assistance programs and small-scale enterprise and on the experience of resource institutions responding to the needs of low income clients in developing countries. In addition, field research with resource institutions has produced the series of twenty-one teaching cases that comprise Part II of this book. These recreate key decision points in the evolution of diverse approaches to enterprise development. They are intended for use in training programs and workshops that feature the case method approach. A separate Case Leader's Guide to the ARIES cases is available.

An important companion to this book is the *AskARIES Knowledgebase*, described more fully in Part III. This system uses the personal computer to organize the core knowledge of small enterprise development and to make it accessible in remote field locations. In effect, it represents a desktop library focusing on the problems of enterprise development and their potential solutions. Organized according to the recurrent problem framework set forth in Chapter 4 of this volume, *AskARIES* extracts from the core literature of the field insights and information of special relevance to each problem area. It also contains conventional summaries of each included document. The organizing framework, developed in collaboration with leading practitioners in the field, is adaptable for institutions to use in communicating new ideas and findings among themselves.

Acknowledgments

This book and the *AskARIES Knowledgebase* are the result of the ARIES project (Assistance to Resource Institutions for Enterprise Support), created in 1985 and funded by the Office of Rural and Institutional Development (Bureau for Science and Technology) and the Office for Private and Voluntary Cooperation (Bureau for Food for Peace and Voluntary Assistance) of the Agency for International Development.[1] The project combined technical assistance, applied research, and training for public and private sector organizations that sponsor enterprise development programs. In this endeavor, ARIES built on the research output and experience generated through the PISCES I and PISCES II projects that were funded by USAID between 1978 and 1985.[2]

As in any large-scale undertaking of this sort, our intellectual debts are manifold. The footnotes and bibliography formally acknowledge many colleagues and resource institution staff members who shared with us their knowledge and insight. However, there are many others we would like to thank here. We have benefited particularly from the opportunity to participate in several working sessions with the project's Technical Review Board. We are grateful to its members—Jeffrey Ashe, Jaime Carvajal, Jacob Levitsky, Carl Liedholm, Harthon Munson, and Howard Pack. Thomas Timberg, ARIES project manager, and his colleagues at Robert R. Nathan Associates have given us many valuable suggestions and leads. Beth Holmgren of ARIES subcontractor Control Data Corporation has provided useful information through CDC's "needs analysis" and surveys of training materials. Subcontractor Appropriate Technology International has made useful contributions.

We are grateful to the members of the SEEP Network (Small Enterprise Education and Promotion) and especially Elaine Edgcomb, its program coordinator, and Peggy Clark, formerly of Save the Children, now with the Ford Foundation. Much of the spirit of collaboration with the small enterprise development community that has enriched this work is due to Elaine's insights and initiatives, and to Peggy's suggestion at a SEEP/ARIES meeting that we organize a case teaching workshop at Harvard. Subsequently, it was members of SEEP who became the case teaching faculty at the pivotal Harper's Ferry Workshop on Credit Management and who continue to carry forward interest and momentum in the use of the case method both for training and for generating new knowledge about enterprise development.

At AID, Ross Bigelow has been a committed and informed project officer (even writing one of the cases); Michael Farbman has been consistently supportive of project activities; and Andrea Baumann has been of great assistance in the development of project components.

The HIID-ARIES research assistants deserve a special place in this acknowledgment. They have helped to develop the substance of the *AskARIES Knowledgebase* that underlies Part I of this book and the cases that comprise Part II. In alphabetical order, they are: Christopher Alden, Charles Alterkruse, Mary Barton, Eva Benedikt, Pia Bungarten, Shubham Chaudhuri, Julia Dubner, Elizabeth Francis, Cynthia Leigh Glass, Heidi Hennrich, Frank Hicks, Anne Hornsby, Gudrun Kochendorfer-Lucius, Rebecca Kramnick, Poh Lian Lim, Andrew Neitlich, Vijaya Ramachandran, Thomas Reis, Catherine Rielly, Elisabeth Rippy, Charles Ruhlin, Douglas Ryan, Laura Elaine Sejen, Stuart Sharp, Patricia Walker, R. Dieter Wittkowski, and Sarah Yeates. Cheryl Cvetic helped to set up the administrative framework for the project. Amy Sanders played a major role in orchestrating the transformation of working manuscript into camera-ready copy. Rajesh Pradhan has played an especially important role in the development of *AskARIES*, not only through his many insightful entries and his authorship of the *AskARIES* User's Guide, but by his indefatigable attention to the myriad details so essential to the success of this large-scale computer-based undertaking. He also was the key individual in what proved to be an extremely complex desktop publishing challenge: twenty-one cases with dozens of exhibits created on a variety of computer systems.

Our thanks also to Donald Morrison and Zach Deal, of Harvard's Office of Information Technology, who helped us select and set up the computerized system through which ARIES information is developed, organized, and shared. In helping to transform this book, and its companion materials, through laser-printed page proofs into typeset copy, we are grateful to Gary Bisbee and Joe Snowden of CHIRON, and to Michael Burner and Scott Bradner at the computer-based laboratory of the Psychology Department, Harvard University. Jeanne Tifft and her colleagues at USAID helped us tap the wealth of information available from previous AID-financed work. Susanna Badgley Place shared lessons from her work with the World Bank on small enterprise development. Although the project had no formal provision for translation, we are grateful to Dr. Maria Rausa, a Spanish visitor at Harvard with a special interest in small enterprise development, for her Spanish translations of ten of the cases.

We are grateful also to the many resource people who shared with us their insights on small enterprise development both informally and as speakers in the ARIES Seminar Series. We thank particularly Professors Judith Tendler and Bishwapriya Sanyal of MIT and HIID colleagues Tyler Biggs and Martha Chen. Their seminal contributions have enriched understanding of the development of small enterprises.

Professors Louis Wells and James Austin and Case Research Supervisor Mary Gentile at the Harvard Business School, Catherine Overholt, Kevin Murphy and Mary Anderson all contributed to the development of the ARIES cases and to the project's case teaching outreach efforts. Most importantly, we thank those institutions and individuals whose experiences and decisions are the subject of the ARIES cases. We and all who learn from these cases owe a great debt to those agencies and individuals who so candidly shared their experiences with the ARIES casewriters. Although all of the situations documented produced useful learnings, some of these were exceptionally painful. We applaud the courage and selflessness of those involved for sharing travail as well as triumph.

At HIID, Director Dwight Perkins and Executive Director Joseph Stern have strongly supported the unusual needs of this project, particularly those relating to the relatively large numbers of part-time research assistants and consequent space and computer requirements. We have particularly appreciated their support for the nontraditional publishing venture that *AskARIES* represents. We are grateful to HIID for providing the additional resources necessary for us to prepare for publication this book and its companion products, The *AskARIES Knowledgebase* and the *Case Leader's Guide*. Christopher Hale, John Pollock, Rosanne Kumins, Anne Rippy, and Leslie Hartie facilitated project administration in myriad ways, contributing importantly to its success. David Stein and Ellen Mitchell in Harvard's Office of Technology Transfer helped to guide all elements of the project into successful publication. In this respect we are especially grateful to Krishna Sondhi not only for her excellent publishing skills vis-à-vis *this* book, but for selecting *AskARIES* as the vehicle for moving Kumarian Press into the publication of non-traditional information resources. The editorial and computer skills of Kumarian's Jennifer Dixon have greatly facilitated bringing this complex publication task to fruition.

An unsung hero of *AskARIES* is Professor Paul Brest, who is Dean of the Stanford Law School, and founder and President of Pro/Tem, the producers of Notebook II™. Not only does his excellent text database system provide the platform for *AskARIES*, but his personal commitment to the objectives of the *AskARIES* user community led him to discount

Notebook II so generously for this application that it could be packaged with *AskARIES*, making the system accessible to far more users, particularly those in field offices throughout the world. Robert Baker, of Notebook's distributor Digital Marketing, has eased the start-up pain for new users by writing for us the *AskARIES* hard disk installation program, as well as helping us with various technical problems as they arose. In the same vein we thank our twelve "beta test" agencies and the individuals there who made so many excellent suggestions to improve the product.

Finally, our deep thanks to the many individuals working in the field of enterprise development who shared with us their knowledge, their insights, and their enthusiasms, particularly those who commented upon drafts of both this work and the ARIES teaching cases. We accept full responsibility for any remaining errors of omission.

We cannot close this acknowledgment without special tribute and recognition to the micro-entrepreneurs of the developing world. The ultimate test of all of our efforts is improvement in their well-being and the contribution that such improvement may make to their societies.

Charles K. Mann, HIID-ARIES Project Leader
Merilee S. Grindle, and Parker Shipton

Harvard Institute for International Development
Cambridge, Massachusetts

Notes

1. US Agency for International Development Contract Number DAN-1090-C-00-5124-00.

2. PISCES is an acronym for "Program for Investment in the Small Capital Enterprise Sector." It was initiated in 1978 by the Office of Urban Development, Development Support Bureau (later, the Bureau for Science and Technology). ACCION International/AITEC was the prime contractor and Partnership for Productivity and the Development Group for Alternative Policies were subcontractors. These organizations were asked to respond to three questions: (1) Is it possible to reach very poor urban dwellers and provide them assistance in respect of their self-initiated economic activities? (2) What methodologies/approaches seem to be effective? (3) What are the implications for donor agencies (Farbman, ed. 1981:vii)? Three volumes present the findings of PISCES I and PISCES II (Farbman, ed. 1981; Ashe 1985; AID 1985). See also Blayney and Otero 1985.

Part I

The Framework

Merilee S. Grindle,
Charles K. Mann,
and Parker Shipton

Introduction

Throughout the developing world, myriad organizations—private and public; local, national, and international—manage programs to assist small and micro-enterprises. Their programs are varied, the institutions distinct, and the beneficiaries different. Yet, almost all organizations attempting to carry out assistance programs for small and micro-businesses could benefit by becoming more efficient in their operations and more effective in responding to the needs of their beneficiaries. The ARIES project (Assistance to Resource Institutions for Enterprise Support) was designed to assist these institutions' own efforts to strengthen their capacity to design, implement, monitor, and evaluate development assistance programs with increased efficiency, effectiveness, and sustainability.

The findings of the PISCES projects (Program for Investment in the Small Capital Enterprise Sector), AID-funded projects carried out between 1978 and 1985, form the point of departure for ARIES. These earlier undertakings demonstrated that it is possible to design and carry out programs to assist small and micro-enterprises in the informal sector. A series of case studies and program interventions indicated that such assistance could help very poor people increase their income and welfare and could make it possible for very small businesses to grow and generate employment opportunities in developing countries. PISCES identified types of small and micro-businesses that correspond to three different levels of potential for generating income, welfare, growth, and employment; different types of programs were deemed appropriate for assisting each level of business.[1] The studies also identified factors that increase the potential success of small and micro-enterprise assistance programs: staff adaptability; commitment; concern for social development; and effective credit, training, and technical assistance.

In ARIES, the main focus shifts from the small and micro-businesses themselves to the organizations that carry out programs designed to assist them. The intention is to help institutions such as private voluntary organizations, cooperatives, public sector agencies, business associations, and public and private banks become more efficient, effective, and sustainable as they design and implement programs.

- Increasing efficiency means that resource institutions will be able to accomplish more with the resources available to them and achieve their goals more rapidly.
- Increasing effectiveness means that resource institutions will be able to respond to the needs of their clients with appropriate development assistance.
- Increasing sustainability means that resource institutions will become less vulnerable to financial uncertainty, project failure, and dependence on particular lenders or donors.

Our central working hypothesis is that the better managed the organizations, the more efficient, effective, and sustainable will be their programs. We believe that well-managed organizations for development assistance have the capacities to:

- establish goals, set priorities, and adopt policies to ensure that goals are achieved and priorities maintained;
- adapt to a changing environment, learn from experience, apply these lessons to improve existing operations, and make appropriate decisions about institutional change and growth;
- become self-sustaining and develop sufficient autonomy from donors and other sponsors to be responsive primarily to their beneficiaries, their own experience, and changing circumstance;
- monitor finances effectively so that management can plan for the future, assess ongoing activities, and make informed decisions about strategic, programmatic, and administrative issues;
- identify, attract, motivate, and retain committed and effective staff;
- work effectively with other organizations—public and private; local, national and international—to increase the impact of development programs;
- learn from others pursuing similar objectives and share with them successes, frustrations, and problem-solving ideas.

We distinguish four dimensions of capacity building from which organizations can benefit—strategic, technical, administrative, and communication capacity. The most important of these is strategic capacity, which refers to the ability of management to establish goals, set priorities, generate appropriate institutional policies, and make choices appropriate to their context. For this priority to be addressed constructively, improved technical capacity is needed within the organization, particularly in terms of improved financial information systems. Similarly, improved strategic capacity requires—but also helps ensure—increased administrative capacity, the ability to manage human resources and to coordinate organizational activities. All three dimensions of organizational capacity are strengthened when a resource institution becomes better able to receive and communicate information and to learn from its own experiences and those of others, including its clients.

Assessing and improving their organizational capacity in strategic, technical, administrative, and communication areas helps resource institutions make better choices about interacting with their clients, responding to environmental constraints and opportunities, and selecting appropriate program designs. The interrelationships among clients, environment, programs, and capacities are addressed in this book. It is guided by and based upon the literature of the field and on an extensive description and data set generated from that literature. The data set has been developed and organized within the framework of the *AskARIES Knowledgebase*: a personal computer-based system focusing on the recurrent problems facing small enterprise programs and their solutions as suggested by the literature.

The broad support for promoting small enterprise as an important avenue of social and economic development is relatively new. For many of its advocates it represents a direct way of reaching and assisting in a sustainable way the poor. Others see it as a means of infusing the development process with the dynamism of the market and the spirit of enterprise. Some see it as potentially diversionary from other, more fundamental structural transformations they consider central to the development process; a potential diversion also of the scarce development resources. The research needed to place small enterprise in its appropriate developmental context is still at an early stage. Nevertheless, organizations in the field of enterprise development have learned much about working with small enterprises and have much knowledge to share.

This book does not assess the relative importance of small enterprise in the development endeavor, but it is intended to help the institutions working with small enterprises do their jobs better. We recognize explicitly that these organizations are continuously learning and adapting their programs. There is no "magic formula," no one right way. The literature and agency experience contain many answers, suitable for varying situations, organizations, clientele, and contexts. Accordingly, the book does not presume to present "solutions" to the problems agencies face, but rather a structure within which to seek solutions. Such structure is central to capacity development. As psychologist Jerome Bruner expressed, "Perhaps the most basic thing that can be said about human memory, after a century of intensive research, is that unless detail is placed into a structured pattern, it is rapidly forgotten" (Bruner 1977:24).

Part I of this book sets out a series of frameworks to help understand better the entrepreneurs themselves, the resource organizations and their programs, and the recurrent problems that these agencies face. Chapter 1 draws upon both the literature of small enterprise development and of anthropology to suggest ways to think about the world of the small and micro-entrepreneurs. Who are the entrepreneurs? Where are they located? What do they do? How are they organized? What resources do they have available to them? What are their needs? Answers to these questions shape the orientation of resource organizations. The chapter therefore presents in general terms significant aspects of the identity, work, environment, and needs of the clientele of the resource institutions.

Chapter 2 focuses on the resource institutions that assist the small entrepreneur: their characteristics, the characteristics of the particular clientele they serve; and the context in which they deliver services. The chapter identifies the principal types of organizations that provide support for small and micro-enterprises—private voluntary associations, cooperatives, government agencies, banks, and business associations— and compares their characteristics. It considers briefly the organizational implications of delivering services to different types of low income beneficiaries and concludes with a discussion of the impact of the policy and socioeconomic environments on the resource institutions.

Chapter 3 takes a closer look at programs to assist small and micro-entrepreneurs. It identifies four components of enterprise assistance—financial assistance, training, technical assistance, and social promotion. The chapter then presents six models of programs that combine these components in different ways and in different sequences. A matrix comparing the characteristics of various models is intended to help resource institutions select an assistance model that is appropriate to their resources, priorities, and capacities.

Chapter 4 draws upon the rich literature documenting experience with small-scale enterprise to identify what seem to be the most important recurrent problems faced by resource institutions. These recurrent problems are grouped into broad clusters of related issues and discussed in terms of the priority in which they need to be addressed. The sources of the problem are identified along with the implications for the performance of the resource institution. Many of the problems can be addressed by strengthening the strategic, technical, administrative, and communication capacities of the organization.

Chapter 5 demonstrates how the four capacity areas can be strengthened in resource institutions. It suggests the extent to which building decision-making and managerial skills can lead to increased efficiency, effectiveness, and sustainability in the performance of the organization and points out a method for improving these skills. The chapter assesses training materials and resources appropriate for strengthening skills in financial, personnel, organizational, and communications management.

This document should help illuminate important issues faced by resource institutions and suggest viable ways of coping more effectively with recurrent problems. Of course, the effective use of these solutions will not ensure resource institutions of a trouble-free future. A stronger and more self-sufficient organization, not a perfect one, is an appropriate and feasible goal for these institutions. The framework presented in Part I of this book is intended to give both structure and insight into this continuing process of capacity building.

Part II of the book consists of twenty-one cases focusing on key decisions that have helped to shape contemporary approaches to small enterprise development. These are intended for workshops and management training programs that use the case method. As argued in the introduction to Part II, the case method is particularly well suited to building capacity to think strategically about alternative models of enterprise development. Because they are designed to be vehicles for discussion and critical examination of experience, the cases are not closed, completed "stories" of various program approaches. Rather, they present actual situations faced by real decision makers, without indicating how the issue was resolved. In exhibits, they include selected contextual and analytical information bearing upon the decision. As an aid to those planning to use the cases for training and workshops, a Case Leader's Guide to the ARIES cases also is available. This includes notes on the real-life outcome of the situations presented in the cases.

Despite the many books and articles about enterprise development, much of the decision making that actually has shaped current programs is not recorded in this literature. Therefore, these cases not only represent useful teaching materials, but also serve to document how some of the major approaches to enterprise development came to their current form. All have been carefully researched by the case authors to recreate as authentically and faithfully as possible the situation prevailing at the decision point of the case, and set forth the facts as they were then known by the individuals involved.

Although the cases were written by different authors, consistency in approach and educational philosophy was encouraged through participation of all but two of the authors in a workshop on casewriting and teaching developed for ARIES by James Austin of the Harvard Business School. Leading trainers in the small enterprise development community were one of the driving forces behind this workshop. Subsequently, they became the faculty for the ARIES Credit Management Workshop at Harper's Ferry. This workshop provided an opportunity to test out and refine both cases and teaching strategies with a large group of project managers and field staff. This collaboration and sharing of experience among the case authors, trainers, and potential users has been important not only in producing a coherent set of teachable cases, but also one that is enriched by the diversity of voices, styles, and perspectives of the individual authors.

Part III of the book presents an introduction and brief explanation of the *AskARIES Knowledgebase*. Its structure and organization grew out of a series of interviews and meetings with key individuals in the resource institutions most experienced with small enterprise development. As they described to us the sorts of problems they experienced in designing and managing their programs, it became apparent that many of the problems were common to virtually all organizations, although they met them in a wide variety of ways. Out of this collaboration with the small enterprise development community came the idea to create a problem-centered framework within which to organize the knowledge about this subject and within which to "seek solutions." The framework itself has been widely circulated within this community and incorporates many suggestions and ideas from these practitioners of enterprise development. At one level, *AskARIES* represents a wide annotated bibliography of the literature of this subject, summarizing all the documents covered by the system. But those who see it only as a richly indexed annotated bibliography will miss its key feature: an ability to deliver sharply focused information about specific problems. The experienced and trained *AskARIES* research team combed the literature to find for *AskARIES* a range of views and analyses relative to these recurrent problems. Often such information was not the central theme of the document and hence would be missed in a traditional annotated bibliography.

With this problem focus, the information content of *AskARIES* responds to the expressed needs of the small enterprise development community. As explained further in Part III, the "community consensus" on the common framework gives *AskARIES* the potential to expand beyond its current level as a store of existing knowledge into a vehicle for sharing new knowledge generated within that community itself.

Note

1. According to the PISCES projects, Level I businesses are extremely marginal; community-based programs stressing social welfare are most appropriate. Level II enterprises are micro-enterprises that generate enough income to allow the owner to meet basic family needs; programs organized around small informal groups of similar size entrepreneurs are most appropriate. Level III businesses are very small enterprises that have the capacity to grow and to enter the formal sector; programs offering assistance to individuals are most appropriate. See Farbman, ed. (1981).

Chapter 1

Understanding Small
and Micro-Entrepreneurs

Fundamental to a resource institution's capacity to serve its clientele effectively is a clear understanding of the nature of these small business people. Based on anthropological and other perspectives, this chapter suggests some ways of thinking about the clients and of understanding their circumstances, motivations, and needs. A main theme is the great extent of local and regional variations in small business people and their circumstances, and therefore the need for careful analysis of local context in program and project preparation. Usually this kind of analysis requires time and close contacts in the field. A number of the observations in this chapter serve as bases for later recommendations in Chapter 5 on components and models of assistance programs.

Who Are the Small and Micro-Entrepreneurs?

There are many ways of defining "entrepreneur" or "enterprise."[1] For purposes of this volume, an "enterprise" will be defined broadly as any business that produces or distributes goods, or provides services, including financial services. Many definitions of enterprise focus on the individual, but these are often inappropriate in developing societies. Some definitions include group-based initiatives like local cooperatives, savings and credit associations, and self-help societies. Micro-entrepreneurs are often self-employed, though this concept too has many meanings.[2]

In the following discussion, "small" refers to enterprises working with no more than twenty-five permanent members (Chuta and Liedholm prefer fifty—1979:12) and fixed assets of no more than U.S.$50,000;

9

"micro" will mean those with no more than about ten permanent members, and no more than U.S.$10,000 fixed assets.[3] The numbers of persons may include family labor. Fixed assets here exclude land (it is often hard to evaluate). Often most of the labor in a micro-enterprise comes from members of a single nuclear or extended family. Generally, a small or micro-enterprise is one whose disappearance would make no appreciable difference to the national or international market in which it operates.

Insiders' and outsiders' perspectives may differ markedly on what constitutes an enterprise, or whom it includes. A common mistake is to assume that enterprises have fixed memberships where they may not. Another is to assume that they have a single manager or head at their core; some are better understood as nexuses or networks. A third common error is to conceive of an enterprise's purpose too rigidly or peg it to a "sector" of the economy when in fact its activities may change quickly and often. Misunderstandings may arise from difficulties of translating terms like "business," "firm," or "enterprise" into other languages. Income, capital, investment, employment, occupation, achievement, and even work and leisure are other ideas likely to be untranslatable or apt to be misunderstood across cultures.[4]

Some Widespread Tendencies of Small and Micro-Entrepreneurs

Though few generalizations about micro-entrepreneurs will apply satisfactorily to all developing countries or societies, some broad tendencies are worth special note.

Multiple Occupations

Micro-entrepreneurs often have multiple occupations, shifting their activities hourly, daily, or seasonally.[5] This pattern is most notably true in agrarian communities. It can serve to avoid or minimize risks and to take advantage of shifting market conditions. Running several small-scale activities can make it easier to avoid taxation or regulation than running a single larger one. Frequently there are also important noneconomic reasons for occupational pluralism, such as the interest of variety, and the advantages of keeping activities inconspicuous to competitors or envious neighbors. Of course, the costs of multiple occupations include some expertise and economies of scale. Since interviewers and informants in questionnaire surveys are often satisfied to report only one economic activity, statistics from surveys commonly underrepresent the proportions of business people engaged in more than one.

Patterns of plural occupations, where they exist, will have these and other implications for support projects:

- Attempts to specialize business people into single "occupations" are likely to make their earnings more irregular and riskier. If these attempts are made anyway, the heightened risks may need to be offset with new savings or insurance provisions.

- Less obviously, assistance projects might most usefully seek to improve conditions in which entrepreneurs work—for example, by small-scale infrastructure or information services—rather than trying to reach particular entrepreneurs.

- Training programs for specific enterprises may have trouble drawing small and micro-entrepreneurs away from their homes or places of work for extended periods.

- Optimal forms of loan collateral, if any is available, may not need to be related to the enterprise for which credit is given. For example, a tailor may be able to offer a cane-crushing machine or hand lathe.

- Numbers of participants may be a poor index of the success or failure of support programs.

Closeness of Business and Family

Small-scale businesses in developing countries generally are tied more closely to family economies than in North America. Often written records do not exist or do not separate family from business accounts. When savings margins are low, families will wish to draw upon resources of the enterprises in times of need. Free interchange between family and business can be a sensible adaptation to poverty, though it seldom helps the businesses themselves.

Family labor can offer decided advantages over wage labor. It can provide efficient long-term training, ensure trust and confidence among workers, keep its own secrets, and respond quickly to changing economic and political conditions (Benedict 1968:10–11). Therefore, it is not always in the family firm's interest to encourage its expansion through hiring labor.

Some cultural family patterns—for instance those with strong internal hierarchy and stable marriages—may be better suited to family enterprise than others (Benedict 1968, 1979). This possibility implies not that resource institutions should seek to change family structures, but that they may be able to decide on the basis of family structures where family enterprises are likely to make the best use of interventions.

Awareness that entrepreneurial families often have multiple occupations, and that the close relations between business and family may be based on sound reasoning, forces a clarification of program goals. Is it the aim to promote particular entrepreneurs and their enterprises, or also the well-being of their simple or extended families and their communities?

The latter goal is normally the more appropriate for newly monetized economies, where placing family wealth suddenly in the hands of only one individual can lead to its irresponsible use and ultimately endanger dependents.

Concern about Risk

Small business people vary greatly in risk averseness, but this characteristic should be respected if it exists.[6] In most developing countries, failing business people fall upon safety nets of near or extended kin, rather than on government relief or welfare systems. In the more egalitarian societies, jealousies and resentments toward rising business people may deprive them of family support in crises. Simply trying to break down clients' risk averseness may damage their well-being in the long run. A more responsible approach is to seek ways of making their investments less risky from the outset.

Invisibility and Elusiveness for Institutions

Many kinds of micro-entrepreneurs have been effectively invisible to investigators, particularly in official surveys. One reason in some areas is seclusion customs for female or child workers. Another is that small-scale trade need not occur in fixed places. Rural-rural, rural-urban, and urban-urban mobility must be taken into account; movements may be one-way or circular. Several kinds of survey bias are identifiable and can be corrected to improve the visibility of the smallest business people.[7]

Business people whose enterprises are small, unregistered, and untaxed are often suspicious of formal institutions. Indeed, some make their living precisely by avoiding them. Illiterate micro-entrepreneurs in remote areas may not differentiate clearly among government bodies, private voluntary organizations, and corporations. Among rural peoples, pastoralists are often the most antagonistic to formal institutions (as well as the most seldom helped by interventions). An implication is that resource institutions wishing to help people like these should consider means involving little or no direct personal contact. One way is to to try to influence policy reforms. Another is providing infrastructure, even on a small scale. A third is to offer instruction, information, or advice through audio cassettes, radio, or other mass media.

Territory and Territoriality

The propensity of small-scale entrepreneurs to recognize, establish, and protect particular territories of operation is enormously variable across cultures, contrary to some popular literature. In some contexts—for instance, among artisans in urban Senegal (Badgley 1978:17)—territoriality is a reason why small-scale entrepreneurs refuse to move into new localities that on the surface might seem economically preferable. Productive enterprises sometimes may be reluctant to expand in size and volume because they would then need to challenge the market "hegemonies" of other producers.

Market territories may be variously understood as belonging to individuals, families, lineages or other kin groups, age sets, castes or classes, villages, chiefdoms, voluntary associations, trades, guilds, unions, religions or churches, ethnic groups, or specific government authorities. These territories may be understood to include trading routes as well as particular places (Cohen 1969), and they may be fixed or may change seasonally. Frequently, too, particular commodities will be considered the province of particular communities or ethnic groups.

Any project designed to promote businesses must be sensitive to locally recognized boundaries of control or market influence, whether these be physically demarcated or not. Tributes, taxes, or tolls demanded by local leaders for operation in particular settings or routes may have more symbolic than economic importance, and they may be negotiable in type or amount, but they should not be neglected lest a project be sabotaged.

Patron-Client Ties

Similarly, it is worth finding out whether small or micro-enterprises have individual ties to powerful figures in local politics or administration. In some societies, politicians favor market vendors or other publicly placed business people with legal protection, contacts for institutional loans, or other benefits, in return for informal campaigning or other support (see Davis 1986). Setting up projects for such business people may mean having to come to terms with their existing patrons.

What Entrepreneurs Belong To: Multifunctional Local Institutions

To understand small and micro-entrepreneurs, one must understand what they belong to: what rights and duties they have with respect to local and regional organizations of any kinds, and which of these connections may be tapped for enterprise support purposes.

An important principle in developing countries is that institutions are more likely to serve multiple purposes than in industrialized countries. Their ostensible purposes often are not the most important. In parts of sub-Saharan Africa, for instance, civic lodges double as chambers of commerce; cooperatives are used as political springboards; family or clan reunion centers are used as capital-raising institutions and legal aid bureaus; churches are used as training centers and work-mobilizing groups for personal or community projects; open-air food markets are also used as information-broadcasting centers, craft fairs, and technological showcases.

A related principle is that economic or social roles are more likely to overlap than in industrialized countries with more mobile populations: business partners are more likely also to be kin, church-mates, sporting partners, and so forth. In many countries, notably in Africa, this is almost as true of urban as of rural communities (see Cohen 1969; Marris and Somerset 1971; Berry 1985). An implication is that for cost-effectiveness, enterprise resource institutions may be able to work imaginatively with, and through, diverse types of local institutions offering appropriate and conveniently situated infrastructure, not just through specialized business associations or training centers, for example.

Classifying Entrepreneurs to Assess Their Relative Needs: What Kinds of People Make Entrepreneurs?

Psychologists, anthropologists, and economists disagree on the extent to which entrepreneurship is a function of drives, culture and values, or market forces and opportunities. Nonetheless, all these determinants play their parts in any setting (see Kilby 1971). There is no single personality trait that produces entrepreneurship. Some frequently cited characteristics include innovativeness, curiosity and openness to new ideas, hard work, orientation toward the future and willingness to save and invest, leadership, risk acceptance, and even selfishness or greed. But all these capacities mean different things in different societies, and some may not be recognized at all. Entrepreneurship is not something that is either present or absent, as a binary variable, but rather is a combination of factors. These are not to be measured on some absolute scale but can usually be understood only in local context.

Small and micro-business people are such an enormous and diverse category of people that any resource institution must make hard basic decisions about what kinds to try to assist, and what kinds to leave alone. It is understandable that institutions starting new programs often are particularly concerned to find the entrepreneurs most likely to succeed, both because they wish their programs to acquire a favorable image among donors and the public, and because they want to establish a firm footing for financial components of their programs such as revolving loan funds. As programs become established they may (and doubtless should) reassess their aims and begin selecting clients more on the basis of need. Unfortunately, these often are not the same kinds of clients.

There is no limit to the number of ways in which entrepreneurs can be classified, but some are indispensable to the design of any project. A few are discussed below: (1) the occupation or nature of the activity; (2) the size of the enterprise; (3) the ethnic and religious identity; (4) the gender; and (5) the age of the entrepreneur. Other essential factors not discussed include: (6) whether the economy is rural, urban, or in between, and the following characteristics of the entrepreneur; (7) wealth; (8) class and/or caste; (9) mobility; (10) formal education, literacy, and numeracy; (11) political party or faction; and (12) membership in voluntary associations, or sodalities.

Some of these factors may be too sensitive, or ethically inappropriate, for explicit policies. But all are dimensions that must be considered, if only to foresee what groups might be excluded from or even actively oppose a program or project.

Occupation or Nature of the Activity: Basic Choices

Many government ministries and departments of labor publish books listing local occupations and job categories, including types of self-employed activities. Resource institutions can compare the activities listed with those they observe on the ground, and can compare the directories of different countries, to perceive which activities are absent, untried, or officially overlooked, or to detect changes through time. (Of course, official descriptions are never a substitute for first-hand observation.)

The evaluation of costs and benefits of different small or micro-level economic activities cannot be covered here, but a few economic criteria of benefits to clients are profitability, direct or indirect employment generation (both backward and forward linkages), possibilities for earning foreign exchange, likely changes in the distribution of earnings, and satisfaction of basic needs.[8]

Particular trades often are seen locally as the province of particular ethnic or religious groups, genders, or ages, as discussed below. There may or may not be economic reasons for these specializations, but usually it is wisest to assume at first that there are.

Issues of Enterprise Size

Sizes of businesses can be judged variously in terms of personnel, capital, turnover, profitability, or other measures. As a kind of shorthand, the PISCES studies classified, by mixed criteria, informal sector micro-enterprises into three "levels" (Farbman, ed. 1981). As noted on page 8, they are: Level I, extremely marginal businesses; Level II, businesses generating enough income to allow the owner to meet basic family needs; Level III, businesses with the capacity to grow and to enter the formal sector. Mixed-criteria classes are often used as well for larger enterprises.

In almost any context, it is a matter of debate what sizes of small or micro-enterprises are most appropriate for interventions, and whether enterprises should be encouraged to expand or only to multiply. The answers, of course, will depend on the activities in which the enterprises are engaged, and on local preferences and market conditions. Expanding enterprises may lead to reorganization problems within them, and possibly to market saturation. Careless interventions to this end may lower efficiency instead of raising it.

Resource institutions seeking to promote enterprise choose among three purposes, realizing that these can be quite distinct: (1) encouraging the formation of new enterprises; (2) helping existing small enterprises to expand (or even to contract); and (3) working to strengthen or stimulate existing enterprises without trying to change their sizes.

Efficiency and Scale. Economists continue to debate the relative efficiencies of smaller and larger enterprises.[9] Much of the literature concentrates on industrial production. It tends to compare what we have defined as "small and micro" with "medium" or larger enterprises having up to hundreds or thousands of employees. Little is known yet about the comparative efficiencies of enterprises of different sizes within the "small and micro" range itself. As further studies on this are done, however, many of the same concepts are likely to be used.

Contrary to popular assumptions, small firms are not always more labor intensive than large ones, nor are large firms always more capital intensive than smaller ones. A general conclusion emerging from size-and-efficiency studies is that capital/labor ratios often vary more among industries than among sizes of enterprise within an industry.[10] Whether smaller enterprises are more labor-intensive than larger ones will depend less upon size than upon whether the enterprise produces, for example, charcoal, cloth, or paint. Generalizations about the efficiency and factor-intensity of enterprises should be treated with caution.

Possibilities of Symbiosis of Larger and Smaller Businesses. The interests of larger and smaller enterprises need not conflict. These businesses should coexist, serving different markets. With subcontracting they can become truly symbiotic. The practicability and durability of subcontracting arrangements may depend on cultural as well as on technical and economic factors.[11]

Cultural Differences: Some Delicate but Essential Considerations

Cultural or ethnic relations usually are best understood as those between groups speaking different languages, though language does not always coincide with other indicators. Most governments of developing countries understandably try to conceal the ethnic dimensions of development, both from nationals and from foreigners. But where members of different cultures may compete bitterly for resources within the same polities, resource institutions should be aware of the schisms, alliances, public stereotypes, and differing ambitions and attitudes of the populations among which they work.

The practical purposes for this understanding are many. They include knowing which groups will accept training or financial assistance from members of which other groups, or will collaborate with them;

knowing what kinds of enterprises, work tasks, or products are appealing or repugnant to particular ethnic groups; and knowing cultural attitudes toward private saving and investment or loan repayments.

Achievement Motivation across Cultures. There is no evidence whatsoever that any culture or ethnic group has stronger inborn propensities or abilities for entrepreneurship than any other. It appears more likely that some place more emphasis on individual achievement than others in their childrearing and early educational patterns (McClelland 1961, 1966), but some studies seeking to explain these differences in terms of "need for achievement" are open to charges of ethnocentric bias.[12] Differences in ethnic attitudes toward enterprise (to the extent they are real) must also be considered a result of resource endowments, climate, demographic pressures, political circumstance, and historical events including colonial contacts, market opportunities, and other factors.

Certainly, societies vary greatly in their cultural emphasis on individualism or group cooperation, on egalitarianism or hierarchy, on concealment or ostentation of personal or corporate wealth, and on innovation or the maintenance of tradition and stability. All these factors may bear directly upon the choices of enterprises, technology, and managerial styles to be promoted.

Minority Entrepreneurial Communities and Diasporas. Examples of small minority groups that excel in particular kinds of enterprise are to be found in all parts of the world.[13] There is no satisfactory single explanation for the ubiquity of this phenomenon, but there is evidence that in many contexts, achievement in enterprise is related (as cause, effect, or both) to personal histories of displacements, migrations and/or social maladjustments, and compensatory rewarding behavior within families (Hagen 1962, 1966, 1980; Hoselitz 1966:189–90; see also Siyagh 1952; Marris and Somerset 1971:58; Shapero and Sokol 1982). In many areas the rise of ethnic-specific entrepreneurial traditions also appears to result partly from land shortage or denial of access to land, and a group's being forced by circumstance into activities other than farming (Barrett 1968; Moock 1976; Paterson 1980a, 1980b). Sometimes, resentments of majority populations about minority successes in enterprise can reinforce aggressive business behavior, through a denial of other livelihoods or opportunities to intermarry. These pressures can lead to a self-perpetuating cycle of accumulation and alienation.[14] But if entrepreneurial minorities are allowed to assimilate, they often will. In any case, the conspicuousness of wealth held by entrepreneurial ethnic or religious minorities should not lead resource institutions to neglect the poorer members of those groups, who are likely to be more hidden from view.

Religious Dimensions in Enterprise. The influences of some religious ideologies on work, saving, risk-taking, and other elements of entrepreneurial behavior vary widely and can be most important.[15] Observations made above about ethnic groups may apply equally well to religions within an ethnic group. Religious prohibitions on loan interest (as in Islam) may or may not discourage participation in schemes with such charges. The charges can sometimes be reclassed as administration fees or profit sharing to the satisfaction of borrowers or lenders. Interest sometimes is concealed also by requirements that a loan issued in one commodity be repaid in another, or by reclassifying loans as sales and resales of objects that never in fact change hands.

Some Inevitable Policy Decisions. Many donor agencies and resource institutions without explicit policies regarding ethnic groups have nonetheless found it necessary to make hard decisions about them. In most developing countries, ethnic groups have specialized in different kinds of enterprise. Inevitably, therefore, the choices by resource institutions regarding which enterprises to promote are therefore also choices about which ethnic groups to promote. Similarly, decisions between geographical locations for programs are often decisions between ethnic groups.

A central issue in program design is whether to try to build upon ethnic groups' entrepreneurial strengths, or to try to enhance them where they have been weak. The former strategy is usually the easier and the more likely to contribute to economic growth, but it risks widening socioeconomic inequalities between ethnic groups within countries. This strategy may also heighten resentments and political instabilities. The second strategy, the harder one, is likely to promote equity between ethnic groups of a country, but it risks widening inequalities within ethnic groups. Compromise strategies are possible, and each resource institution must set its own course according to context.

Regardless of whether resource institutions explicitly consider cultural or ethnic factors in the selection of beneficiaries, they commonly find it helps that the ethnic group(s) of the intended beneficiaries be represented on their own staffs, at the level of contact agents if not also at management levels. Such representation seems important for training, extension, and other kinds of projects, but is particularly so in credit schemes.

In sum, although ethnicity presents some of the most politically sensitive and ethically difficult issues in enterprise development, inevitably these must be faced. The potentially explosive nature of ethnicity in the politics of developing countries may sometimes be a reason for donor agencies and resource institutions to limit explicit references to it in their public presentations and documents. But it is also a reason never to ignore it.

Gender

Official surveys have tended to miss the kinds of businesses women run, or to define them out of existence.[16] In most settings, the observations made earlier about invisibility, part-time and intermittent careers, and close relations between business and family are especially true of women's work.[17] Filling information gaps between women entrepreneurs and resource institutions is a task for both women and men.

Gender issues are closely tied to issues of enterprise scale. "In general, the smaller the size of the business reached by a project the larger the proportion of women business owners" (Farbman, ed. 1981:ix). Changes in enterprise size may be accompanied by shifts in the division of labor and of rewards. In much of sub-Saharan Africa and some other regions, food processing and marketing tasks performed by women are commonly taken over by men when these tasks become mechanized or when marketable quantities rise. Thus programs that aim to raise food production or make processing more efficient in regions like these should include measures to include women directly in incremental earnings.

Societies vary greatly in the extent to which husbands and wives share cash earnings, or information about these. (In some African societies there is almost no such communication.) Sharing between spouses may diminish as incomes rise. It is never a foregone conclusion, therefore, that increased earnings of one sex will find their way also to the other. Among other things, female-headed households should not be neglected in programs aiming at one participant per household (Buvinic and Youssef 1979).

Projects requiring literacy, knowledge of European languages or regional *linguae francae*, collateral, or fixed premises of enterprises before clients can take loans are likely to discriminate *de facto* against women. So, too, may projects requiring legal status as adults, since in some countries women, or unmarried women, are legally defined as minors.

Age

Most of sub-Saharan Africa, most of central Asia including China, and parts of several other regions have systems of respect or reverence for elders, and gerontocratic patterns of authority. (This tends to be the pattern in unilineal societies, that is, those where kin groups are composed by reference to ancestors in the male line or the female line exclusively.) Some of these societies have formal organizations of elders as community leaders. Even in the most gerontocratic societies, however, formal education usually is seen as at least a partial compensation for the inexperience of youth.[18]

Most of the Hispanic, Lusophone, and indigenous societies of Latin America are characterized by rather less emphasis on age seniority than one finds in Africa or central Asia. In these regions project designers and implementers usually will have more scope to use juniors effectively in training, extension, and credit.

The societies where elders are most respected (and control the greatest share of resources) are likely to be those whose junior members seem most in need of extra income-generating activities, and *vice versa*. Here, as in some issues of gender equity, the perspectives of insiders and outsiders are likely to conflict.

Where men or members of a particular age group are found to monopolize project resources intended for equal distribution, it may help to split the projects into separate men's and women's projects, or separate elders' and juniors' projects. Doing so puts the authority for allocation more firmly in the hands of the resource institution.

Perceiving What Kinds of Assistance Are Appropriate

There are many useful manuals and ready-made survey questionnaires available for determining the needs of small and micro-entrepreneurs (see, for example, Ashe, 1978; Dulansey and Austin 1985; Allal and Chuta 1982). To a degree, these can be adapted to fit local circumstances. A set of "rapid rural appraisal" techniques is also evolving for cost-effective yet fairly systematic surveys.[19] But many experienced field officers believe that "slow is beautiful"; that there is no substitute for in-depth interviewing, participant observation, and creative thought together with members of the client population. These things take time.

Entrepreneurs' Perceptions of Their Own Needs

As Harper has observed (1984:26), entrepreneurs, when asked about their problems, will most commonly cite a single need whose fulfillment they believe would solve all their problems, and they will tend to choose one whose solution they consider is beyond their control. Understandably, they most often announce lack of funds (see Chuta and Liedholm 1979: 75; Harper and Soon 1979; Kilby and D'Zmura 1984). This response is especially likely to be voiced in the first meeting with researchers; one-shot surveys often get no further. These needs can be partly illusory and partly real. Certainly shortages of working capital exist everywhere, and Africa's problems in this respect are unusually acute (see, for instance, Geiger and Armstrong 1964:49; Hart 1972:47). But entrepreneurs are much less likely to identify their own managerial shortcomings or gaps in their knowledge where these exist; often they do not know what kinds of information and skills they may be missing. Similarly they rarely mention lack of demand for their goods or services, but this is a problem often clearly evident to an outsider.

One reason why entrepreneurs mention capital shortage so often in surveys may be their expectation that training, extension, or other nonfinancial services will be inappropriate for their contexts. They may be right, particularly where resource institutions are new to an area or are not expected to stay long. For situations like these, financial assistance or other approaches may in fact be more appropriate than training or extension, though these approaches are not mutually exclusive.

Existing Informal Financial Systems: Already Adequate?

As noted above, the ubiquitous clamor for credit among small entrepreneurs around the world should be taken seriously, but not at face value. The preponderance of small businesses in developing countries appears to arise with little or no help in the form of institutional credit.[20]

Before deciding that institutional loans are necessary, wise resource institutions examine and understand the existing local systems of credit. As Firth and Yamey (1964) and others have pointed out, there is no society that does not have borrowing and lending, but the forms these take, and the reliance on credit in general, vary enormously by place and by type of enterprise.

Moneylenders. Moneylenders may be present or absent; where they exist they may lend for production, distribution, and consumption (as in much of West Africa), or only consumption (as in most of East Africa). Frequently small-scale moneylenders are landlords—an especially common pattern in moneylenders in India and elsewhere in South Asia—or shopkeepers. In many countries, people who lend money do not specialize in this as a sole occupation.

Interest rates of moneylenders in these countries often appear usurious to their borrowers and to foreigners, but they may be at least partly justified by high rates of inflation, high risks of lending, high costs of borrower supervision or overhead, and the opportunity cost of capital. Moneylenders from minority groups often lack the social networks of kinship, friendship, or other informal associations by which pressure can be exerted on borrowers to ensure loan repayments.[21] They may therefore need to charge higher interest than other lenders. Of course, new resource institutions often find themselves in the same position, for the same reasons.

Rotating Credit and Savings Associations. Among analysts of rural credit there has been much enthusiasm lately about the perceived successes of rotating credit associations, variously called rotating savings and credit associations, or contribution clubs (in French, *tontines;* in Spanish, *tondas).* Anthropologists have found that these locally organized groups occur in all major regions of the developing world, though not in every society (Geertz 1962; Ardener 1964).[22] The groups are based on the simple principle that in periodic meetings, all members contribute except one, who takes home the total amount, and that each member has a turn as recipient.[23] Commonly occurring as women's organizations (March, and Taqqu 1986), the associations provide credit to borrowers likely to be ineligible to borrow from institutional sources, usually in smaller amounts than the latter lend, and without collateral requirements.

Some governments may discourage these associations, because their assets are hard for them to tax and control. But rotating credit associations combine multiple useful functions for borrowers. They provide not only credit (for borrowers early in the cycle) but also savings (for those later in the cycle); they provide a form of insurance (the order of disbursements may be altered in emergencies); and they serve as a vehicle for social gatherings. Among the advantages that they offer over more formal credit organizations are that they are conveniently located, accessible to the illiterate, and not intimidating as institutional offices. Also, their funds are hard to embezzle. Where rotating credit associations exist, members commonly belong to several simultaneously; the associations thus serve to circulate funds through a capital-short population in useful sums. Because they spring from local initiative, they can generate greater incentive and loyalty than other kinds of lenders. They are participatory development in the strictest sense.

Little is known about the durability of rotating savings and credit associations, though they commonly last well over a decade and may be reconstituted with interchanged memberships after dissolution. Nor is it yet clear whether rotating savings associations can serve as useful links between formal financial institutions and small entrepreneurs, though there are some preliminary signs from Nigeria and Cameroon that they can. They may in any case serve as useful models for group-based institutional savings and credit.[24]

In some regions there may be no readily apparent sources of credit at all. Yet credit may occur inconspicuously, in the form of interfamilial exchanges, tributes to and redistributions by local authorities, bridewealth and dowry, share contracting, and other practices often not recognized as credit. Absence of a lively formal or informal credit market does not necessarily signify absence of need, demand, interest, or potential. But it is a caution to program designers to proceed slowly and with carefully watched pilot phases.

Institutions intending to lend in cash should observe the sums of money that their potential borrowers are ordinarily accustomed to handling. As a rule, they should not lend them much greater amounts of cash than these at the outset. They should also learn whether their clients are used to interest charges. Small-scale business people in regions that have used money for several centuries tend to be familiar with interest charges, if only from dealing with moneylenders or wholesalers. But those in newly monetized economies often are not. Lending to them at high interest might lead them deeply into debt and cause misunderstandings and resentments.[25] Context is almost everything.

Savings. Savings are, and must be, as important a part of small enterprise as is borrowing. The experience of numerous projects suggests that savings components, incorporated into credit projects, not only can provide for capital accumulation but also can help lenders screen borrowers and can generate a sense of commitment on the part of project participants. A savings component also adds members' scrutiny to an organization's management.

Though savings projects appear increasingly to be a welcome and helpful form of intervention, much remains to be learned about their role in small-scale enterprise development. For most regions there is still little firm evidence on the effects of increased savings on family well-being.[26] Resources saved or reinvested in an enterprise are resources at least temporarily denied to family members or others. Studies on individual savings should consider opportunity costs broadly defined: are dependents of the saver losing part of their living, and if so, for how long and with what hope of returns?

The common tendency of small-scale entrepreneurs in many societies to deposit cash informally with friends, relatives, or respected community members helps to ensure that the money, while being saved, remains quickly accessible for emergencies. Moreover, the keepers may consider it a fund of last resort for their own emergencies. Personal break-open cash boxes like "piggy-banks," where common, may suggest a role for more accessible institutional saving mechanisms. Convenience and accessibility frequently outweigh considerations of interest payments in determining depositors' choices of informal moneykeepers or hoarding versus financial institutions like banks. However, informed choice is often difficult because knowledge about rates of interest and currency inflation is hard for small savers to obtain and calculate. Making this kind of information more accessible and comprehensible is a role that not only financial institutions but also other organizations can play. Another issue is trust. Local moneykeepers known for a lifetime may be perceived as more reliable and honest than strangers in a bank—sometimes with good reason.

When assessing needs for savings schemes, institutions should recognize that savings can be converted into nonmonetary assets, and that these need not be related to the purposes of an enterprise. Diverse holdings like land or livestock may produce higher yields than investment in the enterprise. Moreover, in egalitarian social systems, accumulating social credit by lending or giving away resources may be a more rational alternative than savings as conventionally defined. In highly inflationary economies, or those where currency is subject to abrupt manipulation by governments, accumulating nonmonetary assets can make sound sense.

Thinking about savings should not be confined to rigid notions of enterprise boundaries, or even to "sectors" of an economy. Even where savings institutions appear lacking, some less visible form of saving or resource accumulation may be taking place.

Existing Training through Apprenticeships

In nearly all developing societies, children learn valuable production and
service skills in childhood by assisting their older relatives. Commonly
these skills are supplemented in adolescence or later with apprenticeships lasting from a few months to several years. Often they are
paid arrangements between non-kin. In much of West Africa, apprenticeships are highly institutionalized. In a Michigan State University
survey in Sierra Leone, 90 percent of sampled small business proprietors
had previously served as apprentices (Chuta and Liedholm 1979:50; see
also Mabawonku 1979). Other studies have found little relation between
formal education and entrepreneurial success, suggesting the importance
of informal training (Kilby 1965; Liedholm and Chuta 1976; Chuta and
Liedholm 1979).

There is little that can be said in general about the adequacy or inadequacy of local training practices for small and micro-entrepreneurs. A
frequent finding in some regions, however, is that apprenticeships are
gender-specific. Also, handicapped children and youth are not given the
family attention that others receive for acquiring technical skills. They
may therefore need special formal training.

Local patterns of apprenticeship can be duplicated or incorporated in
training projects.[27] Residential apprenticeships may be particularly appropriate for areas of low population densities, where having to travel
long distances discourages participation in courses that do not meet every day. They are less suitable, of course, for people wanting to pursue
several business activities simultaneously, or for women or men with
child care responsibilities at home.

Market Research

One of the most universal needs of small and micro-entrepreneurs is for
better information about market conditions in places with which they
cannot easily communicate directly (Dulansey and Austin 1985:82). They
need more reliable information on supplies, demands, prices, qualities,
competition, regulations, and the status of transporters and routes. For
these kinds of information, small producers and traders most often rely
on traveling relatives and acquaintances who do not specialize in their
trades (and those in their trades may prefer to keep the information to
themselves). Much of their information comes late and third-hand. To
improve their information is to render their ventures less risky, alto-

gether a happier approach than trying to make them more tolerant of risks.

Some ministries of agriculture and parastatal marketing boards compile detailed records of food prices in local markets at regular intervals. As a short-cut to doing their own research, NGOs may be able to obtain these prices and help disseminate them to the public as they are compiled. They should recognize, however, that others close to the sources of this information may wish to monopolize it, or manipulate the statistics, for personal trading ends.

In countries that receive food aid or other material assistance from overseas, resource institutions may provide a valuable service to small traders by finding out and announcing when these shipments are expected to arrive, so that the traders can plan and will not buy too much from local sources to distribute in those places (Morris 1985:30).

Providing information about export market demands, including product preferences and specifications, is a role that international resource institutions are well placed to serve. Better-established, literate business people appreciate being put in contact with potential buyers or distributing agents for their goods; this simple information can be extremely hard to obtain in developing countries. But most small-scale entrepreneurs would need more comprehensive assistance to prepare for exporting (or importing). They might need help organizing themselves into producers' groups. They may need accurate information about tariffs and quotas, shipping logistics, currency regulations, and exchange procedures. Further, they may need help filling out forms until they can arrange to have this done for themselves.

For publicizing market information of simple kinds, like domestic food prices, the radio and other mass media are particularly appropriate. Access to these media too will usually depend on working relations between resource institutions and national governments. But, as noted earlier, the mass media are especially attractive as a way of reaching informal and even illegal traders who wish no contact with officialdom.

Other Needs

The needs discussed above—financial assistance, training, and market research—are the ones resource institutions commonly try to address in assisting small and micro-enterprises, but they are not necessarily the best choices. Conventional approaches focusing on credit and individual or small-group training may be too narrow; certainly their cost-effectiveness and coverage are always limited. Other more or less urgent needs, to name only a few, may include small-scale infrastructure (comprehensive industrial estates, or more selective improvements such as power, light, and water), tool services, grants, legal representation, the organization of guilds or unions, subcontracting assistance, demonstration projects and fairs, newsletters, and educational radio broadcasts.[28]

One final need deserves note: small business peoples' lack of information about the resource institutions themselves. This shortage affects entrepreneurs in all countries. One of the most useful contributions is to prepare directories of all the institutions active in a country, giving their names, addresses, and staff contacts, and describing their policies and preferences, kinds of support offered, geographical and sectoral specializations, volume of lending, training, or other assistance, and giving examples of completed application forms for each. A few examples are currently available.[29] Some government ministries keep directories of PVOs and NGOs for political or administrative purposes; with permission, resource institutions may be able to adapt these for wider dissemination. Resource institution field officers can use these to refer prospective clients to other institutions.

General Conclusion

The central implication of this multipurposed discussion is the need for those engaged in enterprise development work to take time to listen on the ground. The features that small or micro-enterprises have in common are important but few, and assessing their needs beyond these takes time. Thorough and deliberate planning, careful research, patient implementation, limited staff rotations, and realistic project cycles all can heighten the effectiveness of both entrepreneurs and resource institutions, and maximize the benefits of assistance to small and micro-businesses. Trainers train best when they have first stopped to listen; lenders lend best when some of their methods are borrowed from local populations. Taking more time to listen and to observe may slow the pace of development planning, but in the long run it may enable agencies to accelerate development.

Notes

1.   There is little consensus on the meanings of "entrepreneur" or "enterprise." As early as 1937, Fraser distinguished several current meanings of enterprise: the management of a business unit, profit taking, business innovation, and uncertainty bearing (1937, cited in Belshaw 1965). Many economists have focused on innovation: Schumpeter wrote in 1949 that "the carrying out of new combinations we call 'enterprise'; the individuals whose function is to carry them out we call 'entrepreneurs'" (1949:74). Marris and Somerset similarly define entrepreneurship as "a practical creativeness, which combines resources and opportunities in new ways." It "turns invention into profit, but need not originate it" (1971:1–2). Other contemporary definitions of entrepreneur in economics dictionaries include "the owner-manager of a firm"

(Bannock, Baxter, and Rees 1978:152) and "the organizing factor in production" (Pearce 1981:130). Noneconomists will note that this definition omits transporters and retailers, among others.

2. To pick three African interpretations for instance, a Zambian use emphasizes having one's own place of business and determining one's own hours of work; a Ghanaian use specifies working for two or more individuals; a Swazi use emphasizes being paid by the job done or goods sold, rather than receiving a stable salary (International Center for Research on Women 1980:42; Dulansey and Austin 1985:91).

3. The figures are obviously somewhat arbitrary. An often-cited source notes fifty different definitions of "small-scale" used in seventy-five countries (Georgia Institute of Technology 1975, cited in Gordon 1978:18, and in Chuta and Liedholm 1979:12), and of course no country will have just one.

4. These problems have seriously hindered attempts to quantify the economic dimensions of micro-enterprises in developing countries. Statistics on the subject should be regarded with extreme caution, particularly those appearing in secondary literature, where they are often repeated with reckless disregard of definitions, sampling, regional variation, or change over time.

5. Long (1979) analyzes multiple-career strategy in Peru. For a few discussions of the pattern in eastern Africa, see Obbo (1980); Paterson (1984); Shipton (1985). Kilby (1971) gives an unsympathetic view of the pattern in West Africa. These findings challenge conventional ideas about who is an entrepreneur and who is not. Partly for this reason, Shapero and Sokol (1982) have convincingly argued that the focus of entrepreneurial studies should shift from the individuals concerned, to the "entrepreneurial event" itself: the formation of a business, or the act of innovation.

6. The best literature on risk aversion in developing countries concerns small farmers, but most of the lessons apply as well to small business people. See Scott (1976) on Southeast Asia; Popkin (1979) presents a contrasting view on the region.

7. These include (1) spatial biases (urban, tarmac, and roadside biases); (2) project biases (concentrating where money is being spent and staff posted); (3) person biases (concentrating on elites, males, adopters of new techniques, the healthiest and strongest); (4) dry season biases (traveling when it is easy); (5) diplomatic biases (failure to investigate projects suspected as failures); and (6) professional biases (blinkered vision within professions or academic disciplines). This list comes from Chambers (1983:22–23).

8. See Allal and Chuta (1982:64–100) and references cited there. This source gives algebraic formulas for weighting the costs and benefits of activities by these and other criteria.

9. Various arguments about firm size and efficiency based on these criteria and others appear in Staley and Morse (1965); Chuta and Liedholm (1979); Page (1979); Anderson (1982); Steel and Takagi (1983); Harper (1984); Mazumdar (1984); Dulansey and Austin (1985); Biggs (1986); Little (1987).

10. Concluding a recent survey of research on industrial scale and efficiency in India, Korea, Malaysia, the Philippines, and Taiwan, Little comments, "Such differences in labor intensity as there are between size groups within an industry are dwarfed by differences between industries" (1987:230).

11. Japan's rapidly expanding industrial economy relies on subcontracting to a degree that is perhaps unique. In the view of one analyst, subcontracting in sophisticated technology is more easily developed among peoples with a strong sense of hierarchy, as in Japan, than among those with more egalitarian outlooks as in many parts of India (Elwood Pye, personal communication). See also Chuta and Liedholm (1972:27–29) and sources cited there.

12. One source of misunderstandings has been a tendency of some scholars to assume that all societies share the same standards for judging what kinds of activities count as "achievement" and what kinds do not: they suppose that "need for achievement," which some dub "n Ach," is a universal human quality varying in degree but not in kind. It is now recognized that cultures vary enormously in what they consider achievement, so that no simple general model will do; see Cohen (1969); Nafziger (1977); Finney (1971, 1973); Kilby (1971:Chapter 1). LeVine has repudiated some conclusions of his McClelland-inspired 1966 study in subsequent work: he has preferred to consider systems of status mobility and entrepreneurial achievement motivation not as fixed qualities of ethnic groups, but as phases of their histories through which they may pass at different times. Some of McClelland's followers have elaborated an "entrepreneurship training" approach to enterprise development, based on personality tests to screen beneficiaries most likely to succeed. It is a topic of controversy. See McClelland (1961, 1966); Kilby (1971); Hunt (1983) and sources referred to in this last work.

13. A general, categorized appendix and bibliography on what some have called the "minority middleman" or "pariah capitalist" phenomenon appears in Bonacich and Modell (1980). The most conveniently consolidated set of recent writings and bibliographies on the subject is the journal *Ethnic Groups*, especially issues 2(1) (1978), and 2(3) (1980).

14. In most developing countries, of course, minority groups facing discrimination have been encouraged or compelled to specialize in kinds of businesses deemed inferior or polluting by the local majorities. These may variously include activities widely classed as "women's work" such as restaurant food preparation and laundry, or financial specializations like moneylending. Minorities fearing expropriations or expulsions often wish to keep their property in compact, mobile forms, often including jewelry; in many cultures these traditions outlive their initial causes.

15. Weber's classic analysis (1930) remains unsurpassed on the links between Protestantism and entrepreneurial behavior. Long (1968) provides a full-length ethnography of the effects of Seventh-Day Adventism on micro-enterprise in Zambia; Geertz (1963) does this for Islam on Java. See also Benedict (1968) on Ismaelis in East Africa. For shorter general introductions on scriptural, ecclesiastic, and laical attitudes toward work in the larger religions, see

the separate chapters on Hinduism, Buddhism, Judaism, Islam, Catholicism, and Protestantism, in Bieler et al. (1983).

16. Surveys are particularly likely to miss women's businesses when they begin by enumerating businesses, rather than by enumerating people and then their businesses.

17. For reasons of space, only a few of the many important issues of gender and small enterprise development can be touched upon here. For other recent literature of general geographical import, see Boserup (1970); Buvinic and Youssef (1979); March and Taqqu (1986); Crandon (1984); Dulansey and Austin (1985) (Austin includes a useful literature review and list of questions) and their bibliographies.

18. Trainers and extension agents in the more gerontocratic societies should be as senior as possible within the requirements of new knowledge, literacy, or energy for work and travel. Scarce vehicles should be allocated preferentially to older qualified field agents to avoid resentments and misunderstandings. Young officers in charge of credit allocation may be pressured for loans by elders in a community, but elders used as loan collectors will be better able than juniors to exert moral authority over defaulters. Sometimes it is inevitable to use juniors as contact agents in a gerontocratic society for reasons of education or demanding work requirements. In such cases strict scheduling and supervision may be needed to ensure that social frictions with their clients do not discourage them from doing their jobs.

19. Carruthers and Chambers (1981); Chambers (1981, 1983); Collinson (1981); Hildebrand (1981); IDS (1981); Longhurst (1981); Moore (1981); Rhoades (1982); Swift (1981).

20. See, for example, Marris and Somerset (1971); Liedholm and Chuta (1976); Chuta and Liedholm (1979:68–69). This last source reviews several others on the topic. See Anderson (1982) for a cautious approach to the comparative evidence.

21. Cohen (1969), Nafziger (1977), and Strickon (1979) discuss how, in regions with intermixed ethnic or religious groups, informal credit follows ethnic, religious, or kinship lines. These ties form a basis of trust and confidence that ensures borrowers against default.

22. Geertz (1962); Ardener (1964). The latter includes a useful list of questions for research on rotating credit and savings associations. More recent literature on indigenous savings and credit associations is surveyed in DeLancey (1978), and articles therein; in March and Taqqu (1982); and, for Africa, in Rielly (1985).

23. Occasionally there may be more than one recipient. There are many other variations. The contributions may be fixed or variable, and so may the order of rotation. Interest may or may not be paid. The most complex arrangements occur in East Asia.

24. See Siebel (1984) on Nigeria, and Haggblade (1978) on Cameroon. March and Taqqu (1982:52) recommend considering rotating credit associations as among the most appropriate women's informal associations for intervention, on the grounds that they can assert themselves in independent action (as opposed to being merely defensive or reactive), and that they are well bounded as groups, focused in their purposes, good for acquiring productive resources, and highly equitable in their authority, representation, and distribution of resources. The authors further suggest that associations like these provide models for resource institutions to work with by analogy: whether one uses them directly or not, they are patterns of organizations that work. See Ashe (1985, especially Chapter IV) and ILO (1984) for several concise summaries of lessons from group-based institutional savings and credit experiments.

25. This admonition is not meant to deny that high interest charges (those at or near market rates) have some advantages. A new wave of rural credit literature has made these clear. It is epitomized in J.D. Von Pischke, Dale Adams, and Gordon Donald, eds. (1983), and other writings by that book's three coeditors. See also Chapter 3 of this book.

26. Meyer (1985) and several articles in J.D. Von Pischke, Dale Adams, and Gordon Donald, eds. (1983), give current views on rural savings potentials and on needs and strategies for intervention. In recent years the trend has been to pay greater attention to the savings potential of the poor, and to call for more institutional savings opportunities.

27. The youth polytechnics that numerous organizations sponsor in Kenya are an approximation; they keep students in close working contact with a master of a trade for several months or more. These can apparently be effective though seldom inexpensive. A problem they have sometimes faced is market saturation for their particular products in their communities. This problem highlights needs for market research, as discussed in the following section.

28. Chuta and Liedholm (1979:67) give another more detailed list of types of assistance to small-scale businesses.

29. Two examples are Baer et al. (1985) for Senegal, and Mazingira Institute (1985) for Kenya.

Chapter 2

Assisting Small and Micro-Enterprises: The Resource Institutions

Numerous organizations, kaleidoscopic in their variety, pursue programs to assist small and micro-enterprises in the expectation that they are helping raise incomes and welfare levels among low income people and generating much needed employment in developing countries. The number of such organizations is impossible to know with precision. A recent directory lists 1,702 private organizations operating at the international level; a significant portion of these institutions pursues enterprise assistance programs (OECD 1981; Smith, Baldwin, and Chittick 1981:167–80; TAICH 1983). A listing of developing country government agencies, national business associations, private voluntary organizations, banks, and cooperatives providing similar services would be much more extensive. Some organizations focus entirely on enterprise development programs while others carry out a variety of development activities in addition to enterprise support programs. Resource institutions vary widely in size, visibility, and effectiveness. At the same time, they share many concerns, such as the desire to improve program design and the need to ensure that they are effective and efficient in pursuing their goals.

This chapter describes several broad categories of small and micro-enterprise resource institutions and assesses their characteristics as organizations providing development assistance. The chapter will also describe some of the most salient features of the task environment of the resource organizations that make their goals more or less difficult to achieve. Outlining the comparative characteristics of the organizations and describing critical aspects of their environment should assist organizations to assess better which type of program is best suited to their resources, goals, and context. Chapter 3 provides greater detail on the content of the assistance programs undertaken by resource institutions.

Comparative Characteristics

The vast majority of institutions that provide assistance to small and micro-enterprises fall into six general categories:

- international private voluntary organizations;
- national and local private voluntary organizations;
- cooperatives (private, public, and semipublic);
- banks;
- government agencies;
- business associations.

Although there are considerable differences in the activities and standards of performance within categories, each type tends to share a set of similar characteristics.[1] There are many exceptions to the generalizations. Moreover, what may appear to be limitations on particular types of institutions (small size, for example) often contribute to their effectiveness in other ways (such as adaptability to local circumstance). The characteristics assessed are:

- size: number of employees and size of budget;
- scale: extent to which the organization can serve large numbers of beneficiaries;
- institutionalization:[2] durability and extent to which the organization operates on the basis of routine procedures and regulations;
- adaptability to local circumstance: extent to which the organization is able to adapt in response to a changing and varied environment;
- socioeconomic emphasis: extent to which the organization emphasizes community development and social welfare goals as contrasted to a primarily business orientation;
- dependence on donors or government subsidies: extent to which the organization does not generate its own operating budget;
- ability to influence the policy environment: extent of ability to influence government decision-making processes.

The following sections review the comparative characteristics of the six categories of resource institutions.

1. International Private Voluntary Organizations

A large number of well-known institutions are in this category, organizations such as CARE, Church World Service, Catholic Relief Services, the Foster Parents Plan, World Education, International Voluntary Services, Transformation International, American Friends Service Committee, Oxfam, and others (see especially Sommer 1977; OECD 1983; Smith and Elkin 1981; TAICH 1983). In addition, many smaller and less well-known private voluntary organizations have an international focus (see, for example, TAICH 1983). Many of these organizations have long and distinguished records in community development, disaster assistance, and relief work. Increasingly, they have become convinced that development assistance must have income generation as a central component if it is to have a sustained impact on the poor majority in developing countries (see Montgomery 1986:5).

Often, international private voluntary organizations work through local chapters, local affiliates, or local grantees in developing countries. Increasingly, they tend to belong to umbrella organizations of similar institutions, such as Private Agencies Collaborating Together (PACT), Interaction, and the Union of International Associations (Brussels). These organizations have been among those most concerned to develop useful and replicable models for enterprise assistance because of their multicountry focus. They are notable for the extensive commitment of their leaders and staff (see OECD 1983; Sommer 1977; Kozlowski 1983; Tendler 1982). Such individuals generally work long hours, maintain demanding travel schedules, and accept salaries that compare unfavorably with those they might receive in other fields (Wilson 1983:19).

Size. International private voluntary organizations range from very large to small. They may employ as many as several hundred staff people or as few as twenty, ten, or even fewer. A significant portion of their staff resides in developing countries. Budgets range from several million dollars each year to a few hundred thousand dollars (see TAICH 1983).

Scope. The activities of individual organizations in this category may reach a large number of developing countries and the number of individuals and families they assist through their programs can be quite large. In general, however, the scope of their activities in any one country, and thus the number of people they are able to assist locally, is quite limited.

Institutionalization. Large international organizations tend to be well institutionalized, with procedures and regulations guiding hiring, travel, grant making, reporting, budgeting, and other routine matters. They tend to be durable and can take advantage of modern management techniques, including computer-based information and monitoring systems. Smaller organizations tend to be less well institutionalized.

Adaptability to Local Circumstance. When such organizations work through local grantees, they may be able to support particularly well programs that are flexible and that demonstrate creative responses to the needs of small and micro-enterprises at the local level (Wilson 1983:19–20). On the other hand, they may be somewhat less flexible when they operate through local affiliates that must clear many of their decisions with central headquarters. Their commitment to specific models of how to carry out enterprise assistance can affect their adaptability (see Kozlowski 1983).[3] Many international organizations are concerned particularly with program evaluation, an interest that increases their willingness to adapt or try new approaches (see, for example, ACVAFS 1985).

Socioeconomic Emphasis. There is considerable variation and debate among international organizations about whether they should emphasize community development and social welfare goals or the stimulation of business. Many organizations such as CARE, Oxfam, and Foster Parents that have a long history of efforts in community development and relief efforts tend to emphasize social welfare goals and programs that will benefit communities and groups rather than individuals. Other organizations, such as Appropriate Technology International and Technoserve, have a more single-minded focus on enterprise or technology development and tend to be more oriented toward the goal of stimulating entrepreneurship and appropriate business skills and technology.

Dependence. International private voluntary organizations receive funds from a variety of sources, including private citizens, corporations, national and international aid agencies such as USAID, and private foundations (see Sommer 1977; Weisbrod 1977; TAICH 1983). They have often developed sophisticated fund-raising techniques and may have long-term funding relationships with particular granting agencies. In general, they tend not to be extremely dependent on any one donor; this situation has helped many of them to endure. At times, these international organizations compete for funding, even while they maintain collaborative relationships in other areas. Moreover, as has been made clear in recent famine situations in Africa, "The public fund-raising imperative influences NGO [Non-Governmental Organizations] priorities and tends to result in a concentration on situations that lend themselves to dramatization" (Kozlowski 1983:13).

Ability to Influence the Policy Environment. Almost all international voluntary organizations publicly eschew any intent or capacity to influence government decision making in countries where they are active. They are very concerned to promote the image that their activities are humanitarian, not political. In countries where they have large programs and provide large amounts of money, however, they may have some capacity to influence government policy by bargaining over grant conditions. In general, however, their influence is limited.

2. National and Local Private Voluntary Organizations

There are more national and local private voluntary organizations than there are institutions in any other category considered here. These organizations include national institutions such as the Fundación Dominicana de Desarrollo (DDF) in the Dominican Republic, the National Christian Council of Kenya (NCCK), and the National Development Fund of Jamaica. There are also a very large number of more specific or local organizations such as the Carvajal Foundation in Colombia, the Centre d'Education a la Promotion Collective in Cameroon, the Brazilian Center for Assistance to Small and Medium Enterprises (CEBRAE), and the Working Women's Forum in Madras, India.[4]

Many of these national and local efforts began as organizations with community development and social welfare goals; they often focus specifically on the needs of a particular group of people or the needs of a particular locality. These institutions are frequently the creation of zealous or charismatic individuals whose "vision" of development helps sustain the organization (see Tendler 1981, 1982a, 1982b, 1984). They tend to hire individuals who are committed to social action, trusting that specific technical skills can be learned but that motivation and social concern cannot. Staff are frequently poorly remunerated but often continue to offer diligent service because of their commitment. It is becoming more common for national and local private voluntary organizations to join national level umbrella associations or networks of similar institutions (see Montgomery 1986:5). Many have strong links to international donor agencies or international institutions such as religious organizations (see TAICH 1983; Farbman, ed. 1981:*passim*).

Size. National and local private organizations range in size from those with staffs of one hundred or more people to those with ten to twelve people. The very smallest often operate with a staff of two to three people and a number of unpaid volunteers. Their budgets are generally small, rarely exceeding U.S.$2–$3 million dollars annually and often having as little as U.S.$25,000–$50,000 per year with which to operate their programs.

Scope. Such organizations tend to specialize in intensive service to a very specific clientele. When they are small, they may have only a hundred clients; large organizations may benefit directly as many as 5,000 to 8,000 clients over the course of several years (see Farbman, ed. 1981: *passim;* Smith and Tippett 1982).

Institutionalization. While there are a number of well-institutionalized national and local private organizations providing enterprise assistance, many more are loosely organized and casual about the accomplishment of routine procedures such as record keeping and monitoring of programs. Often, their level of informality may be appropriate to their size and may encourage creative response to the changing needs and opportunities of their beneficiaries (see Tendler 1982 for a discussion). In some cases, however, lack of institutionalization affects sustainability and increases the chances for making poor management decisions (see, for example, Gupta 1977:18).

Adaptability to Local Circumstance. Because of their size and focus, national and local organizations are frequently adaptive to local circumstance and responsive to the needs of their beneficiaries. Nevertheless, some of them share with their international counterparts the tendency to be committed to a particular model of enterprise assistance, a factor that may impede their ability to adapt to changing needs and circumstance.

Socioeconomic Emphasis. These organizations vary considerably in terms of the emphasis given to social welfare and community development objectives as distinguished from more specific business assistance. The Urban Community Improvement Program (UCIP) of the NCCK, for example, is principally concerned with the broad community and family welfare impact of its activities among residents of squatter communities in Kenya, while the Carvajal Foundation in Colombia emphasizes the development of business management skills and entrepreneurial talent among its beneficiaries.[5] Often, the difference in emphasis corresponds to the needs of the particular clientele they serve (see Ashe 1981:21).

Dependence. Private national and local organizations often tend to be dependent on donor assistance, and many are highly dependent on one or two principal donors. A large number are dependent almost exclusively on international donors. As we shall see in Chapter 4, dependence is a serious problem. A few organizations, such as the Carvajal Foundation in Colombia, the Fundación Costarricense de Desarrollo (FUCODES) in Costa Rica, the Tahanan Foundation in the Philippines, and the Northeast Union of Assistance to Small Businesses (UNO) in Brazil, have demonstrated an ability to mobilize local funding sources.[6] Others, such as the Kenyan Village Polytechnic Program and the Calcutta "Y" Self-Employment Center have been subsidized by government.[7]

Ability to Influence the Policy Environment. With the exception of a few of the larger institutions, private organizations are not able to exert much pressure on national decision-making processes to bring about a more favorable context for small and micro-business. They are likely to feel vulnerable to government "retaliation" if they become "too political" (see Tendler 1984).

3. Cooperatives

Public and private cooperative organizations are widespread in developing countries. Those most concerned with enterprise development are savings and loan associations, often serving a specific clientele such as farmers, small merchants, or market vendors. Some, however, are production and/or marketing cooperatives, and some have been formed for the purpose of helping members acquire production materials or inventory at reasonable prices. Cooperatives tend to be heavily regulated by governments and often are initiated by them (see Peterson 1982; Quick 1980). The commitment of cooperative leadership to the achievement of organizational goals is often considerable. At times, however, these organizations encounter difficulties at local levels in attracting well-qualified staff (see Peterson 1982; Miller 1977:92). Cooperatives are normally affiliated into national federations or confederations.

Cooperative organizations have been criticized for being inappropriate for the cultural context of some countries or for being dominated by more well-to-do individuals (see especially Peterson 1982; Tendler 1983b; Lele 1981; Widstrand 1970). However, there are well-known successes among cooperatives such as the ones organized into the Indian National Dairy Development Board (Korten 1980; Paul 1982:15–36).

Size/Scale. Individual cooperatives rarely grow beyond a few hundred members, but national federations and confederations can have memberships numbering in the thousands, particularly the government-sponsored cooperatives that are often heavily subsidized by the state. National staff can be large; locally, one to five individuals generally form the paid staff of individual cooperatives. Cooperatives organized on a national scale often reach even remote communities. In some cases, a significant portion of the population may belong to cooperative organizations. In Costa Rica, for example, approximately 30 percent of the economically active population belongs to cooperatives promoted and regulated by a government agency, INFOCOOP.[8]

Institutionalization. National federations and confederations of cooperatives are often well institutionalized. At times, they have been criticized for being bureaucratic and rigid (see Peterson 1982; Quick 1980; Lele 1981). At the local level, poor management and a lack of appropriate procedures or trained staff at times have resulted in cooperatives that are poorly institutionalized and subject to failure or corruption.[9]

Adaptability to Local Circumstance. The necessity of maintaining cooperative forms of organization and the existence of considerable government regulation tend to limit the adaptability and creativity of these institutions. At the same time, effective cooperatives demonstrate the capacity to reflect the needs of their members in initiating projects for them (see Tendler 1983b). Because institutional forms and local economic relationships may make cooperative services more accessible to some than to others, this type of organization may be particularly well suited to certain types of entrepreneurs (better-off small merchants, for example) and less well suited to others (see Peterson 1982; Tendler 1983b, 1984; Lele 1981). If cooperatives are effectively controlled by their members, they can be responsive to local needs.

Socioeconomic Emphasis. Cooperatives strongly emphasize the community and social welfare benefits that result from cooperation and the pooling of benefits and risks. As organizations, however, they depend on the capacity to increase economic performance among their members (see Tendler 1983b:192–95). The services they provide often are directed to the benefit of individual businesses of the membership. Thus, the emphasis in cooperatives tends to be inclusive.

Dependence. Cooperatives are often very dependent on government subsidies and/or donor support (Tendler 1983b). Successfully managed cooperatives, however, have considerable potential to become self-sustaining and productive enterprises. This has been the case with El Ceibo in Bolivia (Tendler 1983b), and the milk producers' cooperatives in India (Korten 1980; Paul 1982:15–36)

Ability to Influence the Policy Environment. In countries where cooperative associations are large and have the potential to be politically important, they may have the capacity to influence government policy with regard to cooperative activities and support. In many cases, governments have developed bodies of laws and policies to regulate cooperatives and their influence on institutions often is limited to this specific set of regulatory measures. In general, public policies affect cooperatives more than cooperatives affect public policies (see Peterson 1982).

4. Banks

Public and private banks often are recommended as potentially appropriate institutions for providing credit to small and micro-businesses. There are some indications that this potential can be realized: the Multiservice Centers of the Bank of Baroda; the Banco del Pacífico in Ecuador; the Grameen Bank in Bangladesh; the BKK in Indonesia; and various branches of Women's World Banking are good examples from recent studies (see Brown 1981a:215–23; Brown 1981b:345–47; Harley 1983; Houghton 1985; Goldmark and Rosengard 1983). However, in general, few small and micro-entrepreneurs have access to these formal financial institutions. Thus, except in the cases of special development banks or special bank programs for small business assistance (for example, the Bank of Baroda, the Grameen Bank of Bangladesh, and the Banco del Pacífico), bank leadership and staff are not committed to assisting small and micro-enterprises (see Fraser and Tucker 1981:216). Banks prefer to deal with larger clients and argue that they cannot afford to lend to the poor (see Fraser and Tucker 1981:216; Miller 1977:72–83; Johnston and Clark 1982:102). Nevertheless, a number of experiences with bank lending to small entrepreneurs as groups or individuals suggest that banks have some advantages for assisting small and micro-entrepreneurs.

Size. Banks tend to be large, with extensive staffs and large amounts of financial resources.

Scale. Banks have the capacity to operate on an extensive scale, particularly in urban areas. Because of added costs, they tend to resist offering services to clients in rural areas, particularly to those in very remote areas. Banks need to operate on an extensive scale in order to keep their administrative costs low and they are often highly competitive with other institutions that offer the same services.

Institutionalization. Banks are highly institutionalized, to the point that it has often been claimed that they are too rigid and bureaucratic to respond to the needs of small and micro-entrepreneurs. Their procedures, regulations, and loan criteria often exclude small and micro-entrepreneurs (see Von Pischke, Adams, and Donald 1983). Development-oriented or special banks, such as the Grameen Bank and the Banco del Pacífico, generally must develop special procedures and hire and train special staff to respond to low income client needs (see, for example, Goldmark and Rosengard 1983).

Adaptability to Local Circumstance. Banks tend not to be adaptable to local circumstance because their procedures and regulations must be uniform and must be applied to broad categories of clients if their activities are to be efficient. A few innovative banks with particular concerns for low income clients, such as the Grameen Bank in Bangladesh (see IFAD 1984; Harley 1983; Houghton 1985), or particular bank programs, such as that of the Banco del Pacífico in Ecuador, have managed to avoid these general tendencies.

Socioeconomic Emphasis. Of all organizations providing enterprise assistance, banks tend to have the most firm commitment to business performance. As impersonal institutions, they can be effective in establishing and maintaining strict criteria for loan repayment, a characteristic of well-functioning programs (see Ashe 1981:42). As single-purpose financial institutions, banks are largely unconcerned with achieving community development or social welfare objectives. Special development banks, such as the Grameen Bank or the BKK in Indonesia, are, of course, exceptions to this general tendency.

Dependence. Generally, banks operate for profit and are not dependent on direct government subsidy or donor funding. Government banks, however, may receive subsidies from public revenues and particular programs of private and public banks may receive subsidized capital from government, donors, or international lending agencies.

Ability to Influence Policy Environment. Banks have considerable capacity to affect government policy related to interest and exchange rates. They also may have some capacity to influence decision makers on industrial and commercial policy. Because a very small portion of their loan portfolio is likely to involve low income entrepreneurs, however, banks are not likely to have much interest in affecting government policy toward this group. Again, special development banks are an exception.

5. Government Agencies

Most governments have programs to assist small and micro-enterprises. These may take the form of technical assistance bureaus, credit agencies, or training institutes. Often such organizations are assigned to the ministries of labor or industry. In some cases, they may be parastatal institutions, such as agricultural banks. The extent to which they are effective or visible varies by country, by administrations within a country, and by agency. Traditionally, these organizations have received funding from international agencies such as AID, the World Bank, the ILO, or international regional banks like the Inter-American Development Bank.

Size. The staff and budgets of government agencies tend to be relatively large, although they often are starved for funds relative to the scale of operations they are expected to accomplish. Inefficiency in the use of funds is a frequent complaint against government agencies.

Scale. Government programs have the potential capacity to reach large numbers of beneficiaries, even in remote rural areas. Although they are similar to banks in size and scale potential, they also have the capacity to provide a multiservice program to beneficiaries, something that is difficult for banks.

Institutionalization. Government agencies tend to be highly institutionalized and many verge on the rigidly bureaucratic. With effective leadership or strong political support, some have been able to maintain their institutionalized characteristics while remaining responsive and adaptable to the needs of their low income beneficiaries. This appears to have been the case with the Tanzania Small Industries Development Organization and PRIDECO in El Salvador (see O'Regan and Hellinger 1981:107–20; Fraser and Tucker 1981:167–91).

Adaptability to Local Circumstance. While bureaucratization tends to inhibit adaptability, some government agencies have been able to be responsive to local circumstances because of the multiservice approach they adopt. A good example of this was the Ministry of Social Services and Development in India reported in the PISCES Studies (Brown 1981a:293–306). In other cases, government agencies can be slow to adapt to beneficiary needs or a changing environment because of the laws and official regulations that shape their activities, including important staffing and administrative decisions.

Socioeconomic Emphasis. Many government agencies have a bias toward community development and social welfare goals. In part, this is a result of their frequent political mandate to mobilize political support among the low income population. Similarly, for political reasons, government agencies may have trouble applying strict criteria of loan eligibility and repayment to clients.

Dependence. Government agencies providing assistance to small and micro-enterprises generally operate with a deficit and receive considerable subsidies from government and from international donors. They often must devote considerable energy to maintaining their public visibility and to promoting agency interests in competitive government budgetary decision-making processes.

Ability to Influence the Policy Environment. In spite of their identification with the public sector, government organizations generally have little capacity to influence national decision makers because of their lack of power when compared to organized economic interests representing other sectors of the economy. However, they may have some capacity to shape decisions about issues that apply specifically and uniquely to small and micro-enterprises.

6. Business Associations

In a number of countries, associations of medium and large businesses have become interested in small and micro-enterprise programs. Usually they set up special foundations, funds, or institutes to carry out these programs (see, for example, Tendler 1984).[10] At times, business associations are motivated by concern over the potential for social unrest if incomes are not raised among large sectors of the population. At other times, they may be interested in engendering links with the smaller enterprise sector in order to provide themselves with a broader base of political support. Or, they may see economic advantages in fostering entrepreneurship in the society, in developing subcontracting arrangements for their own enterprises, or in benefiting from tax incentives that favor philanthropy. Examples of these business associations are COSEP in Nicaragua, the Indonesian Chamber of Commerce, and the Indian Merchants' Chamber; of India (see Tendler 1984; Alliband 1983:56–57; Indian Merchants' Chamber 1977). The commitment of business associations to a low income clientele generally is tempered by their commitment to the economic and political interests of the medium- and large-scale entrepreneurs that make up most of their membership.

Size. The programs of business associations tend to be small and operate with modest budgets. They are often very similar in size and operation to the local private voluntary associations previously discussed.

Scale. The number of beneficiaries of such association programs is also limited, with most of them concentrated in cities. At times, it has proved difficult to increase the size of these programs because they may not be a high priority for a significant portion of association members.

Institutionalization. In many ways, the assistance programs supported by business associations resemble those of the national and local private voluntary organizations. They vary in terms of their degree of institutionalization and their durability.

Adaptability to Local Circumstance. These programs can be quite adaptive to local constraints and opportunities. Their management is generally well informed of laws and regulations that affect business operations and they may have a good understanding of marketing and production opportunities. They offer the potential to link formal and informal sector operations. At the same time, however, some may have rigid ideas about what small and micro-entrepreneurs need and want, drawn from their experience with larger enterprises.

Socioeconomic Emphasis. Programs supported by business associations tend to have a strong bias toward training in business skills and engendering entrepreneurship.

Dependence. Business associations tend to be relatively autonomous, depending mainly on the support of their membership. The programs for small and micro-enterprise support, however, may be very dependent on the goodwill and orientation of the association's membership or on donor assistance (see Tendler 1984). Particularly when the business associationhas a strong ideological commitment and the program is extremely dependent on the parent organization, it may have limited scope for responding creatively to beneficiary needs.

Ability to Influence the Policy Environment. Business associations often have great capacity to influence public policies. However, they may not be particularly motivated to influence the policy environment for small and micro-enterprise, particularly if this emphasis might mean altering the advantages that medium and large enterprises receive from that environment or if small enterprises are seen as a competitive threat (see Haggblade, Liedholm, and Mead 1986).

Comparative Characteristics and Clienteles

All types of resource institutions have produced both successes and failures in carrying out small and micro-enterprise assistance programs. On the basis of a considerable literature, it appears that no particular organizational form is uniquely qualified to pursue such programs. Decisions about which organizational form to adopt or assist generally will depend on local conditions, experiences, available resources, and the particular strengths and weaknesses of existing organizations.

However, there is some evidence that the balance among the characteristics of organizations results in differing capacities to reach particular clienteles. For example, private voluntary organizations, because they tend to be small, focused, and adaptable, and inclined toward community development and social welfare goals, may be the most appropriate institutions for reaching the Level I and Level II entrepreneurs who have been identified by the PISCES projects.[11] Government agencies with a social welfare orientation also may be appropriate for this level of entrepreneur. Cooperatives and government agencies, because of their scale and institutionalization, may be most appropriate for reaching Level II entrepreneurs. Banks and business associations, because of their business orientation, capacity to influence the policy environment, and relative autonomy may be most suited to assisting entrepreneurs at Level III and above. When organizations wish to reach other levels of entrepreneurs effectively, they may have to alter their organizational structures, management styles, or program components. These issues are addressed more fully in Chapter 3.

The Task Environment

In addition to the relative characteristics of the organizations providing enterprise support programs, it is important to consider the task environment that confronts their assistance efforts. The task environment refers principally to the clientele of the organization, the policy environment, and the socioeconomic context. A task environment may be more or less difficult for the organizations as it affects their capacity to achieve program goals. Thus, clienteles can be more or less easy to assist, a policy environment can complicate or facilitate the organization's activities, and a socioeconomic context can be more or less favorable to small and micro-enterprises. Assistance to easier-to-reach clients in supportive policy and socioeconomic environments will be less time consuming, less expensive, and more immediately successful than assistance to clients who are more difficult to reach and who are in unsupportive environments. At the same time, from a development perspective, assisting easier-to-assist clients may be less important than assisting more needy entrepreneurs in a more hostile environment.

Clients

Client characteristics are important to resource institutions because they affect how easily the organization can respond to beneficiary needs. Organizations wishing to assist more difficult-to-reach groups may have to adopt particular program components, hire specialized staff, and spend more time and effort in reaching them. The special problems of helping difficult-to-assist clients can be addressed through organizational structure and management and program design. The literature on resource institutions reports that among the most significant characteristics of the clientele for assistance organizations are: the newness of the enterprise; the size of the enterprise; the sector in which it is operating (retail, manufacturing, or service); the income level of the beneficiary; and the location of the enterprise. Each of these factors can be summed up in a general working hypothesis about the ease or difficulty of assisting those who share the particular characteristic. They are denoted working hypotheses because the literature provides us with a reasonable sense that they accurately reflect a wide body of experience but they have not yet been subject to rigorous testing. These hypotheses are presented below.

Existing enterprises are more easily assisted than enterprises that are newly created through the project. There is a high failure rate for new businesses. Entry barriers and start-up problems are often great. Frequently, new enterprises fail because their owners are not committed to or skilled at a particular activity or may have misjudged a business opportunity. Existing enterprises, on the other hand, have proved a minimum level of survivability and indicate the business acumen and aptitude of the owner. Existing enterprises also have collateral that can serve as the basis for formal institutional assistance.

Larger enterprises are more easily assisted than smaller ones. Tiny enterprises, often involving only one person, may require more intensive assistance than larger ones, although accumulating evidence suggests that simple credit schemes may be effective in assisting the smallest businesses (see Ashe 1981:19–23). The entrepreneurs are generally poorer and suffer more from the cumulative disadvantages of poverty—malnutrition, illiteracy, vulnerability to personal disasters, and other problems. Larger businesses, in contrast, tend to have owners with some cushion between themselves and dire poverty and to have collateral that makes them more riskworthy for financial assistance. Nevertheless, larger small businesses may face constraints on their growth in contexts in which there are barriers to entering the formal sector. Some experience suggests that the larger small firms have a greater impact on employment while tiny enterprises are most effective for increasing welfare levels and income among the poorest sectors (see Farbman, ed. 1981).

Retail and service enterprises are more easily assisted than manufacturing enterprises. The amount of capital, technical assistance, and marketing expertise required for manufacturing is greater than that for other sectors. Aassistance programs for manufacturing enterprises will therefore need larger amounts of capital and more sophisticated technical assistance for production and marketing than is the case for other types of enterprises. At the same time, manufacturing enterprises generally have the greatest capacity to generate productive employment and to make substantial contributions to economic growth (see Haggblade, Liedholm, and Mead 1986; Anderson and Leiserson 1980).

Better off beneficiaries are easier to assist than less well off ones. As indicated in the PISCES studies, very poor beneficiaries may require commitment to the time-consuming development of group solidarity and social welfare benefits. The poorer the clientele, then, the more effort might be required for organizational activities, training, support functions (nutrition and health programs, for example), and monitoring client performance. More advantaged clients may need only one or two types of assistance and are less vulnerable to the kinds of problems caused by extreme poverty—ill-health, lack of permanent residence, debt, and discrimination. At the same time, assisting poorer clienteles tends to have a greater humanitarian, distributional, and welfare impact. Moreover, simple credit programs appear to have had some success with very poor clients without extensive supplementary services.

Urban enterprises are more easily assisted than rural enterprises. The urban location of clients often means they are more integrated into a national economy, have more access to markets, and have more opportunities for growth (see Tendler 1982b). For resource institutions, an urban clientele means that fewer resources are expended in getting to where clients are and in assisting them and monitoring their performance. In many countries, however, the majority of small enterprises are located in rural areas and stimulating urban enterprises can add to already high rural-to-urban migration rates (see Anderson and Leiserson 1980; Chuta and Liedholm 1979; Steel and Takagi 1983; Page 1979).

Women entrepreneurs may require services distinct from those offered to male entrepreneurs. Women are often excluded from the institutions, resources, and skills that are necessary to make a going concern of their business activities (see Obbo 1980; March and Taqqu 1982; Bourque and Warren 1981). Because they often undertake entrepreneurial activities in addition to heavy household responsibilities, their time, energy, and interest may be constrained. In general, women are less educated and poorer than males and in many countries may not have control over personal property. At the same time, assisting women can have considerable impact on socioeconomic structures and can result in real developmental advances (see March and Taqqu 1982; Crandon 1984; Dulansey and Austin 1985).

Resource institutions should not be discouraged from undertaking programs to help more difficult-to-assist clients in favor of programs for those easier-to-assist. If this standard were followed, inequities in resource distribution and access to benefits of programs would become even more highly skewed than they already are in developing countries. However, when resource institutions make decisions about the types of clients they wish to assist, they are also choosing a series of needs they will have to address if they are to be effective. They will need to consider the special requirements of the clientele they decide to serve and to shape their organization and service delivery programs accordingly. In some cases, resource institutions may lack the resources, personnel, or experience necessary to address the problems of particular groups, however extensive their commitment. In such cases, they should be encouraged to make alternative choices or to modify their goals to fit the institutional and contextual reality.

The Policy Environment

There is increasing consensus that aspects of a national policy environment strongly affect the nature and existence of small and micro-enterprises (see Haggblade, Liedholm, and Mead 1986). A list of the policies thought to affect enterprise and employment is presented in Table I–1 (page 47). Aspects of the policy environment also affect how resource institutions operate and the degree of ease or difficulty with which they assist small and micro-entrepreneurs. As yet, there is little direct evidence of these effects, and specific statements about the policy environment must be treated as hypotheses. It is important to present these hypotheses because they can aid resource institutions in becoming sensitive to the factors in the policy environment they need to consider when making choices about organizational structure, activities, and program design. Thus, just as organizations need to plan on what the characteristics of the clientele mean for the institution, they must also consider how the policy environment will affect their activities.

The policy environment may affect small enterprises differently from how it affects the resource institutions. Many studies indicate that government regulation—minimum wage legislation, licensing, trade restrictions, mandatory social insurance programs—often leads to a flourishing of activities in the informal sector, where there are fewer barriers to entry (see, for example, Greaney 1986:18; Portes and Benton 1984). But for resource institutions, government regulation means that it is more difficult for their clients to "graduate" to the formal sector or to become clients of formal sector institutions such as banks. Extensive government regulation also means that small and micro-entrepreneurs can be extremely vulnerable to police and official harassment.

Among the most important aspects of the policy environment for resource institutions are interest rates, regulation, exchange rates, and scale discrimination. A set of hypotheses about how these factors affect the task environment of the resource institution is presented in the following paragraphs.

Government policies that set artificially low interest rate ceilings or credit controls increase the difficulty of assisting low income clients Artificially low interest rates tend to exclude low income borrowers from formal financial markets (Von Pischke, Adams, and Donald 1983; Steel and Takagi 1983). Such exclusion can increase client dependence on the resource institution, curtailing their ability to "graduate" to formal financial institutions, and limiting the ability of the organization to serve more clients. Moreover, when resource institutions lend money to their clients at subsidized—even negative—rates of real interest, they increase their costs and the likelihood of dependence on donors or government subsidies (see Tendler 1984). This makes them more vulnerable to failure. Low interest rates also discourage savings mobilization, which is increasingly recognized as an important mechanism for helping low income people help themselves (see Rielly 1986; Meyer 1985).

Table I–1

Inventory of Policies Affecting Employment and Enterprise Growth

(by functional groupings)

1. **Trade Policy**
   a. import tariffs
   b. import quotas
   c. export taxes or subsidies
   d. foreign exchange rates
   e. foreign exchange controls

2. **Monetary Policy**
   a. money supply
   b. interest rate
   c. banking regulations

3. **Fiscal Policy**
   a. government expenditure
      —infrastructure
      —direct investment in production, marketing, or service enterprises
      —government provision of services
      —transfers
   b. taxes
      —corporate income
      —personal income
      —payroll
      —property
      —sales

4. **Labor Policies**
   a. minimum wage laws
   b. legislation with regard to working conditions, fringe benefits, etc.
   c. social security
   d. public sector wage policy

5. **Output Prices**
   a. consumer prices
   b. producer prices

6. **Direct Regulatory Controls**
   a. enterprise licensing and registration
   b. monopoly privileges
   c. land allocation and tenure
   d. zoning
   e. health

Source: Haggblade, Liedholm, and Mead 1986.

The more extensive the government regulation of business, the more difficult it is to assist small and micro-enterprises. Government regulations about wages, taxation, social welfare contributions, licensing, and other business-related issues are among the important reasons why informal sector businesses develop. Entrance into the formal sector is too expensive and raises too many barriers for low income people. Of course, governments have the right and duty to ensure that workers are not exploited, that businesses contribute to national security and welfare through taxes, and that certain kinds of information on business activities are available. However, extensive regulation also can create a hostile environment for the work of the resource institutions. Resource institutions can be most effective when they can "graduate" some of their clients to the formal sector and deter them from becoming dependent on the programs of the institution. Conforming to laws, regulations, and reporting requirements or helping their clients do so also can be time consuming and expensive for resource institutions.

The more overvalued the exchange rate, the more difficult it is for resource institutions to help small and micro-enterprises to develop and grow. Overvalued exchange rates reduce the price of imported goods and generally lead to rationing of foreign exchange or import restrictions, which in turn generally discriminate in favor of large firms (Haggblade, Liedholm, Mead 1986:23–29; Greaney 1986:19). Thus, small and micro-businesses often cannot compete because of differential access to foreign exchange; they may be restricted to producing goods that do not require imports of machinery or raw materials. While this enforced reliance on indigenous resources may provide informal businesses with a niche in the economy, it also tends to limit the market available to such firms and to hinder their expansion. In such a context, resource institutions serving small and micro-enterprises must increase their marketing and production assistance, especially to their manufacturer clients. Providing services thus becomes more costly and technically complex.

The less government policy discriminates on the basis of scale, the easier it is to assist in the development and growth of small-scale enterprises. Policies to encourage industrialization often result in access barriers for small-scale enterprises (see Tokman 1985). Interest rates, exchange rates, import restrictions, tax benefits, and other policies, in addition to infrastructure development, often favor larger firms and make it more difficult for small firms to compete effectively in national and international markets (Haggblade, Liedholm, and Mead 1986). Such factors impede the potential for growth of the smaller firms. Moreover, such policies generally require small and micro-firms to operate illegally, greatly increasing the chances that they will be harassed by police officials and subjected to "shakedowns" and other pressures. Indeed, often it is municipal level regulation and discrimination as much as national that work against the interests of small and micro-entrepreneurs. Again, in this kind of a policy environment, resource institutions must generally provide more services to their clientele than they would in a more neutral policy environment.

As indicated in the first part of this chapter, resource institutions have variable capacity to press policy makers to alter an unfavorable policy environment. Generally, they are wary of becoming "too political," for they fear retaliation by government (see Tendler 1984). A recent trend toward the creation of national umbrella organizations of private voluntary institutions may, of course, increase the leverage of NGOs in representing the interests of small and micro-entrepreneurs (see Montgomery 1986). There is also a general trend of greater political support for the economic and social welfare contributions of the small enterprise sector that may translate into an impetus to change existing policy where it is discriminatory or unfavorable. Currently, however, most institutions must take the policy environment as a given for their short- and medium-term activities and work within it as best they can. If policies discriminate substantially against their programs, resource institutions need to consider adopting special compensatory features in the programs they design. If interest rates are kept artificially low, for example, resource institutions can assess modest user charges that will help ensure their own financial viability (see Rielly 1986).

The Socioeconomic Context

There are, of course, factors in the general socioeconomic environment that make it more or less difficult to assist small and micro-enterprises, factors such as the dynamics of economic growth, the extent of infrastructure development, existing domestic and international market linkages, and societal traditions of entrepreneurship. Many of these more general factors are discussed in the PISCES reports (see Ashe 1985:20–22; see also Blayney and Otero 1985). They are summarized here to complete the picture of the task environment that has been developed in this chapter. Ironically, aspects of the socioeconomic context that increase the difficulty of assisting small and micro-enterprises at times may help the enterprises themselves in the sense that growth of the informal sector is often encouraged and stimulated by poor socioeconomic conditions. Important aspects in the socioeconomic environment can be stated in terms of a series of hypotheses about the ease or difficulty with which resource institutions carry out their assistance programs.

The more dynamic the local and national economy, the easier it is to stimulate the creation and growth of small and micro-enterprises. Economic growth tends to increase the size of markets available to enterprises and creates opportunities for growth. These provide resource institutions with more options for assisting their clients and may facilitate their graduation to greater independence and linkages to formal sector institutions.

The lower the rate of inflation, the easier it is for resource institutions to manage their finances effectively. High rates of inflation increase the difficulty and frequency of assessing, setting, and revising interest rates, staff salaries, credit limits, and budgets. Hyperinflation may require a resource institution to adopt a barter system, as has occurred at times in Bolivia. Organizational management, record keeping, and administration are more difficult under such conditions.

The more developed the physical and social infrastructure, the easier it becomes to stimulate the creation and growth of viable small and micro-enterprises. Resource institutions can limit the services they must provide for their low income clients when markets are easily accessible, when businesses can get access to basic services such as electricity and water, and when schools, clinics, and social welfare agencies are widely available. In such conditions, the small and micro-enterprises that develop must be able to compete with the production of goods and services by larger enterprises.

The more extensive the market linkages, the easier it becomes to stimulate the creation and growth of the small and micro-enterprise sector. Extensive market linkages open up opportunities for enterprise creation and growth and facilitate graduation to formal sector institutions.

The more extensive the societal tradition of entrepreneurship, the easier it is to pursue assistance programs for small and micro-enterprises. Entrepreneurial traditions reduce resource institution expenditure of time, talent, and budgets on training and technical assistance in their small and micro-enterprise assistance programs.

With the exception of the last factor—entrepreneurship—most resource institutions in developing countries face a socioeconomic context closer to the "more difficult" side of the continuum than to the "less difficult" side. Moreover, these aspects of the task environment change only slowly and cannot be altered through the activities of the resource institutions. Nevertheless, it is important for resource institutions to assess the socioeconomic context for elements that may pose problems for their assistance programs. How to cope with problems can then be considered explicitly in organizational decision making and program design.

Conclusions

Resource institutions have a variable set of characteristics that affect their capacities to carry out small and micro-enterprise assistance programs. Whatever their comparative advantages as institutions, however, they must address a task environment that will ease or impede their efficiency, effectiveness, and sustainability. The choices they make about how to assist a low income population should be shaped by an understanding of both their own institutional characteristics and the aspects of the task environment that will affect their activities: the characteristics of the clients, the policy environment, and the socioeconomic context. Despite the complexity, there are recognizable patterns and some clear choices. However, the easiest options are not always the most charitable; the most charitable, not always the most cost-effective. Every institution must trade off some objectives for others it deems more important. Even the nature of the trade-offs themselves will vary with the task environment. It is no surprise, then, that the resulting assistance programs themselves vary widely. Within this variety, nonetheless, one can discern patterns and categories of approaches. In Chapter 3 we suggest some that we believe useful.

Notes

1. The identification of institutional characteristics is based on a review of the literature on small and micro-enterprise assistance programs and on the more general literature dealing with institutional analysis. Numerous examples of such institutions are provided. To the extent possible, we have drawn these cases from the PISCES studies so that readers can easily refer to more extensive analyses of empirical examples. We have also drawn examples from other easily accessible sources. In addition, we have added a few examples from field interviews with resource institutions in Latin America and Africa. In general, examples refer to institutions that had demonstrated some success in carrying out small and micro-enterprise programs, at least at the time they were studied.

2. Institutionalization has both positive and negative connotations. "According to organization theory [institutionalization], can produce greater efficiency, reliability, and accountability, but an organization's need for control often results in rigidity, inertia, and resistance to change, as well as in ritualism and insularity." (Kramer 1982:265)

3. For example, a director of one international organization observed, "...NGOs [Non-Governmental Organizations] sometimes 'idealize' their roles and believe that theirs is the only or the best solution to the particular problems at hand. This attitude does not normally ingratiate them with host country officials nor does it facilitate understanding of, or cooperation with, official aid agencies." (Kozlowski 1983:13)

4. Each of these organizations is described in Farbman ed. (1981), as a part of the work done under the PISCES Project or in Smith and Tippett (1982). On the DDF and the NCCK, see also AID (1985).

5. The UCIP is described in O'Regan and Hellinger (1981:60–81); the Carvajal Foundation is described briefly in Chapter 3. See also Sanders (1983a) and (1983b).

6. FUCODES and UNO are the subjects of teaching cases developed by HIID/ARIES. The Tahanan Foundation is described in Brown (1981b:307–16). UNO is described in Tendler (1983a).

7. These are described in O'Regan and Hellinger (1981:83–99) and Brown (1981b:367–73).

8. Interview, San José, Costa Rica, June 17, 1986.

9. Tendler (1983b:224–29) argues that evidence of corruption often surfaces in a cooperative as a result of other problems or dissatisfactions among members.

10. Associations of small and micro-entrepreneurs are becoming more common in developing countries. These are generally organizations formed by entrepreneurs in already existing firms who come together for the purpose of discussing and resolving common problems, political representation, joint advertising, or joint purchasing or marketing. A good example is CANAPI in Costa Rica, which represents its membership politically, provides training courses, organizes artisan fairs, operates shops to sell products made by its members, and publishes an advertising directory. There is little information available on these kinds of associations and they are not included in the text discussion. We have limited our focus to business associations formed by medium and large entrepreneurs that have initiated programs for small and micro-enterprises.

11. See Ashe 1981:19–23.

Chapter 3

Assisting Small and Micro-Enterprises: Program Components and Models

No single program design is "best" for assisting small and micro-enterprises. Rather, there are a variety of ways to aid this sector of the economy. Program design should be varied in order to meet the specific needs of diverse types of small and micro-entrepreneurs. Some enterprises may require credit, some may need technical assistance, and others may need several services offered together in order to improve operations. In addition, programs that assist small and micro-enterprises should respond to the changing needs of their clients over time. At one point in its development, a business may need credit in order to expand; at another point, its principal need may be marketing assistance. Because needs change over time, responses to them will also be varied.

The resource institutions discussed in Chapter 2 use a variety of approaches to assist small and micro-enterprises. Of these, several have been widely adopted. This chapter describes the components of various types of assistance programs. The resource institutions combine these components in distinct ways, resulting in at least six principal models. Each of these program models has implications for cost, staffing requirements, and the type of client most easily assisted. The chapter considers the characteristics of the various models in a way that should help resource institutions assess their capacities to pursue individual models.

Program Components and Models

Four components are widely found in various combinations and sequences in small and micro-enterprise assistance programs: (1) financial assistance; (2) technical assistance, also called extension; (3) training; and (4) social promotion. Provision of financial assistance is found in almost all such programs, although its importance within a program "package" may vary considerably. The other components are adopted or not, sequenced differently, and delivered with varying degrees of seriousness. A single resource institution may adopt only one program type or it may pursue two or even more types for different kinds of clients. Moreover, a resource institution may try out and discard different assistance programs as it develops and discovers more effective modes of operation (see, for example, Tendler 1983a; Montgomery forthcoming:Chapter 5).

The Components: Ingredients of Assistance Programs

Financial Assistance. Almost all small and micro-enterprise programs include means to provide credit to their clients. Nevertheless, there is considerable debate about whether small entrepreneurs need as much access to credit as is frequently claimed. Certainly the entrepreneurs generally claim they need credit, but this claim may reflect their own realistic assessment of what they consider to be an immediate and tangible benefit. The emphasis on credit should not be allowed to obscure factors such as marketing or technology assessment, which may be just as critical to the success or failure of small and micro-enterprises (see Marris and Somerset 1971; Liedholm and Chuta 1976; Harper 1984). Why, then, does credit figure so centrally in assistance programs?

Resource institutions most often answer that lack of access to capital is a critical constraint on small and micro-enterprises (Chuta and Liedholm 1979:68–69; Blayney and Otero 1985). This corresponds closely to what the entrepreneurs generally say they need most and to what donor and lending agencies have traditionally supported (see Farbman, ed. 1981:xii). A second answer appears to be that many resource institutions are convinced that they must offer credit if they are to attract clients.[1] Even programs in which credit is not a central ingredient make access to capital available to their clients as an inducement for them to benefit from the other services. Yet another reason is that credit should generate income for the institutions and allows them to sustain themselves more effectively. Thus, even where resource institutions emphasize other services, they believe that offering credit will enable them to support these activities more effectively.

Credit is offered in two ways, to individuals or through group mechanisms. With individual credit, the entrepreneur usually presents some form of collateral, a guarantor of the loan, or personal testimony to his or her character and serious intent (see Blayney and Otero 1985). In group credit programs, small groups of individuals co-guarantee loans for specific members. Subsequent loans to any member of the group are made contingent upon repayment of prior loans. Peer pressure and group cohesion are considered important to the success of repayment (see Ashe 1985:40–41 for an example; see also Houghton 1985). This kind of credit system is generally used with the poorest entrepreneurs, while individual credit tends to be offered most frequently to better-off business people. Most resource institutions offer credit directly to their clients, but some act as conduits to formal institutional credit by preparing their clients to be effective in applying for such loans. There appears to be a growing consensus among resource institutions that, to the extent possible, credit should be disbursed through formal financial intermediaries.[2] Often credit can be extended through special program funds for enterprise development. Both clients and financial intermediaries learn how to deal with each other more effectively through credit disbursement mechanisms and client graduation to formal sector institutions is made easier.

Other forms of financial assistance, such as mechanisms for mobilizing savings effectively, are much less frequently adopted. As savings mobilization becomes more widely appreciated as an effective means to assist the poor—the research literature strongly supports this idea—resource institutions are likely to begin adopting it more widely.[3] Currently, many appear to hold the "too-poor-to-save" belief. This has blinded them to the important role savings mobilization can play in assisting small and micro-businesses (see Rielly 1986).

Technical Assistance. The second most frequent ingredient of enterprise support programs is business extension or technical assistance.[4] Frequently, it is provided as an aspect of a credit delivery program. Technical assistance is a broad label that includes assisting small and micro-entrepreneurs with routine business practices such as bookkeeping and costing of inventory and more specialized forms of aid such as marketing, production, and choice of appropriate technology. In general, business extension is provided on a one-to-one basis, with program staff working individually with the enterprise owner at the site of the business. The most common pattern is that technical assistance is provided free to the clients; many resource institutions fear that if they charge for such services, clients will not utilize them (see Tendler 1984). Unfortunately, in the absence of user charges, resource institutions often have no way of knowing if the technical assistance is needed, appropriate, effective, or efficient (for a discussion, see Blayney and Otero 1985).

Generally, resource institutions have staff—often called promoters or extensionists—who school beneficiaries in routine business practices. For specialized assistance, resource institutions either hire a full- or part-time specialist in a particular area—marketing, for example—or contract on a need-specific basis with an expert from an appropriate consulting firm or a technical or training agency. Technical assistance efforts often are criticized as inappropriate to the needs of beneficiaries or for being carried out in an overly casual or haphazard manner (see, for example, Fraser and Tucker 1981:169–82). At the same time, few resource institutions believe they can do an effective job of assisting their clients without it.

Training. A number of resource institutions are committed to providing group training to their beneficiaries. Training components emphasize business skills and entrepreneurship or are geared toward inculcating job-related skills. In the case of business training, the resource institutions frequently claim that the entrepreneurs have a specific skill—repairing bicycles, for example—but lack skills such as bookkeeping, cost accounting, marketing and sales, and enterprise administration (see Ashe 1981:42–43). Entrepreneurial training often contains a strong motivational dimension. The resource institutions believe that business and entrepreneurial skills can be taught effectively to small-scale entrepreneurs, even those with very low levels of schooling. Manuals, workbooks, and learning tools such as games, using simple concepts, bright colors, and cartoon figures, are frequently used in this training. A sequence of formal or semiformal courses often is offered for which entrepreneurs pay a small sum to defray part of the costs or to encourage their commitment to learn something from the course. Teachers usually come from the staff of the resource institution or may be employed part-time as they attend universities or teach in other jobs. Training modules at times are integrated with individualized extension components.

In the case of job skills training, the emphasis is placed on preparing students for employment opportunities in the formal or informal sectors through teaching specific job-related skills such as metalworking, masonry, tailoring, weaving, mechanics, and baking. The purpose is to allow trainees to find employment or to begin their own small businesses. Some programs combine job skills training with employment advisory or placement services. The costs of this type of training program can be significant because of equipment, repairs, and replacements. Trainees may pay a fee for participation in a course or they may generate program income from the activities they undertake to learn a specific task (for an example see O'Regan and Hellinger 1981:83–99).

Social Promotion. Resource institutions often add a social promotion component to their programs to assist small and micro-entrepreneurs. Such a component most frequently is part of assistance programs to the poorest or most marginal groups in society. Social promotion activities stress the provision of social welfare and community development benefits to a particular clientele or locality and the inculcation of attitudes and behaviors such as cooperativeness, mutual trust, and self-esteem. Social promotion efforts require considerable commitment of staff time and are difficult to measure in terms of their effectiveness. Moreover, the effects of even very successful social promotion efforts probably do not become evident in the short-term time frame of many funding or evaluation cycles. The resource institutions that undertake social promotion efforts believe they are particularly important if the very poor or groups such as women or low castes are to develop greater capacity to generate income (for an example, see Brown 1981:293–306). Resource institutions offer social promotion services free of charge by staff who have community development or social work training.

Other Ingredients. In addition to the four principal ingredients of enterprise assistance programs—financial assistance, technical assistance, training, and social promotion—some resource institution programs offer other services. For example, beneficiaries may be able to join into groups for program design. Resource institutions may make raw materials or supplies directly available to individual beneficiaries. Some programs include the opportunity to form or join associations that promote small business interests, publish advertising directories, or meet to discuss common problems. Still other institutions have developed special "incubator" programs for new enterprises as a specialized service. Programs with a specific clientele may make services available to meet unique needs, such as day care centers for the children of market women (see Tendler 1984). The forms of service delivery and the effectiveness of these assistance components vary considerably among resource institutions.

The Models: Combining the Ingredients

The four components most frequently found in enterprise assistance programs are combined in several ways and sequences by resource institutions. Particular combinations and sequences of service delivery are instructive as alternative forms of assistance. Moreover, when combined into particular models, they may differ in how appropriate they are for meeting the needs of particular types of clients. Setting out several of the most frequently adopted models, and discussing particularly successful ways in which they have been used, should assist resource institutions and others in assessing how programs to reach particular clienteles might be designed most effectively.

Six principal models are used by most resource institutions:

- individual financial assistance;
- integrated financial assistance and technical assistance/social promotion;
- integrated and sequenced financial assistance, technical assistance, and training for individuals;
- integrated and sequenced training, technical assistance, and financial assistance for individuals;
- group-oriented social promotion, financial assistance, and technical assistance;
- training.

Each of these models is described briefly below, along with a specific case of a program that uses the model and a brief discussion of the strengths and weaknesses of each. The data for this discussion are drawn from the literature on small and micro-enterprise assistance programs, especially those that have been relatively effective in delivering services to a low income clientele. Table I–2 provides a listing of a number of the more well-known programs using particular models and a bibliography of where additional information about each can be found. Resource institutions may pursue more than one model in order to benefit different

Table I–2

Small and Micro-Enterprise Assistance Models and Examples of Programs That Utilize Them

			Models		
1	*2*	*3*	*4*	*5*	*6*
Banco del Pacifico	CANAPI	UNO	DESAP (Carvajal)	PRODEME	Calcutta Y Self-Employment Center
PCIB Money Shops	ADEPE	NCCK	CNPAR	PRIDECO/ FEDEC-CREDITO	Village Polytechnic Program
Bank of Baroda	CEOSS	SEAP	MSCI	Working Women's Forum	Lesotho Opportunities Industrialization Center
ADEMI	NAESEY	Carmona Social Development Center	PROJUVEN-ENTUD	CEOSS	Rural Enterprises Extension Service
BKK		PfP/Upper Volta	COLMENA	SEDEMEX	CEOSS
		ASEPADE	Dominican Development Foundation	Dominican Development Foundation	
		SIDO	PfP/Botswana	FUCODES	
		FUCODES		Banco Mundial de la Mujer	
				Institute of Cultural Affairs, Nairobi	
				Women in Development, Kenya	
				Grameen Bank	

types or levels of entrepreneurs. Thus, individual lending models often are pursued side-by-side with a group-oriented social promotion, financial assistance, and technical assistance model as a way to assist both better-off and less well-off clients. Resource institutions often "try out" models before settling on one that best suits their resources and the needs of their clients.[5] The models are not rigid and there is considerable capacity to innovate in terms of services and sequences within each one.

The models can be compared in terms of their cost, the level of beneficiary they serve most easily, the kinds of skills they require of program staff, their labor intensity, their appropriateness for new or established business, and the extent to which they require the active involvement and time commitment of beneficiaries. These criteria for assessing the models are defined in the following way:

- Cost: program resources, including staff time and resources, necessary to deliver a standard "package" of services;

- Beneficiary level (adopted from the studies): Level I: subsistence level with very limited potential for growth; Level II: micro-enterprise level with some basic skills and limited potential for growth; Level III: micro- and small enterprise level with basic skills and some potential for growth;

- Skill requirement of staff: extent to which program requires staff with business skills and/or community development skills;

- Labor intensity: extent to which the program requires the commitment of staff time and resources to provide a standard "package" of services;

- New or established enterprises: appropriateness of the program for assisting new or established enterprises;

- Beneficiary commitment: extent to which clients must actively participate in program services in order to receive benefits.

The discussion in the following pages will compare each model to the others in terms of these factors. Table I–3 presents a comparative overview of their relative characteristics.

Model 1: Individual Financial Assistance. This model often is adopted by banks and large government programs for enterprise assistance. The model focuses on the delivery of credit to a specified population, usually small businesses that can offer loan collateral or that have been in existence long enough to make them more credit-worthy than new businesses. This type of program generally operates with earmarked or subsidized capital that forms the basis of a loan fund. In principle, this kind of program can be relatively cost effective to pursue as it minimizes costs for specialized staff and eschews some of the more labor intensive components of the other models. With careful design of interest rate or user charges, strict repayment monitoring, and escalating loan amount procedures, this model has demonstrated considerable potential for reaching small and micro-entrepreneurs. Its effectiveness can increase when savings mobilization efforts are added to the financial assistance offered (see Rielly 1986).

Table I–3
Relative Characteristics of Enterprise Assistance Program Models

Model	Cost	Beneficiary Level	Staff Skill	Labor Intensity	New or Established Business	Beneficiary Commitment
1	Low	I, II, III	Simple Business	Low	Established	Low
2	Moderate	I, II, III	Simple Business and Community Development	Moderate	New or Established	Low
3	Moderate to High	II, III	Business	High	Established	Moderate
4	High	III and above	Business	High	Established	High
5	Moderate to High	I, II	Comunity Development	Moderate	New or Established	High
6	High	I and above	Specialized	Moderate	New	High

The Banco del Pacífico makes particularly effective use of this model. It is a private commercial bank in Ecuador, studied by the PISCES Project (see Fraser and Tucker 1981:216–23). The bank offers loans to very small businesses that have a physical locale (not street vendors, for example), that produce goods of acceptable quality, whose owners have reputations as "serious" people, who can provide suitable documents about their business and personal credit-worthiness, and who present a solvent co-guarantor of the loan. Small loans are made in two *tranches* per year and part of the funds are deposited in the client's savings account. Strict repayment and collection procedures are used. According to PISCES researchers, the emphasis of the Banco del Pacífico program is rapid delivery of loan funds to suitable clients; the process takes as few as ten days for many applications. The study indicates that costs to the institution are kept very low. The entrepreneurs assisted are generally those with fairly well-established businesses and program results have been positive.

Model 1 is the simplest of the six discussed. Compared to the other models, it is likely to have the lowest cost, assuming it is properly designed and managed (see Goldmark and Rosengard 1983; Houghton 1985). It can be appropriately designed for beneficiaries at all three levels of enterprise development, although it is perhaps most easily directed at entrepreneurs at Level III and above, as in the Banco del Pacífico example. Model 1 does not require a highly skilled staff; those with a good basic understanding of financial operations and routine procedures can be effective, as long as they have personal qualities that allow them to interact easily with low income clients (see, for example, Goldmark and Rosengard 1983). The Banco del Pacífico program utilized university students who worked part-time. This model is not as labor intensive as other models, as each staff person may be able to attend to a significant number of clients. It is generally appropriate only for already existing businesses. Beneficiaries need only commit the time necessary to apply for a loan and to make repayments. If the experience of the Indonesian BKK is any indication, it is a model with considerable potential for scaling up. The weakest point of Model 1 appears to be its limited ability to assist small business clients in making the best possible use of loan capital (see Wines 1986). Institutions adopting the model need to be particularly concerned about client selection and the potential for default and failure rates among beneficiaries.

Model 2: Integrated Financial Assistance and Technical Assistance/Social Promotion. This model is designed to provide services to individual entrepreneurs. It is similar to the first model except that as part of a credit application or monitoring process, entrepreneurs receive individualized assistance with bookkeeping, marketing, or other needs. Alternatively, entrepreneurs become members of groups that meet to discuss and resolve a series of similar problems. In such cases, community development and group cohesion goals are emphasized. A number of cooperatives conform to this model, whereby individuals join a group in order to receive individual credit but also are expected to contribute to the institution through their participation in its activities. Associations of small businesses may utilize a similar model. At times, groups may cooperate to acquire access to raw materials or necessary inputs or to establish and maintain projects to benefit the community such as fair price stores, wells, roads, or productive projects. An institution maintains a corps of business extension or social promoters and specialists to carry out these activities.

An example of a relatively effective integrated financial assistance and technical assistance program is ADEPE in Costa Rica (see Grindle 1986). This is a small private sector organization with a clientele that is primarily rural. It works with micro, small, and medium industry so that the small and medium categories provide subsidies for the micro-enterprise sector. It provides credits that are monitored closely by its technicians as a way of providing training in business management. Through considerable learning from experience, it has developed a model that appears to be flexible and efficient as well as relatively cost-effective. An example of a cooperative organization using a financial assistance and social promotion mechanism is CIDES in Colombia (see Fraser and Tucker 1981:194–210). CIDES stresses self-improvement through a series of meetings, short courses, and group activities.

Programs based on this model generally are less expensive than more complex models. When effectively designed, they can generate income for the institution that helps defray administrative costs. They can be designed to be appropriate for all levels of entrepreneurs; staff need basic competence in simple business administration practices, the capacity to interact effectively with low income clients, and skill in community development. The model requires a larger staff than for the first model because of the individual nature of the technical assistance delivered and the time and effort needed in social promotion. In many cases, part-time workers such as university students and volunteers have been incorporated into such programs. The model appears to be replicable, although its capacity for growth is limited by the need to maintain a staff commensurate with the services offered. It is appropriate for new or established business. Financial assistance and technical assistance programs require relatively little from the beneficiary; financial assistance and social promotion programs require considerably more commitment from them. A recurrent problem noted in the pursuit of this model is the need to ensure that technical assistance and social promotion are appropriate for the entrepreneurs and that suggested practices are actually adopted.

Model 3: Integrated and Sequenced Financial Assistance, Technical Assistance, and Training for Individuals. This frequently used model provides credit and, in addition, offers extension and training as options for borrowers. Individual clients are drawn to the resource institution through the availability of credit. In assessing an application, program staff visit the enterprise, interview the owner, look at the books if any exist, and evaluate the credit-worthiness of the applicant. At the same time, an assessment is made about whether the entrepreneur should receive technical assistance and/or training. If accepted as borrowers, entrepreneurs are visited by program staff and offered assistance with routine business responsibilities or special problems they may have. Experts may be contracted to handle very specialized problems of production or marketing. After technical assistance has been initiated, the entrepreneurs are encouraged to enroll in an appropriate training course, for which a small fee is usually assessed.

An effective application of Model 3 is the integrated and sequenced financial assistance, technical assistance, and training program used by the Northeast Union of Assistance to Small Businesses (UNO) program in Brazil (see Tendler 1983a; Smith and Tippett 1982:73–76). UNO assists existing Level III type entrepreneurs to gain access to formal institutional credit by helping them prepare proposals for submission to participating financial intermediaries. Business extension begins during the proposal assistance phase and continues after the loan is granted. Entrepreneurs are encouraged to participate in formal training programs after they have been accepted as borrowers; approximately half of the assisted entrepreneurs do so. According to researchers, administrative costs and default rates have been held reasonably low by this model and it is often cited as a success story for small and micro-enterprise assistance.

This model is relatively expensive because of the need to subsidize the technical assistance and training. It is a model that probably best meets the needs of Level II, III, and larger entrepreneurs because these individuals are most able to apply the business skills and training to their activities. Staff with an understanding of appropriate business practices are required as well as those who are effective in teaching and relating to low income clients. It requires a relatively large staff to deliver this package of services, although students and university teachers are often used on a part-time basis. Established businesses are usually those most effectively served through this kind of model, and beneficiaries are encouraged—but not compelled—to devote considerable energy to learning. Model 3 programs may encounter difficulty in providing effective technical assistance and training as they have little leverage over the client once a loan has been granted. They must persuade the borrower to avail himself or herself of the additional services. Drop-out rates in the extension and training components may be high unless both are of high quality and relevant to the entrepreneurs.

Model 4: Integrated and Sequenced Training, Technical Assistance, and Financial Assistance for Individuals. This model is distinct in that training is emphasized as the most important need of small and micro-entrepreneurs. Training may consist of a series of courses interspersed with individualized extension that is linked to the content of training. Alternatively, a training sequence can be completed before the initiation of the extension. Only after a required training and technical assistance sequence has been completed are entrepreneurs eligible for credit. In this way, creditworthy clients are effectively identified; as a result, credit programs tend to have considerable potential to assist the enterprises most likely to survive and grow. The credit may be disbursed through a financial intermediary other than the resource institution. In this case, passing through the sequenced activities can qualify the borrower for particular lines of credit.

This model is identified closely with the DESAP program of the Carvajal Foundation in Cali, Colombia, Cali (see Grindle 1986; Sanders

1983a; 1983b). It has been adopted widely by other institutions in Colombia and in other Latin American countries. The Carvajal Foundation has become a training forum for the replication of this model; managers of resource institutions have attended seminars in Cali and elsewhere about the program and its components. In the model, entrepreneurs sign up to take a sequence of three courses, beginning with principles of accounting, then moving to cost analysis, and finishing with marketing and sales. Additional courses on investment projects and principles of administration are offered to those desiring further training. Trainees pay a small fee for the courses and use workbooks as an aid to semiformal classroom sessions. After the trainee has completed each course, an extension agent visits her or his establishment to ensure that the course content is being applied in practice. Additional assistance is offered at these individualized sessions. Successful "graduates" of the training and extension phases are then eligible for special lines of credit made available by the Carvajal Foundation with a local financial intermediary. DESAP clients appear to have considerable potential for growth and graduation to formal institutional credit and other support. The Foundation also supports a number of other programs to which DESAP beneficiaries have access, such as a self-help housing scheme and provision and marketing assistance.

A model that emphasizes training and extension more than financial assistance is a relatively costly form of providing services to a low income clientele. Technical assistance is generally provided free and the cost of training programs to the beneficiaries may or may not be covered by fees. The model is most appropriate for enterprises that have some capacity to grow and to become part of the formal sector—generally those at Level III and above, although those at Level II can also benefit from this model. The relatively large staff is markedly business-oriented and stresses the inculcation of business skills and entrepreneurial motivation. When resources are available to adopt this model, its replication is facilitated by the careful borrower selection process resulting from the sequencing of activities. That is, those selected as borrowers have become well known to the organization through its training and assistance components. In comparison to the other models considered, it requires significant commitment from beneficiaries of their time and effort.

Model 5: Group-Oriented Social Promotion, Financial Assistance, and Extension. This model focuses on the promotion of small groups that join together to guarantee loans for individual members of the group and to assist each other in resolving business problems that may face several of the members in common. Considerable effort is put into promoting the ideas of self-help and organization. Community development goals are stressed through promotional meetings with prospective group members. This model has been found particularly appropriate for very low income entrepreneurs or those who are termed pre-entrepreneurs. Small groups are believed essential, with no more than ten individuals participating per group. Credit is given in small initial loans, sometimes in amounts as low as U.S.$12–$25, often in amounts of U.S.$50–$250. When these initial loans have been repaid, subsequent loans may be applied for. Program staff accompany their promotional and community development activities with very simple technical assistance to individuals or groups of credit recipients.

This model is the basis of the "solidarity" group approach widely promoted by Acción International/AITEC and used by the Grameen Bank and Women's World Banking (see especially Ashe 1985:38–60; Houghton 1985). The "solidarity group methodology" explicitly recognizes "empowerment" as a program goal, encouraging group members to develop problem solving and leadership skills during their meetings and interactions. Small groups of five to ten members meet for one to several months to prepare themselves for the responsibility of taking out a loan. They then formulate credit proposals and submit them to the enterprise support organization. Group members monitor their co-members because all co-sign for individual loans and no new loans are made to anyone in the group until a loan has been fully repaid. Extension is made available to groups through the organization as the groups require it. Acción experience with the approach, such as the PRODEME Program in the Dominican Republic, EUS in Costa Rica, and PRIDECO/ FEDEC-CREDITO in El Salvador, indicates that marginal entrepreneurs—street vendors, market women, individual shoemakers, and others—can be assisted effectively through this model. In Bangladesh, large numbers of extremely poor landless rural villagers have been assisted by the Grameen Bank program and others based on similar models.[6]

The solidarity group model is less expensive than the training model but still requires considerable resources to deliver a "package" of services to the groups. This model appears to be highly appropriate for Level I and II entrepreneurs and is effective in reaching very low income people. Staff need social promotion and community development skills more than strictly business-related skills. Working with groups rather than individuals reduces the amount of staff time required for effective performance. Nevertheless, staff must spend much time working with individual groups or promoting the program. It is a model that appears appropriate for both new and established businesses. Beneficiaries must make a substantial commitment of time to their group.

Model 6: Training. This model concentrates on providing job skills training for low income people. It is less concerned with the promotion of small businesses and entrepreneurship than with employment. It is a model used by a number of government training agencies. Programs based on this model work most effectively when research has been done on the kinds of skills that are most in demand in a locality and when efforts are made to place graduates in appropriate jobs. Trainees usually receive the training free or pay only a nominal fee. Often, Model 6 programs attempt to defray costs through the sale of goods and services produced by the trainees. Where goods are manufactured, programs may need substantial investments of capital for machinery and other inputs.

The PISCES projects describe the training programs of the Coptic Evangelical Organization for Social Services (CEOSS) in Egypt, the Calcutta "Y" Self-Employment Centre, the CNPAR in Upper Volta, and the Village Polytechnic Program in Kenya.[7] Each program had some success in providing skills training and in channeling trainees into appropriate jobs. The Village Polytechnic Program, for instance, spread rapidly from four experimental projects to over 270 community projects in the 1980s. Courses are organized in each village center after a committee formed of community representatives and government officials has determined the demand for various types of skills. Local staff, numbering from five or six individuals to as many as twenty individuals, offer training in carpentry, masonry, tailoring/dressmaking, metalworking, motor mechanics, and other areas. This large program, which receives assistance from the government, international donors, and a variety of private voluntary agencies, trains some 20,000 people in various skills at the same time. Goods and services are produced through the program on contract and part of the proceeds are used to support the local program and to capitalize a trainee loan fund.

Model 6 is an expensive type of program to operate, necessitating considerable investment in buildings, equipment and machines, and training staff salaries. Generally, programs using this model are subsidized by governments or donors. The model is appropriate for reaching Level I and above beneficiaries. The skills required by staff include special knowledge of production techniques or other technical skills, in addition to the capacity to teach low income clients effectively. The number of personnel required to teach courses may be modest if trainers have a wide range of basic skills. The Kenyan program has demonstrated the replicability of the program, but cost and technical capacity may slow the extent to which it can be effectively adopted. Model 6 probably is carried out most effectively on a large scale because of the investment and staff expertise that are required. It may be an appropriate model for new businesses as it can give trainees the skills to initiate their own enterprises. As with other training models, it requires considerable commitment on the part of beneficiaries to learn and apply new skills.

Conclusion: Models and Resource Institutions

As noted earlier, there is no "one best way" to design an enterprise assistance program. However, program models can be selected that increase the chances for a resource institution to achieve its goal of serving a particular client group. Moreover, categorizing the typical characteristics and requirements of various models may help the organization determine the extent of financial and human resource commitment required to accomplish the goal.

In cases where resources do not match program requirements, support institutions have several choices. They may:

- set out to acquire appropriate levels of financing and staffing to pursue a particular model;
- adjust program components to tailor a particular model to the resources available;
- adopt some combination of these two choices.

An institution lowers its chances of success when it offers a program that is inappropriate to its priorities, size, or resources.

Notes

1. This observation results from interviews with directors and staff of a number of resource institutions in Latin America and Africa.

2. This observation is also based on interviews with resource institution leaders.

3. The research literature is extensive. See, for example, Von Pischke, Adams, and Donald (1983); Meyer (1985); Vogel (1982); and Rielly (1986).

4. Technical assistance, as the term is used here, is distinguished from training activities. Both technical assistance and training may stress the same content—business skills, for example—but we use technical assistance to refer to one-to-one encounters between staff and clients, usually at the site of the entrepreneurial activities, and training to refer to more formal classroom-type learning experiences.

5. This observation was confirmed in a number of interviews with resource institution leaders.

6. ILO (1984) and Hunt (1984:185–87 and notes) provide general discussions and further references on the merits of grouping beneficiaries for credit, training, and technical assistance. They discuss a number of innovative attempts that have had impressive results.

7. These two programs—the Calcutta "Y" Self-Employment Center and the CNPAR in Upper Volta—also had extension components geared toward developing business skills and loan components.

Chapter 4

Diagnosis: Recurrent Problems of Resource Institutions

A reading of the literature and discussions with professionals in the field suggest that institutions providing services to small and micro-enterprises share many of the same sorts of problems as they manage their organizations, design and implement projects, and interact with donors, governments, and other organizations. These problems vary in number and intensity among the resource institutions and they may be particularly abundant or acute in organizations moving from a social welfare orientation to an income generation strategy. If they remain unresolved, these recurrent problems seriously diminish the performance of the organizations, impairing efficient and effective operation. If, however, the problems can be addressed successfully through improved management, planning, and outreach, the resource institutions can provide more useful services to their clients, the small entrepreneurs.

Organizations are not static, but change over time as they are created, grow, respond to new exigencies and opportunities, and, at times, disintegrate. Organizations learn from their experiences, their failures, and their successes, often through a process that resembles "floundering around" (Tendler 1984). A successful organization, therefore, is not a "blueprint" of a perfect institutional prototype (see Korten 1980). Rather, an efficient, effective, and sustainable institution is one that learns from its experiences, that is adaptive and able to change and to improve its decision-making processes and problem-solving capacity. Such an organization is able to plan and carry out efficient, effective, and sustainable programs.

In the Introduction to Part I, a well-managed organization was described as one with the following characteristics:

- the capacity to establish goals, set priorities, and adopt policies to ensure that goals are achieved and priorities maintained;
- the capacity to adapt to a changing environment, to learn from experience, to apply these lessons to improve existing operations, and to make appropriate decisions about institutional change and growth;
- the capacity to become self-sustaining and to develop sufficient autonomy from donors and other sponsors to be responsive primarily to their beneficiaries, their own experience, and changing circumstance;
- the capacity to monitor finances effectively so that management can plan for the future, assess ongoing activities, and make informed decisions about strategic, programmatic, and administrative issues;
- the capacity to identify, attract, motivate, and retain committed and effective staff;
- the capacity to work effectively with other organizations—public and private; local, national, and international—to increase the impact of development programs;
- the capacity to learn from others pursuing similar objectives and to share successes, frustrations, and problem-solving ideas with them.

Recurrent problems faced by resource institutions often are responsible for the failure of institutions to develop their capacities. The purpose of this chapter is to identify a set of recurrent problems that directly affect the performance of resource institutions and to link these problems to the notion of capacity building . Capacity building occurs in four interrelated domains—strategic, technical, administrative, and communications. Improved performance can be achieved among resource institutions by directing primary attention to improving the decision-making and managerial skills of organizational leaders, that is, by strengthening their strategic capacity. As this occurs, improvements in technical, administrative, and communications capacities in the organization will be required to support improved decision making.

Through a review of the literature on resource institutions and the programs they carry out, we have developed a framework for examining the most significant problems faced by such organizations. The information generated suggests that the most important recurrent problems fall into nine general categories: (1) setting objectives and priorities; (2) becoming efficient; (3) managing change; (4) creating independence; (5) project design; (6) accounting practices; (7) personnel and organizational management; (8) information management; and (9) institutional linkages. Going beyond the diagnosis facilitated by the data, we shall suggest in this chapter and the next that each of these categories can be addressed most appropriately through one of the four types of capacity building. Table I–4 presents an outline to clarify the relationship among capacity building domains, problem categories, and specific problems. In the remainder of the chapter, each problem is briefly explained, its sources are explored, and its implications for the performance of the resource institutions are considered. The next chapter presents a prescriptive response to this diagnosis, suggesting methodologies and materials for addressing clusters of related problems.

Strategic Capacity Issues: Making Better Decisions

The literature suggests that the first priority for strengthening resource institutions is to improve the strategic vision of their leaders. The strategic capacity of an organization refers to the ability of its managers to establish goals, set priorities, and pursue policies to ensure that goals are achieved and priorities maintained. Strategic capacity includes the ability of managers to respond to questions such as: "What are we doing? Why are we doing it? Who are we doing it for? How can we do it most effectively and efficiently?"

Managers of resource institutions that provide services to small and micro-enterprises generally have become active in the field because of deep commitment to assisting in grassroots development efforts and humanitarian concern for the problems of low income people in the developing countries. Just as frequently, however, the commitment to aiding the poor and stimulating local self-help initiatives makes it difficult for these managers:

- to be completely objective about how much they need to know about small enterprises before initiating activities;
- to consider what is feasible for the organization to accomplish;
- to appreciate how much improved financial management can contribute to effectiveness; and
- to make good choices about growth and change in the activities of the organization.

Building strategic capacity within resource institutions is a critical step in translating idealistic motivations into effective and efficient implementation of programs to assist small and micro-enterprises.

Table 1–4

Capacity Domains, Problem Categories, and Problems Affecting the Performance of Resource Institutions

Capacity Domain	Recurrent Problem	Problem Subcategory
STRATEGIC	SETTING PRIORITIES	Assessing the need Knowing the environment Considering feasibility
	BECOMING EFFICIENT	Cost effectiveness Staffing and support Centralization/decentralization
	MANAGING CHANGE	Expansion/contraction Reorientation
	CREATING INDEPENDENCE	Independence from funders Independence of clients
TECHNICAL	PROJECT DESIGN	Appropriate designs for credit and marketing projects Pricing of services Interest rates Appropriate technical assistance Sequencing of activities Participation Client selection and monitoring
	ACCOUNTING PRACTICES	Short-term budgeting Medium/long-term financing
ADMINISTRATIVE	PERSONNEL AND ORGANIZATIONAL MANAGEMENT	Hiring staff Training staff Motivating staff Coordinating staff
COMMUNICATIONS	INFORMATION MANAGEMENT	Learning from feedback Program evaluation
	INSTITUTIONAL LINKAGES	Networking with other resource institutions Linkages with governments and international donors

Four problem categories can be addressed through efforts to improve management's strategic capacity. These are: (1) setting objectives and priorities; (2) becoming efficient; (3) managing change; and (4) creating independence. In responding to problems in each category, managers need the ability to identify goals and priorities that reflect real development needs and good financial management practices. These skills derive from an appreciation of the needs of their clients and the needs of the organization if it is to be efficient, effective, and sustainable. With this kind of information, managers are able to make better decisions about what goals are appropriate for the institution and how best to achieve them. Each of the four problem categories is discussed below.

Setting Objectives and Priorities

The principal task of all organization managers is to determine the goals and priorities of an institution and to ensure that its objectives reflect what is feasible to achieve. Yet, many institutions have only vague objectives or flounder for long periods while they experiment with different approaches and models (see, for example, Lassen 1980; Tendler 1984). Most are highly motivated to assist small enterprises, but may have limited knowledge about the dynamics of this sector or how the institution can most effectively aid its development (see Tendler 1982; Ashe 1985; Kilby and D'Zmura 1983).

Assessing the Need. Resource institutions, despite the best intentions, may have inadequate knowledge about small enterprises (Ashe 1985; Tendler 1984). There is ample reason for this lack of knowledge: information about small enterprises is difficult to collect and interpret (see Chuta and Liedholm 1979; Page and Steel 1981; Snodgrass 1979; Anderson and Leiserson 1980; Liedholm and Mead 1986; James 1982; Blayney and Otero 1985; World Bank 1978). By their nature, such enterprises tend to operate beyond the purview of census takers, tax collectors, and chambers of commerce. As discussed in Chapter 1, many of them operate in homes, back alleys, and remote villages. Their links to the local, national, and international economies are often obscure or subject to debate even among academic specialists. Whatever the reasons for the problem, lack of knowledge about the small enterprise sector limits the effectiveness of institutional efforts and results in considerable waste of time and financial and human resources.

Knowing the Environment. Managers of resource institutions can fail to appreciate the importance of the policy and socioeconomic environments that surround small enterprise development (see Ashe 1985; Squire 1981; Marsden 1981; see Chapter 2). But these issues are critical to the effectiveness of efforts to assist small entrepreneurs (Anderson 1982; Ashe 1985; de Vries 1981). The economic environment shapes opportunities for entrepreneurship and determines demand for the goods and services produced. Government policy provides a set of opportunities and constraints, determining tariffs, exchange rates, tax policies, and regulations that affect the day-to-day operation of small enterprises. Successful resource institutions have the capacity to catalog the conditions of the economic and policy environment for small enterprises and to assess the potential for their development in the present and future.

Considering Feasibility. Resource institutions frequently attempt to achieve too much in relation to their resources (Lassen 1980; Smith and Tippett 1982). If they are underinformed about the sector they want to assist and the environment within which the sector operates, they may set unrealistic goals and establish infeasible time structures. Their motivation, drive, and high ideals can keep them working hard at achieving their objectives for long periods, but ultimately they become overextended and their projects begin to falter and fail. Carefully weighing client needs and environmental constraints against available and projected human and financial resources can do much to help management establish feasible program objectives and priorities.

Becoming Efficient

Resource institutions often lack good financial management (Tendler 1982; Scurrah and Podesta 1984; Kubr 1983). Their leaders have limited knowledge of budget analysis, program monitoring, and cost accounting. They have insufficient appreciation of how decisions about staffing and support or decision-making structures affect the overall efficiency of the organization. These shortcomings can waste an organization's scarce funds and valuable human resources and endanger the sustainability of its projects. Organization managers must be able to put on a financial management hat and wear it effectively.

Cost Effectiveness. A considerable body of evaluation literature indicates that resource institutions typically have high unit costs for the services they offer to their clients (Tendler 1984; Ashe 1985; Adams, Antonio, and Romero 1981). In particular, costs per loan are often high in credit programs and technical assistance efforts generally operate in the red. High unit costs are coupled with approaches to small business assistance that generate little or no income for the institution, increasing their dependence on donors for operating expenses as well as for investment capital. These problems point to the need to improve managerial skills in budget analysis, programming, and human resource allocation. Cost effectiveness in general is a strategic capacity issue both because resources are scarce and because many donors make it an important criterion in judging institutions and the projects they carry out.

Staffing and Support. Many resource institutions typically rely on volunteers and professional staffs who are not well paid for the work they perform (Tendler 1982; 1983). Offices operate on shoestring budgets and institution managers are loathe to expend their limited funds on equipment such as typewriters, vehicles, computers, and calculators. However, these very conditions can increase the costs of providing services. Volunteer staff, however well motivated, can be unreliable or poorly trained (see Tendler 1983). Low salaries can cause high turnover of professional staff, increasing the longer-term costs of hiring and training personnel (see Goldmark and Rosengard 1983). Lack of typewriters, vehicles, and computers can mean that staff—both volunteer and paid— spend inordinate amounts of time accomplishing even simple tasks such as completing reports or monitoring clients through visits to their establishments (Smith and Tippett 1982; Tendler 1983). Low morale and frustration can ensue, further diminishing staff performance.

The solution to these problems, of course, is not to lavish funds on salaries, office equipment, and transportation. Few resource institutions have the kind of budgets that would allow them such luxuries. The solution is rather an increased ability to make decisions about staffing and support on the basis of the criteria of efficiency, effectiveness, and sustainability, rather than counting on goodwill to compensate for the effects of minimal expenditures. The latter situation leads to high real costs, not low ones.

Centralization/Decentralization of Decision Making. Despite considerable rhetoric to the contrary, resource institutions themselves often have centralized and top-down decision-making styles (Lassen 1980; Tendler 1982; Honadle and Hannah 1981; see also Goldmark and Rosengard 1983). In some cases, the institutions may be the creations of their leaders, who use them to fulfill a personal vision. Or, because of deeply held commitment and a certitude about their view of development, some leaders want to ensure that all decisions conform to their views. At the other extreme are overly decentralized organizations. In these cases, management may have little insight into what is occurring, who is benefiting, or in what direction the institution is moving.

The degree of centralization or decentralization in decision making is a cost-effectiveness issue because managerial time is expensive in terms of opportunity costs. Managers need time to assess alternatives, think through medium- and long-term plans, promote organizational commitment, determine policies, raise funds, and promote smooth relations with potential donors and governments. They will not be efficient in these responsibilities if they are heavily involved in day-to-day decision making, putting out "brush fires," and mediating minor conflicts. At the same time, they require information about the organization's progress and they need to stay in touch with the realities of management, requirements that argue against their complete aloofness from the day-to-day problems of the organization.

Managing Change

Serving small enterprises is an expanding field in development assistance. Many organizations originally established to promote community development and social welfare are expanding or changing their objectives toward income-generating projects. In addition, new institutions are emerging with the express purpose of encouraging the development of small enterprises and entrepreneurs. Well-established institutions are also expanding their operations. Managing change has therefore become a central ingredient of the effective management of resource institutions. Knowing when to expand, when to consolidate, or when to contract is a vital and difficult decision for organization managers. Changing an institution's orientation requires hard-headed decisions about staffing, skill requirements, and appropriate programs; these decisions have implications for who is assisted and how effective new programs are. More than any other set of decisions, bringing about change within an organization tests the strategic capacity of its management.

Expansion/Contraction. Managers of resource institutions often mistake the favorable short-term liquidity of the organization for its long-term solvency. They may decide to expand their operations without adequate attention to issues such as depreciation of capital assets and their replacement costs, projections of old and new funding sources, and future personnel costs. As a result, after expansion, managers may find themselves hard pressed to maintain new programs, experiencing serious cash flow problems, and frantically trying to raise survival funds from donors. Knowing when to expand, when to consolidate, and when to contract is preeminently an issue of knowing how to interpret and make decisions on the basis of appropriate and timely financial information.

Reorientation. Offering services to small enterprises requires objectives, priorities, and skills different from those needed in offering social welfare services. In particular, successful resource institutions learn to think like their clients, business people whose future will depend on accurately identifying economic opportunities and weighing the risks of failure. Assessing the financial needs of small businesses, assessing market conditions, and determining the risks involved in production and marketing activities are important skills required in enterprise-oriented programs. They are not skills necessarily found among concerned and committed staffs of resource institutions that are initiating such programs. In assuming new objectives, organization managers may not anticipate the special skills and understanding required, and may not recognize that commitment and experience in dealing with low income populations cannot substitute for specific skills related to the economic management of small businesses (Lassen 1980; Crandon 1984). On the other hand, their greatest strength is their idealism and their skills in working with low income and disadvantaged groups. Business skills must not be purchased at the cost of these qualities or the organizations will endanger their identity. The deep sense of commitment that motivates these institutions must remain their central feature.

Creating Independence

For many reasons, resource institutions often are characterized by dependence. Many receive donor and government subsidies and in turn lead their clients to become dependent upon subsidies from resource institutions. Heavy dependence on donor or public subsidies can make the internal budgeting process mainly a frantic effort to manage recurring financial peaks and valleys in funding; soon, medium- and long-range becomes virtually impossible. When the future depends heavily on donor support or official subsidies, programs may blossom and expire in short order and cycles of expansion and contraction may become both endemic and unpredictable. In addition, dependence of clients on the institution can lead to a failure to encourage self-sustained development.

Independence from Funders. The "godfather syndrome" is one of the most frequently encountered problems in the management of resource institutions that assist small enterprises—their heavy reliance on donor funding (Tendler 1984; Adams, Antonio, and Romero 1981:224; Scurrah and Podesta 1984:19; Sanyal 1987). Some institutions may be particularly dependent on the largesse of a very few donors or on government subsidies, a dangerous situation. Among other things, dependence means that organization managers spend too much time pursuing funders; budget cycles can be extremely erratic and characterized by unexpected shortfalls when funding sources do not come through as expected; institutions compete with each other—often intensely—for the attention of the funders; and program planning becomes vulnerable to the whims of the godfathers and the fads that affect development thinking among such donors. The management of the resource institution is affected by this kind of dependence but so, too, are the programs they initiate and pursue. Clients may discover that expected loans are not forthcoming, technical assistance is cut out at critical moments, or a program is redefined or eliminated.

Independence of Clients. Resource institutions can fall unwittingly into a trap of dependence on donors; they may have their own organizational dynamic tending to promote dependence of their own clients upon them (Tendler 1984; Leonard and Marshall 1982; Lassen 1980). Resource institutions benefit from demand for their services by being able to point to widespread need in fund-raising activities. They benefit from being able to demonstrate good performance on the part of clients—loan repayment, for example—which often is achieved through close supervision. They may believe that the small and micro-entrepreneurs they work with are unable to make decisions on their own or they may wish to instill a particular model of business development. For these reasons, re-source institutions may not wish to see their clients graduate to other sources of credit, technical assistance, or related services. When they exist, such institutional imperatives can thwart the very characteristics of self-sustained development among clients that the institution espouses.

Building Strategic Capacity

The four problem categories of setting priorities, becoming efficient, managing change, and avoiding dependence present institution mana-gers with a series of recurrent problems. All of these problems can be ad-dressed through improved goal setting, planning, and financial manage-ment. Building the strategic capacity of management should be a priority as resource institutions work to become more efficient, effective, and sustainable. There are, of course, myriad ways to help people become better managers. There are also a number of technologies that can help, particularly in analyzing information for decisions. Especially critical skills deal with decision making and its relationship to the analysis and application of appropriate information. Chapter 5 considers appropriate methods for pursuing the goal of improved organizational management.

Technical Capacity Issues: Providing Better Information

Regardless of the assistance model that is adopted or the characteristics of the resource institution, small and micro-enterprise programs often experience recurrent problems rooted in program design. Poorly de-signed projects lessen the earning potential of clients; many resource in-stitutions can relate histories of their own efforts that have ended in fail-ure and disillusion. There are, of course, no fail-safe project designs. Nevertheless, most resource institutions can benefit from more knowl-edge of what has proved successful in credit and marketing services, frameworks within which to consider user charges and interest rates, ex-amples of effective technical assistance required by small entrepreneurs, techniques to encourage participation, methods for selecting clients who will benefit from the project, means to monitor their performance, and assistance in reaching specific target groups such as women, refugees, the unemployed, or the very poor.

In addition, resource institutions often can benefit from increasing their technical capacity to monitor finances. Improving technical skills will result in better information for institutional managers to use in their strategic decision-making activities. Thus, improved technical capacity is a vital support for organizational management and will have a direct im-pact on the efficiency, effectiveness, and sustainability of the organiza-tions. To a considerable degree, improving technical capacity means learning to ask the right questions and to generate information appropriate for answering them.

Project Design

Appropriate Designs for Credit and Marketing Components. The provision of credit and marketing services requires considerable knowledge about how small entrepreneurs need, use, and repay loans and how their products or services are related to local, regional, national, and even international economies (Ashe 1985; Page and Steel 1984). A recurrent complaint among resource institution managers and evaluators is that the organizations have moved precipitously into projects that were ill-conceived or inappropriate to the needs of the client population (Lassen 1980; Wasserstrom 1985; McKean 1982; Scurrah and Podesta 1984; Korten 1980). Hobbled by basic design flaws, such projects often exhibit poor loan repayment records; others fill warehouses with unsalable merchandise produced by low income artisans. The most effective of the resource institutions know a great deal about the components of effective credit delivery and marketing projects—scale of credit to be offered, interest rate structures, repayment schedules, channels of commercialization, performance monitoring. Helping them deepen this knowledge and share it more widely can improve still further the performance of the resource institutions. The best project designers ask such questions as: "Do small entrepreneurs really need credit? What alternative sources of investment and operating capital are available to the small entrepreneur? Is there really a viable market for the good or service produced? Are input markets reliable enough for sustained operation?"

Pricing of Services. Resource institutions frequently charge little or nothing for the services they offer their clients (Tendler 1984; Ashe 1985; Anderson 1982). Frequently, this practice results from attitudes held about who the clients are and what their needs are: resource institutions desire to help the entrepreneurs, tend to see them as destitute, and assume they cannot pay market prices for the services they receive (see Rielly 1986). Often, resource institutions justify their work by pointing to the exploitative charges of middlemen and usurious interest rates of moneylenders (Tendler 1982). They may believe that their primary purpose is to offer low-cost services to these exploited people. They may also believe that, however much clients may need the services, if higher prices are charged, they will not use them. Nonetheless, undercharging for services can increase dependence on donors, reduce cash flow below the level needed to sustain the program, make it difficult for the institutions to know if the clients value and benefit from the services, encourage clients to treat the services as free goods, and discourage client demands for improvement (Tendler 1984; Ashe 1985; James 1982). In contrast, appropriate user charges for services can contribute importantly to financial viability. Moreover, managers will receive better information on the use and effectiveness of services, and clients will be encouraged to provide better feedback to the institution as to their value.

Interest Rates. Interest charges in credit programs are a chronic problem in project design. Resource institutions typically charge below market rates for loans. Projects often lack components for savings mobilization (see Adams, Antonio, and Romero 1981; Blayney and Otero 1985). Particularly in highly inflationary economies, interest rates in credit programs tend to fall well below market prices and money is often loaned at negative real rates (see Scurrah and Podesta 1984). Savings mobilization capacity that can be encouraged through appropriate interest rate structures is generally ignored (Meyer 1985; Vogel 1982). As with the more general problems of the pricing of services, supporting institutions frequently hold paternalistic attitudes about those they assist, consider that below market rates are just and that market rates are exploitive of the poor, and fear that client demand will dry up if higher interest rates are charged. In contrast to these perceptions, there is ample evidence that low interest rates distort programs intended to assist the poor, do not really reflect the ability of low income entrepreneurs to repay, and impair the institutions' ability to plan for their own futures because they become chronically dependent upon outside funding (Von Pischke, Adams, and Gordon 1983). The consequences of charging low interest rates are generally adverse for resource institutions, affecting their ability to grow or even to maintain themselves in the medium to long term.

Appropriate Technical Assistance. Several of the models reviewed in Chapter 3 include technical assistance components. Often, however, program clients complain that the technical assistance offered is not relevant to their particular business or is too general to be of assistance to them (Tendler 1984; Crandon 1984; Wasserstrom 1985; Fraser and Tucker 1981:167–91). In some instances, resource institutions assume that their clients are ill-informed or ignorant about business and that even cursory or extremely basic assistance will improve the performance of small businesses. The dangers of this assumption are compounded in cases in which the resource institutions have only rudimentary knowledge of business practices. This situation may lead to staffing with extensionists who have little experience in the small business field and assistance programs that may not encompass the very skills most necessary and appropriate for the small entrepreneur. Waste of time and resources result. More damaging, however, is the potential harm that can result if a small business person adopts inappropriate or bad advice. Thus, assessing what kind, if any, of technical assistance is appropriate and designing projects in accordance with this information are vital skills for successful resource institutions.

Participation. Effective and efficient projects to assist small and micro-entrepreneurs are designed with the particular needs of the clients in mind (see, for example, Paul 1982:201). They must reach the groups they are intended for, and they must inform potential clients of the benefits to be derived from participation. These requirements place a large burden on project designers. Acquiring information and feedback is important to improving project success. A cost-effective way to generate this result is to encourage the extensive participation of clients in project design, monitoring, and evaluation (Cohen and Uphoff 1977; Reichmann 1984; Korten 1980; Esman and Uphoff 1984). Project managers then receive continuous information directly from the clients, encouraging in this way flexibility and innovation when problems emerge. The reasons for encouraging participation are numerous but often are overlooked as resource institutions seek to begin projects as soon as possible or to pursue their own ideas about what is best for the clients (Lassen 1980; Tendler 1982; Kilby 1979). Moreover, techniques for securing constructive client participation in project design and implementation are not well understood or easily learned.

Client Selection and Performance Monitoring. Some projects incorporate elaborate methodologies for selecting beneficiaries, screening their needs, and monitoring their performance. Often, there is a strong component of control and even distrust of potential clients. The result frequently is to increase administrative costs and to delay unnecessarily the provision of services to the clients who are selected. Recent experience with small-scale enterprises suggests that program designs can be simplified by peer screening and reputational methods for selecting clients and through procedures that encourage peer and self monitoring (Ashe 1985; Reichmann 1984; Blayney and Otero 1985). In some cases, however, more complex measures may be needed if groups such as women or the very poor are the targets of business assistance programs. These groups often are not incorporated into programs because business assistance projects can be utilized most readily by better-off, usually male, small entrepreneurs (Ashe 1985; Crandon 1984; Buvinic 1984). Good project design displays sensitivity to the issue of the inequality in benefit distribution that results from client selection procedures.

Accounting Practices

Resource institutions providing services to small businesses often are weak in the very skills and practices they seek to instill in their clients— appropriate accounting procedures and systems for budgeting and planning (Scurrah and Podesta 1984; McKean 1982; Vogel 1982). Institutions' staff may have little interest in the seemingly mundane facts that appear on balance sheets and income statements or have limited patience for thinking about such issues as cash flow management or fund accounting and depreciation. They may be loathe to consider their organization, committed as it is to development and a vision of a better future, to be also a business operation that must make cold judgments about the best use of its capital and other assets. Staff may lack the skills to do much more than simple bookkeeping; they may not follow accounting practices that allow them to uncover problems of financial management and suggest alternatives to make better use of available resources. And ultimately, they may not appreciate the extent to which improved accounting practices can strengthen financial management at the level of institutional leadership. When they do not, resource institutions typically suffer recurrent budget shortfalls, their equipment wears out with no provision for its replacement, cash surpluses that could be generating income are not invested, is confused with solvency, and a host of other problems occur and recur. Improved accounting practices relating both to short-term budgeting and medium- and long-term planning can help an institution address these problems and in doing so, increase the efficiency, effectiveness, and sustainability of the organization.

Short-Term Budgeting. Resource institutions often experience annual budget shortfalls. In part, these are related to their dependence on donors or government subsidies for operating and investment funds. If a grant proposal is rejected, donor monies are delayed, or official subsidies are cut back, a resource institution can experience several months of uncertainty and shortages before funding becomes available. When these occur, its projects slow down and clients are left hanging on promises for the future. One solution, of course, is to become less dependent on donors, as discussed earlier. But accounting practices can also respond to the problem (Scurrah and Podesta 1984; McKean 1982). Improved capacity for keeping financial records, for managing annual budgets, and for considering options to avoid unexpected shortfalls facilitates producing timely financial tracking reports so that managers know where the organization stands. Managers should know how cash surpluses can be invested to generate income and how short-term lending can smooth the typical pattern of peaks and valleys of funding needs and expenditures that arise during the course of an annual budget cycle. And, perhaps most important, improved budgeting capacity can clarify the difference between long-term solvency and short-term liquidity so that managers can make informed decisions about when to expand, consolidate, or contract the institutions' operations.

Medium- and Long-Term Financial Planning. Resource institutions may be so absorbed in meeting short-term budget needs that they fail to consider longer-term options that could ease the overall resource shortage of the organization. Annual budgets may be produced, but these are often not derived from multiyear budgetary projections that are used for financial planning. Depreciation of equipment may not be considered in relation to encumbrance or fund accounting to absorb the financial drain of having to replace capital assets. Too frequently, locally available banking services are not used effectively and little thought is given to projecting future funding needs and opportunities. In the absence of better medium and long-term financial planning, resource institutions have little chance of escaping recurrent crises caused by the godfather syndrome or the need to respond to unexpected problems such as acquiring or replacing equipment.

Building Technical Capacity

Improved program design capacity would strengthen the overall performance of resource institutions. Managers of resource institutions need program staff with the technical skills to provide them with timely information, advice, and sensible alternatives for program design. Relevant skills in program design can be improved through a variety of methods. Many skill-specific materials already exist for this purpose. The case method, described in Chapter 5, can be particularly useful in improving program design capacity. Case method workshops can help sensitize participants to the constraints and opportunities faced by small businesses and the particular rationales that lie behind the decision making of their owners. In addition, project designers need a good understanding of credit and marketing systems, interest rate structures, and appropriate user charges. Computer-based training with hands-on experience and immediate feedback can be useful in improving this understanding. In cases where computers are not available, workbooks and applied learning modules can be used. "How-to" manuals and applied exercises can help to develop skills needed to improve technical assistance and client monitoring and evaluation. These training methods can be important tools for resource institutions moving toward becoming more effective, efficient, and sustainable in delivering needed services to small entrepreneurs.

Improved capacity to manage current and longer-term accounting issues can help to strengthen the overall management and performance of resource institutions. Many skill-specific training materials and methods exist to build technical capacity. For example, hands-on learning using computer programs for teaching accounting practices, linked to the use of an accounting workbook, can be an effective tool for strengthening technical capacity in accounting practices. In addition, some methods are available for helping those responsible for accounting understand how their expertise can most effectively aid institution managers. These approaches to technical capacity building are discussed in Chapter 5.

Administrative Capacity Issues:
Developing Human and Organizational Resources

Resource institutions assisting small and micro-enterprises require and generally have highly committed staffs. The hours are long, the work is arduous, the evidence of success is often far in the future, and pay and material support are minimal. Given these conditions, the evidence of enthusiasm, commitment, and creativity among resource institution staff is impressive. But commitment and energy are not enough for effective operation. Good management requires the capacity to hire, train, and motivate staff and to deal with logistical problems arising from the need to visit clients, monitor their performance, and produce timely reports. Thus, another component of improving the management of resource institutions is improving their administrative capacity.

Personnel and Organizational Management

Hiring Staff. Resource institutions operate with highly motivated people who generally lack the business dimension of the skills for assisting small entrepreneurs (Scurrah and Podesta 1984). Again, this is particularly the case in organizations moving from a social welfare orientation to a small business development approach. Training can inculcate needed skills and performance, but hiring practices need to be strengthened also. Hiring appropriate staff is an especially pressing need for resource institutions in Africa, where expatriate personnel typically play a large role in organizational management and operation. In many cases, expatriates may not be well attuned to local problems or business practices or they can be so wedded to imported models that they do not recognize the possibility of their inappropriateness to local circumstance. In hiring new staff, the availability of skills, ethnic divisions, and gender may also need to be considered. When appropriate skills are not available locally, administrators need to be able to identify easy learners among applicants. In addition, effective personnel management includes being able to identify and contract short-term technical assistance to supplement staff resources. Improving personnel management skills can increase the possibility of identifying the right person for the appropriate task.

Training Staff. Because requisite skills often are in short supply, resource institutions must consider how to train their staff in appropriate skills. For example, promoters and extensionists often have been criticized for giving poor or irrelevant advice. Or, projects may be endangered because staff with important skills are not available. At times, project monitors may not know what is going wrong (or right) with a program unless they understand the complexities of operating small and micro-businesses. Once again, the need for requisite skills is often masked by enthusiasm and commitment among staff, but the failures that can result from this situation directly affect the lives and livelihoods of large numbers of clients (see Honadle and Hannah 1981). An important ingredient noted in successful programs is adequate and appropriate staff training (see Paul 1982:201).

Motivating Staff. Commitment to the "cause" is not enough to ensure effective and efficient performance. In particular, incentives are needed to encourage staff to continue to work actively in pursuit of common objectives in the face of difficult working conditions, considerable frustration, and frequent failure (Ashe 1985; Paul 1982; Goldmark and Rosengard 1983). Staff "burn-out," familiar in small enterprise support programs, not only can hurt and slow down service, but also can quicken personnel turnover. Good and dedicated personnel are not an abundant resource in any environment and are in particularly short supply for the kinds of work done by micro-enterprise resource institutions.

Coordination. Resource institutions often grow and contract like mushrooms. They develop myriad projects, respond to numerous crises, and expand rapidly when they become flush with donor funding, only to suffer rapid shrinking when funds dry up. What often is sacrificed in the frequently tempestuous life of such organizations is coordination. When internal coordination is weak, however, financial management is made difficult and the organization may fail to learn appropriate lessons from its experiences. Administrative capacity building implies strengthening the ability to coordinate the activities of diverse groups of people and to establish enduring systems for monitoring their performance and for assessing problems as they arise. Organizational management can be greatly improved through the introduction of mechanisms to improve internal coordination.

Building Administrative Capacity

Improving staff quality, durability, and coordination takes managerial innovation. Among the tools to help improve performance are human resource planning, incentive systems, and organizational restructuring. Chapter 5 suggests a series of concrete tools and methods for addressing these recurrent problems. In addition, increased communication among resource institutions can encourage sharing of ideas about how to deal with these recurrent administrative issues. We consider in the next section this issue of communications capacity.

Communications Capacity Issues: Solving Problems Collectively

A frequent failure of resource institutions is their inability to learn from their failures or from their clients and field agents (Lassen 1980; Tendler 1982). Just as frequent is the need they express to contact other organizations in order to coordinate activities, share experiences, pool resources, or learn from common problems and mistakes. They often express the feeling of being cut off from knowledge of kindred organizations, of being reluctant to interact with governments, and of being unable to establish constructive working relationships with international donors. Each of these recurrent problems relates to the communication capacity of the resource institution. Improving communication capacity means increasing the ability to receive and impart information effectively and to learn from feedback and experience. Problems of information management and institutional linkages, discussed below, indicate the importance of improving communications capacity and the impact such capacity would have on the issues that have been considered in previous pages.

Information Management

Learning from Feedback. In enterprise development, numerous pitfalls can beset resource institutions. Often very creatively, they may flounder around for long periods, trying to find a way out, searching for an appropriate model for service delivery, or experimenting with a variety of alternatives (Tendler 1984; Lassen 1980). Alternatively, they may be so committed to a rigid model that they do not listen to client complaints or absorb evidence of problems or failure. Many institutions do not learn from their experiences—either successes or failures. The most effective organizations learn to listen and to ask the right questions so that they can monitor their own performance and that of their clients. Not only do they learn to listen, they also develop the ability to interpret and analyze what they hear and then, where necessary, to change practices, personnel, or procedures (see Paul 1982:201; Young and Nellis 1985).

Program Evaluation. Donors and lending agencies often stress the importance of monitoring and evaluation of development programs, particularly those directed toward low income clienteles. This also represents a good source of project feedback for resource institution managers. There are a large number of monitoring and evaluation methodologies available, complete with "how-to" manuals (see, for example, ACVAFS 1983; Cotter 1986; Markey 1986; DAI 1985). Resource institutions that deliver credit to small and micro-enterprises have demonstrated considerable capacity to improve their monitoring systems. Well-managed organizations almost always adopt systems for following up borrowers and encouraging prompt repayment. The same cannot be said for overall program evaluation, in spite of the ready availability of methods to do so. Typically, resource institutions feel pressed to assign scarce financial and human resources to the more immediately operational aspects of their programs. They may need and want evaluations of their activities and the performance of their clients, but believe they do not have the resources to undertake routine assessments. If program evaluation is to become more useful, methods are needed that use little staff time and re-sources. (For a *Guide to Guides* for evaluating small-scale enterprise pro-grams, see Hennrich 1987.)

Institutional Linkages

Networking with Other Resource Institutions. A multitude of resource institutions provide services to small entrepreneurs. Some are more effective than others, some are larger than others, and some have a longer history than others. In spite of such differences, they frequently carry out remarkably similar projects and face remarkably similar organizational and environmental problems (James 1982; Kilby and D'Zmura 1983; Leonard and Marshall 1982). Together, their experience represents a vast store of knowledge about effective responses to the needs of small en-trepreneurs. Isolated, they may have limited repertoires for responding to common problems that beset large numbers of organizations. Thus, in practice, each time an institution initiates a new project, the wheel may have to be reinvented and many unnecessary failures may result. The process of learning to be more effective and efficient could be improved greatly through more contact among resource institutions. This possibil-ity is discussed in greater detail in Chapter 5.

Linkages with Governments and International Donors. Private re-source institutions typically believe that they provide better services at lower cost than do public sector organizations offering similar services or that they provide services to groups that are forgotten, overlooked, or discriminated against by government (Tendler 1982; Sanyal 1987). Given this perspective, such organizations often display lack of interest or hos-tility toward government programs or the public sector in general. Nevertheless, many development specialists are concerned that private organizational efforts will never achieve a significant impact unless they can find ways for increasing their capacity to affect more beneficiaries. Such scaling-up of development efforts requires more effective collabo-ration between public and private sector programs. Barriers to such interaction need to be addressed.

Just as governments often are treated with disdain, donors often are treated with considerable circumspection. International donors are courted assiduously by resource institutions, but donors also monitor performance, send evaluation teams, insist upon reforms, and stipulate how their funds are to be spent. Governments and donors can provide useful services to resource institutions but they can also be seen as threatening outsiders that do not or will not understand the particular dilemmas or problems faced by the institutions or who may harbor de-sires to take over the programs of the organization. If such attitudes were overcome, resource institutions could often benefit. For example, gov-ernment agencies might provide alternative sources of funding or might cooperate in useful ways in the achievement of common goals. There is even the possibility that, with better communication skills, resource institutions could play more effective roles in altering policies and regulations that discriminate against small and micro-businesses. Similarly, donor agencies could make technical assistance more available, offer other training opportunities, initiate institution building grants, and facilitate access to other organizations if they were better informed about the problems faced by the institutions. The large donors could synchronize better the structures of their application and evaluation forms so that smaller institutions spend less time on paperwork for multiple funders. Greater capacity to communicate with the outside agencies could help to resolve a number of the organizations' recurrent problems.

Building Communications Capacity

By increasing their communications capacity, resource institutions can become better informed, better able to apply the lessons of experience, and better connected with their environment. More knowledge of available technology can help. Learning to listen effectively is a critical skill that can alter attitudes toward clients, governments, and donor agencies. Specific tools and resources to help them are discussed in Chapter 5.

Conclusion

In summary, there is no single or immediate panacea for addressing issues of efficiency, effectiveness, and sustainability in resource institutions. Rather, improving their ability to offer timely, useful, and low cost services to small entrepreneurs involves an on-going and simultaneous effort to build capacity in four interrelated areas, beginning with the priority of improving strategic capacity among institution managers and supporting this with improvements in technical, administrative, and communications areas. Increasing capacity in these four areas will not make the performance of the resource institutions faultless. However, it will help them to make problems more detectable, to ease the difficulties in managing them, and to avoid their recurrence in the future. The next chapter offers some suggestions to help accomplish these improvements.

Chapter 5

Prescription: Capacity Building for Resource Institutions

How does a resource institution become more efficient, effective, and sustainable? In the previous chapter, a series of recurrent problems of such organizations was surveyed with the intent of indicating how they inhibited the management and operations of resource institutions, ultimately affecting the capacity to provide the best possible services to small and micro-enterprise clienteles. We suggested that the problems that emerge repeatedly in resource institutions of all types—private and public; small and large; local, national, and international—can be effectively addressed through building organizational capacity in four critical areas. Assisting them to strengthen their strategic, technical administrative and communications; abilities will result in organizations that are better able to meet the needs of their low-income beneficiaries and more able to contribute to the process of development.

Helping resource institutions to strengthen their strategic capacity generally is the first step and highest priority for improved management and performance. This should be supported by improvements in technical, administrative, and communications skills within the institution. The relationship among the capacity areas is interactive. As managers improve their abilities to establish goals, set priorities, make effective decisions, and respond creatively to problems as they arise, they will need better financial information, a stronger and better organized staff, and more informational linkages to their clients, financial supporters, and sister organizations. But improved strategic capacities will also help managers set in motion the changes needed to get the information and responsiveness they need. Thus, helping to enhance strategic capacity in an organization can produce positive changes in other capacity areas.

In this chapter, capacity areas are discussed in terms of the approaches and methods that are most appropriate for strengthening the performance of resource institutions. The chapter suggests a series of tools that are available for improving organizational efficiency, effectiveness, and sustainability. Some of the tools are particularly appropriate for strengthening particular capacity areas, while others have more general application. Thus, it is possible to indicate what approaches are most useful for addressing particular recurrent problems and to associate topics with distinct categories of materials.

Tools and Topics

The four capacity areas are required in varying degrees by different personnel in the resource institution. Management, for example, needs to have a strategic vision of the organization to be able to see it in the context of its larger social and political setting, to have a coherent idea of its strengths and weaknesses, to appreciate where it is now and where it should be going, and to have a sense of the fundamental decisions about the nature and course of its development. Management is uniquely able to assess these factors and to make the big decisions about the institution's future, decisions that must be made correctly if the organization is to thrive and prosper.

Others in the organization require technical skills to implement its activities. An effective management information system, for example, may demand a certain level of systems design and computer expertise. Managing resources effectively requires expertise in answering questions such as: How will responsibility be delegated, performance supervised, results measured? How will staff be selected and trained? How will levels of resources be matched to tasks to be accomplished? Thus, the technical and administrative capacity-building areas require organizational staff to increase their skills in relatively technical areas such as accounting, financial planning, and personnel systems.

Communications capacity often is perceived to be simply a task of getting management's messages out to others, both inside and outside the organization. A fundamental aspect of communication, however, is the ability to receive, process, and act upon information, as well as to send it. Thus, enhancing communications capacity includes understanding and responding better to the situation and needs of clients, developing an ability to learn from the experience of sister organizations, interacting more effectively with those whose decisions set the policy environment for small and micro-enterprise development, and making funder-recipient relationships more mutually productive.

Effective approaches to enhancing technical and administrative skills often are different from the approaches to enhancing strategic and communications capacity. In the former case, there is generally a body of reasonably settled knowledge and technique to be transmitted. Various media, materials, and settings are known to be effective in transmitting knowledge and skills and can be adapted to local situations, resource constraints, and organizational needs.

Building strategic and communications capacities is more difficult. By their very nature they require accumulating, assessing, synthesizing, and acting upon large amounts of information from multiple sources. This is particularly true of strategic capacity building. There is no "right answer" or settled body of knowledge for effective decision making and problem solving. However, there are ways of thinking, frameworks to help organize and understand problems more clearly, and general approaches for decision making that have proved useful. Helping managers to develop these broad-gauge skills will require approaches to learning that are more innovative and less well-established than those for technical and administrative capacities. Such approaches generally capitalize on the experience of similarly situated institutions and information about how their plans and strategic choices worked out in reality. For example, with the benefit of hindsight it often is possible to see key opportunities seized or missed, key decisions that opened or closed possibilities, and clear or cloudy perceptions of mission and strategy.

In the following pages, methods for building capacity in four areas are described. The case method, manuals and workbooks, audio and visual training materials, and computer-based training materials are the most appropriate tools for increasing strategic, technical, administrative, and communication capacities. Some of the tools are especially appropriate for addressing particular sets of recurrent problems.

The Case Method

Managers of resource institutions assisting small and micro-enterprises face many common challenges and issues. A variety of differences in circumstances, pressures, beliefs, cultures, histories, and personalities produce wide variation in institutional responses to these comparable challenges. Some responses have been more successful than others. For senior executives facing common problems in managing their organizations, the case method provides a framework within which they can learn from each other as they analyze and discuss cases with which they can identify. An effective caseleader can catalyze fruitful discussion and help structure the input of the participants in a way that helps to clarify issues and facilitates the drawing of conclusions. Well-selected and well-written cases highlight important decisions that faced real managers, decisions that shaped the evolution of the institution and/or its relationship to its environment.

In addition to helping to build managers' capacity to think strategically, the case method also can be an effective methodology for staff to become more sensitive to the world of the small and micro-entrepreneurs and the decisions and dilemmas they face in their business activities.[1] Effective use of the case method also can increase staff understanding of the components of effective assistance programs, the need for appropriate financial information, the consequences of alternative organizational structures and incentive systems, and the results of various forms of communicating with "significant others."

The method can be used in short training programs tailored to the needs, interests, and skills of managers and staff. Using cases that focus on the real world problems they face, the case methodology engages managers and staff both intellectually and emotionally. Moreover, good case teaching not only develops decision-making abilities, it also contributes to communications capacity as well. Participants learn who has what sort of expertise, how it can be tapped and utilized, and what can be learned from the careful observation of the experience of others. Part II of this book contains a discussion of the case method and an introduction to the twenty-one cases that follow.

Manuals and Workbooks

A wide variety of manuals and workbooks for organizational management and substantive skill building exist that are appropriate for resource institutions.[2] In general, they tend to be less "engaging" than computer-based training. At the same time, they are inexpensive, widely available, and useful for subsequent reference after initial training has been completed. Manuals and workbooks are particularly useful for training in substantive areas and are appropriate for use by staff of various levels of education because they are available for a variety of skill levels. Some useful manuals and workbooks in substantive areas have been developed by the resource institutions that have training components in their assistance programs for small and micro-entrepreneurs. Some of these can be useful for initial orientation of nontechnical staff in business activities such as basic accounting and business administration.[3]

Training Videos, Filmstrips, and Audiocassettes

A surprising number of resource institutions have equipment for displaying videotapes, filmstrips, and audiocassettes. Often, the organizations have invested in the development of videos that explain their programs or present a history of the organization.[4] According to resource institution staff, videotapes particularly are useful for fund raising, the orientation of newly hired staff, and visitors to the organization. A few institutions that provide training for small and micro-entrepreneurs also use videos and filmstrips in classroom settings to complement the activities of teaching staff. Video and audio training materials exist that deal with issues such as business applications of computers, budgeting, accounting, communications skills, personnel supervision, financial analysis, organizational design and control, and other substantive areas.

Many existing training materials are most appropriate for staff with relatively advanced educational levels. These materials offer the advantage of stimulating trainees through visual presentation. Nevertheless, they do little to encourage active and interactive learning. Thus, they are most appropriately used in combination with other teaching methods. For example, they can be used to support classroom teaching in substantive areas and the presentation of some aspects of training cases could be effectively produced on videotapes.

Although it has not yet been used widely as such, videotape has the potential to be used much like a field notebook to bring into training sessions a greater sense of the reality of the small business person's situation. Today's small format video recorders are light-weight, mobile systems that can be operated effectively by amateurs. Light-weight, portable equipment is suitable to document the entrepreneurs' conditions, and the tools and techniques they use, and to record their options. Portable video represents a powerful medium for developing a more realistic understanding of the business person's perspective of the types of policies that would improve production; of problems within the distribution system; and of the constraints facing small enterprise.

Ideally, the managers of resource institutions get a sense of the entrepreneurs' reality by frequent visits to the field. However, even with the best of intentions and frequent visits, reality is substantially distorted by the visit itself. The advance preparations for official visitors plus the deference accorded to them makes it virtually impossible for an accurate impression of the villagers' perceptions and village conditions to emerge (Chambers 1980). Compounding the problem are the vehicle and gasoline shortages that severely limit the field travel even of those most determined to see conditions for themselves. As a result, speculation about the entrepreneurs' circumstances serves as their knowledge base, and often this speculation emerges from an inappropriate or outdated mental image of village life.

The new generation of field video equipment now makes it possible to use a video to supplement survey and other field data. Small enough to be relatively unobtrusive, the video camera distorts less the reality of village life than does a visit of high ranking officials. Small business people will often be more candid with a relatively low status interviewer than they will with a high status official. In the context of in-depth interviews and group discussion, the video camera has the potential to provide a far more accurate record of the reality of daily circumstances and problems. It can capture what in many cases are highly constructive suggestions for program improvement.

Computer-Based Training Materials

Increasingly, resource institutions are using computerized systems for tracking finances, budgets, and client performance.[5] Although these systems continue to be out of the reach of the smaller organizations, particularly private nonprofit ones, it is reasonable to expect that in the future computerized management and administrative systems will be adopted even more widely. Capacity building in response to particular recurrent problems can be done effectively through a variety of computer-based training materials.[6] They provide hands-on experience for trainees that can build substantive skills, logical analysis of problems, and effective decision making. Well-selected materials have considerable potential to strengthen resource institution management and staff in the substantive areas of planning, project design, financial and administrative management, monitoring, and evaluation.

Computer-based training materials have several advantages for capacity building efforts. For institutions with access to computers, they are relatively inexpensive, generally ranging in price from less than U.S. $100–$500. Once this investment has been made, the materials are available for use by large numbers of staff. Compared to the cost of sending individuals to formal and traditional training sessions or organizing such activities locally, their cost is minimal. Computer-based training can be carried out on the premises of the resource institutions and tailored to other time demands on trainees.

Computer-based training materials are widely available and cover a large number of topics, such as accounting, planning, financial management, communications, inventory control, project management, proposal analysis, and personnel management. Moreover, appropriate packages of training materials can be developed for the particular needs of specific resource institutions. Finally, extensive experience with this training format has resulted in a number of software packages of high quality that have proved effective in engaging participant interest and commitment. Some of the materials already in use are appropriate for the management of many resource institutions; in other cases, packages that consider language, culture, and educational differences need to be developed.

Computer-based education products for small business management are included in the evaluation of training materials prepared by the Control Data Corporation as a part of the ARIES project (CDC 1986). Of particular note are the variety of materials developed by CDC for small business training in the United States. Although too sophisticated for most Third World micro-entrepreneurs, the presentation of the principles involved may be of interest to many small enterprise program managers.

There is another dimension in which the computer may serve as a powerful training tool. The *AskARIES Knowledgebase*, described in Part III, contains a wealth of information about enterprise development, structured around specific problems. It provides a valuable resource for anyone developing training materials about enterprise development. At the students' level, however, the knowledgebase represents a truly revolutionary resource. Not only does it put the core literature of the field at their fingertips, but the multifaceted field structure allows them to explore relationships among such factors as project content, client characteristics, geographic areas, and so forth. This encourages the sort of active questioning and analysis that characterizes the most powerful learning experiences. Moreover, in the future, digital audio and interactive video will allow both audio and full-motion video to be a part of *AskARIES*, so that the user can call up, say, an interview with Grameen Bank founder Professor Muhammad Yunus or a segment from the more than 200 hours of video tape that the Grameen Bank has recorded as a part of its own training program. *AskARIES* represents only a starting point in using the computer as a training resource—a platform to build on for the future.

Selecting Tools for Capacity Building

Resource institutions can be assisted in improving their effectiveness through tailoring capacity building in strategic, technical, administrative, and communications skills to the particular needs of organizational management and staff. For example, organization managers do not require intensive substantive knowledge-building in accounting practices —these skills should be developed among those responsible for accounting services—but do need to develop a manager's-eye view of what financial information they need, how to interpret such information, and how to use it for long-range planning and strategic decision making. Different training approaches can be introduced to respond effectively to the distinct but interrelated needs of managers and staff. The following brief discussion suggests the kinds of materials that can help to build capacity in the four capacity areas.

Strategic Capacity Building

The case method is particularly appropriate for building managerial capacity to set goals, establish priorities, and pursue policies that allow the organization to achieve its goals. Cases can introduce managers to the world of the small and micro-entrepreneur and sensitize them to the constraints and opportunities faced by small businesses, including the particular rationales that lie behind the decision making of their owners.

This approach is useful for encouraging managers to develop skills in assessing the needs of small entrepreneurs, understanding the environment in which they work, and considering the extent to which the human and financial resources of the institution allow them to respond to the needs they measure. With greater capacity to gather and assess such information, institution managers will increase their ability to establish reasonable objectives and determine priorities for their organizations. Similarly, cases can help managers develop appropriate organizational structures by assessing what the most important decisions are, who are the most appropriate decision makers for various types of issues, and how to ensure that appropriate information flows in a timely fashion to these decision makers. In a more general sense, cases can increase managerial capacity to forecast, plan, and create new alternatives.

Computer-based training materials, "how-to" manuals, and workbooks can help managers develop substantive knowledge in the areas of financial planning and organizational systems. For example, these materials can be packaged to help managers consider the cost-effectiveness problems raised in Chapter 4, investigate alternatives for raising operating and investment capital, scale their programs to a level of resources they reasonably can expect to command, and become aware of the issues of liquidity and solvency already discussed. They can become more familiar with issues such as user charges, investments in local financial institutions, and loan capital from local banks.

Technical Capacity Building

Although the case method can be used also for building technical skills among resource institution staff, it is probably less important than other approaches. Where resource institutions have suitable infrastructure, computer-based materials can be used in teaching accounting fundamentals, cost analysis and reporting, budget control, program budgeting, cash management, inventory control, and financial analysis of programs. "How-to" manuals and workbooks cover the same topics and can be used as supplements or as the primary tool where computer technology is not available. Video and audio training materials covering some of these substantive areas is most appropriately used to reinforce learning that is occurring through other methodologies. The case method is more useful in addressing problems in program design. Cases can sensitize management and staff to the particular problems faced by small and micro-entrepreneurs, the ways in which various program components affect them and their businesses, and the potential consequences of making choices about investments in technology, marketing systems, and production processes. Computer-based systems can assist in program planning, monitoring and evaluation, effective allocation of program resources, and assessment of marketing and interest rates structures. "How-to" manuals are particularly appropriate for designing technical assistance components, carrying out feasibility studies, and developing record-keeping systems.

Administrative Capacity Building

Cases can increase the ability of management and administrative capacity staff to make effective staffing and organizational decisions and to communicate more effectively within the organization. They can also encourage sharing of ideas about how to deal with these recurrent administrative issues. Computer-based training materials can be particularly useful in building skills in personnel planning, personnel record systems, resource allocation, and monitoring; skill-building seminars can stress issues such as those related to motivation and incentives within organizations. Modules for assessing needs and diagnosing administrative problems can be effectively presented in "how-to" manuals. Visual and audio materials can be particularly useful in building skills in interpersonal relations, cooperativeness, and supervision.

Communications Capacity Building

Case materials can encourage resource institution management to listen more effectively to the organization's clientele and to use this feedback in program design, staffing, and communications. Moreover, by bringing managers together in short training courses structured around the case method, sharing of ideas, experiences, and responses to common problems is encouraged. Computer-based modules for program monitoring and evaluation can also increase use of feedback information. In addition, technologies are available for strengthening the ability of organizations to communicate with important individuals and groups in their environment—clients, donors, governments, and sister organizations. For example, a communication technology such as CARINET[7] can increase networking and make information retrieval and sharing less time-consuming and more effective. Similarly, the personal computer-based *AskARIES Knowledgebase* described in Part III can encourage greater communication related to alternatives for addressing recurrent problems. Seminars in information management, hands-on problem-solving experiences, and introduction to already existing networks and services can do much to build this important capacity.

Conclusion:
Taking the First Steps toward Diagnosis and Prescription

Chapter 4 presented a structuring of the recurrent problems of resource institutions. In this chapter, the focus has been on capacity building in specific areas and the methodologies that are appropriate to this task.

Often, resource institutions will be able to identify their own needs, particularly when these relate to one of the specific recurrent problems that have been discussed. When they do so, they may also be able to identify an appropriate means of addressing the problem area—managerial training, staff training, reorganization, or the introduction of new accounting, personnel, and communication systems.

In other situations, however, managers of resource institutions will be aware that "something is wrong" in the performance of the organization and its programs, but may be too close to the problems to assess and address institutional or program malaise. At times, then, resource institutions will need help diagnosing their needs and prescribing appropriate remedies to recurrent problems. This is particularly the case when resource institutions require a "package" of capacity-building efforts. In such instances, technical assistance should be sought to help resource institutions identify needs, diagnose recurrent problems, and prescribe appropriate courses of action, including the design of specific packages of appropriate training materials.

As indicated at the outset of this book, even the most skilled and dedicated effort to increase strategic, technical, administrative, and communication skills will not produce perfect organizations and flawless programs. But such efforts can improve decision making, problem solving, and other abilities to produce more efficient, effective, and sustainable organizations. Improvement in these skills, using their own and outside resources, will help organizations to cope better with the recurrent problems that characterize their difficult, demanding, yet highly productive task of assisting small and micro-enterprises.

Notes

1. This pedagogy requires cases structured very differently from most of the "case study" literature of small enterprise development. Much of the latter consists of descriptive "stories" about particular projects or organizations. In contrast, the teaching case presents a particular decision situation, along with such background information as is necessary for a productive discussion in terms of specified teaching objectives. The ARIES cases, for example, are designed to analyze specific recurrent problems and responses to them. The idea is to create with the case and a good case leader an environment within which to examine various institutional responses to these problems, and the degree of success that was achieved.

2. Control Data Corporation has identified and assessed a large number of these materials for their appropriateness in addressing the particular recurrent problems faced by the resource institutions.

3. For example, the manuals produced by the Carvajal Foundation in Colombia for Level III and above entrepreneurs might be useful in training staff with

minimal educational attainments who are responsible for providing very basic technical assistance to Level I and Level II entrepreneurs. Particularly useful is the manual produced by PACT: *Small Business Projects: A Step by Step Guide* (PACT 1987).

4. These observations result from field visits to resource institutions in New York, Washington, D.C., Latin America, Asia, and Africa.

5. This observation results from field visits to resource institutions in New York, Washington, D.C., Latin America, Asia, and Africa.

6. Within the ARIES Project, identifying and developing such materials for use by resource institutions are the primary responsibility of Control Data Corporation (CDC 1987).

7. Created by Partnership for Productivity, CARINET is an international, low-cost computer communications network used for electronic mail and computer conferences.

Part II

The Cases

Introduction to Part II

A major objective of this book is to help resource institutions enhance their capacity to serve more effectively small and micro-enterprises. An important vehicle for this capacity development has been the creation of a series of management teaching cases tailored expressly to the situations of these resource institutions. Part I of this book presented a framework for assessing the kinds of recurrent problems faced by resource institutions and identified models of small and micro-enterprise assistance that are frequently adopted by these organizations. In Part II, the cases address the issues of institutional management and program design that are analyzed in the first part of this book. The cases draw on the actual experiences of resource institutions and the dilemmas and opportunities faced by their managers. Each case places the reader in the position of a decision maker, presents information about a critical decision that needs to be made, and asks, "What would you do if you were this person?" As is true of most such institutions, the issues faced are usually complex, and in the process of considering them the decision maker must often assess institutional goals, the strengths and weaknesses of the organization, its capacity to respond to the needs of its clients, and its relationships with other organizations. Moreover, as indicated in Part I, institutional characteristics, the needs and conditions of clienteles, and country contexts all differ, adding to the complexity of the dilemmas faced by resource institution managers.

The richness and variability of the issues that emerge in each case make it difficult to categorize and sequence them in this volume. For ease of access, we have arranged them alphabetically by resource institution name. Before presenting an integrative overview of the cases, we first present a general introduction to the case method itself.

What Is the Case Method Approach and Why Use It?

Senior managers of any organization require a variety of skills to guide the organization effectively toward the accomplishment of its goals, indeed to assure that the goals themselves are appropriate. One requirement surely is substantive knowledge about a variety of subjects relevant to the organization's activities. Of great importance, however, are other skills: effective approaches to problem solving, ability to see problems and goals in context (to think strategically), and interpersonal and communication skills.

The case method has proved effective in helping people to develop this combination of skills. Although there are many variants of the method, most share the following characteristics. The centerpiece is the "The Case"—sometimes called "The Case Report"—a carefully researched description of a particular problem or situation that faced the management of an organization. A "case analysis" of this situation then is prepared by participants. In The Harvard Business School's use of the method, individual reading and reflection on the case are followed by small group discussion where much of the case analysis takes place. This is followed by the case discussion, where an experienced case leader orchestrates an exploration of the issues raised by the case. At the conclusion of the discussion, there may be a brief statement of what actually was done and the subsequent outcome. Ideally this is provided by one of the individuals from the actual case situation (who also may have observed the discussion). It may involve comments upon the case analysis and conclusions of the group and response to questions.

Writing about the case method, HBS Professor Benson Shapiro stresses that the two concepts of *metaphor* and *simulation* are central to the case method approach. Each case describes a real situation and serves as a metaphor for a particular set of problems. On simulation, Professor Shapiro states that "the case method of management instruction is based upon the belief that management is a skill rather than a collection of techniques or concepts. The best way to learn a skill is to practice in a *simulation*-type process" (emphasis his, Shapiro 1984).

More than conveying specific subject matter knowledge, the case method fosters a systematic approach to problems. It builds understanding of how to use an appropriate analytical framework to pull from a welter of information the significant elements needed for decision. It develops the ability to recognize limitations to action posed by the societal, economic, institutional, and personnel context of the problem. An important skill is developing these frameworks—often a set of questions—to define the problem accurately. "Problem definition," writes Professor E. Raymond Corey, "also involved delineating a framework within which to deal with what may be posed as an immediate question. For example, the manager in the case may be asking, 'Why isn't our advertising effective?' That could be the tip of the iceberg; the fundamental problem might be 'What should be our target market segment, and how do we develop an overall strategy for reaching it?' It becomes possible, then, to deal with the specific query regarding advertising effectiveness within the framework of the broader question" (Corey 1976).

The fact that the analysis and understanding of the case take place through interpersonal give-and-take moderated by the case leader delivers at least two important messages. First, in management situations, much information must be drawn out through discussions to which different individuals bring different perspectives. Like the case leader (who in some sense serves as a role model) the manager must be able to use discussion leadership skills to tap the wisdom and perspectives of his or her people. To an important extent in the case method, "the medium is the message," to use McLuhan's language. This is apparent in Professor Charles Gragg's classic article "Because Wisdom Can't be Told" when he describes three phases that students pass through in making the adjustment from lecture style teaching to the case method. The first phase, he says, "is that of discovering the inability of the individual to think of everything that his fellow students can think of ... The second phase is that of accepting easily and without fear the need for cooperative help." The final phase is "recognition that the instructors do not always or necessarily know the 'best' answers" (Gragg 1940).

Second, the case method reflects the manager's reality that, in Thomas Bonoma's words, "cleverness and even brilliance unpresented, or presented poorly will not necessarily dominate mediocrity presented with persuasive genius." He continues, "Because administrative cases are dissected in a community of learners, not only 'goodness' of analysis but also persuasiveness of presentation enter the discussion arena as factors with which to be reckoned" (Bonoma 1981).

An additional benefit of the case method for senior managers is its action orientation. There is an insistent pressure to develop actionable plans suited to the situation being presented. In advising new case teachers, for example, Professor Shapiro urges, "The instructor should *understand that in the discussion process action drives analysis*" (emphasis his, Shapiro 1984). Having experienced this sort of pressure themselves, executives tend to be impatient with approaches they consider "academic."

Several fundamental principles of effective learning underlie the case approach. First, people absorb new knowledge most effectively by integrating it with their existing knowledge. The case approach emphasizes that participants draw upon their own experiences for insights, sharing these perceptions with the group. This encourages participants constantly to integrate new case material with their existing store of knowledge. Indeed, a major premise of the case method is that most of the learning comes not from the "teacher" but from the group: from its analysis, the perspectives that come out in the discussion, and the experience of seeing peers functioning as resource people. Speaking to a group of senior managers entering Harvard's Advanced Management Program, Malcolm McNair forewarned them that they would not depart the program with "answers." "On the contrary," he said, "the principal value to you of this training at the Business School will lie in the power that you will develop to analyze a situation, to formulate a program of action, and to carry that program into effect through the people in your organization or in your community" (McNair 1954).

Second, active learning is more effective than passive learning. Participants constantly are seeking to relate each new contribution to their own analysis; to modify it, to extend it, to enrich it. The value of this style of active learning is Charles Gragg's main theme as he assails "the decidedly questionable ... assumption that it is possible by a simple process of telling to pass on knowledge in a useful form. This is a stumbling block of the ages. If the learning process is to be effective something dynamic must take place in the learner" (Gragg 1940).

In selecting the situation presented in the cases that follow, we first sought to identify key problems and issues facing managers of small enterprise programs: essentially the recurrent problems described in Chapter 4. In some form, all resource institutions working with small enterprises encounter these recurrent problems and issues. Each deals with them in some fashion, some with great successes, others with less. In these experiences lie many useful lessons.

In case workshops, the systematic study of the cases that follow can help managers build up a framework within which to examine the problems they face. Analysis and discussion of some of the main ways these problems have been dealt with help to build up a sense of patterns in the problems and in various solutions worked out to them. ACCION, for example, talks about its "methodology." They have worked out a particular approach to small enterprise development that they find mitigates some common problems. The Carvajal Foundation has evolved quite a different model of enterprise development. Both have influenced the design of many projects beyond their own. Much can be learned by examination and discussion not only of "the model" but also of how it came into being. Both organizations began with quite different approaches from their present ones. It is far more instructive to study *why* and *how* they changed their program design than it is simply to have the result described as in many of the existing "case studies."

The set of cases that follow focuses on key turning points in the evolution of major approaches to dealing with recurrent problems and issues. Used in the context of case method management education, analysis of these cases can help participants to build up a repertoire of patterns—metaphors in Shapiro's word—that can help them to analyze more insightfully the problems of the institutions they manage. Rather than being told or reading about the "ACCION Model" or the "Grameen Bank Model," participants examine through cases the set of circumstances that led ACCION to shift from its original approach to its present "methodology"; they study the findings that led eventually to the creation of the Grameen Bank from a very different sort of predecessor project. How were the circumstances similar; how were they different? What options were considered and discarded in arriving at the current approaches? The cases focus less on describing current models and more on illuminating the dynamic turning points in the evolution of current approaches to small enterprise development. This approach emphasizes the model as a response to a particular problem or opportunity rather than the model as just the way a particular organization does business.

The cases presented here differ sharply from those in most of the "case study" literature. Much of the latter is purely descriptive, "stories" about particular projects. Relatively few materials are designed to analyze the circumstances to which the model represents a response. Thus, these cases represent a vehicle for discussion and analysis—not a recounting of the decision finally taken and its effects. In the context of the case method, the latter is relatively incidental information and is briefly presented by the case leader at the end of the session. This outcome information, and suggestions on the teaching of each case, is presented in a companion to this volume *Seeking Solutions: A Case Leader's Guide*. A well-prepared case leader can create an environment within which to examine major recurring problems of resource institutions, responses to these problems, and the degree of success achieved.

An Integrative Overview of the Cases

To provide a general overview of the issues each addresses, we shall introduce the cases here in terms of the strategic choices they pose about models of small and micro-enterprise assistance. Most of the cases deal with the search for an institutionally and contextually appropriate method of providing assistance to a clientele of small and micro-entrepreneurs. Decisions that center on how best an institution can assist its low income clients bring together a series of issues about institutional development, capacity building, and viability and require decision makers to consider its relationship to its environment, its funders, and its clients. Thus, the search for an institutionally appropriate model of small and micro-enterprise assistance almost inevitably implies an examination of the range of management issues addressed in Part I.

Making these kinds of decisions often amounts to critical junctures in the growth and development of resource institutions. These arise, for example, in a series of cases that center around designing programs for credit provision. In one, the executive director in the *FUCODES* case in the Dominican Republic must decide whether the institution should develop credit programs to assist individual entrepreneurs or whether it would achieve its goals more effectively by dealing with groups of clients. This critical choice necessitates assessing the prior experience of *FUCODES*, its resources, its goals, its financial viability, and the perspectives of its directors and funders. Similarly, in the *Senegal (A)* and *Senegal (B)* cases, institutional goals and capacities and individual perceptions and experiences come into play—and conflict—as the institution grapples with selecting a model for credit delivery. In these cases, institutional managers consider and debate the appropriateness of a minimalist model of credit provision for the Senegalese context and assess how such a model should be implemented within the organization. The cases therefore provide insight into the minimalist model and also demonstrate the range of institutional and contextual factors that need to be considered in reorienting the goals and activities of an existing organization. The choices made in Senegal, however, may not be appropriate for all institutions and contexts. In Bangladesh, managers of a rural development program, challenged to make credit provision self-sufficient, are oriented toward a more complex and integrated scheme that differs considerably from the minimalist approach. In this *BRAC (A)* case, the financial viability of a credit scheme becomes a critically important issue because of the variety of tasks that managers believe need to be carried out in order to reach the poorest sectors of the population with effective assistance.

Other cases address institutional aspects of effective credit provision. In the *Save the Children* case, the difficulties involved in decentralizing a credit program to the community level in Honduras are addressed. Here, concern for altering the management structure within a resource institution is coupled with issues of defining policies and procedures, assuring credit program sustainability, facilitating participatory management, and training staff at all levels to ensure that the program is contributing to broad-based community development. Participatory management of a credit program is also central to the *IIRR (A)* and *IIRR (B)* cases. Managers in these cases consider and then design measures to bring about more collaborative relationships between the International Institute of Rural Reconstruction and its grantee organizations in the Philippines. Again we find managers at a critical juncture in the development of their organization grappling with issues that range from how participation in credit management should be defined to how to manage relationships of dependence and independence between donors and their clients.

At times, the impetus to reassess program strategy comes from unexpected sources. In the *UNO* case in Brazil, for example, a donor organization uses a critical evaluation of this resource institution to think through its own approach to small and micro-enterprise assistance. In the evaluation, UNO was charged with inefficiency and failure to reach the neediest clients; directors of ACCION International, who helped establish the Brazilian organization, explore new options for program design and consider what "success" really means in a small-scale credit program and how best to reach a poor clientele. In the *PRODEME* case, an ACCION consultant to the organization struggles with a similar set of issues and must consider his own ideas and goals for credit programs as it becomes clearer that the resource institution sponsoring PRODEME is not willing to reorient its activities, so convinced is it of its own success. The consultant, already questioning the appropriateness of the program he has helped to design, is confronted by an external evaluation report that presents evidence of high loan default rates and reconsiders how to develop a viable credit program that meets client needs.

Meeting the credit needs of a very low income population is also a central issue in *The Grameen Bank Project (A), The Grameen Bank Project (B)*, and *The Grameen Bank Project (C)* cases. Designing a very large scale program to provide credit to the very poor in Bangladesh involved visionary management and experimentation over a period of time before an appropriate model emerged. Despite its evident success, however, expansion of the program was not easily accomplished. Managers had to convince national political and bureaucratic leaders of the need to reorganize the national banking system in Bangladesh to facilitate delivery of very small loans to a very large number of extremely poor clients throughout the country.

These cases indicate that there may be several models of effective credit delivery to small and micro-entrepreneurs. These range from the minimalist approach in *Senegal (A)* and *Senegal (B)* cases to the multifaceted approach considered in *BRAC (A)*; from the locally managed approach pursued in the *Save the Children* case to the large-scale national approach developed in *The Grameen Bank Project (A), (B), and (C)*; from methods that provide credit to individuals to those that operate through the solidarity group model, as considered in the *FUCODES, UNO*, and *PRODEME* cases. The choices about which path to pursue raise issues of financial viability, organizational philosophy, and institutional structure. In addition to presenting a variety of models of credit provision, some of the cases can also be read as histories of the development of important models that are now well known in enterprise assistance. For instance, the *The Grameen Bank Project (A), (B), and (C)* cases trace the history of the important Grameen Bank approach to credit delivery, and the *UNO*— one of the earliest programs—and *PRODEME* cases detail the evolution of the solidarity group model within ACCION International. Other cases are sequenced to indicate how resource institutions have thought through issues of choice of an appropriate model of credit delivery and then how they have applied this thinking to the actual design of a delivery system and the administrative system to support it. This sequence is apparent in *Senegal (A)* and *(B)* and *IIRR (A)* and *(B)*, as well as in *CARE-Philippines (A)* and *(B)*, which deal with issues other than credit.

Not all the cases deal with credit programs, of course. An important aspect of the development of an institutionally appropriate model can be found in the *Carvajal (A)* case. Learning from the experience of others is an important aspect of this case, in which a manager of the Carvajal Foundation assesses the UNO experience to determine its relevance to an organization that is philosophically committed to the importance of training as a way of assisting small and micro-entrepreneurs. The manager must consider what lessons UNO has to offer and which of these lessons is appropriate to his organization. Then, once a new model has been developed and has demonstrated its usefulness, managers are required to address the issue of its financial viability. In *Carvajal (B)*, the viability of an integrated training model is considered in light of the program's success in Cali, Colombia. Viability becomes critically important to program managers when they consider replicating their program in a number of other locations in Colombia.

In addition to credit and training, some assistance programs identify marketing as a critical need of small and micro-entrepreneurs. Accordingly, two cases, the *Indonesian Rattan Basket Exporting Company* and *BRAC (C)*, consider how to market the goods produced by low income clients. In the Indonesia case, a critical issue is the potential tradeoffs between assistance to the poor and employment creation on a larger scale. The issue of scaling up to meet export quality and quantity demands also requires an examination of the issue of financial viability. In *BRAC (C)*, marketing outlets for goods produced by rural groups constitute a major strategic choice for managers in the context of very incomplete information and high potential for failure. In this case, marketing poses dilemmas for an organization that is already heavily committed in terms of time and financial and human resources and that faces an environmental context that offers little support for marketing endeavors.

Some of the cases are less concerned with models of assistance than they are with issues such as appropriate institutional management of staff and relationships with donor or grantee organizations. Thus, in several of the cases, the problem of appropriate training for managers and field staff is addressed, but nowhere as explicitly as in the *BRAC (B)* case. Here, BRAC's Management Development Committee must assess the content of a training program for the organization's middle managers and, in the process, consider the kind of competencies required by managers in rural development programs and determine the extent to which training can develop such skills. *CARE-Philippines (A)* and *(B)* address issues of interinstitutional relationships when a major organizational reorientation is being considered and implemented in the Philippines. In *CARE-Philippines (A)*, assessing experience with income-generating activities provides an opportunity for the resource institution to consider this new program thrust in relation to its other programs and to determine whether it has the capacity to integrate income-generating projects effectively into its Philippine portfolio. In *CARE-Philippines (B)*, the organization's complex relationship with a grantee of the income-generating project raises issues of control and autonomy between such organizations and considers how "partner" organizations should be selected and evaluated. These cases present an inside view of the dilemmas and tensions that beset organizations as they determine their priorities and attempt to implement new programs in "real world" contexts.

Many issues emerge in each of the cases and each can be read and analyzed in a variety of ways and sequences. They provide opportunities for rich discussions of models of small and micro-enterprise assistance, internal management problems, relationships with clients, and contextual constraints and opportunities.

The cases also can be used to focus on the capacity domains and recurrent problems set forth in Part I. Such a focus allows the designers of workshops, for example, to tailor a series of cases to the needs of a particular group of participants. For instance, the *Senegal (A)* case is well suited to bring out strategic issues of setting priorities: assessing the need, knowing the environment, considering feasibility. Table II-1 presents a map the issues in the twenty-one cases in relation to the broad categories of the recurrent problem framework. By design, the cases tend to cluster within the general category of strategic capacity. Such issues lend themselves particularly well to the case method approach. Therefore, within the ARIES project, the Control Data Corporation training packages tended to carry the main training materials burden within other dimensions of capacity, particularly the technical and financial aspects.

Conclusion

The comparative approach suggested above represents only one way to study these cases. The cases themselves are rich in possibilities because they reflect the real dilemmas and decisions that confront managers in a complex and multifaceted task. The situations presented underscore the fact that solutions to the problems of resource institutions are a result of an ongoing process of strategic management. They illustrate also how solutions often depend upon institutional and cultural contexts, and indeed upon the visions and capacities of individuals. Not only do these continuously interact; they change over time. The management challenge, therefore, is not mounting a one-time search for some universally best solution, but building the capacity continuously and creatively to seek solutions—solutions that realize effectively the aspirations and goals of each institution and the population it serves.

Table II-1
Capacity Domains and Recurrent Problems Addressed by Cases

1   ADEMI

Strategic	Becoming efficient: staffing and support; centralization/ decentralization. Managing change: expansion/contraction.
Administrative	Personnel and organizational management: training staff; motivating staff.

2   BRAC (A)

Strategic	Becoming efficient: cost effectiveness.
Technical	Project design: appropriate designs for credit and marketing projects; pricing of services; interest rates.

3   BRAC (B)

Strategic	Becoming efficient: staffing and support. Creating independence: independence from funders.
Administrative	Personnel and organizational management: training staff.

4   BRAC (C)

Strategic	Setting priorities: assessing the need; knowing the environment; considering feasibility. Managing change: reorientation.
Technical	Project design: appropriate designs for credit and marketing projects; sequencing of activities.

5   CARE-Philippines (A)

Strategic	Setting priorities: considering feasibility. Managing change: reorientation. Creating independence: independence of clients.
Technical	Project design: participation.
Communications	Information management: program evaluation. Institutional linkages: networking with other resource institutions; linkages with governments and international donors.

6 **CARE-Philippines (B)**

Strategic Creating independence: independence from funders.

Administrative Personnel and organizational management: coordination.

Communications Information management: learning from feedback; program evaluation.
Institutional linkages: networking with other resource institutions; linkages with governments and international donors.

7 **The Carvajal Foundation (A)**

Strategic Setting priorities: assessing the need; knowing the environment.
Managing change: reorientation.

Technical Project design: appropriate designs for credit and marketing projects; appropriate technical assistance; sequencing of activities.

8 **The Carvajal Foundation (B)**

Strategic Becoming efficient: cost effectiveness; staffing and support.
Creating independence: independence from funders.

Technical Project design: appropriate technical assistance.

Communications Institutional linkages: linkages with governments and international donors.

9 **FUCODES**

Strategic Setting priorities: considering feasibility.
Becoming efficient: cost effectiveness; staffing and support.
Managing change: reorientation.

Technical Project design: appropriate designs for credit and marketing projects.

10 **The Grameen Bank Project (A)**

Strategic Setting priorities: assessing the need; knowing the environment; considering feasibility.

Technical Project design: appropriate designs for credit and marketing projects.

11 **The Grameen Bank Project (B)**

Strategic Setting priorities: assessing the need; knowing the environment; considering feasibility.

Technical Project design: appropriate designs for credit and marketing projects.

12 The Grameen Bank Project (C)

Strategic   Setting priorities: considering feasibility.
                     Becoming efficient: cost effectiveness;
                     staffing and support.
                     Managing change: expansion/contraction.
Technical   Project design: participation.
Administrative   Personnel and organizational management:
                     training staff; motivating staff; coordination.

13 IIRR (A)

Strategic   Managing change: reorientation.
                     Creating independence: independence of clients.
Technical   Project design: participation.
Communications   Information management: learning from feedback.
                     Institutional linkages: networking with other
                     resource institutions.

14 IIRR (B)

Technical   Project design: participation.
Administrative   Personnel and organizational management:
                     coordination.
Communications   Information management: learning from feedback.
                     Institutional linkages: networking with other
                     resource institutions.

15 Indonesian Rattan Basket Exporting Company

Strategic   Setting priorities: knowing the environment.
                     Becoming efficient: cost effectiveness.
                     Creating independence: independence from
                     funders.

16 PRODEME

Strategic   Setting priorities: assessing the need.
                     Becoming efficient: cost effectiveness.
Communications   Institutional linkages: linkages with governments
                     and international donors.

17 Save the Children

Strategic   Becoming efficient: cost effectiveness;
                     centralization/decentralization.
                     Creating independence: independence from
                     funders; independence of clients.
Technical   Project design: appropriate designs for credit and
                     marketing projects.

18 Senegal (A)

Strategic   Setting priorities: assessing the need; knowing
                     the environment; considering feasibility.
                     Managing change: reorientation.

Technical   Project design: appropriate designs for credit
                     and marketing projects; sequencing of activities.

19 Senegal (B)

Strategic   Becoming efficient: staffing and support.

Technical   Project design: appropriate designs for credit
                     and marketing projects; interest rates;
                     appropriate technical assistance; client selection
                     and monitoring; sequencing of activities.

Administrative   Personnel and organizational management:
                     motivating staff; hiring staff.

Communications   Information management: learning from feedback.
                     Institutional linkages: networking with other
                     resource institutions.

20 Tototo Home Industries

Strategic   Setting priorities: assessing the need;
                     considering feasibility.

Technical   Project design: appropriate technical assistance;
                     participation; sequencing of activities.

Administrative   Personnel and organizational management:
                     training staff; hiring staff.

Communications   Information management: learning from feedback.
                     Institutional linkages: networking with other
                     resource institutions.

21 The UNO Project

Strategic   Setting priorities: assessing the need;
                     knowing the environment.
                     Becoming efficient: cost effectiveness;
                     staffing and support.
                     Managing change: reorientation.

Technical   Project design: appropriate designs for credit and
                     marketing projects; pricing of services; interest
                     rates; appropriate technical assistance; client
                     selection and monitoring; sequencing of activities.

Communications   Information management: learning form feedback.

Case 1

ADEMI:
Scaling Up and Decentralizing
a Loan Program

This case was written by Margaret Bowman. It is intended as a basis for class discussion rather than as an illustration of either effective or ineffective handling of an administrative situation. The collaboration and support of the Executive Director of ADEMI and his staff are gratefully acknowledged.

Pedro Jimenez was by no means a newcomer to the Association for the Development of Micro-Enterprises Inc. (ADEMI) and to the world of small enterprise assistance programs. He had been the original Executive Director of the ADEMI program when it was started in 1983. Three years later, Pedro was asked to return to the same position he had held earlier. Much had changed in ADEMI since he left the organization to manage a factory in one of the Dominican Republic's free trade zones. The organization had grown considerably in terms of the number of small enterprise clients it served and in the number of branch offices that existed around the country. However, the credit and technical assistance services ADEMI provided and the goals of the organization had remained the same. Therefore, Pedro felt very comfortable taking over his old position.

To the credit of the previous director, the program had attracted considerable attention from donors because it seemed successful at lending money to poor business clients, maintained relatively low default rates on those loans, and earned enough interest on loans to cover the bulk of its administrative costs. These were attributes that similar credit programs were not able to attain. Several donors therefore were willing to fund ADEMI's expansion through grants and loans. Pedro was confronted with (1) analyzing the existing program to ensure that it warranted expansion in its present form, and (2) planning for the expansion of the program in a way that would facilitate management of an increased number of client loans without compromising quality.

114

Pedro Jimenez, ADEMI's Executive Director

Pedro Jimenez was deeply committed to the ideals of the organization and had a good sense of the future directions it should follow. He seemed to have unlimited energy and enthusiasm, which he relayed to the organization. He was a leader with the ability to motivate staff members and to inspire a sense of social service. Pedro also brought skills as a professional manager to ADEMI, as he had held several management positions in private sector firms. This experience provided Pedro with insights into efficiency, cost-effectiveness, and public image that the Board of Directors considered assets to ADEMI. Because of his previous involvement with ADEMI, Pedro also had the advantage of knowing most Board members and was a close friend of the Board President.

ADEMI's Objective

ADEMI is a private, nonprofit organization located in Santo Domingo, Dominican Republic. It was established in April 1983 by the Dominican private sector to confront the problem of unemployment and underemployment in the country. Its goals were to create employment and increase incomes through credit and technical assistance programs to a countrywide clientele of small businesses.

ADEMI is one of several programs started with technical assistance from ACCION International, a Massachusetts-based nonprofit organization. ACCION assists programs that provide loans and technical assistance to small businesses in several Latin American countries.

ADEMI lends to businesses in the "informal sector," characterized by small businesses, started by the poor, which crop up in cities all over the developing world. These enterprises have been considered very risky business investments for banks because they are not registered with the government and do not follow established business practices, particularly with respect to financial and inventory accounting.

ADEMI's clients are micro-businesses; that is, they usually have fewer than six employees and own less than U.S.$10,000 in assets.[1] Through the program, participants are first eligible for small loans and gradually qualify for larger loans as they repay previous loans. (This process is described in the next section.) Clients are also required to maintain savings accounts in commercial banks. Through this process, a client builds up a credit record and gains valuable experience working with banks, which improve the client's chances of obtaining commercial credit in the future.

ADEMI has two loan programs designed to reach two categories of beneficiaries. The first program offers individual credit for micro-entrepreneurs who have a fixed place of business such as shoemakers, carpenters, printers, mechanics, seamstresses, food vendors, and crafts-people. The objectives of this micro-enterprise program are to increase incomes and employment.

The second program is for "solidarity groups" of five or six business people who are held jointly responsible for repayment of the group's loans. One group member is elected as a representative and is responsible for collecting payments. Solidarity group members are the smallest and poorest enterprise owners and do not have a fixed place of business. Many of the solidarity groups are comprised of mobile vendors. Such businesses represent an extremely high credit risk, and individually would not meet the requirements for the micro-enterprise loan program. The objectives of the solidarity group program are not only to increase incomes and employment, but also to increase "empowerment" by developing mutual support and leadership through group processes (Farbman 1985:1). The solidarity group structure both allows ADEMI to meet the needs of the poorest businesses, and has generated higher repayment rates than those of the micro-enterprise loans.[2]

ADEMI's Method of Extending Credit

ADEMI's program focuses on access to credit, advice on business organization, and simple administrative assistance. Most client contact is made by advisors who visit the client's place of business. Advisors visit potential client businesses to assess their capacity for investment and employment generation. They continue to work with the same clients whenever possible. At first clients are only allowed to borrow small sums of money, similar to the sums they may have obtained from moneylenders. The amount a client becomes eligible to borrow increases as the client demonstrates that she or he is credit-worthy. Financing is based on the business owner's production cycle, which varies from one to six months. Initial loans are for raw materials and wages. As the business grows, ADEMI offers supplementary loans for the purchase of fixed assets. (See Exhibit 1, Flowchart of Credit Process.)

Since the initial loan is small, the credit analysis is simple and usually takes only a few days.[3] There are no initial training requirements, so clients do not have to spend much time away from their shops.[4] As a client qualifies for progressively larger loans, ADEMI provides accounting and management training through advisors sent to the client's place of business. The program requires clients to open a savings account, and clients are urged to deposit part of their loan in the bank.

ADEMI's protection from financial risk lies in the incremental structure of its loans. The prospect of receiving larger loans in the future provides the incentive for the owners to repay. Co-signing of loans by all members of a solidarity group encourages repayment in that program.[5]

Advisors make personal visits to the business several days before loans are due to stress the importance of repayment, and a 0.5 percent finance fee is charged for every day payment is late. If these are not sufficient impetus, ADEMI takes legal action against those who default.

ADEMI does not subsidize interest rates, but charges market rates that are considered very reasonable relative to the usurious rates charged by moneylenders.[6] ADEMI can generate large savings for its clients and still cover its direct operational costs. Pedro reported that "last year, ADEMI reached its goal of sustained operational self-sufficiency by covering its administrative costs from interest earned on its loans."[7]

ADEMI's approach supports the entrepreneurial talents of micro-business owners. It starts with individuals who have displayed entrepreneurial talents and who have at least one year's business experience. ADEMI does not try to reshape the business plans of its clients, but helps the business owners to carry out their own plans. ADEMI requires that business owners play a major role in identifying and solving their own problems. This step discourages clients from becoming too dependent on the ADEMI advisor.

ADEMI's Expansion

ADEMI was started in 1983 to address the needs of Santo Domingo micro-entrepreneurs. According to the previous Executive Director and the Board of Directors, after several years of operation the program's impact was so positive in terms of the number of jobs created, the increase in client incomes, and low program cost that they decided to expand ADEMI's activities to other cities. (See Exhibit 2, ADEMI Program Statistics.)

An important part of the expansion to new cities involved a relationship with a local "host" organization such as a development association or a business organization. ADEMI usually was invited to open a new office in a city by such an organization; it would not open an office without this support. The purpose of this relationship with a local organization was to facilitate local relations with banks and business people, to help locate a qualified advisor, to provide low cost (or free) office space, to identify possible social and business funders in the area, to lend more credibility to the new office, and to lend support to the ADEMI program through advertising and recuperation of bad debts. The local associations were eager to form relations with ADEMI because doing so brought much needed services to their region and because ADEMI's success and activity would become associated with their organization. To formalize their commitment, ADEMI and the host organization signed a contract in which they both promised to support the local office.

A Typical Branch Office

A new branch advisor was supposed to receive training in Santo Domingo for two weeks and in another branch office for one week. After training, the new advisor would open up the branch office. With the assistance of the host organization, the branch advisor would then make arrangements with a local bank to open up savings accounts to facilitate disbursements and recuperation of beneficiary loans. One day each week, the advisor would send the completed loan applications to the ADEMI credit analysts in Santo Domingo for approval. The approved loan checks were then returned to the local city where the advisor gave the check to the beneficiary (ADEMI 1985:54,55). Once the branch was established, the loan procedures were similar to those in Santo Domingo.

History of Expansion

At the request of a local Chamber of Commerce, the first branch office was opened in Bani in the southern region of the country in December 1984. Like most other offices, the Bani office was run by a local advisor and a secretary.[8] The office was located in the same building as the local host association, it was small, and was furnished very simply. Typically, ADEMI purchases only a file cabinet, a desk, chairs, and an adding machine. With these few resources, the advisor and the assistant-secretary run programs for up to 135 clients. The other five offices in the south were opened in late 1985, mostly in cooperation with local Chambers of Commerce. In 1986, seven offices were opened in the eastern region. ADEMI opened its eastern offices in cooperation with FUNDESIRE, the regional development association. (See Exhibit 3, Map of Branch Offices.)

ADEMI's Organizational Structure

In ADEMI's organizational structure, control was fairly centralized; the Director and the Sub-Director held all the decision-making power. (See Exhibit 4, Organizational Structure.) The Director was responsible for managing the organization and maintaining outside relations with donors and other supporters. The Sub-Director supervised the advisors in Santo Domingo and became responsible for the direction of the other branch offices as they were added. The staff members were carefully chosen and were well educated, but were not included in decision-making processes. Pedro himself had been involved in designing this original structure for ADEMI. As a new organization, it required strong direction from top management. He was not sure that the structure still suited a now four-year-old organization that had grown so considerably.

Future Expansion

In the future, the Director planned to expand the size of each of ADEMI's offices in the eastern and southern regions of the country, and to open new offices in cities in the northern region, which is currently not served by ADEMI. To provide a sound base for making these decisions, he wanted first to take stock of the existing program.

Advice from a Consultant

At this crucial time when Pedro was considering how to expand the program, the ACCION home office sent a consultant to add some insight to the existing situation and to offer Pedro some options. Among the areas that the consultant identified as being potentially problematic for a scaled-up program were: the structure of the organization, centralization of decision-making power, poor communications between the main office and field offices, inadequate staff training, lack of staff motivation, lack of strategic planning capacity, and inadequate attention to field offices in general. (See Exhibit 5, Excerpts from Consultant's Evaluation.)

Although Pedro was surprised that all of these issues were identified as potential problems for the expansion of his program, he was willing to consider the consultant's advice. As a manager, he was aware that successful expansion of an organization was not merely a matter of increasing resources proportionately. The Santo Domingo office could not support the planned increased volume of loan processing given its existing processes and structure. Moreover, as the new Director, he had little stake in preserving the *status quo*—he would be expected to make changes to accommodate the expansion.

Notes

1. Most ADEMI clients own much less than U.S.$10,000 in fixed assets.

2. See Exhibit 2: The rate of late repayment for solidarity group loans is currently 6 percent for solidarity groups and 17 percent for micro-enterprise loans. This higher rate of repayment of solidarity group loans is attributed to the social pressures exerted by the group structure. Solidarity group loans have maintained a better repayment record for several years and this trend is expected to continue.

3. Approval of the first loan is supposed to take fifteen days (see Exhibit 1). Subsequent loans take only two days to approve; this time period is normally longer in the case of branch office loans because of the longer transport time.

4. Other credit programs require that business owners participate in lengthy training programs before they are eligible for loans. Some micro-enterprise

owners cannot afford this time away from the job. As a result, the more needy businesses may not qualify for loans.

5. Each member of a group is liable if one member falls behind in payments.

6. A study conducted by Jeffrey Ashe (1984) disclosed that business owners use moneylenders who charge interest rates up to 20 percent *per month*.

7. In this calculation, ADEMI does not include any assistance provided by ACCION International. ACCION provided regular consultation during the first three years of operation, conducted evaluations, assisted in fund raising, advised in high-level staff recruitment, and provided consultants to assist with key decision making such as the expansion of the program.

8. Recently the office in Barahona has operated with two advisors. All other offices have only one.

Exhibit 1
FLOW CHART OF ADEMI CREDIT PROCESS
INDICATING NONMONITORED STEPS

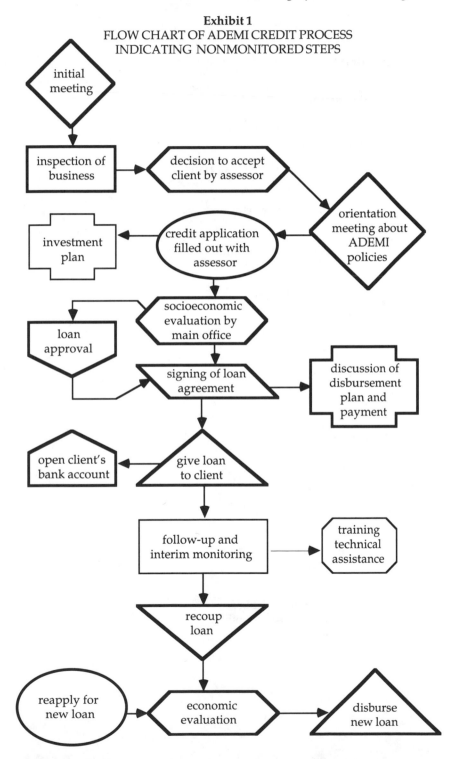

Legend for Exhibit 1

 Process step monitored/no question that step occurs.

— Process step not monitored, no record of activity.

◇ Meeting between advisor and client.

▢ Inspection/monitoring by advisor.

⬡ Credit evaluation by ADEMI.

⬭ Client application for loan.

✚ Planning discussion between advisor and client.

▽ First approval based on potential of clients.

▱ Client signs loan agreement in branch offices.

△ Loan disbursement to client.

⌂ Advisor takes client to bank to open account

⯃ Advisor provides assistance as needed, at place of business.

▽ Advisor reminds client of due-date; client deposits monthly payment in bank.

Exhibit 2
ADEMI PROGRAM STATISTICS

According to Pedro Jimenez, ADEMI had achieved outstanding levels of loan repayment, income growth, and employment generation—especially in comparison with similiar credit programs in other developing countries. In just three years of operation, the program achieved self sufficiency and covered 102 percent of its direct administrative costs with interest earned on its loans. (Costs do not include advisory services that the U.S.-based ACCION office has provided to ADEMI to start the program or short-term consulting and monitoring visits they make.)

	1983	1984	1985	1986
Rate of Self-Sufficiency (Interest Income ÷ Operational Costs)	0.43	0.52	0.74	1.02
Percent Late Payment, Both Programs (less than 1 yr.)	1	17	26	20
Percent Nonrecuperable, Both Programs (1 yr. or more)	0	0	0	5
Total Amount Loaned (in pesos)	1,033,770	2,099,633	2,871,600	3,425,515
No. of New Jobs Created	596	418	211	1,341
No. of Jobs Strengthened	2,202	1,819	2,344	7,544
Cost per $ Lent (1983 pesos)	0.12	0.12	0.08	0.06
Exchange Rate (U.S.$1/RD$)	1.56	2.74	3.09	3.06
Solidarity Groups Only				
Rate of Late Payment (%)	2	0	0	6
Portfolio Amount (pesos)	71,936	18,666	4,941	89,816
No. of New Clients	215	0	4	58
Microenterprises Only				
Rate of Late Payments (%)	1	17	26	17
Portfolio Amount (pesos)	177,025	511,566	996,388	1,700,812
No. of New Clients	572	208	4530	1,262

Growth Statistics	*Start of Program*	*Present*	*Percent Increase*
Average Beneficiary Income (pesos)	$3,461	$4,746	37
Average Profit (pesos)	$839	$1,275	52
Average No. of Employees Hired	3	5	66
Average Savings (pesos)	$22	$277	1,159

Source: Arelis Gomez and Vanessa Saladin, "ADEMI: Programa de Financiamiento a Microempresas y Grupos Solidarios—Informe de Evaluacion de Impacto," Santo Domingo, February 1987.

Exhibit 3

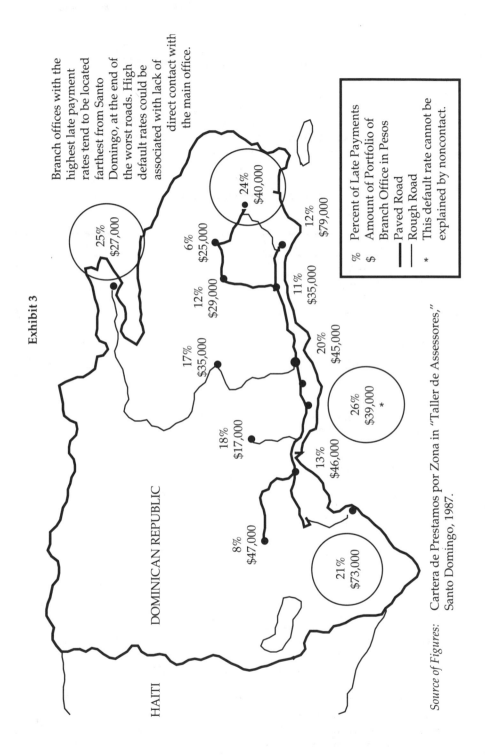

HAITI

DOMINICAN REPUBLIC

Branch offices with the highest late payment rates tend to be located farthest from Santo Domingo, at the end of the worst roads. High default rates could be associated with lack of direct contact with the main office.

25%
$27,000

24%
$40,000

6%
$25,000

12%
$79,000

12%
$29,000

11%
$35,000

17%
$35,000

20%
$45,000

18%
$17,000

26%
$39,000
*

13%
$46,000

8%
$47,000

21%
$73,000

%   Percent of Late Payments
$ Amount of Portfolio of
      Branch Office in Pesos
——— Paved Road
——— Rough Road
*   This default rate cannot be
      explained by noncontact.

Source of Figures: Cartera de Prestamos por Zona in "Taller de Assessores,"
                     Santo Domingo, 1987.

Exhibit 4
ADEMI: INITIAL ORGANIZATIONAL STRUCTURE

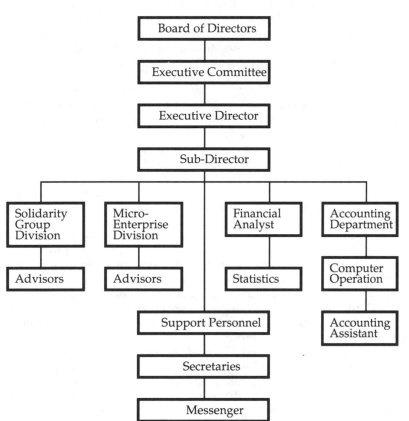

Source: Arelis Gomez and Vanessa Saladin, "ADEMI: Programa de Financiamento a Microempresas y Grupos Solidario—Informe de Evaluación de Impacto," Santo Domingo, February 1987.

Exhibit 5
EXCERPTS FROM CONSULTANT'S EVALUATION

Problems with Expansion
The expansion of the program to branch offices has lacked management and supervision from the beginning. ADEMI assumed that conditions would be similar to those in Santo Domingo and did not foresee all the administrative complications of running programs in the Dominican countryside. Feasibility studies were conducted, but they focused more on demand for credit services than on the ability of an ADEMI branch office adequately to provide those services. The program design that worked in Santo Domingo was applied to the branch offices, using basically the same loan policies, requirements for beneficiaries, and technical assistance.

No special infrastructure was developed to deal with the particular needs of the branch offices. Since main office and branch office personnel interacted more often by mail than in person, a system should have been developed to relay information and procedures. New forms had been sent to the branches without directions. The branch office secretaries said they did not know to whom to talk about questions when they called the main office, so they filled out the forms to the best of their knowledge—each secretary a bit differently.

Also, there was no regular system of disbursing supplies to the offices. Because many supplies were not available in the countryside (or they were much more expensive than in Santo Domingo), the secretaries would come to the main office to get supplies themselves. This was an inefficient use of their time. Still, every office visited lacked some simple but necessary items such as forms, typewriters, or working calculators. The offices that did not have access to what the main office considered "cheap" photocopying facilities would actually send the originals to the main office and wait an unpredictable amount of time for copies to be sent back. Meanwhile the secretaries would handcopy forms—all to save a few cents. More efficient systems should have been devised to avoid these problems since they affected every branch office.

Planning problems were not detected because the branches were not monitored closely enough. The Sub-Director received monthly reports (which were not adequate without other communication) and data on branch expenditures, but did not use that information to its full potential. Until recently, the main office did not break down its costs according to city (to calculate an average loan cost per city). This breakdown would have shown that differences in loan costs among offices more than accounted for variances in transportation costs. Additional investigation could have identified certain cities that had less effective loan practices or credit needs that warranted different loan amounts or terms. Closer monitoring of the offices could have helped identify problems earlier and the program could have been adapted over time to provide assistance to an advisor or to change the loan terms to fit the market.

Although training was planned, in practice there was little time for it. Also, since most of the branch offices had been established at the same time, there were no other offices from which to learn. The branch advisors were all new to ADEMI when they opened their offices, had received little training, and had to learn on the job by trial and error. Although advisors are supposed to have development experience, in practice, hardly any of them did. Since they generally received only two to three days of training (instead of the specified three weeks), the advisors were unprepared for their mission as the sole representative of ADEMI in a city. There was little communication between offices as well, so they did not even have the advantage of learning from one another as their programs developed.

ADEMI advisors contacted local associations before opening new offices. In addition to the host organization, many other organizations agreed to support the branch offices. However, there is little evidence that the host organizations have helped ADEMI beyond providing office space or that the other organizations helped at all. The problem seems to be that the advisors have not requested support and have not kept the associations informed of ADEMI's activities. Thus, most of the benefit of the relationships has been untapped.

Because of the lack of attention to the branch offices, it does not seem surprising that they should have some problems. As the program expands further, the inefficiencies that existed will become more burdensome if they are not addressed. An office with only 65 clients will have more time to learn by trial and error or to recopy forms by hand than one with 165.

Suggestions

Assign a branch office liaison in the main office. One person should be in charge of regular communication with the branch offices. This person should become familiar with the branch offices by participating in the regional meetings to learn first hand how frustrating it is to run a loan program when the loan checks and supplies do not arrive. This would not have to be a full-time position at this time, but it should take priority over that person's other duties to prevent branch office requests from being put off. The branch offices are much too important to ADEMI and to the expansion program to be ignored.

Develop better systems for delivering supplies to the branch offices. The coordinators could be used to deliver supplies and copies to the field. The coordinators should be given the authority to secure supplies from the main office and secretaries can fill a request form upon delivery. Someday they will have vehicles to facilitate delivery.

Establish loan guidelines for advisors. Designate an acceptable range of terms and amounts for different circumstances. Add guidelines to advisor manual; alter individual office policies later as necessary.

Advisor reports should be qualitative as well as quantitative. The monthly advisor report forms should include a brief explanation of the major changes in program indicators, a discussion of their ability to meet their program goals, and requests or suggestions from the field. These comments could be written on the back of the existing form. They should be read by the coordinators, the Operations Manager, and the Programming Manager—all of whom are responsible for improving the branch offices.

Develop a policy to determine when and how to add a new advisor. The planning staff should analyze whether 95 clients per advisor is indeed a desirable ratio for ADEMI branch offices. How do solidarity groups figure into this number? A similar policy should be developed for coordinator/branch office ratios.

Develop a policy for hiring and training advisors, and plan ahead. An advisor can plan to have more time to train an assistant if he or she knows one is coming. The managers should identify which offices are most in need of an assistant and contact the local associations to start identifying candidates. The hiring process might be improved and streamlined if it were preplanned. The best advisors (who would be the best trainers) can only train one person at a time. Also, there are times of the year when the Director or other key personnel will not have time to give adequate attention to trainees.

Strengthen the solidarity group program. The solidarity group coordinator should participate in a regional meeting to explain the benefits and concepts of group lending. He can later travel to the offices to work with advisors to improve their programs.

Give the coordinators the responsibility for analyzing the program statistics of their region. If the coordinator has to develop a monthly regional report, he will not only save the main office time but he will necessarily have to understand the causes of fluctuations and be able to perform analysis to produce the report (a check on his skills). This task will give the coordinator responsibility for investigating as well as clearing up the problems.

Develop a training program for mid-level managers without experience. The Director should spend time with the new managers to talk about management. The managers should be encouraged to talk and share experiences with one another and should be allowed to run regional meetings to gain experience with the Director close by.

Establish requirements for opening new offices. ADEMI should provide support services to all offices. These require that the office have regular mail or bus service, have access to a telephone and a bank, and be a reasonable working distance from a regional coordinator.

Train someone to program the existing ADEMI computer. ADEMI needs to train a staff member who works with the Planning Department to program the existing ADEMI computer. The organization manipulates computer information sufficiently to warrant this (the consultant is budgeted at twice as much money as an employee is paid), and an in-house expert would allow more flexibility since he or she would be more accessible than the consultant is.

Enlist active support of ADEMI by local organizations. Some local organizations even signed a contract agreeing to support the local ADEMI office. ADEMI has to think of constructive ways to involve them in ADEMI activities. One suggestion is to ask the Chambers of Commerce to promote an entrepreneur of the year from among ADEMI clients. In any case, the advisors should certainly keep the associations up-to-date by giving them copies of the monthly progress reports produced for the main office. If the main office produced some advertising materials, the Chamber of Commerce offices could more actively promote ADEMI's services.

Verify that communications channels are working as they are supposed to. The advisors should understand ADEMI policies and know where they should be concentrating their efforts; coordinators should have summary statistics of the branch offices in their charge and should be able to explain any irregularities or trends; the Operations Manager and the Planning Manager should have a basic understanding of what is right and wrong about each office and should know what is being done to solve any problems. To verify this, the Director can check on the Planning Department, and the Planning Department evaluators could ask the coordinators if they can explain issues relating to the branch offices and check to see that important information is feeding up to the main office. Likewise, the evaluators could ask the advisors and the secretaries if they understand certain policies flowing down from the main office.

Exhibit 6
NUMBER OF ADEMI CLIENTS FINANCED BY CITY PER BY YEAR (1983–86)
AND PROJECTED NUMBER OF NEW CLIENTS FOR 1987

City	1983	1984	1985	1986	Total, 1983– 1986	1987[a]	Approx. Total, 1987
Santo Domingo	787	189	330	277	1583	335	1918
Bani	—	19	40	26	85	60	145
Barahona	—	—	31	10	141	102	243
San Juan	—	—	15	65	80	48	128
Azua	—	—	13	95	108	128	236
San Cristobal	—	—	14	76	90	98	188
Ocoa	—	—	14	60	74	34	108
Samana	—	—	—	121	121	44	165
Monte Plata	—	—	—	97	97	75	172
San Pedro	—	—	—	81	81	61	142
Hato Mayor	—	—	—	54	54	101	155
El Seybo	—	—	—	58	58	73	155
La Romana	—	—	—	99	99	100	199
Higuey	—	—	—	101	101	86	187

Source: Arelis Gomez and Vanessa Saladin, "Programa de Financiamiento a Microempresas y Grupos Solidarios: Informe de Impacto" (Santo Domingo: Inter-American Development Bank, 1987), p. 8.

[a] Micro-enterprises only, does not include number of projected solidarity groups.

Exhibit 7
DIFFERENCES IN BRANCH OFFICES

City (and months of operation)	Description of Area	No. of Clients	U.S.$	Default Rate (%)	Popular Activities	Per-cent
Azua 13 months	Agricultural	86	45922	13	Food Carpentry Tailors	29 17 20
Ocoa 14 months	Hilly Area Agricultural	59	16974	18	Food Tailors Carpenters	41 21 17
San Cristobal 10 months	Dense Agricultural	75	45301	20	Carpentry Tailors Food	22 18 11
Barahona 13 months	Large Zone No Development Organization	134	73399	21	Tailors Food Carpentry	41 22 21
Bani 22 months	Agriculture Some Industry	82	39119	26	Food Carpentry Tailors	32 20 12
San Juan 13 months	Agricultural	89	46722	8	Tailor Carpenter Tinsmith	25 23 6
San Pedro 10 months	Under Develop-ment by Actual Enterprises	—	34604	11	Carpenter Tailor Shoe Repair	22 27 10
La Romana 10 months	Industrial Zone with Commercial Activity	—	78716	12	Tailor Carpenter Food Prep.	28 24 9
Hato Mayor 10 months	High Unem-ployment No Industry	—	28700	12	Tailor Carpenter Food Prep.	27 13 12
El Seybo 10 months	High Unem-ployment No Industry	—	24950	6	Tailor Carpenter Food Prep.	27 13 12
Higuey 7 months	Agricultural High Unem-ployment	—	40319	24	Tailor Food Prep. Carpenter	30 20 14
Monte Plata 7 months	Easy to travel from the office to the communities	—	35376	17	Tailor Food Prep. Carpenter	35 17 17

Case 2

BRAC (A):
How to Define "Self-Supporting"
in the BRAC Rural Credit Program

This case was written by Professor Catherine Lovell, assisted by Murshid Shah. It is intended as a basis for class discussion rather than as an illustration of either effective or ineffective handling of an administrative situation. The collaboration and support of the Executive Director of BRAC and his staff are gratefully acknowledged.

In August 1986, Karim, Program Coordinator of the Rural Development Program of the Bangladesh Rural Advancement Committee (BRAC) faced an important decision. Within three days he needed to develop an operational definition of "self-supporting" for the rural credit program, one component of the Rural Development Program (RDP), which he managed. A visiting foreign donor evaluation team needed BRAC's definition of self-supporting for its Evaluation Report on the RDP. The definition was also required for a grant proposal for forward funding for RDP, which was being prepared that week. The foreign donors, as well as BRAC, were committed to the concept of self-reliance in development, but an exact definition to measure whether a credit program could be considered self-supporting had not yet been developed because of various complicating factors that made defining it difficult both conceptually and practically. But now Karim must construct such a definition.

Bangladesh and BRAC

Exhibit 1 provides a brief description of rural conditions in Bangladesh and describes BRAC, the organization in which Karim works.

Rural Credit Programs in Bangladesh

As a part of its Evaluation Report the foreign donor team briefly summarized the rural credit situation in Bangladesh as follows:

Because of the need to generate rural employment opportunities in Bangladesh, there are at present (1986) some seventeen Non-Governmental Organizations (NGOs) and five government or semi-government institutions or projects that are providing savings and credit programs to the rural poor. Three of the NGO programs and one of the semigovernment programs are large. Almost all of the programs target their savings and credit programs directly to the landless poor or to small farmers.

It is difficult to state exactly how many million *taka* have been loaned over the ten years prior to 1986 by these NGO and semi-governmental credit programs. Best estimates place the amount at over Tk 300 million (about U.S.$90 million). Savings accumulated and invested by the target people themselves have been estimated at close to Tk 100 million (over U.S.$30 million).

Interest rates in these programs have ranged from 10 to 30 percent per year. Repayment rates have showed wide variation in the different programs, but what is of particular importance is that the several NGOs with the most widespread and large-scale programs have been able to achieve on-time repayment levels between 80 and 96 percent. They have also succeeded in generating millions of days of employment. These agencies have developed methods that work well on a wide scale.

A key question remains, however, about all of these programs: *Can they become self-sufficient? If so to what extent?* That is, can the profit from the investment in loans more than pay for the costs of making the credit available and collecting paybacks, so that capital can be generated for continuing loan investments? Since subsidized credit can result in inefficient allocation of scarce resources, nonsubsidization may be an important target. The answer to the question of whether or not the programs can become self-supporting seems to depend at least partially on how the concept of self-supporting is defined. Few of the organizations have given sufficient careful attention to this definition.

The Bangladesh Rural Advancement Committee (BRAC) operates the largest of the NGO rural credit programs. As a part of our evaluation of BRAC's program we have attempted to understand the difficulties related to defining self-supporting and have asked BRAC to provide us with its definition.

Exhibit 2 describes BRAC's Rural Development Program and the credit program that is an important part of it. This exhibit provides the information that Karim has available to him in making his decision.

Karim's Alternatives

After accepting his assignment, Karim immediately called a meeting of his regional managers. Also included in the meeting were two of the branch managers who happened to be in the head office that day for reporting purposes. The rest of the day was spent in discussion of the problem and careful study of the financial records of the past few years. By the end of the discussion the group had developed some possible definitions but could not agree. In concluding the meeting Karim asked each of those with strong opinions to summarize his point of view. Here are the main arguments as they were made.

Muhammad argued that *all* costs of RDP must be included or the program really could not be said to be "self-supporting." He said that since the credit program could not be successful without all the organizing, training, logistical aids, and so forth, those things had to be considered part of the program. He argued that even head office RDP costs must be included.

Ahmed, on the other hand, argued that only those costs directly related to making and collecting the loans, such as the time of the Program Organizers (POs) in working with potential borrowers to analyze projects, to fill out loan papers, to collect interest and principal payments, and to keep necessary records, should be included. He also suggested that the cost of obtaining the loan capital at the lowest possible rates be included. He did not think it would be fair to include all of the general rural development costs of RDP. He argued that even if BRAC did not have a credit program it would still be organizing and helping rural people to make use of their own talents, energies, and resources; therefore it would have Centers, POs, and so forth.

Ferouz restated his opinion that all reasonable costs directly related to making and collecting the loans should be included (also the cost of capital at a reasonable rate of 6 to 10 percent) but that only part of the other costs of RDP should be included. He said that although the various organizing and infrastructure development activities are essential, the costs cannot all be borne by the profits from lending to these small business ventures at the 18 percent interest rate that the ventures can bear. He argued that some fair share of the overall costs of the organizing, training, and support costs should be allocated to the credit program. He suggested that half of all PO time, all of training, and most of the facilities costs would be reasonable.

Karim has until Tuesday, the day after tomorrow, to present and be able to defend his definition to the Executive Director and the donors. Which of these alternatives, or combinations of alternatives, should he choose? Does he have other options that have not been proposed?

Exhibit 1
THE BANGLADESH RURAL ADVANCEMENT COMMITTEE (BRAC)

Bangladesh

Bangladesh is the second poorest country in the world. The average annual income is about U.S.$140 per capita; literacy is only 20 percent overall and is lower among women. The population, with the highest density in the world outside a few of the city states, was over 100 million at the end of 1986 with a population growth rate of 2.6 in spite of a well-financed family planning program.

Nearly 90 percent of the population live in rural areas. Agriculture employs roughly 72 percent of the labor force and accounts for more than half of the GDP. Over half of the rural families fall into the category of "functionally landless," having less than 0.2 hectare of land. Nearly all of the landless are also "functionally unemployed" since wage employment other than part-time work on farms is nearly nonexistent and declining in relation to demand. For the most part the landless eke out an existence as seasonal wage-laborers on farms, on foreign donor–supported food-for-work programs, on subsidized rural works programs, or in petty trading.

BRAC

It is in this context that the Bangladesh Rural Advancement Committee (BRAC) operates. BRAC, an indigenous Bangladeshi organization, began as a small relief organization in 1972 following the war of independence. It is now the largest NGO in Bangladesh (and one of the largest in the developing world) with a paid staff of over 2,500 people, and a variety of social mobilization, employment generation, health, education, and other programs conducted in many different areas of the country.

BRAC's headquarters are in Dhaka, the capital of the country. The Executive Director and head office staff of about 100 people are quartered there. The remainder of the staff are quartered in or work out of some seventy centers and camps in other parts of the country. The staff is entirely Bangladeshi although occasionally BRAC employs short-term foreign consultants for special assignments. At the present time BRAC's funds come from foreign donors, primarily Canadian, Dutch, Norwegian, Swedish, Swiss, and German aid agencies, UNICEF, and in smaller amounts from Ford and other foundations, and from its own business operations. The operating budget in 1986 was about U.S.$4.0 million.

After meeting initial relief demands with its first project, BRAC expanded to other areas with a community-wide rural development strategy. By 1976, however, it had become apparent to BRAC workers, in dialogue with the community people in the villages where BRAC worked, that because of the existing stratification in the communities available services and resources were being retained in large measure by the upper socioeconomic strata, leaving little to "trickle down" to the more disadvantaged. Consequently, BRAC changed its strategy for its basic development efforts to a "target population" concept. The focus since that date has been the landless poor—those who must sell their manual labor for survival. Although the benefits of BRAC's work are often felt community-wide, those who benefit most directly are the landless, marginal farmers, fishermen, and artisans without implements and raw materials—categories that comprise about 50 percent of village families.

The fundamental intention of BRAC's work is to help individuals and communities to become self-reliant so they can function effectively without external assistance. The ultimate objective is to end the long-standing exploitative relationships that dominate rural life in Bangladesh. BRAC is registered with the government under the Societies Registration Act and the Foreign Donations Act. BRAC works primarily in areas where other organizations are not working, and concentrating on building model development activities to pave the way for others.

BRAC Activities

Rural Development Programs. BRAC has four integrated rural development programs, each with a slightly different mix of activities. Fundamental to all of them is the organization of landless men and women into cooperative groups who plan, manage, and control collective activities and facilitate individual endeavors. Social and economic advances and self-reliance are the goals. The basic approach is to form male and female groups in each village; assist them with functional education and consciousness-raising activities; provide training in leadership, management, and income generation skills; and provide or help them to obtain the other tools necessary for self-sufficiency.

Credit and Infrastructural Supports. BRAC's RDP, the most far reaching of the programs, had established, by the end of 1986, forty-three Centers covering nearly 1,200 villages, and over 2,000 village organizations with a membership of 114,000 villagers—60,000 females and 54,000 males. BRAC views the institution-building activities of RDP as its front-line program to provide the foundation for later multisectoral, integrated programs. Between 1979 and the end of June 1986, group members in RDP had generated Tk 11.7 million from their own savings, and during the same period BRAC provided credit to groups or individual group members in the amount of Tk 75.6 million (about U.S.$37 million). In the year 1985 the village group projects generated nearly one million person days of employment. Not included in this figure are such household-based activities as poultry raising and small-scale livestock rearing.

The three other older, more integrated rural development programs (one of which is entirely for women) cover another 450 villages. The landless groups in these villages are now in various stages of federation into area-wide, self-managed confederations. The people in these federations have added many health, educational, and infrastructural programs to their basic RDP activities and are now significant forces in the political lives of their communities. BRAC's encouragement of federation into Union-wide, or Upazila-wide federations (the Union, which includes between ten and twenty villages, is the level of Bangladesh government closest to the people; the Upazila is the next highest level which includes about ten Unions covering about 200,000 people), has resulted in such sociopolitical activities as wage bargaining, election of landless to Union Councils, protest actions, and pressure for local government services.

Health Programs. In addition to the general rural development programs, BRAC conducts several very large primary and preventive health care activities in rural areas. The largest is a nationwide program to teach oral rehydration techniques (for diarrhea) to all the rural mothers in Bangladesh. By the end of 1986 the program was in its sixth year, and had reached 7 million households. The program would continue until 1990. Also in 1986, in a third of the country, BRAC began a four-year program to assist the government in a child and mother immunization and Vitamin A distribution program. Model-building activities in preventive and primary health care, planned to cover fifteen Upazilas over a four-year period (about 3 million people), also began in 1986. More than a thousand BRAC health workers are active full-time in these health programs.

Nonformal Education. BRAC assists landless villagers with a nonformal primary education program, which completed its model building stage in 1985. By that time the nonformal education schools were providing education to over 5,000 rural children, over 60 percent of whom were girls, in some 125 schools. In 1986 there were 430 schools; by 1987 there will be 730 schools with nearly 30,000 children regularly attending.

In addition to primary education an essential part of BRAC strategy is adult functional education classes. Before village groups can be formed, target villagers are required to take functional education classes that combine consciousness raising about their life and environment with basic numeracy and literacy. Teachers for these programs are selected from the villages and especially trained as teachers.

Support Activities. To support its rural development activities BRAC has three training centers with a staff of nearly fifty trainers (two more centers will be completed by the middle of 1987), a materials development unit, a publications unit, a research and evaluation division, a logistics unit, and a computer center.

BRAC also initiated a Rural Enterprise Project in 1986 whose objective is to increase the potential for long-term, income generation projects for the landless by investigating, testing, and demonstrating new or improved kinds of economic activities that it would be possible for the landless to undertake.

Another important adjunct to the rural development programs are four BRAC-operated retail outlets, the Aarong Shops, located in three cities in Bangladesh. They were originally organized to provide outlets for village-produced goods. The shops themselves now employ more than eighty people. Domestic sales were about Tk 22 million in 1986.

BRAC also has two commercial enterprises, BRAC Printers, and a potato cold storage and ice plant. All profits from the businesses are used to help support BRAC's rural development activities.

Exhibit 2
THE BRAC RURAL DEVELOPMENT PROGRAM (RDP)

BRAC's Rural Development Program (originally divided into two programs called the Rural Credit and Training Program and the Outreach Program) started operations in 1979. The main components of the RDP are four:

1. consciousness raising, group formation, and resource mobilization by group members;
2. training to improve income generation skills and management and entrepreneurial capabilities;
3. credit;
4. technical, logistical, and marketing supports.

Each of the four is described in more detail below.

Consciousness Raising, Group Formation, and
Internal Resource Mobilization

Selection of the target people in a village, group formation, and education are the first steps; economic activities follow.

After initial selection of villages to be covered by an RDP Center, a baseline survey is conducted in each village to identify the poor. Then individual contacts and informal discussions are started by BRAC's Program Organizers (POs). In these discussions target people are made aware of the causes of their plight and the critical need for united action. The size of the discussion group tends to grow and more and more poor people are involved. This growth leads to the formation of the village organizations, one male and one female for each village. The time required from initial individual contacts to group formation is usually three to four months.

During initial discussions over many weeks between BRAC POs and landless men and women in the villages, potential leaders are identified. These leaders, with the assistance of the BRAC POs, take initiative to educate other poor people and to organize them. Formation of a landless organization is followed by introduction of a Functional Education Course organized by BRAC for the members. The course is the main tool of consciousness raising. The daily functional education meetings include activities to develop group norms and discipline and to foster group cohesion as well as to teach the members basic numeracy and literacy. Completion of a Functional Education Course is usually required for all members and is one of the main criteria for securing an individual loan later when credit is offered. Once a group is formed and completes functional education, group leaders are selected by the members and weekly meetings become the norm.

The weekly group meetings, usually attended by BRAC POs, are used to motivate group members to mobilize their own local resources before external credit aid is considered. Members save regularly, perhaps only a few taka per month (1 taka is about 3 cents) in order to accumulate funds to be used later for economic schemes. Members are also encouraged to utilize to the fullest extent possible all other resources that they may control: if they have a small piece of household land, for example, they are encouraged to plant trees or vegetables; if they have any silted ponds, no matter how small, they are encouraged to clear and reactivate them for fish cultivation. They are encouraged to use, if needed, government health services that are available and any other services they are entitled to. They also use their group strength to improve the part-time wages paid to them by the farmers.

The average group has between sixty and seventy members, the size depending somewhat on the number of people in a village. For efficient management of economic schemes and credit operations each village organization is subdivided into small groups made up of five to seven members who formulate loan proposals for individual projects, which are then submitted to the whole group for approval.

Training. The second component of RDP is training. Experience in the field has showed that training is necessary to ensure efficient income-generating projects. Human potential and managerial capability, as well as occupational skills, must be enhanced before projects are successful. As a response to the demand for training, BRAC developed its own Training and Resource Centers (TARC), which now provide training in residential centers or in village locations to group members as well as staff. The Center trainers are experienced BRAC workers or experts in particular fields, such as fisheries, who have been especially trained as trainers. The Centers have about forty full-time trainers.

Training for group members can be broadly divided into two areas: (1) human development training; and (2) occupational skills training. Human development training includes functional education, and consciousness raising, and also management skills such as leadership, funds management, project appraisal, and planning. In addition to improving leadership and management skills the human development training helps the group members to look at their own potentialities and helps them to analyze their own social and economic problems.

The second category of training, occupational skills training, teaches villagers specific skills they need to undertake particular economic activities. Usually this type of training is a part of the planning and implementation of an economic activity (for example, if the project is one to raise fish in village ponds, special training about types of seedlings to buy, feeding, seasonal aspects, costs, and marketing is offered). Usually the group members decide who should go for training at BRAC Training and Resource Centers and who should attend if the training is offered in the village. For many kinds of economic projects, the training course includes preparation of an implementation plan for the particular project.

The RDP must pay the Training and Resource Centers for all training provided. (In other words, training is provided through a marketing system internal to BRAC that is designed to make the training centers responsive to the needs of the various BRAC programs.)

Credit. Credit is an essential component of the RDP. Loans are given to individuals or to groups to finance economic activities. The loans can be short term (repayable within a year), medium term (up to three years), or long term. Examples of types of business ventures that have been given credit include: (1) rice, potato, and other crop cultivation on land leased from the government or private owners; (2) irrigation businesses in which the landless own the tubewells and supply water to farmers; (3) rice and oil seed husking businesses; (4) cattle and goat rearing; (5) rural transport businesses, primarily rickshaws and push carts; (6) rural industry including rice mills, brick fields, textile weaving, seri and ericulture (silk production); (7) market management (in which the group leases the market building from the government and then subleases to various vendors); (8) petty trading; (9) fish culture operations; (10) poultry keeping (for sale of eggs and chicks); (11) vegetable and horticulture nurseries; and (12) food processing.

The smallest loans that have been made are Tk 500, the largest Tk 800,000. Interest rates are 18 percent; however, some loans carry additional service charges. No service charge is applied to collective schemes that involve all members of a group. A 3 percent service charge is applied to all individual loans. For effective supervision of individual loans, a management committee of five to seven members, selected by all members of a group, is formed by each village organization. For their supervision activities the committee members receive the 3 percent service charge.

Before a group is eligible for loans it must meet certain requirements. (1) It must have regular weekly meetings and make regular savings deposits; (2) it must have a bank account; (3) it must be able to manage its own finances and administration; (4) it must have savings equivalent to 10 percent of the loan requested; and (5) it must have proved group cohesiveness.

In order to meet these conditions a group usually has to have been in existence at least one year. In the early stages of the credit program a six-month period was thought sufficient to create group cohesion but experience has shown that this period was too short.

Nine basic rules serve as guidelines for the issuance of loans:

1. A loan will be granted on a self-liquidating basis. Repayment of principal and interest must derive from the profit from the business that the loan is financing;
2. No loan is given for consumption purposes;
3. No loan is given to a borrower to buy land from another borrower who owns less land than he or she does;
4. Since poor people have competing demands on their incomes, loan repayment must follow closely the receipt of income from the project;
5. Loans are never given for the full investment. The borrowing group must invest some of its own resources so that all members have a significant stake in the success of the venture.
6. No "collateral" in the normal sense is required, unless it is available from previous projects or group resources;
7. There will be continuous and intensive monitoring of the venture during the life of the loan;
8. Priority in loans is given to projects that have a strong development component; and
9. Loans are given only to ventures with visible economic and social profitability potential determined by the feasibility analysis.

Loan proposals are screened and approved by the groups during their weekly meetings. A loan can be approved only if two thirds of the membership is present, and 75 percent of those attending approve. Participation and group responsibility are thus an essential element of the loan process. The BRAC Center manager must sign off on all loans.

RDP POs help the individuals or groups to formulate their business ventures and help them to do the simple feasibility analyses required. Loan interest and principal payments are paid to the PO; once groups have been operating for some time, credit activities are an important part of each PO's work. In 1986, new loans were made to 4,291 income-generating ventures, approximately one hundred new ventures for each center.

Technical, Logistical, and Marketing Supports. As BRAC gained experience with the RDP program, it learned the many infrastructural constraints that surround income generation activities. At the beginning of the credit program, as schemes were examined and implemented, it became apparent that organization, credit, and training were not sufficient for successful ventures. Technical, logistical, and marketing supports were also needed.

Finding ways to overcome infrastructural barriers through various kinds of technical and logistical supports is a continuous process for BRAC field operations. Some of the supports that have been developed include:

1. *Facilitating the supply of necessary inputs:* At the time of making a loan, RDP helps the group examine its input needs. If the required inputs are unavailable in the local market, the branch office assists the group with procurement. In fish culture activities, for example, where a steady supply of fish seedlings was not available, RDP helped some of the village groups to develop and maintain fish nursery ponds from which they now sell needed seedlings to other groups. Some of the BRAC Centers also stock and supply inputs required by other kinds of ventures, for example, improved seeds for vegetable production, improved tree seedlings, fertilizers, and parts for machinery.

2. *Facilitating the supply of needed technical supports:* Borrowers may face technical problems for which they do not have solutions. For example, a leased rice field may be attacked by a pest and the borrowers do not know which pesticides to use. The PO will help the project leaders to consult government agricultural extension officers or BRAC's own Training and Resource Center agricultural experts to find out the correct pesticide, and if necessary they will help in procuring it.

As another example, special program supports such as vaccination activities for livestock and poultry have been developed. Borrowers in livestock and poultry schemes were incurring losses due to diseases, and no government infrastructure was operating to supply adequate vaccination services. RDP began by training the village women to vaccinate poultry and livestock. Then gradually, with BRAC's help, the groups have encouraged the government agriculture extension workers to supply vaccines and to train on a regular basis new women vaccinators who are now paid for their services.

3. *Creating warehousing facilities:* Facilities for warehousing were very scarce in the right locations. Warehouses with capacities for storing one hundred tons of grain each have been constructed in many of the RDP Center compounds. These are used for storing both inputs and produce, which can be held in the warehouses to take advantage of favorable price changes at different times of the year.

4. *Creating market linkages and outlets:* Sales outlets for certain kinds of products produced by village groups—particularly those produced by women—were lacking. Demand was not linked to supply. One example of marketing support is the chain of Aarong shops established by BRAC to provide retail outlets for textile, leather, jute, wood, and other handicraft products.

Administrative Structure of the RDP

Each of the 43 RDP field Centers covers 30 villages. Each village has one male and one female group. Each Center employs three POs, each of whom works with twenty groups spread over ten villages. To assist the POs in their work, village men and women who have completed at least ten years of school are employed.

They also work with the male and female groups to help them with group accounts, banking services, and technical assistance.

Each Center has a manager in charge of administration and coordination and an accountant who records loans, payments, and so forth. Each Center is supervised by a Regional Manager based at the Dhaka head office of BRAC. An RDP Program Coordinator heads the program and reports to the Executive Director.

As RDP has scaled up, accounting and other central financial support service requirements and monitoring and reporting requirements have enlarged. BRAC has found it necessary to develop a computer center to provide support for this program as well as for its other programs.

Financial Information

In 1986 the expenditure of BRAC for all of its programs was about Tk 132,000,000 (U.S.$4 million). The following is a summary of the expenditures of the RDP, with which this case is concerned. RDP represents about 16 percent of BRAC's total budget.

Annual Financial Summary of RDP, 1986	
A. Cost of Center Managers, POs, Other	
1. Salaries and benefits	9,074,200
2. Training	1,704,176
3. Transportation	899,109
4. Depreciation (motorcycles and bicycles)	158,787
	Tk 11,836,272
B. Facilities	
1. RDP building depreciation	376,672
2. Rent	230,985
3. Utilities	291,184
4. Maintenance	342,992
5. Rural facility development	6,660
	Tk 1,248,493
C. Training of Landless	
1. Group members training and workshops	891,435
2. Education materials	436,711
	Tk 1,328,146
D. Administrative and General Expenses	
1. General expenses	323,652
2. Recruitment and training	98,617
3. Supplies	172,776
4. Stationary, forms, etc.	219,720
5. Depreciation (furniture and equipment)	141,529
	Tk 956,294
E. Technical Support	
1. Books and journals	859
2. Consultancy	20,476
3. Technical follow-up	4,464

	4. Plant nursery	43,154
	5. Evaluation	90
		Tk 69,043
F.	Emergency	Tk 857,331
G.	Head Office Overhead	
	1. Salaries and benefits	773,258
	2. Training	36,492
	3. Transport and travel	51,245
	4. Recruitment & training	400
	5. Facility development	5,775
	6. Consultancy	2,595
	7. Books & journals	6,250
	8. Logistics^a	3,563,525
	9. Depreciation	375,470
		Tk 4,815,010
TOTAL		**Tk 21,110,589**

Notes: The above expenditure figures do not include the cost of obtaining the capital that was used for making the loans.

The average amount of credit outstanding during the year was Tk 37,284,617. The interest income for the year was Tk 6,693,855. The on-time payment of interest and principal throughout the year was about 90 percent.

^{a} Includes RDP's portion of overhead costs such as computer, accounts, audit, research, and head office logistics.

Case 3

BRAC (B): Management Development Program

This case was written by Professor Catherine Lovell, assisted by Murshid Shah. It is intended as a basis for class discussion rather than as an illustration of either effective or ineffective handling of an administrative situation. The collaboration and support of the Executive Director of BRAC and his staff are gratefully acknowledged.

In May 1985, Shahid, Shabbir, Murshid, and Ahmed, key members of BRAC's new Management Development Committee, must make a final decision as to priorities for the content of a middle manager training program that will begin in six weeks. If modules are to be developed in time for the first four-day session and for subsequent monthly sessions, final decisions about subjects to be covered, and the relative importance of each, must be made by Wednesday, the day after tomorrow. Each of the four men must come to the meeting on Wednesday with his recommendations about content priorities so that a decision can be hammered out at that meeting. Each must make a decision about what he will push for as the three or four most needed competencies that can be enhanced by training sessions.

BRAC and the Management Development Program

For background information, see Exhibit 1 of the BRAC (A) case.

In Spring 1985 the Bangladesh Rural Advancement Committee (BRAC) decided to intensify its ongoing management capacity-building program. As BRAC had grown in size, program variety and geographical coverage, management capacity had become increasingly important. BRAC top management, realizing that management capabilities have lagged behind growth, has made a major decision to institute an enlarged management development program for both top and middle managers.

For several years BRAC has had an ongoing institution-building program (financed primarily by a grant from the Ford Foundation) under which management development has been taking place. Most of the in-

143

stitution building had involved: travel by selected managers to other Asian countries to visit development projects; bringing in of consultants for management systems development; improvements in internal management systems (for example, personnel and finance, including computerization); and advanced management courses taken overseas by a few managers each year.

A Management Development Program (MDP) Committee has been set up and a management expert from the United States, now living in Dhaka, has been hired to work with it. The Committee's role has been to think about and decide what types of management capacity-building programs should be enlarged or added. The Committee has so far decided that the current institution-building programs (travel, study abroad, internal systems development) should be enhanced but also that a special intensive management training program for all managers should be introduced.

As one part of this program, a special management training program for about seventy-five middle level (mostly field) managers is being planned by the MDP Committee. The Committee has held several meetings in which the members have examined the constraints that surround their plans for this training and have made certain basic decisions.

They decided that BRAC's own top trainers from its Training and Resource Center (TARC) will be the trainers. Training will be done in Bengali and all training materials will be in Bengali. The Committee decided at the outset that the consultant would work along with the trainers from TARC in such a way that TARC's trainers will be able to provide future training without her assistance or the assistance of any other outside consultant. The trainers and selected managers will be taught to develop their own management cases to be used in future training. They also agreed to maintain in written form all module plans and materials and to document experiences with the modules for use in future training.

The training methods to be used will include specially prepared management cases (based on BRAC experience), simulations, games, group and individual projects, readings, and discussions. All training will be grounded in BRAC's philosophy of training: participatory, learner centered, experience based, and action oriented.

The committee members realize that not all the seventy-five field managers can be withdrawn from the field at the same time. Also, since training groups optimally should not be larger than twenty-five each, the committee has decided that the seventy-five managers will be divided into three groups of twenty-five persons each. Each group will be organized to include managers from various programs in order to enhance cross program learning. The first set of training sessions will be held during a six-month period, then evaluated at the end of that period. Monthly sessions will be held for each group but for periods not to exceed four to six days each, since this group of managers cannot be spared from the field for more than one week at a time and at least one day's travel time on each end of the training sessions must be included in time away from work. The training days themselves will run from seven to ten hours each.

Once priorities for content have been decided, assistance in module preparation will be obtained from the management consultant and from persons at Dhaka University Business School as required. All the sessions will be held at BRAC's own residential training centers where space has already been reserved.

Competencies Required

The key decision that still remains to be made is the subject content to be covered in the training sessions and the relative emphasis to be given to each subject.

As background for its decision about content, the Management Development Committee has spent nearly two months doing a management development needs assessment. The Committee members have interviewed most field and head office managers, and have administered questionnaires to many members of the field staffs who work under the managers. The interviews and questionnaires were designed to obtain data about backgrounds, about key tasks, about perceptions of purposes and processes, about behaviors, and about the broader working environment. The managers were asked to describe day-to-day activities and recount critical incidents and their responses to them. Those interviewed were also asked to define what they perceived as their own management development needs as well as what they saw as the needs of their bosses and of those who worked as managers under them.

As an outcome of this assessment, the Committee prepared a first draft of a chart outlining the competencies that seemed to be required by the various levels or spheres in BRAC. A day-long meeting with BRAC's twenty top managers was held to discuss the draft. Based on the inputs from that meeting, they prepared a final Competencies Chart. It is appended as Exhibit 1 of this case.

The Competencies Chart divides BRAC managers into four spheres: top managers (Sphere 1), middle managers (Sphere 2), first-line supervisors (Sphere 3), and leaders of the landless groups (Sphere 4). The chart briefly describes the competencies that individuals within each of the spheres should bring with them when they join BRAC (the first three columns), and those competencies that they can develop through experience and training after joining.

The training sessions now being designed by the MDP Committee are expected to improve the competencies of the seventy-five Sphere 2 managers who work in all the different programs. The needs assessments showed that almost all these managers have worked with BRAC for at least five years. Most started out in the field as Program Organizers and have been promoted two or three times with increasing management responsibilities assigned each time. All are university graduates, most with what are called master's degrees in Bangladesh, the equivalent of bachelor's degrees in the United States. Their average age is about thirty. Only two of them have had any formal management training; two-thirds of them studied general liberal arts subjects, one third science. Since joining BRAC all of them have participated in from two to four short (one- to three-week) training sessions covering interpersonal communication and other behavioral skills, and project planning.

Each of the field managers supervises from ten to twenty-five staff members. In the core Rural Development Program activities each manager heads a branch that relates to several thousand members in BRAC-organized landless groups. The managers' jobs are particularly complex because their work is carried out in difficult working conditions and in an environment in which governmental and elite resistance is high but acceptance is essential. Living accommodations are minimal (usually field staff members live in bachelor camps in more or less remote areas), infrastructural supports are minimal, communication and transportation channels are very underdeveloped, and the political situation is somewhat unstable. Domination of poorer people by richer farmers and government officials is the norm.

Because communication with the BRAC head office is difficult and the nature of the work is far from routine, field managers must take extraordinary initiative and make decisions without reference to the head office much of the time. Besides leading and supervising their staffs, a large part of a field manager's time must be spent on liaison and representational activities with various elites and governmental agencies. Conflict resolution is an essential part of their work. Also, as credit programs to facilitate small-scale entrepreneurial projects by the landless have become an important part of their work, many managers are handling large sums of money and increasingly are being called upon to take the lead in assisting their staff members and the landless group leaders to do feasibility analyses for small-scale economic projects.

The Committee members realize that not all of the competencies listed on the chart can be learned through training sessions no matter how well designed. Many must be acquired in other ways. And maybe some competencies that are required didn't get on the chart.

Shahid, Shabbir, Murshid, and Ahmed must now decide on priorities for the subjects to be covered in the training. Each must make his decision by Wednesday.

Exhibit 1

MANAGEMENT DEVELOPMENT PROGRAM: COMPETENCIES CHART

Spheres of Management BRAC	Foundation Competencies			Knowledge/Skills That Can Be Learned				
	Intellectual	Personal	Conscientization, Awareness	1. Interpersonal	2. Planning	3. Management Information Gathering, Storage, and Processing	4. Analytic	5. Scheduling
Sphere 1 Executive Director	Logical thought.	Self-confidence. Spontaneity. Perceptual objectivity.	Thorough national and global perspective.	Concern for others. Concern with impact.	Strategic and indicative planning.	Conceptualize needs.	Systems analysis.	Inter-project programming.
Deputies		Accurate self-assessment.		Use of unilateral socialized power. Oral communication.	Major project and work activity design within participatory framework.	Develop management information collection, storage and analysis system.	Theoretical frameworks.	Prioritizing.
Program Department Managers	Conceptualization.	Stamina.					Conceptualizing tools. Statistical techniques.	Logistics.
Regional Managers	Diagnostic use of concepts.	Adaptability. Integrity.		Positive regard for others. Group process.			Comparative analysis.	
Sphere 2 Branch Managers	Logical thought.	Self-confidence.		Concern for others. Concern with impact. Oral communication. Positive regard for others.	Project and work activity design within participatory framework.	Collection, filing and analysis of data.	Conceptual frameworks.	Logistics.
Camp Head	Conceptualization.	Spontaneity. Perceptual objectivity.	Advanced awareness.				Simple data analysis.	
Area Head Program Organizer	Diagnostic ability.	Accurate self-assessment. Stamina. Adaptability.		Group process.			Simple statistical techniques.	

Exhibit 1 (cont'd)

Spheres 1 and 2 (cont'd)		Knowledge/Skills That Can Be Learned					
6. Supervision, Leadership	7. Productivity	8. Financial	9. Communication	10. P.R., Representational	11. Developing others	12. Conflict Resolution	13. Development studies
Objective setting. Develop structural systems and incentive systems. Monitoring system for performance. Motivating. Role modeling.	Economic analysis. Input-output and impact analysis. Measuring system performance.	Financial system development. Financial analysis. Auditing. Program budgeting and control.	Bilingual. Sophisticated oral/written communication conceptually organized.	Understanding of BRAC programs. Program analysis and packaging both oral and written for various audiences.	Coaching, counseling. Developing training systems. Building teams. Developing responsibility.	Developing organizational systems for conflict resolution. Mediation. Defusing. Judging. Sanctioning. Confrontation.	Analytic understanding of development theories and knowledge of various development experiences and approaches. Understanding of national-global socioeconomic/political context.
Understanding/interpreting systems. Motivating. Role modeling. Objective setting.	Simple input-output analysis against targets. Input-output impact monitoring.	Account generation and reporting. Project budgeting, analysis, and control.	Oral/written communication clear, organized, accurate. Bilingual.	Understanding of BRAC programs and purposes. Oral/written communication to villagers, government officers, donors, elites.	Coaching, counseling. Building teams. Developing responsibility. Developing informal learning processes.	Mediation. Defusing. Judging. Sanctioning. Confrontation.	General knowledge of development theories and approaches. Understanding of national socioeconomic and political context.

Exhibit 1 (cont'd)

Spheres of Management BRAC	Foundation Competencies			Knowledge/Skills That Can Be Learned				
	Intellectual	Personal	Conscientization, Awareness	1. Interpersonal	2. Planning	3. Management Information Gathering, Storage, and Processing	4. Analytic	5. Scheduling
Sphere 3 Program Organizer Head Office Mid-level Staff Village Aides	Logical thought. Reasoning.	Self-confidence. Self-control. Stamina. Adaptability. Patience.	Basic awareness.	Concern for others. Concern with impact. Oral communication. Positive regard for others. Group process.	Project and work activity design within participatory framework.	Collection, analysis, and understanding of data.	Understanding of relationships. Information verification. Simple data analysis.	Simple scheduling of time and events.
Sphere 4 Landless laborers	Logical thought.	Self-confidence. Self-control. Stamina. Adaptability. Patience.	Basic awareness.	Concern for others. Concern with impact. Oral communication. Positive regard for others. Group process.	Project and work activity design within participatory framework.	Collection and understanding of simple data.	Understanding of relationships. Information verification.	Simple scheduling of time and events.

Exhibit 1 (cont'd)

Knowledge/Skills That Can Be Learned

Spheres 3 and 4 (cont'd)

6. Supervision, Leadership	7. Productivity	8. Financial	9. Communication	10. P.R., Representational	11. Developing others	12. Conflict Resolution	13. Development studies
Setting activity objectives. Monitoring individual and group performance.	Setting and following output targets. Output-impact monitoring.	Account keeping. Simple project budgeting and control.	Understanding of BRAC programs and purposes. Oral communication to villagers and officials.	Understanding of BRAC programs and purposes. Oral communication to villagers and officials.	Coaching, counseling. Giving responsibility to others.	Mediation. Defusing. Judging. Sanctioning. Confrontation.	General knowledge of development theories and approaches.
Setting activity objectives. Monitoring individual and group performance.	Setting and following output targets. Output monitoring.	Keeping simple accounts. Simple project budgeting.	Oral communication clear, accurate.	Ability to express purposes and needs to other villagers and to government officers.	Coaching, counseling. Giving responsibility to others.	Mediation. Defusing. Judging. Sanctioning. Confrontation.	Ideas about meanings of development.

Case 4

BRAC (C):
What to do about
Market Outlets?

This case was written by Professor Catherine Lovell, assisted by Murshid Shah. It is intended as a basis for class discussion rather than as an illustration of either effective or ineffective handling of an administrative situation. The collaboration and support of the Executive Director of BRAC and his staff are gratefully acknowledged.

It is January 1978. The Executive Director of the Bangladesh Rural Advancement Committee (BRAC), Fazle Hasan Abed, is faced with a major strategic decision. He must decide whether or not BRAC should be involved in opening a marketing outlet for products produced by the rural groups that BRAC and other NGOs have organized for productive efforts. Women are making nearly 70 percent of the products that need to be sold. For almost six months the issue has been discussed and rediscussed, but now Abed must make the final decision about BRAC's involvement. Should BRAC add yet another major project to its already multifaceted activities?

Bangladesh and BRAC

For a brief description of conditions in Bangladesh and the programs of BRAC see Exhibit 1 of the BRAC (A) case.

The Marketing Problem

In the early 1970s numerous NGOs, many from Western countries, and some indigenous ones, like BRAC, had initiated programs in Bangladesh to attempt to alleviate the worst miseries resulting from the terrible cyclone of 1970 and the havoc from the independence war with Pakistan in 1971. By the mid-1970s some of these groups had turned from relief activities to programs to help the poorest, primarily the landless, to become self-reliant through production efforts. The government had also introduced several similar projects. Most of the projects had encouraged home-based, handicraft production, but some had organized cooperative efforts at production centers.

One of BRAC's major self-reliance projects (centered in the Manikganj area about forty miles north of Dhaka) had organized and trained women to produce silk and also to do block printing with colorful dyes on cotton to be used for saris and other garments, or for tablecloths, bedcovers, and various other uses. By January 1978 more than one hundred women are employed in silk production, from silkworm culture to spinning and weaving, and nearly a hundred others are involved in block printing or sewing. Both quantity and quality of products have been steadily improving. Groups organized by BRAC and other NGOs in many different villages all over the country are also producing various kinds of jute, straw, bamboo, wood, and other handmade products.

Marketing of the handicrafts, however, has become a serious problem. Several of the NGOs have established small retail stores in Dhaka. Caritas, for example, has a small store in one of its church compounds, primarily for jute products. The Mennonite Central Committee (MCC), whose many groups are making various handicraft items, among them unusual wheat straw picture cards, is exporting most of its products to small NGO stores in Europe or the United States. Several small private shops and boutiques, including some in or near the major hotels, are selling handicrafts from these artisans.

The principal existing marketing outlet is a cooperative handicraft shop called Karika. Karika, a quasi-governmental organization funded by a German Foundation, "Bread for the World," had been founded to help solve handicraft marketing problems. It buys products from the various artisans and sells them in its store.

Many of the producers, however, are having serious problems in dealing with Karika. They deliver their finished products to Karika agents who pay them by check about a month after delivery. Another month to two months is required for the rural banks to collect the money from Karika's Dhaka bank. As a result of this process the artisans do not receive payment for two to four months. Since the producers are normally very poor people, they have neither the working capital to invest in required raw materials, nor the income to buy food while waiting for payment. Another major problem is that Karika does not have the capacity to help the village people with product and design ideas. BRAC is increasingly being approached to loan the producers working capital. In some cases it is making such loans. But BRAC has believed that when it makes these loans it is helping to subsidize Karika rather than being of most benefit to the producers. If a market outlet could be run more efficiently and could make a profit, couldn't the producers be paid immediately in cash on delivery?

BRAC's capacity to provide start-up credit financing for new producer groups has just been enhanced by the introduction of a new, very large, foreign donor–financed program, the Rural Credit and Training Program (RCTP). Abed realizes that this new program will organize and train many new people for productive capabilities and that the number of products requiring markets will increase even more. Quantity and variety will be enlarged and the market problem will get worse. He also realizes that this big new program will take a great deal of his attention.

Another key problem with the Karika shop as a primary outlet is that it is mainly a small handicraft outlet and does not provide a market for the silk and other textile production of the Manikganj women, who are by now producing beautiful varieties of silk cloth and other textile products in rather large quantities.

At the same time another major BRAC project for women is getting off the ground in Jamalpur, where women are starting to produce many products using the traditional Kantha quilt embroidery, and are experimenting with other textile products as well. As he thinks it over, Abed anticipates that within two years the types and quality of these products, too, will need a special kind of market.

During the last six months, the MCC and BRAC have taken the lead in trying to work out some of the marketing problems with Karika (particularly payment arrangements), but no progress has been made. MCC and BRAC have set up a joint committee of representatives of their two organizations to review all the marketing problems and to explore alternative solutions to them. That committee has also tried to make projections about directions that production and marketing activities to support rural artisans may need to take over the next few years.

In the last committee meeting many important points growing out of several months of discussions had been expressed. Abed thought over the key considerations that were put forward at that meeting. As careful minutes unfortunately had not been kept, he now had to reconstruct the main points in his mind. Following that, he reviewed the results of a quick feasibility study that the committee had requested.

1. If production continues to increase, enlarged markets are necessary. Current market outlets are insufficient.

2. If more variety in types of products occurs, more versatile market outlets will be required.

3. If kinds and quality of products are to be improved, the producers will need more assistance in design ideas and product development methods and quality standards. To be successful, any marketing operation must think about incorporating a design research and quality control division or at least capability. Preliminary discussions have been held with Appropriate Technol-

ogy International in the United States, which appears willing to fund such a research center if it can be combined with a marketing outlet.

4. Producers must have access to ongoing working capital. Should a retail shop be expected to pay producers cash upon the delivery of products, and if so, where can it get its working capital?

5. Can a shop make enough profit to accumulate its own working capital? Can a shop make enough profit to be entirely self-supporting? How many years would it take to become self-supporting? Could the initial investment capital be obtained commercially or from donor groups?

6. If a new market outlet were to be be established by BRAC or by BRAC together with other NGOs, could the management capability be found to operate on a business-like basis, not as an "NGO type" unbusiness-like operation? In the discussions at the meeting this problem loomed as one of the most serious risk factors. BRAC has no one on its current staff who could be spared to run such an enterprise and its management capabilities will be stretched very thin between current programs and the big new RCTP program just beginning.

7. If a new market outlet were started, should the market be defined as primarily domestic or should the focus be on export? After a lot of discussion the idea that outlets would be export oriented was discarded as being too risky. The committee members realized that artisans are used to producing in small quantities. For profitable export larger quantities of the same product are usually required. One canceled or unfulfilled big order, or unmet quality standards, could mean ruin. But, the committee members argued back and forth, is there sufficient local market? Dhaka has about four million people, but is there enough upper and upper-middle class purchasing power in Dhaka to provide a market? There are other large cities in Bangladesh: Chittagong and Sylhet, for example. Could outlets be introduced there? Is there a potential market in those cities?

8. If a new marketing outlet were to be established, should it be a wholesale outlet, serving as intermediary between producers and retail stores? Or should it be a store directly connecting producers and consumers to provide the producers with maximum possible income? Could that be managed logistically?

9. How important to the whole marketing scheme is the idea of developing uniquely Bangladeshi designs and products? One of the committee members kept insisting that the products being produced now are primarily second-rate copies of Indian designs

and products. But other committee members had asked "Is there enough potential in indigenous Bangladeshi designs to establish a unique market?" Several volunteers connected with MCC and BRAC have been insisting to committee members that an emphasis on Bangladeshi uniqueness would pay off. Among them were fine arts graduates willing to volunteer time to try to put their concern into practice.

10. If a new market outlet were to be started by BRAC, how much employment might it provide and could enough profit be made to help finance some other activities of BRAC?

Feasibility Study

With the above questions in mind, Abed and Paul Myers, the Bangladesh director of MCC, had asked one of the MCC staff members, Mr. Sajid, to do a very rough financial feasibility study. For the purposes of the study he was to assume that the market would be domestic, that the outlet would be one modest but professional type store in Dhaka. Since he did not have the capability or resources to do a scientific market analysis, he was to assume that a small local clientele did exist—as Karika and the other small shops did have a steady clientele and a few of the shops were actually making a profit, although their marketing techniques were less than professional.

About all Mr. Sajid could do within his time and assumption constraints was to calculate a simple break-even analysis. In his calculations he investigated the start-up costs: potential space cost factors, rent, utilities, and licences; costs of initial fitting of the shop; and the amount of working capital needed for initial stock purchases. He decided on a small, three-room shop with small adjacent *godown* (warehouse) space. He included the costs of shelves, showcases, required racks and counters, air conditioners, and so forth, to make a first-class, professional-looking shop. He also assumed that three full-time employees, supplemented by volunteers, would be all that were required to handle the anticipated clientele for the first two years and he calculated labor costs based on that assumption.

He assumed a markup of 30 percent on all products sold. He also assumed that producers would be paid cash upon delivery of merchandise (products would not be accepted that did not meet quality standards set by the shop).

The conclusion of his break-even analysis was that average sales per month of Tk 186,000 (U.S.$11,625) would be required to break even. The costs of the initial fitting out investment, amortized over the first two years, were included. The break-even analysis did not include the costs of the research-design center that the committee thought would be a necessary adjunct to the ultimate success of the shop.

Since the committee members, like Mr. Sajid, had no way to do a sophisticated market analysis, they had made an educated guess that for the first two years, at least, they would not be able to reach the Tk 186,000 in sales per month, but they did believe that a properly run shop could build up to that figure within about two years. The committee members also realized that to meet that target the outlet must be assured of sufficient quantity and quality of supply.

Abed himself (although he had no hard data to consult) calculated that with a start-up grant of Tk 2 million (about U.S.$125,000) all initial investment and losses for the first two years would be covered. Although he was a good businessman (he had been a chartered accountant and regional manager with a large international company before starting BRAC), it was clear to him as well as to the committee as a whole that acting upon such a rough estimate would be primarily an act of faith.

What Should Abed Do?

As Abed considered his several options he kept thinking about the hardworking women who made up 70 percent of the BRAC producers. They were the least advantaged and the most in need of help. They had already proved what they could do. Now they deserved an effective means for marketing their products.

Option 1. Do nothing. Hope that other NGOs, the government, or private entrepreneurs will eventually provide the market outlets since the supply is now guaranteed, or that Karika will find ways to improve its operation.

Option 2. Actively encourage another NGO or private entrepreneur to open a professionally run operation. Offer to help raise the money from private investors or external donors. (BRAC has an excellent track record at raising money from donors for worthwhile projects.)

Option 3. Join with another NGO with similar concerns and ambitions and open a shop together. Work out the management problems together. Actively solicit external donors for the investment capital on a grant basis. At some point pursue Appropriate Technology International for the funding to set up a design research center as a support for the shop.

Option 4. Go it alone, pursue all the donor paths suggested in Option 3, and assume that qualified management can be found or developed.

Option 5. Don't act right now with insufficient information; try to develop more information and try to generate additional options.

Case 5

CARE-Philippines (A): The Income-Generating Project

This case was written by Francisco Roman. It is intended as a basis for class discussion rather than as an illustration of either effective or ineffective handling of an administrative situation. The collaboration and support of the Executive Director and his staff, CARE-Philippines, and the Director of SED Programs, CARE-NY, are gratefully acknowledged.

The IGP

The Income-Generating Project (IGP) was initiated in 1981 by the CARE-Philippines Mission Director, Charles Lasky. By 1987, the IGP had gone through an "experimental" and an "expanded" phase, and a new Mission Director, Stanley Dunn, had been assigned to CARE-Philippines. In December 1987, an internal reorganization of CARE-Philippines was in progress, and changes would also affect the IGP staff. Stanley Dunn was in the process of sorting out in his own mind the past, current, and future situation of the IGP within the CARE-Philippines program.

Background

CARE-International

According to its Agency Organizational Profile, CARE was organized on 27 November 1945 "... as a private, voluntary, non-profit agency to distribute urgently needed food packages to destitute peoples in the war-torn Europe after World War II ... As Europe recovered, CARE gradually withdrew from the war-torn countries it had served, and became increasingly involved with assisting needy millions in other continents."

CARE's initial image was built on the millions of food packages that it distributed in the early post-war period. In the 1950s, with the enactment of U.S. Public Law 480, CARE expanded into large-scale, bulk shipment of food commodities. In 1962, CARE established health and medical services. And, "Currently, CARE has projects in 36 individual countries. These projects involve feeding and nutrition; self-help (food production, income generation, education, water/health, community development) conservation and energy relief ... In over forty years of its existence, CARE has provided more than U.S.$4.8 billion worth of goods and services to 86 nations in four continents."

"CARE's purpose is to help the developing world's poor to achieve long term social and economic well-being and self-sufficiency and to offer relief in times of crisis." CARE's operating policy is to work with partner organizations in recipient countries (see Exhibit 1, CARE's Program Principles). In 1986, CARE-NY added Small Enterprise Development (SED) as one of its major worldwide program themes. It hired an experienced small enterprise specialist, Larry Frankel, to develop and lead a Headquarters staff capability to help its field missions develop their small enterprise activities. CARE also added four regional technical advisors in SED, one of whom—based in Bangkok—has responsibility for providing technical assistance to the IGP.

CARE-Philippines

CARE has operated in the Philippines for over thirty years, and has provided over U.S.$131 million in development and relief assistance. Its objectives in the Philippines are to:

- improve the health and nutrition of the undernourished, especially children and pregnant and nursing mothers in lower income levels;
- encourage the production and consumption of highly nutritious foods;
- promote the development and strengthening of indigenous private sector groups to facilitate provision of effective assistance to community participants in self-help and income-generating activities;
- respond to emergency or crisis as circumstances and resources permit.

Funding for the Philippine programs is channeled through CARE World Headquarters and comes from individual and corporate donations in various CARE donor countries and from grants from USAID and other country governments and international agencies. "The Philippine government provides a budget through its counterpart agencies, for operating, handling, and internal transportation expenses." Counterpart funding is also provided as a condition for CARE support of individual development projects.

CARE has six major activities in the Philippines: The Emergency Response is a fundamental CARE activity, and provides food and relief supplies that "clearly cannot be met by national relief agencies," and rehabilitation and recovery assistance through follow-up projects based on specifically identified needs.

There are two other long-running CARE programs: The School Nutrition Program (SNP), implemented by the Philippine Ministry of Education, Culture and Sports, and supported by CARE since 1958, "aims to reduce malnutrition by encouraging school efforts in nutrition education, health and sanitation as well as increased food production in school gardens ... the FY 1987–90 project will provide over 16.3 million pounds of nutritionally appropriate food commodities annually to approximately 763,000 targeted child beneficiaries in over 5,000 elementary schools in nine regions ..."

The Targeted Food Assistance Program (TFAP), implemented by the Ministry of Health, and supported by CARE since 1977, meets the "immediate calorie and protein deficiencies of the second and third degree malnourished pre-schoolers from 1–6 years old as well as the pregnant and nursing mothers." The program expects to reach 220,000 beneficiaries by 1990. A related activity, Nutrition Program Enhancement, "... seeks to enhance the quality and integration ... of all ongoing CARE-supported food and nutrition projects. Also, to identify and develop new approaches as a permanent solution to nutrition problems in the Philippines."

The next two activities are relatively recent and are less directly related to the food and relief programs for which CARE has been known in the Philippines; they also involve working more with grassroot partner organizations than with CARE's traditional government partners. The Family Income Generating Project (later known as IGP) began in 1981, and "... seeks to improve the well-being of the lowest income rural families by increasing their ability to obtain additional basic needs through the generation of additional cash income. Rural families are provided with short-term loans in the form of production materials for intensified farming and other appropriate livelihood activities ... with loan returns recycled ... to reach out to new additional beneficiaries." At the outset there was no real emphasis on or plan for local institution strengthening, including strengthening of formal lending institutions or mechanisms.

The Negros Occidental Development Assistance Program, initiated in July 1986, reflects a national and international concern over the poverty of displaced and underemployed workers and their families dependent on the area's sugar industry. The program "... seeks to initiate long term development activities which will help bring about a smooth transition from the economic base of sugar growing to a more diversified and self-sufficient means of livelihood for the workers of the province." While CARE's immediate activities in Negros involved reducing malnutrition, CARE also began to shift to crop and livestock production activities aimed at the displaced sugar workers and farmers. CARE works in Negros with local NGOs, cooperatives, and church-based community groups: "Individual projects focus on rice production and marketing,

corn, cassava, legume and vegetable production, cattle and swine fattening, and carabao, goat and duck raising breeding. Land-based programs
for landless sugar workers include provisions for land use for a minimum of three years." The ongoing commitment amounts to approximately U.S.$350,000 per year.

The Evolution of the IGP

The Experimental Income-Generating Project

The IGP began in December 1981 on a trial basis. The original concept
was to provide supplementary or secondary activities to rural farm families to augment the household income over and above the basic inflow
derived from the family breadwinner's "primary" activity, such as farming. The experimental IGP started as an extension of support to
beneficiaries already involved in the food programs of the government
agencies with whom CARE worked. CARE considered phasing in a
livelihood component into the SNP and TFAP. "The emergent project
provided in-kind livelihood activities, such as cash value loans, with repayments to be used for extending the assistance to new participant
families. The project was directly implemented and managed by CARE-
Philippines utilizing its existing staff of field officers, whose primary job
was to supervise and monitor the various food programming operations
in the field." At this time, CARE-Philippines staff, unlike staff at some
other CARE country offices, had little experience in income-generating
activities and the intricacies of managing a revolving loan fund or
analyzing the commercial viability of enterprises.

CARE had long dealt with government ministries and agencies. By
1984, it became apparent that CARE would have to deal also with private
voluntary organizations (PVOs) and non-government organizations
(NGOs). CARE engaged the issue of selecting a suitable "partner" to
carry out the IGP. "... Pilot sub-projects were developed and funded
with key organizations to test the operational aspects of the partnership
approach ... the initial partner organizations supported the development
principle of working with and strengthening existing indigenous PVOs
with CARE-Philippines assuming a program of training and policy-mak-
ing rather than a direct implementing role." By 1985, with the changing
political situation, almost all sources of rural small sum credit had dried
up, and CARE-Philippines found it necessary to establish its own independent loan fund.

The IGP concept implied a rethinking of basic policy: "CARE-Philippines believes that it is not enough to merely feed people in order that
they do not starve. The real and greater challenge lies in CARE's capacity
to increase people's ability to increase incomes. With the PL-480 Food
Assistance Program in a phase-out mode, an increasing involvement in

small sum credit development and self-help programs will characterize CARE-Philippines operational thrust in the coming years." To develop and implement such a project, CARE identified and hired small enterprise or business specialists who brought technical capacity to the IGP project and to CARE-Philippines. They in turn trained other CARE staff and CARE counterpart staff.

The Expanded IGP

The Multi-Year Plan (MYP) for FY 1987–90 described the latest phase of the IGP: "The CARE-Philippines Expanded IGP is a U.S.$1.8 million four-year effort built on the basic concepts and experiences of the Experimental IGP [FY 1981–84] … The expanded IGP seeks to assist low-income individuals and their families to increase their incomes by providing small amounts of production capital inputs as loans for such agro-based activities as vegetable farming, livestock raising, and for off-farm small enterprises such as food processing/marketing."

One major difference between the experimental and the expanded IGP was the "concept of commercial viability of enterprises"—that "… they should be able to operate and survive in the market place on a commercial basis after the IGP ends."

Another difference was the change in focus from developing secondary sources of income, to sustaining, increasing, and diversifying income activities related to the household's primary source of livelihood; the latter were usually farm-related tasks. This change occurred in the course of the experimental IGP when CARE found that the targeted recipients were most concerned with the viability of their primary income-generating activities. The households were in no position to undertake secondary activities while their basic income source was still in doubt.

The IGP differed from the traditional CARE-Philippines programs in part because of the use of NGOs as counterparts. NGOs had been a regular part of the Philippine social and economic development infrastructure but had received more prominence and attention, and increasing fund support, with the change in political administrations. Government agencies were in the process of reorganization, and were considered too unwieldy and too inflexible to undertake the diversity of entrepreneurial and managerial tasks involved in generating income for the rural poor. Moreover, NGOs, as well as selected local government groups, had established the necessary grassroots support at the community level.

IGP Operating Objectives

Partner Organizations

The role of the partner organizations was "… to manage agricultural and non-agricultural production credit and marketing support; and to give the business management consultancy and technical assistance necessary to achieve the goal of income increase of the beneficiary communities." Eventually, these partner organizations were expected to take part in CARE's traditional programs of health care and disaster relief.

The criteria for selecting a partner in the IGP were "... track records that indicate management capability for social development projects and some experience with credit delivery." However, since partners were likely to display varying degrees of managerial competence, "... one focus of the IGP will be to strengthen indigenous organizations which assist the poor ... through sharing the project management and financial management consultancy skills of the CARE IGP staff and through networking the staff skills of the different partners themselves at workshops and training centers."

Loan Recipients

CARE identified several types of loan recipients "... who have been left out of the already inadequate formal credit channels," such as landless farm workers, tenants, small farm owner-cultivators, sustenance fishermen, and market center slum dwellers, with a yearly cash and noncash household income below U.S.$900. The latter figure translated into U.S.$150 per person; the country's average annual per capita income was approximately U.S.$600. The IGP's initial operations would cover approximately 3,000 rural families located in the distant provinces and islands south of Metropolitan Manila.

These recipients were caught in the traditional economic cycle of poverty: insufficient credit = low productivity and yields = low income = low savings = low asset base = insufficient credit (in the next cycle). CARE proposed to use production credits from its funds sources, and through the management and technical assistance from the partners, to enter this cycle and help the poor break out of it.

CARE ultimately expected that the loan recipients would channel the increased income into savings to replace the existing loan and even to build up funds for "... emergency health and consumption needs." Over the long run, the recipients' income-generating activities would expand from the micro-enterprise stage to become small- and medium-scale enterprises. Thus the average sub-project loan was expected to increase from U.S.$3,200 in 1986 to $5,000, $7,000, and $8,000, respectively in FY 1987, 1988, and 1989. By FY 1989, a few relatively "large" loans of U.S.$20,000 and U.S.$30,000 would be made available for sub-projects deemed ready to move into the "formal" financial sector. FY 1990 outlays would consist entirely of loans for small (as opposed to micro-) enterprises. However, CARE realized that the process "... will necessarily involve high-risk commercial activities with the recipients' loans because these are the people left out of the formal banking system (even in earlier government-subsidized loan programs). Therefore, the need for intensive monitoring will be of utmost importance." All these aspects were carefully analyzed in projected income, cash flow, and ROI statements.

Procedures

The partners were expected to develop and implement "commercial" activities, sub-projects in CARE's terminology, for their loan recipients. CARE would provide the initial funds for the partners to intervene among their constituencies, first through the financing of production inputs, and later by providing technical and management assistance. The latter was expected to prove critical as the sub-projects expanded and evolved beyond the familiar production and farming activities, into further processing, or into marketing or trading, for example. In addition, the IGP was prepared to support selective income-generating activities to provide income for the partner organizations themselves. At this time, the IGP staff did not realize the length of time involved in training and upgrading local institutions.

The basic procedure required that "... each potential partner first develops with one of its grassroots organizations (i.e., credit coop, mothers' club, farmers' association) a 'sub-project' for 12 to 20 loan recipients' individual enterprises (generally all of the same module or type, i.e., cattle fattening) to be supported initially through a single loan agreement with CARE that is guaranteed by the partner." The procedure implied a process of "learning-by-doing": "... the IGP can cross analyze sectors according to profitability and develop technical assistance modules appropriate for the entire sector, e.g., cattle feeding manuals."

The procedure was expected to reduce CARE's exposure to a particular partner: "This sub-project by sub-project approach allows CARE to become familiar with the partner's management capability and potential without committing large amounts of funds. When a number of small sub-projects are being managed well by a partner, these are consolidated under a separate project agreement into a single revolving loan fund ..." Furthermore, "... this approach is aimed to strengthen indigenous organizations by developing their organizational skills and management effectiveness."

The partners in turn were expected to benefit from the relationship in several ways: They were expected to charge reasonable but competitive interest on loans, the income from which could be used "primarily to support the services of the partner organization" to provide the means for expansion. Partners were also able to develop income-generating activities for their own organizations. Third, the CARE relationship would help in developing additional, international, sources of funding. And the "networking" with other partners, through CARE workshops, was expected to improve further partner capabilities in management.

CARE had developed over the course of the IGP fairly extensive procedures as well as documentation on partner selection, sub-project monitoring and appraisal, and financial supervision and control. The procedures included analyses of the partner, the sub-projects, and the target community. The IGP was also the subject of site visits by both Philippine and international CARE staff. For instance, the General Terms and Conditions covered such items as counterpart funding, interest charge computation, separate bank accounts and books and financial statements, and funds liquidation procedures. The General Procedures for Submission and Development of Proposals covered guidelines for the selection of beneficiaries and small enterprises, policies and procedures on loan processing and approval, schedules on releases and repayments and capital build-up, and systems for recording and reporting the income-generating activities of both borrowers and partners, and for maintaining financial control, a business evaluation project study.

By 1986, the IGP staff was in place, a computerized information system was designed (by outside consultants) and installed, and two systems—a core system for project screening and a support system for sub-project monitoring, reporting, and control—were incorporated into a Manual of Operations (to be revised further) for use by CARE and its partners.

Three Perspectives on "Lessons Learned" in the IGP

The IGP had screened forty sub-projects, and approved thirty one; loans approved totaled U.S.$110,000, of which U.S.$90,000 had been released; there were 592 loan recipients and 4,164 indirect beneficiaries.

CARE-NY Staff Report

In September 1986, a member of the CARE international staff in her field trip report wrote about problems with the key link in the IGP–partner organizations.

It takes more time to work with the partners than the IGP had originally thought.

Even though the partner organizations accept the idea that it is necessary to have detailed financial management systems, it takes time for them to implement these systems.

It is essential for the (CARE) IGP staff to establish their credibility from the beginning of the (sub) project ... by offering specific extension inputs such as financial management assistance. This type of assistance requires a very professionally skilled staff.

The NGO networks that are on the brink of dissolving are often the best prospect for the IGP ... They realize that the IGP is their last chance for survival and thus are thoroughly committed to the program.

A major issue ... is how to support ... increased staff costs ... of partner NGOs until they have the capacity to support themselves ... I support the concept of lending funds to partner organizations to establish enterprises whose sole purpose is to support their organization. These enterprises, however, must not be detrimental to the project participants or contradict the partner organizations' or CARE's development approach and philosophy.

Outside Observer's Report

An academic researcher working on NGO issues in the Philippines made the following comments on the partners:

> Each partner organization moves at its own pace ... Some organizations which are very well established feel they have "all the answers" ... Young/new organizations ... those who recognize they don't have everything it takes ... often are better risks ... simply because they "want to learn" ... Very few NGOs, no matter how entrepreneurial, can understand a micro-enterprise loan program, without some temporary administrative support program ... it takes TIME ... for the partners first to decide what they want to do and how they want to do it. It also takes time to review with them how to improve it. Thus, this project is not one that immediately moves large volumes of money ... Yet there is pressure to move money.

Another problem observed in the report was that the partner's image of CARE as a relief agency creates the "... illusion that 'if the loans run out CARE will forgive them' ... For example, CARE has encountered this attitude in a major organization with which it was forced to terminate its relationship. The organization believed it should not be liable for the loan because CARE was conducting the monitoring process. When CARE was monitoring the sub-projects it discovered that the organization was not providing the technical assistance which they had promised." This problem was not exclusive to CARE. A substantial portion of the Philippine government's loan programs had been converted into grants and the local NGOs and project participants expected CARE to follow suit.

CARE-Philippines IGP FY 1986 Year-End Report

In its own year-end report, CARE noted the following lessons learned:

1. Networking and capacity-building of partner organizations entails intensive IGP inputs ...
2. A series of conferences between CARE and partners has proven very valuable in getting participation in IGP systems development ...

3. A strong and reasonably wide network of private partners is a workable goal ...

4. Work with the current number of partners required the identification of a field or range of potential partners from which to choose because some of these potential partners eventually backed out or were screened out.

5. There is a need to emphasize from the very start ... the role of CARE as a facilitator of institution or capacity building of partners rather than that of a grant making agency ... to make it easier for CARE to address the needs of the target beneficiaries through partners ...

6. The use of business management techniques is a must for effective credit delivery projects with the poor ... Capital build-up is a necessary objective of income-increase.

7. For a new project of this complexity it is unrealistic to try to raise funds without a track record and to operationalize the project simultaneously in the first project year.

8. Basic tenets of the original MYP, i.e., working through and with private non-profit organizations as partners, use of specific criteria for choice of partners, sub-project types and loan recipients, and the need for credit for food based agricultural production and processing, have all proven valid.

As he reviews the experience with the IGP to date, Stanley Dunn knows that both the mission and CARE-NY will be looking to him for leadership on the issue of "where do we go from here with respect to the IGP."

Exhibit 1
CARE'S PROGRAM PRINCIPLES

Fundamental Program Principles

- Significant Scope
- Working with Poor People
- Participation
- Adaptability
- Sustainability
- Fundamental Change

These principles should form the basis for all CARE's work in development. They should also be seriously considered in CARE's relief work, since—in the long term—all CARE's programming should be viewed as developmental.

Each CARE program and all its projects are expected to embody all six principles.

Recognizing the formative nature of these principles, staff at all levels within CARE are called upon to commit themselves to the continued development and incorporation of these principles into all we do.

Significant Scope

CARE should identify and address problems that are common to a significant number of people while being appropriate to CARE's other program principles, purpose, and philosophy.

While CARE programs and projects are designed to have direct and permanent impact for our counterparts and partner communities, they should also affect similar problems of other people and communities not directly involved in the program or project.

Whether a broad approach to a problem is adopted elsewhere or on a larger scale, or an appropriate technology is copied by those on the periphery of a project, good programming has a multiplier effect that can only occur when it addresses conditions common to many.

This principle recognizes that projects small in scale may represent an effort to develop new approaches to significant problems.

Working with Poor People

This principle reinforces commitment to "People." CARE was founded as a "People to People" organization and would like to stress the central nature of "People" to its program and project planning.

In particular CARE is concerned with poor people and those in greatest need.

CARE views its relationship with poor people as a partnership; respecting the experience, culture, and dignity of the people and recognizing the important roles both partners play in the development process.

CARE's resources are intended to be of direct benefit to poor people. Although it is recognized that resources can be channeled through groups who are not necessarily the "Poorest" people, providing positive impact upon poor people is the primary goal.

Participation

CARE will strive to facilitate community-based programs and projects recognizing "participation" can take many forms whether it is working with villagers, local indigenous organizations, or national counterparts.

Meaningful participation requires a joint responsibility for project planning, implementation, and evaluation among all participants, with control and ownership of the project being assumed by the community. As such this principle is seen as a necessary condition for "Fundamental Change," "Adaptability," "Sustainability," and the creation of a "Critical Mass."

CARE recognizes that to become effective in applying this principle at the project level, "Participation" must also be operationalized within the organization and be manifested in its dealing with donors.

Adaptability

Designing an adaptable project implies a choice of problem (see "Significant Scope"), goals, processes, and activities that could be made again in another setting. A key factor in designing an adaptable project is awareness of the assumptions on which project success rests and consideration of possible secondary consequences.

An adaptable project is one in which significant aspects of the project can be undertaken elsewhere. It should be stressed that it is not sufficient for a project to be implementable by "CARE" elsewhere given similar resources.

Furthermore, CARE should *actively* promote the adaptation of its projects by local institutions.

Sustainability

All CARE-supported projects should be designed in recognition of the fact that CARE's intervention is short term whereas the development process is continuous and infinite. Every project should therefore incorporate a strategy that at the lowest level allows a community to maintain and continue a project as long as it is needed, and at a higher level builds capability within the community to control and manage a development process that will lead to other community-initiated development projects.

Fundamental Change

Not only does good programming address significant problems of poor people in a participatory, adaptable, and sustainable manner; it also strives to affect their lives in a significant way.

CARE projects should ideally address basic needs and raise people's awareness about the causes of underdevelopment whereby reducing the limitations imposed on people's lives.

Good projects strive to bring about a fundamental change in society as traditional barriers to mobility are weakened and new opportunities are grasped. Thus, interventions not only should have impact but, where feasible, should promote positive attitudinal change and enable people to take greater control over their own lives.

Recognizing the ambitious nature of this principle, CARE would hope to see its future programming move in this general direction to the extent local and financial constraints allow.

Case 6

CARE–Philippines (B): The Relationship with REACH

This case was written by Francisco Roman. It is intended as a basis for class discussion rather than as an illustration of either effective or ineffective handling of an administrative situation. The collaboration and support of the Executive Director and his staff, CARE-Philippines, and the Director of SED Programs, CARE-NY, are gratefully acknowledged.

The Case Study

Stanley Dunn, the Country Director of CARE-Philippines, responded to an inquiry he had received from CARE-NY on the possibility of developing a case study on CARE-Philippines' Income-Generating Program (IGP), with the following "initial ideas":

> ... We would like the case study to focus upon the REACH Foundation—our major partner organization in the IGP.
>
> The nature of the case study must be such that it is of use to the CARE mission in future decision making. Consequently, the study should focus on:
>
> 1. What were the criteria used in selecting REACH?
> 2. Were the criteria correct? What additional or different criteria should be used in the future?
> 3. What adjustments in original objectives vis-à-vis strengthening the partner organization have been necessary? Why?
> 4. How successful has the project been in reaching targeted objectives? What were the reasons for the achievement/non-achievement of objectives?
>
> Note that we wish the study to focus on the partner organization—not on beneficiary objectives. Needless to say, the latter achievement need certainly be considered in examining the success of the partnership relation ...

Background

The IGP

The basic objective of the IGP was to "... enhance and diversify the primary source of income of the rural poor on a sustainable basis" by providing "... revolving loans to fund small, community-based family-operated 'sub-projects' such as cattle fattening, vegetable farming, rice trading, etc."

The targets were those borrowers "... that are excluded from the inadequate rural banking system and government loan programs: small farm owners/tenants, upland shifting cultivators, and market center slum dwellers ..." At the end of the IGP, the program's participants or beneficiaries were expected to "... move into the rural banking system and the formal financial sector of the Philippines."

The mechanism to achieve the basic objective was to include and develop Private Voluntary Organizations (PVOs) or Non-Government Organizations (NGOs) as the "... counterpart or partner organizations as implementing and administrative conduits for the sub-projects and as sources of counterpart capital for these sub-projects." The NGO-partners had to "co-finance and manage production credit, furnish marketing support, and give business management consultancy and technical assistance to their affiliate groups, i.e., farmer associations, cooperatives, mothers' clubs." Partner organizations were to be selected on the basis of "... track records that indicate management capability for social development projects and some experience with credit delivery." However, since NGOs would demonstrate varying levels of competence, a second, important objective was "... to strengthen these indigenous organizations which assist the poor ... both through sharing project management, financial management, and consultancy skills of the CARE-IGP staff and through networking the staff skills of the various partner organizations themselves at workshops and training conferences."

REACH (Rural Enterprise Assistance Center) Origins

REACH was founded by staff who came from a now defunct state corporation, the Farm Systems Development Corporation (FSDC). The REACH "clients" also came from the FSDC. The latter had organized small-scale farmers who worked on small, community-based irrigation systems (of a hundred hectares or less) into Irrigation Systems Associations (the initials ISA mean "one" in Tagalog). The ISAs were formed into a federation, one per province in the Philippines. REACH itself was an outgrowth of the ISA in Cebu.

The FSDC objectives included an "income-generating component" that predated CARE. The FSDC expected the ISAs to become private, self-supporting enterprises; this goal was to be attained by securing large institutional loans for rice and feed mills. The income from mill operations would then support the ISA federation and pay back the loans.

Implementation of the FSDC plan was not particularly successful: For example, the land needed as collateral for the loan (to finance the rice mill) proved difficult to secure. The choice sites were expensive or unavailable, and land that was donated was usually not conveniently located for the prospective rice mill to service its potential clients. Furthermore, the oil crisis of 1979 raised both capital and operating costs; the peso depreciated further, and the interest burden increased on dollar-denominated loans for the mills and irrigation pumps. Most of the ISAs defaulted, farmers stopped paying for the use of irrigation facilities, and many mills went bankrupt. In 1984, the ISA federations were still financially dependent on FSDC, particularly for staff salaries. These problems were compounded by the national scale of the operation, by the depletion of international fund sources, and by the internal disintegration of the FSDC following the changeover in political administrations in 1986.

The ISA-Cebu federation did not contain a large, rice-growing population; it was therefore too small to obtain loans for the rice mill operation. It thereby had avoided the problems of high debt on fixed assets and high cost of operations. The ISA-Cebu staff, under its manager, Ramon "Monching" Barriga, evolved its own national plan "... to offer farmers diversified training in farm production, technology and credit." However, because the ISA-Cebu was low on the FSDC's list of priorities, it had to seek funds sources elsewhere.

The first contact between CARE and REACH occurred when the REACH staff were still part of FSDC and the ISA federation, and CARE was still running its experimental IGP, and directly servicing community groups. The ISA-Cebu manager, Monching Barriga, contacted the CARE Cebu field staff in September 1984, and later the CARE Country Director, Charles Lasky, on the possibility of funding the ISA. The inquiry led to an invitation for Barriga to attend the CARE annual meeting as a guest speaker. The two managers then went on to explore the concept of CARE's use of indigenous organizations as the intermediary mechanism for the IGP, in order to expand CARE's IGP operations. ISA-Cebu was CARE's first major and regular partner; eventually it was reconstituted in 1984 as REACH, emphasizing a new identity distinct from the organization's FSDC-ISA origins.

CARE-REACH: 1984–86 Operations

REACH originally planned its projects for the subsistence upland farmers, who had no access to irrigation. However, the upland projects, such as tree farming and orchard development, required long-term investment, and CARE was then only able to provide medium-term loans of two or three years. REACH then designed a project to combine rice and vegetable farming. However, a typhoon intervened, partially destroying the irrigation system. REACH therefore first asked and received from CARE funds to repair this damage. REACH repaired the damage on schedule, below budget, and expanded the irrigation system in the process.

By mid-1985, FSDC funds, and indeed the FSDC itself, were in jeopardy. The ISA infrastructure was shrinking rapidly, and REACH reduced its staff to anticipate the cutoff of funds. At the same time, other colleagues in the ISA community approached REACH searching for other sources of funds. REACH in turn took the matter up with CARE.

The "networking" concept seemed applicable to the ISAs. Individuals in the different ISAs had valuable skills: in cattle or rice production, for example. Since all the ISAs had to trim their staff, survival now depended on sharing the resources of the remaining core staff with their respective resident experts. By early 1986, the ISAs were bereft of funding from their parent, FSDC, and some ISAs had joined REACH.

REACH created a working board from the different managers of the old ISAs, and CARE joined the board as a nonvoting member. The board screened new members and new projects. For instance, one idea, which CARE agreed to, was to lend the ISAs funds "... to purchase a plot of land which would function as a demonstration center for integrated farming. This land would also be a form of collateral base for them, so that, as owners of land, they would be able to secure other funds for their organization."

CARE in turn assigned its project officers to review REACH decisions and operations regularly, and CARE began providing REACH with management tools for project analysis and financial control. CARE provided REACH with documentation for project proposals, financial projections, farm planning budgets, and loan status reports.

CARE also offered management advice. Consultation between CARE and REACH at the area office, sub-project level usually took place during monitoring visits. For example,

> One ISA was having trouble calculating their collection rate ... In this case, the CARE staff person would go through the calculations with them and make sure that they understood the calculation and what they were looking for. In the field, CARE would also show them how to put together systems of a particular Area Office that would collect accurate data. This is done by helping them to identify where the problems exist with data collection: Is it out in the field with the technician? Is there a gap in time before the harvest comes? ... CARE helps them identify and correct the "break-down" in the system. By working on a one-on-one basis with the rural manager, CARE hopes to offer the assistance and education needed so that the ISAs become sound businesses.

CARE also ran several training courses for REACH and its affiliates in 1986 on group building, designing action plans, project management and needs assessment, and technical transfer communication and formal presentations. At the REACH board meetings, CARE posed such questions as: "What is a well-managed organization?" Each area office then analyzed its organization and designed a plan to "upgrade" the organization.

CARE and REACH Organization Charts

The core IGP staff numbered about a dozen, or approximately 10 percent of the total CARE staff. The upland project in Mindanao was not part of the original IGP. (See Exhibit 1 for the partial CARE organization chart.) REACH itself was never a large organization. In 1987, it had a core staff of five men and three women, almost all in their early thirties or younger. Each REACH Field Manager had a corresponding monitoring CARE Project Officer. Exhibit 2 represents the casewriter's depiction of the REACH organization chart.

CARE IGP Staff's Views on REACH

Nancy Hopkins

Nancy Hopkins was the IGP Program Officer. She had previously worked with USAID on a short-term contract dealing with project co-financing for local PVOs; her prior experience included liaison work between family planning programs and funding agencies and PVOs. In 1984, she met Charles Lasky, CARE's Country Director, who was in the process of rethinking the 1981 IGP. The new IGP was to work with NGOs rather than directly with village groups, and her task was to begin discussions with NGOs and to write up the new IGP project proposal for CARE-International's evaluation.

The proposal was submitted to New York in early 1985, while Nancy Hopkins continued working with possible partners. The proposal emphasized CARE's role as a "catalyst," that is, CARE would design the program and the PVOs would be the primary channel to implement the IGP. CARE would initially provide a financial "umbrella" for the PVOs to operate, and would be the "hub" through which the PVOs would operate.

The concept of counterparts was acceptable to CARE; however, its traditional partners were established government line agencies, and not NGOs. Furthermore, CARE did not see itself as a lending institution, but more as a service organization for technical, logistics, and management functions, and at best a possible broker for other, larger, financially oriented organizations. According to Nancy Hopkins, "Lasky thought it [the new IGP] was a long shot." But the old IGP had stretched CARE's organizational resources. As the old IGP expanded, funds were being disbursed without sufficient supervision and evaluation; there was no regular or formal mechanism for feedback other than collection and receivables reports.

The proposal was approved after six months. An executive from New York came to Manila to discuss the project and to look over the activities in Cebu. While he was apparently somewhat skeptical about the project, the new IGP was approved on a one-year trial basis for several reasons: the farmers interviewed believed that they did benefit from the IGP; CARE-Philippines could not expand the IGP much further with its existing staff; CARE-Philippines and Charles Lasky expressed their confidence in the IGP concept and in its partners, REACH in particular; the project could start small, but could "expand like an accordion"; and there were funds left over from another program.

The expanded IGP proceeded on several tracks: other funding sources had to be found, partners screened and "sub-projects" evaluated; CARE staff for the IGP was increased; expert consultants (for example, for small enterprise development) were sought. But the key locus of activity was between CARE and REACH.

The relationship started with the meeting in 1984 between Charles Lasky and Monching Barriga. It was strengthened by REACH's demonstration of competence in the rehabilitation of the irrigation project, and expanded as Barriga brought in more ISAs to REACH and to CARE. (CARE already had been screening sub-projects that Barriga's colleagues in the ISAs had brought to them.)

By late 1985, the relationship was firm enough for the two organizations to think about how REACH could maintain itself over the long run. REACH had originally asked CARE to fund a rice mill. CARE was unwilling to enter into fixed asset financing and sought out other sources for REACH. However, the notion of direct lending to support partner organizations began to take shape, as did the concept of each partner's developing its own income-generating activities to support itself.

REACH significantly expanded in 1986 and began exploring entrepreneurial, income-generating projects for itself. One activity was to move into rice trading, which REACH thought was a natural extension of its rice production sub-projects. REACH also began exploring other activities for landless farmers. As "squatters" on the land, they had no incentive to improve it, so cattle grazing or fattening emerged as a project for them. Monching Barriga also met with other ISAs, and CARE's "networking" concept was becoming a reality. Under Barriga, the ISAs discussed their future, for example, as one unit, or as a federation of local foundations. REACH was also interested in making contact with other national and international foundations. Barriga provided the vision and enthusiasm to get people together; he also used these skills when he became a city counselor in mid-1986.

At this time, the ISAs and REACH were in an organizational limbo. They were still part of a disintegrating FSDC, which was rapidly proving unable to provide regularly for staff salaries and the upkeep of its assets (offices, supplies, and jeeps). The small staff of REACH had been depending on FSDC-employed "Institutional Officers" (IOs) for maintaining field operations. FSDC experts, for example, rice technicians, were being absorbed into the Ministry/Department of Agriculture, under the new administration. In the last quarter of 1986, salaries had not been fully paid. FSDC was dissolving, and CARE procedures for salary support for REACH were still being worked out; morale among the ISAs and REACH was faltering.

In early 1987, Nancy Hopkins was becoming concerned about REACH's situation. She made a field visit in February, and she noticed the concern of Monching Barriga over salaries for the staff. At the same time, the financial problems—outstanding receivables, delays and defaults in collections, and poor sub-project performance—began to emerge. Most of the sub-project loans were made to rice farmers, and the lending process tended to follow the agricultural harvest cycle of roughly six months. Cash needs therefore reflected high seasonal peaks and valleys, rather than exhibiting a balanced stream of cash flow in and out.

By March, it was necessary to evaluate the existing sub-projects before considering new activities. One of the CARE IGP staff officers "read the riot act" to REACH. He was upset that the farmers' organizations were not cohesive and were not keeping their accounts up-to-date; these current observations were the opposite of his own observations a year before. He believed that REACH had not acted enough on his recommendations for loan control and accountability that he had made in mid-1986. Nancy Hopkins thought that REACH might have been too confident about its abilities in rice production and trading and in community development and group building, and had not realized how much it still depended on the FSDC support structure (for example, on the IOs, the rice technicians).

Orlando "Boy" Abelgas

Boy Abelgas was the Assistant Program Manager of the CARE IGP. He was hired by Nancy Hopkins in mid-1985 as the IGP Project Officer. Boy Abelgas' career was in the social development area: He had entered a Jesuit diocesan seminary in Cebu, but after spending a year as a volunteer among slum dwellers, he decided to continue his social development activities outside the priesthood. In 1975, he joined the Philippine Business for Social Progress (PBSP), a PVO funded by contributions from private corporations. He stayed with PBSP until 1983, in several of its regional offices, but was basically interested in Cebu. He shifted to a UNFPA-PCF (Population Center Foundation) pilot project for the urban poor on a professional consultant's contract; while there, a friend introduced him to CARE.

At CARE, Abelgas assisted Nancy Hopkins in refocusing the MYP (Multi-Year Plan) of the IGP. His first major task was to draw up the IGP operating guidelines, which he developed in part from his PBSP experience. By 1986, he was more heavily involved directly with the ISAs—evaluating their organizations and their activities with their beneficiaries.

Abelgas followed the partner selection guidelines that were common to PBSP, CARE, and other national agencies: a track record of social development work, and indications of organizational and financial stability. He thought that some of the partners identified by CARE would not have immediately qualified for assistance under PBSP's more stringent application of the criteria. But he believed that CARE was not interested in "tailgating PBSP"; rather, that CARE wanted to establish itself with a broader partner base and clientele, by transferring its expertise into providing operational support funds for production inputs (instead of food) and technical and management services (in lieu of health and nutrition delivery).

Boy Abelgas offered his views on the CARE experience with REACH: Monching Barriga apparently foresaw the dissolution of the FSDC and began seeking other funds sources and "parent" organizations for his ISA federation in Cebu; he found CARE. The relationship was tentative at first; the FSDC "family" of organizations had a poor image. But he and CARE were apparently convinced by the dedication and enthusiasm of the ISA-Cebu that they could carry out its work with its clients regardless of FSDC's dissolution.

On the other hand, Abelgas, and others at CARE noticed that the REACH staff was still "in-bred," that is, it was accustomed to the FSDC support structure and was clearly unfamiliar with the requirements of an international foundation and the approach of CARE in particular. There were problems with fitting REACH's needs for sub-project funds and for salaries into the CARE budget procedures. More critical was the dependence of REACH on the FSDC field staff, the IOs, for field visits to the sub-project beneficiaries. The organizational layers were also stretching REACH's limited core staff. Funds, reports, and some decisions on sub-projects traveled back and forth between CARE's Manila head office to the offices of CARE and REACH in Cebu, to the REACH IOs, to the ISA "offices," and to its members.

Boy Abelgas also felt that REACH was, in his words, "taking in too much, too soon," given the simultaneous expansion tasks in 1986 of financing, sub-project development, and the search for its own entrepreneurial income-generating activities. All this took place at a time when

REACH's manpower resources were effectively declining with FSDC's dissolution. Rice trading proved extremely difficult for REACH, which had apparently assumed that the skills of rice production, with which its staff were somewhat familiar, were similar and transferable to this activity. The latter became "... a working capital drain, and by early 1987, the damage had been done."

With regard to operations, 1987 also required more intensive monitoring by CARE, particularly when the rice trading operations "got caught up in receivables"; poor accounting resulted in selling prices below total costs, cattle fattening technology and markets were proving unsatisfactory, and a fire damaged REACH facilities. However, Boy Abelgas believed that the financial distress was only a symptom of more basic problems: He thought that REACH staff "... suffered from misplaced intentions ... and used credit as a social objective, not as a business objective. REACH's strength was in its idealism, but it lacked the balance of realism." For example, the rice trading operation may have been an indication of enthusiasm and optimism and a "can-do" philosophy overtaking competence and sound judgment. CARE did not react to this potential problem at once, because REACH in fact had developed some of its own control procedures for the rice trading project: "... solid procedures which looked good on paper but suffered from problems of implementation ... they took exception to their own procedures." CARE then undertook stronger action after its initial attempts to use persuasion and suggestions proved unsuccessful. So Abelgas spent May to June "getting our act straight" with REACH, and using the financial data to "temper" its optimism.

CARE'S Assessment of REACH'S Problems

Assessing REACH (May 1987)

CARE made an assessment of the IGP and REACH in its mid-1987 Planning, Implementation, and Evaluation (PIE) Report. By this time, CARE had eleven partners, including REACH. CARE had the largest financial commitment with REACH. However, another foundation, TOUCH, was recently formed from another ISA in another major island, Mindanao, and CARE's exposure there was rapidly increasing. Because of the similarity of origins and activities, CARE carefully analyzed the REACH situation in order to avoid repeating its problems.

The assessment brought out two major problems, those related to technology or production, and those related to participants—either the partners or the beneficiaries. For example, the cattle fattening project resulted in below-average actual incomes to the target beneficiaries because "(a) the participants did not adhere closely to the recommended technology; (b) quality stock were not available; (c) alternative protein substi-

tutes were not available; and (d) the partner organization failed to monitor and interact with the beneficiaries." The rice trading project also
failed because "(a) the partner organization staff deviated from the the
basic strategy; and (b) ineffective implementation of the revised marketing strategy worked-out with the CARE Program Officer." The PIE Report arrived at the following assessment of REACH:

> REACH ... was beset with the following problems ...: key was
> that the General Manager's time was split off by political/civic duties
> and that the newly recruited Executive Officer was unable to begin
> when expected due to delays in the completion of his thesis followed
> by emergency surgery.
>
> Structural problems and faltering morale ... led to: Financial
> problems (e.g., inability to meet cash operating needs, particularly
> the salaries of field staff due to low collection rate from sub-projects).
> This resulted in the loss of several field staff ... We have held off
> funding additional projects until they could stabilize their staff situa-
> tion.
>
> Limited expertise of the field staff in rice trading and livestock
> technology ... caused part of the problems in collections. These staff
> were replaced.
>
> Poor marketing management and lack of entrepreneurial skills in
> rice marketing. When cash sales faltered, they turned to credit sales
> in direct disregard for their own policy and tied up large chunks of
> operating capital in delinquent accounts.

The result was closer coordination between CARE and REACH staff.
Regular and more formal consultations were set up, and CARE staff
"dug deeper" into the REACH situation. At the same time, the PIE noted
the REACH staff's "... willingness to take a hard look at itself and make
necessary corrective actions."

The ARIES Strategic Overview Paper

In early 1987, when CARE was exploring various avenues for analyzing
the performance of REACH and its other partners, it received a draft
copy of the ARIES Strategic Overview Paper. CARE decided to use the
framework of that paper as a part of its evaluation of REACH's performance. Abelgas thought that the framework was somewhat similar in
structure to PBSP, and offered several advantages: it made explicit the
proponent's (for example, REACH's) development program and expressed the need for REACH to develop a "mission statement." Abelgas
thought that the ARIES framework could be exploited to develop
REACH. (See Figure 1.) The framework was given an acronym: SCAT—
for Strategy, Communications, Administration, and Technical. SCAT was
used in the review of REACH sub-projects and, as a means to specify

Figure 1. Applying the ARIES Framework to REACH

Cebu Area: Cattle & Hog Fattening   *Bohol Area: Cattle Fattening*

Strategic

Area management showed weaknesses in planning and setting up priorities.

Same. Inability to foresee marketing constraints and market for the cattle.

Communications

Weak in community organizing and ineffective community extension services. Overall communications of the partner is not very effective. Inability to link with government agencies and other associations for coordinated technical assistance and training necessary for effective implementation.

Good organizational development and community extension services. No internal reporting system in writing from the IO to the area manager on field visits. Data on the income, weight gain, and expenses for the farmer participants were not established. Improve accuracy and analysis of reports to CARE to become effective. No linkage for technical assistance was established.

Administration

Monitoring, supervision, implementation, and control was weak, and monitoring visits at area level were seldom done. Lack of capability to handle livestock technology for cattle and hogs and limited ability to handle technical assistance by the partner to the participants.

Limited technical ability of the area manager and institutional officer about cattle fattening; technology management attention was divided and not focused on CARE's project.

Technical

Weak in financial planning/ accounting; system encountered problems of collection which greatly affected their operations; failed to establish effective credit and collection management; under-utilization of loan-fund balance.

Financial planning/projections need improvement; limited knowledge of accounting and financial analysis.

---

the inputs and responsibilities of the REACH officers, to replace the diffused group decision making that prevailed at REACH after Barriga's job as city counsellor took up more of his time.

After the meeting, REACH drew up a list of recommendations, which included reviewing the strengths and weaknesses of its managers in the above areas, an action plan, and an annual operation and financial plan.

Internal Controls

CARE had also set up monitoring and control procedures for the IGP, based on its long experience in health care delivery services as well as on the "on-the-job" experiences of the IGP staff; CARE also used external consultants and procedures used by other NGOs, such as PBSP. The procedures evolved over the course of the IGP, and were not completely in place in 1987, but they were extensive; the manual of operations in 1987 consisted of a hundred pages of forms, from the selection and screening to performance audit and evaluation.

The documents were quite detailed. For example, there were ten "Basic Principles of Internal Control" in the IGP manual, as follows:

1. Fixing of responsibility. Without proper charge of responsibility, the quality of control will be inefficient.
2. Segregation of the accounting and operations functions.
3. No one person should be in complete control of the whole business transaction.
4. Use of available proofs of accuracy.
5. Careful selection and training of employees.
6. Rotation of employees on a job.
7. Bonding of employees.
8. Writing down instructions for each problem.
9. Use of controlling accounts as extensively as possible.
10. Use of mechanical equipment whenever possible.

The manual noted eight "Minimum Internal Control Requirements":

1. Use of double-entry system of bookkeeping.
2. Prompt recording of transactions and balancing of accounts.
3. Deposit of all cash receipts intact daily and making all payments by check signed and scrutinized by authorized signatories. If cash receipts cannot be deposited intact daily, a member of the group or a properly designated officer should conduct surprise cash counts for all funds kept by the custodian at least twice a week.
4. Preparation of monthly comparative statement of operations for review by management.
5. Use of serially numbered forms and proper control over these forms.

6. Monthly reconciliation of bank balances.
7. Periodic audit by a designated internal auditor, or, as an alternative, submission to CARE-Philippines of audited yearly financial statements.
8. Use of adding machines, cash boxes, and physical safeguards.

Finally, the "internal control checklist" contained items such as: "vouchers should be executed in ink ... to make alteration difficult" and "beneficiary ledgers should be balanced regularly with the controlling account ... to check on the accuracy of the records."

CARE Field Report on REACH

The CARE Program Officers (POs) were primarily concerned with project development, monitoring and evaluation of sub-projects, management and technical advisory services to partner organization, and related documentation. They discussed the development of sub-projects with REACH, and tried to reach agreement on action plans. However, REACH was the implementing agency and until the financial crisis, "moral suasion" was the main tool available to CARE.

The reports of the CARE POs highlighted the operating problems of REACH's activities: The ISA rice and feed mills were poorly located because they depended upon donated land for their locations; the piggery projects to complement the feed mill operations were not feasible because REACH could not attain economies of scale and cost of feed was uncompetitive. The REACH staff depended too much on the auxiliary-FSDC support staff, particularly the IOs, and became desk-bound managers instead of field managers. One result was poor management and supervision over the beneficiaries. The latter entered and left sub-projects without sufficient control by REACH; the beneficiaries of some activities were scattered and had small land holdings, so a sub-project had too many beneficiaries for the core REACH staff to monitor; there was insufficient follow-up among the farmers of the technical package, the utilization of farm inputs, and the farm budget.

CARE demonstrated its concern with the viability of REACH by increasing its visits to the field from its main office staff. One memo in early September documented the following problems:

The books of account are in a state of shambles. This is only partially attributable to the destruction of records during the fire which gutted the REACH office in May.

Longstanding unliquidated cash advances to employees have tied up a substantial portion of the working capital of the sub-projects (e.g., 20–25% of the Rice Trading Project) ... Such advances can only be partially attributed to the delayed release of support funds for salary expenses.

Not only did the Rice Trading operation extend credit sales, they imposed no interest or penalty charges on unpaid accounts of individual customers ...

REACH is now essentially without field staff as its two previous Institutional Offices opted to be absorbed by the Department of Agriculture upon the abolition of the FSDC ...

With the abolition of FSDC and the fire in May, REACH is almost completely without assets ...

Three projects are located in an isolated area which is also experiencing severe peace and order problems ... Consideration should be given to phasing out of this area ...

... Baseline data [are] lacking. Repayment rates are very low. Working capital has been depleted through losses or is tied up in receivables and unaccounted advances. REACH lacks the resources to meet even the most minimal of operating expenses.

... The current policy of rotating project officers ... including assigning of a project officer based in Manila, undermines CARE's ability to provide the required support ...

In discussing the memo, Nancy Hopkins noted that:

... the problems have all been discussed and specific verbal and written recommendations made by the CARE program officer in March both to the area manager and to the REACH Board as a whole. The problem is not a lack of knowing the problems or knowing how to solve them. The answer is teaching REACH staff how to manage their priorities, time and resources through appropriate planning ... In summary, REACH ... has few material resources. This has been well known from the beginning ... What impressed us from the beginning was the ability of these people to take almost nothing and make it something. The human resources are there, not in number but in experience and in willingness to do what must be done to survive as an organization and to make the sub-projects viable.

Nancy Hopkins believed that the new REACH organization, with an executive officer to check the drift following the reduced involvement of Barriga, was the first positive step. The executive officer was a REACH staff member who was formerly with one FSDC area office. He had a clear mandate to work with the rest of the REACH staff (1) to firm up the control systems, (2) to improve REACH's financial position, (3) to consolidate existing sub-projects and to review the performance of the beneficiaries, (4) to rethink REACH's policies and procedures, and (5) to develop a short-term action or survival plan for REACH.

Boy Abelgas thought that after CARE "put its foot down" in August, REACH had started "to own up" to its problems. The entry of a new Country Director and the operations audits by CARE Manila office staff had brought the message home. Abelgas, as a nonvoting member of REACH's board (who were also its operating managers), stated in no uncertain terms that if REACH failed to "turn around" while under CARE, no other institution was likely to accept it. At the same time, Abelgas thought that the REACH staff officers had "become fat cats, and were now back to being hungry, and that was good for them." REACH was back to the basics, and focusing on its survival, through "probationary action plans" subject to monthly review and revision.

REACH'S Self-Assessment

REACH's Response

The REACH staff responded to its problems by carrying out, on its own, an analysis of its organization and policies, based in part on the above CARE analysis. A REACH conference in mid-1987 applied three elements of the ARIES framework in terms of the organization's strengths and weaknesses; by this time, the IOs were no longer functioning, and "Communications" was a direct effort between REACH and its beneficiaries. (See Figure 2.)

Figure 2. REACH Strengths and Weaknesses in Key Capacity Areas

Strengths	*Weaknesses*
	Strategic
Knowledge of farmer clients	Inadequate comprehensive strategy
Network of farmer associations	Lack of clarity about REACH policies
A production base	Inadequate operating plan
	Technical
Credit and technical expertise and institutional competence	Poor credit management
	Inadequate market monitoring
Actual experience in crop and livestock production	Must update technologies
	Improve community building
	Improve enterprise management skills
	Administration/Organization
Committed, motivated staff	Inadequate policies, procedures and systems in budget and audit
Close contact with clients	
Links with NGOs and other agencies	Inadequate fund sources
	Lack of manpower
	Rapid action = hasty decisions

As a result of the preceding analysis, REACH prepared an action plan to remedy its perceived weaknesses. The plan included organizing training sessions, designing and implementing systems, and working out

operating plans on a month-to-month basis, for monthly review. The entire organization was involved in the plan, given its small size.

In late 1987, REACH also completed a review of its internal controls.
Some problems noted were: "Cash fund vouchers are not cancelled after
payment ... Cash receipts are sometimes not deposited daily ... bank
reconciliations are not prepared ... doubtful account allowances are not
maintained ... inventory on hand (belonging to the rice mill operator) are
stocked inside the warehouse and without proper accounting control."

REACH's Philosophy

REACH reassessed its "reason for existence" by attempting to articulate
clearly its organizational philosophy at an August 1987 Conference. At
the conference, a number of ideas surfaced during a brainstorming session:

Beliefs
- farmer as entrepreneur, to manage farm resources for higher productivity and income
- respect for farmers
- entrepreneurship
- farming as a "no-nonsense" activity

Values
- excellence in what we do
- hands-on interaction
- pioneer appropriate
  technology in the locality
- bias for action

Roles/Norms/Standards
- output/result oriented
- awareness of commitment
- flexibility
- optimum use of resources

Behavior
- approachability
- open-mindedness
- humility

Structure
- simple and lean
- staying close to client-farmers
- active participation of farmers
- accessibility to farmers

REACH Reassesses the Assumptions

At another discussion in its mid-September meeting, the staff asked
itself two questions: What is the situation we are in? How did we get
there? The answers were summarized as shown in Figure 3.

The discussion resulted in a twelve-point "principles for action" that
corrected the erroneous presumptions noted above—for example, "check
that farmers are clear and knowledgeable about the project objectives."

The above organizational soul searching notwithstanding, REACH
still had to deal with the issue of project viability and its financial problems. REACH evaluated each sub-project and the beneficiaries involved.
Most sub-projects could be sustained only at reduced levels. A few activ-

Figure 3. Situation and Causes

Situation We Are In	The Thinking That Led to It
Did not discuss thoroughly with farmers	"It's enough to discuss once"
Did not conduct regular meetings and project visits	Expected farmers to act on their own; "no meeting, no problem"
Not familiar with project beneficiaries	Left responsibility to auxiliaries (IOs)
Did not study IGP proposal	"Just a proposal" "CARE is not a strict monitor"
Slow release of funds	"Puede na" (it's OK) attitude
No collection plan; sloppy	Trusted the beneficiaries to act without supervision
No project documentation	Documents serve no purpose
Inadequate record keeping	Did not feel the need for it
No management control system	Funds can be moved around; no sanctions for lack of it; "we trust the people"
No working capital analysis No formal reports	Did not see its purpose "Puede na"
No follow-up on activities	Activities will happen by themselves

ities had to be terminated; for instance, after a field visit to the San Roque ISA, where REACH exposure amounted to over RP P 90,000, the Executive Officer reported in late October that "... the farmer members ... decided to terminate our San Roque ISA Cattle Fattening Project due to the losses incurred by a majority of the beneficiaries attributed to the absence of good market for fattened cattle in the area during the disposal of the stocks and our inability to assist them in looking for markets outside our province as committed to by our office before the start of the project."

REACH was also concerned with maintaining direct contact with its client-ISAs and their members. In general, each REACH Field Manager tried to visit the sub-project once each week, spending a day in each project. Some variation occurred among the areas, depending upon road access, peace and order conditions, and the sub-project's distance from the area main office. One day might be sufficient to evaluate a sub-project, but the managers thought that three days in a locality were needed to make contact with the ISA members, particularly for collections.

The financial constraint affected field visits in so far as the managers felt that a three-day visit per project would require additional daily living expenses, and such a schedule might not be sustainable through the use of public transport. The staff limitations were more critical, since during the rice harvests the managers "had to be everywhere at once" and had to deal with the sub-project as well as with the beneficiaries themselves. For example, the opportunity for collections from rice farmers was after the harvest, when farm income was at its peak; beyond that time, the income tended to dry up quickly, and collecting became more difficult. Beneficiaries were issued promissory notes, and they were organized into groups (usually based on the ISA). But the presumption that a group could police itself and collect from its members proved to be a "fair-weather" assumption.

Financial Information on REACH Activities

REACH also hoped to expand its operations despite its current difficulties. However, it was still dependent upon CARE, and in mid-November it submitted a request for additional CARE support in loans and grants. A projected cash flow for the first six months of 1988 showed the necessity of CARE financial support. (See Exhibit 3.) The projection reflected the peaks and valleys of agricultural loan financing; harvests occurred roughly every six months, and loans were recorded on a semestral basis. REACH prepared a request to CARE for salary and working capital support up to U.S.$5,000. The financial activities of REACH are illustrated further in Exhibits 4–6.

Conclusion

Initial Results

By year-end 1987, REACH had begun (1) to cluster sub-projects, (2) to restructure its own and its sub-project loans, and (3) to improve collections. According to Nancy Hopkins, REACH appeared to have reasserted its "will" to continue, and the new recognition of financial rigor and control over field operations should begin to bear fruit.

According to Boy Abelgas, the REACH financial performance was obviously unsatisfactory, but his estimate of a 25 percent failure rate in collections was probably no worse than other understaffed and overextended NGOs, or even rural banks, that were trying both to become entrepreneurs and to develop entrepreneurs (among the beneficiaries) in a notoriously fickle agricultural environment. He did not feel uncomfortable with CARE's guidelines or its procedures, and he thought that the problem lay not in the criteria but in the "nature of the individual organizations," that is, some NGOs would be stronger than other NGOs in some aspects, and weaker in others. Each partner would have to be monitored and evaluated on a case-by-case basis; otherwise, "the alternative is to just pick and choose from the established organizations" for partners, and to forego the partner-development aspect of the IGP. He concluded by noting that the IGP belonged to an emerging "family" of similar programs (for example, rural capital formation, small enterprise development) run by other international agencies, and that the IGP had a future with CARE.

CARE had already begun to apply its experience to its new partners. Its IGP staff were more aggressive in insisting on basic control mechanisms, and more vigilant in monitoring sub-project expansion. The REACH experience offered "rules of thumb," for example, on avoiding the dispersal of sub-projects, on ascertaining the technical requirements of sub-projects, and on realizing the difference in skills needed to manage marketing (as opposed to production) activities.

Key Decisions

By year-end 1987, CARE had to decide what measures to take with respect to REACH. These included methods of control as well as support for the foundation. In addition, as the Dunn memo indicated, CARE itself had to learn from the REACH experience, in dealing with its other partners. The IGP was expanding, based on the multi-year plan, and new problems had to be anticipated. Finally, the IGP itself had to be reviewed in the light of CARE's experience with REACH.

The New IGP Operating Manager

By year-end 1987, CARE had also completed its reorganization in the Philippines. Under a new area-based setup, the IGP would still exist as a distinct unit, although the staff were located in the respective CARE field offices. However, the present IGP operations would be under a new area manger, Gilda Martinez, who was based in Cebu, and was familiar with IGP operations, but whose major responsibility in CARE was with its food program. As the Area Manager for the East Office, she would supervise both the food and IGP operations.

Exhibit 1
CARE ORGANIZATION CHART (Partial)

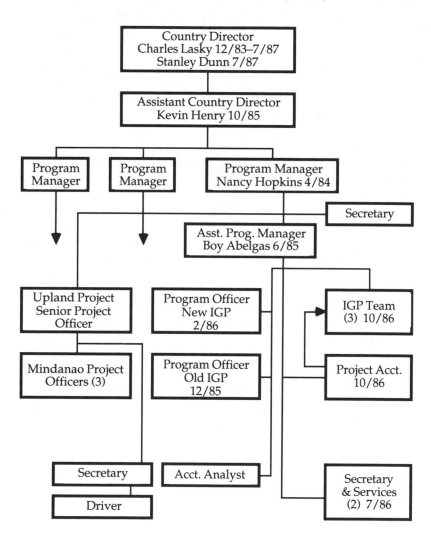

Exhibit 2
REACH ORGANIZATION CHART

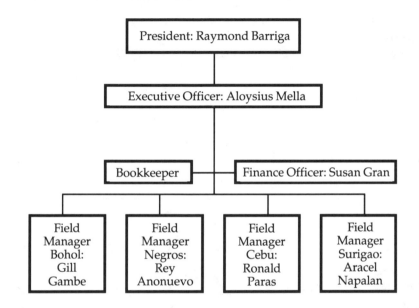

Exhibit 3
PROJECTED CASH FLOW STATEMENT (12/87–6/88)
(RP Pesos 000's)

	Dec.	Jan.	Feb.	Mar.	Apr.	May	Jun.
Inflow							
Beginning Balance	1	338	(32)	(41)	(55)	(30)	417
Repayment of Principal	311	72	9	65	35	421	29
Repayment of Interest	44	8	1	6	4	54	3
Income from Enterprises	29	7	4	11	19	16	13
Totals	385	425	(18)	41	3	461	462
Outflow							
Loan Releases	11	438	4	77	15	25	458
Operating Expenses	35	19	19	19	19	19	19
Totals	46	457	23	96	34	44	477
Ending Balance	339	(32)	(41)	(55)	(31)	417	(15)

Note: ( ) denotes negative.

Exhibit 4
REACH FINANCIAL ACTIVITIES

	12/85	6/86	10/86	3/87	11/87
Sub-Project Loans Outstanding (RP P Millions)	1.93	1.68	1.17	1.44	1.44
Grant Support Funds Outstanding (RP P Millions)	—	0.25	0.25	0.40	0.40
No. of Sub-Projects	3	23	23	27	27
No. of Direct Beneficiaries	106	496	530	552	552
No. of Indirect Beneficiaries[a]	—	2,844	2,844	2,994	2,994

[a] Includes rice trading operations.

Exhibit 5
SUB-PROJECT BREAKDOWN, 1987
(RP Pesos)

	Cebu	Bohol	Negros	Surigao
Rice Production	107,500	152,255	91,160	97,853
Cattle Fattening	146,819	93,016	52,500	20,537
Hog Fattening	6,300	—	19,800	—
Rice Trading[a]	30,000	119,952	80,000	99,900
Integrated Farming[a]	138,310	—	—	—
Crop and Livestock Center[a]	—	—	145,176	—
Totals	428,929	365,223	388,636	218,290

[a] These activities were undertaken by REACH in order to generate income for the REACH overhead and organization.

Exhibit 6
OUTSTANDING LOANS AS OF NOVEMBER 30, 1987
(RP Pesos)

Province and Sub-Project	Principal	Interest	No. Semesters Past Due (1 sem. = 6 mos.)
Cebu			
Rice Production	30,000	22,000	3
Rice Production	900	1,400	1
Cattle Fattening	19,000	14,700	3
Cattle Fattening	11,000	18,000	1
Rice Trading	7,500	7,000	2
Bohol			
Rice Production	12,000	27,000	1
Rice Trading	15,000	24,000	2
Cattle Fattening		15,000	1
Negros Oriental			
Rice Production	6,500	11,800	1
Rice Trading	10,000	16,000	2
Cattle Fattening	6,500	11,000	1
Hog Fattening	2,500	3,700	1
Surigao del Norte			
Rice Production	—	10,000	1
Cattle Fattening	—	3,500	1
Demo Farm	600	900	1
Rice Trading	12,000	20,000	2
Total	133,500	206,000	

Case 7

The Carvajal Foundation "MICROS" Program (A): Reorienting an Organization and Choosing a Model

This case was written by Margaret Bowman, in collaboration with Merilee S. Grindle. It is intended as a basis for class discussion rather than as an illustration of either effective or ineffective handling of an administrative situation. The collaboration and support of the President and Executive Director of Carvajal Foundation and their staff are gratefully acknowledged.

In 1976, Weimar Escobar, a young economist, was hired as an advisor by Pedro Sardi, to help start a micro-enterprise assistance program at the Carvajal Foundation. Because assistance to small businesses was a new undertaking for the Foundation, the President of the Foundation sent Pedro, the Foundation's Micro-enterprise Director, and Weimar to visit UNO, a highly regarded micro-enterprise program in Brazil. Their purpose was to analyze which elements of that program could be transferred to Cali. Weimar and Pedro were particularly interested in learning the details of how the program was run and how it balanced the provision of credit, management assistance, and business training. Both were convinced by the President of the Foundation that the program would need to provide some combination of these services. To their disappointment, however, they discovered that the UNO project, like many other enterprise projects, focused almost exclusively on providing credit.[1] It therefore seemed of little assistance in helping them determine how to provide the other services. It became Weimar's responsibility to recommend a program design that was consistent with the Carvajal Foundation philosophy based on the scarce empirical evidence to which he had access.

The Carvajal Foundation

The Carvajal Foundation is located in Cali, a city with a population of 1.2 million. The Foundation was started in 1961 when members of the Carvajal family decided to make 40 percent of the shares of the Carvajal Company, one of the largest corporations in Colombia, available for philanthropic development projects. The Carvajal Foundation is the largest Colombian foundation and continues to be financed and managed by the Carvajal family.[2] The Carvajal family has a strong sense of civic consciousness and formed the nonprofit foundation to enable it to respond to the problems of the city and the region. The family is highly respected within Colombia and has close contacts with government officials and business leaders. As a result, the Foundation has a level of financial security and influence that is rare among private development organizations. The Carvajal Foundation has been influential in setting government policy in a number of fields, but it has played a particularly prominent role in developing educational institutions.[3] The management of the Carvajal Foundation believes firmly in the importance of education in national development and, as a result, has a strong philosophical commitment to promoting education in most of its philanthropic undertakings.

Originally, in the early 1960s, the Carvajal Foundation had a "social service" approach in its work and focused on providing a range of social services to disadvantaged communities through "parochial centers" run by the Catholic church in Cali. Those centers were located in the slum areas—barrios—and provided health programs, natural family planning, organized sports, and cultural activities. Each center also included a primary and secondary school that were built and staffed by the Foundation. The primary schools focused on formal educational training while the secondary schools provided academic as well as vocational training in automobile repair, electrical repair, electronics, and commercial skills.

Although the parochial centers were run by the Archdiocese of Cali, they were funded by the Carvajal Foundation at a cost of roughly U.S.$400,000 each per year. The Foundation believed in the principle of charging user fees for the services it provided, but realized that the poor could not always afford to pay the full cost of those services; it therefore subsidized some of the more expensive services.[4] Mr. Jaime Carvajal was especially willing to underwrite the cost of education because he believed in its value to the community and to society. As he said, "Education is highly valued in most societies and has always be subsidized. Why should practical education for the poor be any different?"

In addition to the parochial centers, the Carvajal Foundation supported a radio program to bring classical music to Cali, an AM station that broadcast high school courses for which credit could be obtained, and a self-help housing project where building plans and construction materials were provided to the poor at reduced costs.

Over the twenty years that the program had been in operation, the barrios in which the parochial centers were located gradually evolved into communities with adequate levels of housing, health, and education.

During that period the government had assumed increasing responsibility for the health and educational needs of the *barrio's* inhabitants. As a result the Foundation began to think that the *barrios* no longer required the same level of assistance, and decided to dedicate a greater portion of its resources to more experimental projects that might provide models for replication by other foundations.[5] Consequently, the Foundation began to pass on responsibility of the centers to other community development institutions and to shift the emphasis of its assistance.

Jaime Carvajal's Desire to Work with Micro-Enterprises

In the course of the Foundation's work with parochial centers it came into contact with many micro-enterprises.[6] Mr. Carvajal was impressed with the entrepreneurial talents of the many experienced shoemakers, bakers, tailors, and other tradespeople who had small shops around the parochial centers. Even so, he recognized that without some form of business assistance their potential to grow and succeed was limited, and, over time, he came to realize that the Carvajal Foundation could play a central role in providing that support.

The Carvajal Foundation had several practical reasons for wanting to start a micro-enterprise program. First of all, as in many other Latin American cities, more than 50 percent of the working population in Cali are employed in the informal sector. Therefore, Mr. Carvajal saw the provision of aid to small businesses as a concrete way of strengthening the economy and a solution to problems of high unemployment and uneven income distribution. And, because micro-enterprises were typically labor-intensive and located in poorer areas of the city, Mr. Carvajal was convinced that such assistance would effectively target the poor. Moreover, he strongly believed in the concept of free enterprise and considered micro-enterprises to be the "embryo" of that system; by incorporating informal sector businesses into the economic mainstream the capitalist system would be strengthened, thereby adding to the political stability of the country. Mr. Carvajal cited several of the largest corporations in Colombia as evidence of micro-enterprises that had flourished in the hands of able businesspeople. The multinational Carvajal Company had itself evolved from a small print shop since its founding in 1904.

Although he believed that the Foundation should assist small businesses, Jaime Carvajal also believed that it should concentrate on assisting viable enterprises. He did not want to encourage businesses that would not succeed. His many years of business experience had convinced him that some people simply did not make good business people. He knew that more than 50 percent of the legally registered small businesses ended up bankrupt, and he imagined that the failure rate for micro-enterprises in the informal sector would be even higher. Therefore, he decided not to try to "create" micro-entrepreneurs, but rather to work only with people who had established businesses, as they had already overcome many risks, had demonstrated entrepreneurial talents, and were, therefore, more likely to succeed.

In deciding on this course of action, Mr. Carvajal assumed that although a micro-enterprise owner with several years of experience would have fairly good knowledge of his profession, that person probably lacked the training and guidance needed to make sound business decisions. Jaime Carvajal was convinced that management skills were the missing link required to improve micro-enterprise productivity and profitability. In his words:

> Although the economic system does permit the small businessman to operate his business, it does so by creating the illusion that all that is necessary is some limited technical know-how and a small investment. Our businessman is then left to his own means. If the system would only give him a chance to acquire some knowledge of business administration, he could be in a favorable position to really do well.[7]

Micro-Enterprise Census

To investigate the demand for a micro-enterprise assistance program in Cali, the Carvajal Foundation conducted a census of enterprises with fewer than 10 employees to determine the number of small businesses and to discover their specific location, their demographic characteristics, the activities they were engaged in, and their business needs (see Exhibit 1 for census results). Upon joining the Foundation, Weimar was placed in charge of conducting the census, and, in reviewing the results, he found that the size of the informal sector was much larger than many people realized and that the thousands of micro-enterprises were engaged in a wide variety of manufacturing, commerce, and service activities. The survey results convinced him that many of the businesses had good growth potential and could become significantly more profitable with relatively modest levels of assistance. The survey also showed that the micro-entrepreneurs' most commonly expressed need was for credit, but that the great majority were unable to qualify for bank credit either because they lacked sufficient collateral to secure a loan and/or because they were not legally registered and did not keep records of their business transactions. Their only alternative was therefore to borrow money from friends and relatives or, more typically, from moneylenders at exorbitant interest rates. Thus, the census enabled the Foundation to define the micro-enterprise landscape in Cali, and convinced it that micro-enterprise assistance would have a beneficial impact on the economies of the slum areas.

Lack of Information on Micro-Enterprise Assistance Models

Having determined the need for a micro-enterprise assistance program, Weimar attempted to investigate how such programs were run elsewhere to see what lessons he could learn, but quickly discovered that very few such programs existed. In fact, he was hard pressed to locate descriptions or evaluations of programs designed to assist "small" businesses (which, with ten to fifty employees, were considerable larger than micro-enterprises), let alone information relevant to the needs of the very small enterprises the Foundation was interested in assisting. The only program that seemed to offer any hope of guidance was the UNO project in Recife, Brazil. All reports suggested that it was a very successful micro-enterprise program, and so, in 1976, Weimar and Pedro Sardi traveled to Recife to discover more about the UNO program and to see what lessons they could draw for designing a program in Cali. (See Exhibit 2 for a description of the UNO program.)

What Weimar Learned from his Brazilian Experience

Overall, Weimar was impressed with the UNO program. In the three years since it had been operating, it had lent U.S.$259,000 to 147 clients, and the clients, who seemed happy with the program, had repaid 95 percent of their loans on time. Weimar was concerned, however, about several aspects of the program and also doubted that all of the methods UNO used would be applicable to Cali or acceptable to the Carvajal Foundation.[8] Weimar's main concern was that the program concentrated almost exclusively on credit. Although the UNO Director acknowledged that clients could have benefited from managerial assistance or training, he believed that those other services were not as essential as timely credit and too expensive to provide. UNO's primary goals were to reach large numbers of clients and to keep operating expenses low. To minimize its costs, it used student advisors who had some financial background but lacked sufficient training and experience to provide comprehensive business advice to clients.

Weimar also believed that that UNO program was not participatory enough for the type of program that Mr. Carvajal envisioned. In order for clients to receive loans from UNO they were supposed to fill out a series of forms, but because the clients usually did not keep any records, the student advisors filled out the forms for them based on estimated inventories, sales, and so forth. Although that procedure was undoubtedly the fastest way to complete the loan forms, it did not teach the clients about the loan process itself. As a result, the clients played a very passive role, were given little opportunity for direct input, and continued to be dependent upon the advisors. Weimar was also concerned about the quality of the accounting information on which loans to clients were based. Because UNO did not require the advisors to construct a balance sheet to determine the overall profitability and viability of the businesses, the program had no real way of knowing whether the businesses it financed were profitable in the long run or whether they were losing money.

While Weimar felt that the UNO program had developed a system for providing credit to micro-entrepreneurs in a cost-effective manner, he was disappointed about the lack of emphasis on complementary training. He was particularly concerned because, from what he saw of the UNO program, it was not clear that the loans were increasing the profitability of clients' businesses even though the owners were able to repay them on time.[9] And from his discussions with clients about their businesses, Weimar concluded that their business decisions could have been enhanced by receiving some basic managerial training in addition to credit.

Situation Facing Weimar

Even though the Cali survey indicated that credit was the single input that micro-entrepreneurs thought they needed most, Weimar's experience with UNO made him reluctant to suggest that the Carvajal program provide credit alone. Another reason for his reluctance was Jaime Carvajal's insistence upon the need for training and education. Mr. Carvajal explained to him:

> ... without the educational process and close managerial scrutiny, credit can do more harm than good ... it is likely to be used inappropriately and lead to spiraling indebtedness and eventual bankruptcy. Although entrepreneurs usually cite credit as their major constraint, what they really require is management training. In fact, management training alone will often improve small business performance more than simple provision of credit.

Mr. Carvajal believed that it was easier for business owners to blame their problems on a lack of credit but that lack of management skills was often a more fundamental, albeit less obvious, cause of poor business performance.

Despite Mr. Carvajal's sentiments, Weimar was concerned that the Foundation would be perceived as paternalistic if it insisted that poor micro-entrepreneurs receive administrative training when all they said they needed was credit. Even so, he thought that it might be possible to provide training in conjunction with credit and hoped that if the Carvajal Foundation did offer training courses, people would come to see the benefit of the training over time. Given that business owners might be reluctant to participate in training courses, however, he realized that he would have to ensure that any training the Foundation provided was appropriate to the micro-entrepreneurs' needs.

He was not sure what sort of training would be appropriate, especially given the low average educational level among the poor. Weimar also wondered if the Carvajal Foundation were the appropriate organization to provide managerial and production training or if some other organization could assume that role more effectively. If the Foundation opted for training, Weimar wondered how he might proceed in developing a training program—especially as no other organizations seemed to be offering such training. One of Weimar's major concerns was that he had no prior experience with micro-enterprise training.[10] He was very conscious of the fact that it would be risky both for his own reputation and for the Foundation to embark on an untried path of assistance, and that developing a novel program from scratch would be time consuming.

Given the various difficulties Weimar saw associated with a training program, a less comprehensive program at times seemed more attractive to him. And even though the UNO program had some shortcomings, at least it had the benefit that it was tried and tested. An added incentive to use the UNO model was that an international organization had offered to pay the costs of an advisor from the UNO program to assist the Carvajal Foundation in replicating the program.

While Weimar was convinced that credit was necessary, it was not clear to him how best to provide this assistance given that Mr. Carvajal did not like the idea of the Foundation's lending directly to clients. Jaime Carvajal believed that clients would be confused about the Foundation's intentions if, while it was trying to assist them, it was at the same time charging interest and collecting on unpaid loans. He did not want his Foundation to be perceived as a bank by the poor, as he thought that its image as a philanthropic organization would suffer. UNO had developed a means of avoiding that problem through its affiliation with a government development bank that disbursed and collected clients' payments. That relationship allowed UNO to play a limited role in financial transactions with clients. And while a similar type of arrangement would separate the Foundation sufficiently from lending, Weimar was not sure whether the Colombian government was sufficiently convinced of the economic value of micro-enterprise lending to undertake such an effort. A private bank, however, might consider an arrangement if it had to assume only limited risk on the loans.

Weimar also had to consider the question of whether training should be offered before or after credit. If credit were offered first, the Foundation would not know which businesses were profitable and how much to lend them. Because most clients did not keep financial records, there was little information on which to base financial analysis of the firm, or to determine a business owner's capacity to repay loans and which investments made the most sense for the business. On the other hand, Weimar questioned whether the poorest clients (who would have to take valuable time from work and possibly pay for courses) would be financially able to participate in training sessions if training were offered before credit. Likewise, clients might not be willing to take courses unless they knew in advance that credit would be forthcoming.

Another issue that concerned Weimar was the ability of clients eventually to "graduate" from the program. His prior experience as an advisor in a government-run credit program for small businesses taught him that programs needed a strategy for moving clients beyond its services if clients were to become independent. He suspected that management skills might help clients to become independent and to be self-sufficient in the long run. The program participants would also have to be aware of the laws and requirements that apply to larger businesses so that they could someday move on to borrow money from a commercial lending organization. Since the UNO program did not attempt to encourage its clients to graduate to the formal sector, Weimar did not know if it was realistic for the Carvajal Foundation to expect small businesses either to want to or be able to legalize their businesses and seek commercial bank loans. Even if those expectations were not realistic, he wondered whether it was sensible actively to prepare clients for that process or to concentrate on more immediate concerns instead? Weimar did not want to spread the Foundation's efforts too thin by attempting to address too many components at the outset of the program (which would also add to the program's cost, start-up time, and complexity). After all, he would have to help implement the program.

Mr. Carvajal had asked Weimar to review three options for the Carvajal Foundation program and to recommend one and defend his recommendation:

1. Model the Carvajal Foundation program closely after UNO's credit-oriented program;

2. Borrow some aspects of the program from UNO and add-on other components to meet Carvajal Foundation objectives;

3. Depart completely from the UNO model and create a program focused on administrative training.

Weimar also hoped to resolve some of the other issues described above and to suggest to Jaime Carvajal an outline for a program that would fit the Foundation's objectives in assisting micro-enterprises.

Notes

1. Since the period covered in this case, UNO has expanded is business advisory services.

2. Manuel Carvajal was not only the first President of the Foundation, but was on the Board of the Carvajal Company as well. Mr. Jaime Carvajal is now President of the Foundation.

3. Colombia is an atypical Latin American country in that there are several large private foundations that play an active role in national development efforts. These foundations have a long history of working in conjunction with the government to provide services to socially disadvantaged citizens.

4. The community schools charged about U.S.$15 per month per student; scholarships were available to those who could not pay.

5. Thomas G. Sanders, "Promoting Social Development: Private Sector Initiatives in Cali, Colombia," *UFSI Reports,* No. 21, South America, 1983, p. 4.

6. For the purpose of this case, micro-enterprises are defined as unregistered businesses of ten employees or less that operate in the informal sector of the economy, not directly connected with formal institutions.

7. Jaime Carvajal in a speech to the "Regional Meeting of Donor Agencies on Small-Scale Enterprise in Latin America," Quito, 1985.

8. Although Colombia and Brazil are different in many respects, the informal sectors in which micro-enterprise owners operate are very similar. Those micro-enterprise owners confront many of the same barriers to legalization and do not have access to bank credit. Consequently, Weimar was confident that a model that worked in Brazil had a good chance of working in Colombia.

9. Most clients had not taken advantage of an optional accounting course offered and did not know how to keep simple accounting records.

10. Weimar had prior experience with a credit program targeted toward small- and medium-sized businesses that offered credit and technical advice to clients. That program assumed that the clients had sufficient knowledge of their businesses and therefore focused on credit. It did not consider training part of its role.

Exhibit 1
RESULTS FROM CENSUS OF MICRO-ENTERPRISES IN CALI[1]

Micro-enterprise owners could be male, female, old and young, but the average age was roughly forty years.

Micro-entrepreneurs were engaged in a wide variety of activities in the service, manufacturing, and commerce sectors.

Micro-enterprise owners were usually in the "medium," "medium-low," and "low" economic strata.

Micro-entrepreneurs had an average of two to five years of formal education.

Average household size was six persons.

Most micro-entrepreneurs set up shops in their homes.

Micro-enterprises employed an average of two to five workers, depending on the sector.

The greatest perceived barrier to growth was credit, followed by lack of administrative skills.

Source: Adapted from census data collected by the Carvajal Foundation by Weimar Escobar and Jairo Cordoba in "Las Microempresas y la Generación de Empleo," Cali, 1986.

[1] Gender comparisons of micro-entrepreneurs were not available in this study.

Exhibit 2
BRIEF DESCRIPTION OF BRAZILIAN MODEL

The Northeast Union of Assistance to Small Business (UNO) was started in 1972 by members of Recife's business community with the assistance of Accion International[1] and support from foreign donors and the Brazilian government. UNO offered credit to existing small businesses that were unable to obtain credit from banks. In order to help the poorest clients, UNO restricted its services to businesses with less than ten employees, an annual income of less that U.S.$8,200, fixed assets of less than U.S.$37,000, and annual sales of less than U.S.$45,000.

UNO loans were mainly for working capital and were repayable in one year, but occasionally for fixed asset investments, repayable in up to three years. Although first loans were for very small amounts, once a loan was repaid, the client could become eligible for a larger loan. In this way, the loan amounts could be gradually increased as clients learned how to handle larger amounts of money, up to a limit of U.S.$3,000. Although all types of businesses were eligible in principle, UNO lent mainly to retail firms rather than to riskier manufacturing and service sectors. These factors contributed to UNO's high repayment rates by reducing its lending risks.

The UNO program worked with local banks to disburse funds provided by a variety of national and international donors. The interest rate it charged borrowers was 25 percent, of which it retained 3 percent interest as a commission[2] while the remainder accrued to the institutions that supplied the credit funds. Even though the interest rate charged was quite high since inflation in Brazil ranged from 30 to 100 percent per annum, the UNO interest rates had always been negative in real terms. Thus the credit funds could never be self-sustaining in any meaningful sense.

UNO used part-time student advisors to identify the borrowers, fill out loan forms, and monitor loan recipients—and was therefore able to provide those services to all clients free of charge. UNO staff spent most of their time with clients during the selection and loan application stage, rather than after the clients received the loan. Once UNO approved a loan and the loan money was disbursed, clients paid monthly installments directly to the bank. When loan payments were late, the bank would send a list of delinquent borrowers to UNO advisors, who would investigate reasons for the delay. UNO maintained a loan guarantee fund in the bank to cover unpaid loans which allowed it to recommend actions to the bank based on its analysis of the reasons for the delay in payment. (The guarantee was also important in causing banks to lend to the poor.) UNO could recommend that the bank accept late payment and charge a late fee or that the bank proceed with its loan collection procedure. However, these procedures were not often used, as delinquency in the program had never been more than 8 percent.

UNO provided no managerial assistance or extension services except for a series of optional courses in simple bookkeeping, sales promotion, and check writing.[3] The UNO staff believed that since poor business owners' greatest demand was for credit, the organization could best use its limited resources by concentrating its efforts on providing credit in small amounts to as many clients as possible—and would offer managerial assistance on a limited basis to those who thought they needed it. According to an evaluation of the program, few clients attended the courses or considered them valuable.

In general, the results of the program were impressive. In evaluating the UNO program, Judith Tendler noted:

> Everyone's eyes are on UNO in the Brazilian city of Recife. Considered a model of how to provide credit to small businesses, UNO seems to have achieved what many similar programs have not. Its repayment rates, at about 95%, are unusually high. Its management is dedicated and talented, with a continuity that is impressive for an organization paying salaries that are lower than the public sector. It has succeeded in lending to firms with no previous access to bank credit, and has not allowed political pressures to influence its lending decisions—a remarkable achievement given the lure of its highly subsidized interest rates. UNO has not succumbed to the temptation to lend larger amounts and to better-off firms, in order to achieve the economies of scale inherent in making fewer and larger loans. By lending to small firms without access to credit, UNO has been a pioneer in Brazil, working where no other agency has, showing that it could be done, and opening a path for the public sector.[4]

Source: Judith Tendler, "Ventures in the Informal Sector and How They Worked Out in Brazil," AID Evaluation Special Study No. 12, March 1983.

[1] ACCION International, a U.S.-based private organization, had worked with community development projects in Latin America; this was its first attempt at a small business credit program.

[2] Apparently, the 3 percent represented a negligible contribution to UNO's costs.

[3] UNO started offering technical assistance and more intensive training later in the program's development.

[4] Tendler, 1983, p. ix. (The majority of Tendler's comments in this evaluation reflect flaws she saw in the UNO program. These were omitted here because they had not been identified as of 1976.)

Exhibit 3
SAMPLE OF UNO CLIENTS' FOOD STORES:
AVERAGE MONTHLY SALES, IMPUTED WAGES, AND GROSS PROFITS
(constant U.S. dollars)

Visit	Sales		Gross Profits		Imputed Wages[a]	
	U.S.$	No. of cases	U.S.$	No. of cases	U.S.$	No. of cases
1st[b]	3,754	42	974	42	228	42
2nd	3,481	42	781	41	236	42
3rd	3,605	42	825	36	209	40
4th	3,086	32	657	27	195	26

Source: Based on UNO loan files, copied from Judith Tendler, "Ventures in the Informal Sector and How They Worked Out in Brazil," USAID, March 1983, p. 149.
[a] Wage to the firm owner, as estimated by interviewing each business owner about monthly household expenses and value of items taken out of the store for family consumption.
[b] The first visit is a preloan visit during which the data for the loan application are gathered. The three subsequent visits are either for supervision or for preparing subsequent loan proposals.

Exhibit 4
CREDIT- VS. TRAINING-BASED PROGRAMS

For lack of adequate nomenclature, I will use "Type A" and "Type B" to distinguish between two generalized models as I see them in Latin America today. Before entering into a discussion of the following outline, a word about premises at the root of the differences between the models: Type A: The micro-entrepreneur does not know how to use credit effectively. For this reason, before loans may be disbursed, the perspective borrower must receive training in accounting, costs, marketing and personnel management. The entrepreneur does not know his business sufficiently well, either. Therefore, he should pass through the stages of pre-selection, selection, diagnosis, and training, which will enable him to better understand his business. Without this educational process, credit will probably do more harm than good for the entrepreneur, indebting him to the point where he cannot cancel his loan, effectively eliminating his chances of receiving other credit. Besides, many micro-entrepreneurs really do not need credit. What they really require is management training. Thinking that their primary need is credit, many micro-business people take the required training courses in order to receive it. During the management training period, they learn how to use their own resources better and realize that, in reality, they do not really need credit.

The premise of the Type B model may be summarized as follows: Like their counterparts of the large, medium, and small business sector, the micro-business needs capital to function. The major obstacle to expansion of the micro-business is not management training, but credit assistance. The micro-entrepreneur knows how to use credit, if it is disbursed in the small amounts he is accustomed to using. The micro-entrepreneur needs training in the use of credit, but the most efficient manner to learn how to use credit is precisely by using it in his business.

Since the following outline is of generalizations, probably no micro-business program will fit neatly or clearly into either of the two categories or program types. However, since all programs do share many of the aspects described, the following table is submitted for reflection and discussion.

Source: This discussion of the merits of credit vs. training based programs was excerpted from *Models for Microbusiness Support in Latin America* by Stephen H. Gross of ACCION International, as presented in the "Regional Meeting of Donor Agencies on Small Scale Enterprise Development in Latin America" in Quito in April 1985. (ACCION generally supports the Type B model in its programs.)

Support Programs for the Informal Sector

Aspects	Type A	Type B
Objectives	create and strengthen jobs; increase income	create and strengthen jobs; increase income
Types of Businesses	manufacturing, services	manufacturing, services, commerce
Business size	tend to be larger	tend to be smaller
Emphasis	training	credit
Amount Loaned	U.S.$800–$3,000	U.S.$30–$1,000
Guarantee	co-signer	co-signer and/or group
Uses of Credit	fixed assets and working capital	working capital
Interest Rates	subsidized	nonsubsidized
Payback Periods	6 months to 2 years	2 weeks to 6 months
Time Between First Contact with Program and Loan Disbursement	1 to 2 months	4 to 8 days
Learning Processes in the Use of Credit in the Course of One Year	1	4 to 6
New Clients Serviced in One Year	250 with training; 150 with training and credit	3,000 with credit; 400 with training and credit
Number of Loans Disbursed in One Year	400	12,500
Amount Disbursed in One Year	U.S.$300,000	U.S.$800,000–$1,000,000
Jobs Created in One Year	450	900
Jobs Strengthened in One Year	900	3,000
Administrative Cost per Unit Loaned	40 to 50 cents	5 cents or less
Financial Self-Sufficiency	difficult	1 to 2 years
Promotion and Selection	program is responsible	clients do it
"Graduation" to Formal Banking	little incentive due to subsidized interest rates and terms	positive incentive due to nonsubsidized interest rates and short terms

Case 8

The Carvajal Foundation "MICROS" Program (B): Considering Feasibility—Developing Outside Financial Support

This case was written by Margaret Bowman, in collaboration with Merilee S. Grindle. It is intended as a basis for class discussion rather than as an illustration of either effective or ineffective handling of an administrative situation. Though the basic elements of this case are based on facts, the timing of events and their relative importance were altered to form a more condensed case for discussion. The collaboration and support of the President and Executive Director of Carvajal Foundation and their staff are gratefully acknowledged.

In 1980 the Carvajal Foundation MICROS program had been in existence for three years, providing comprehensive training and credit to micro-enterprise business owners in Colombia. The MICROS staff thought that the program was very successful, having been carefully developed over the years to meet the specific needs of its micro-enterprise clients. During the program development, the quality of the program had been of greater concern to the Foundation than the cost. But now that MICROS was gaining more attention and other Colombian foundations were interested in replicating it, the cost of delivering services was becoming an issue. The challenge before Jaime Carvajal was to develop ways to make the micro-enterprise program less expensive which did not compromise the objectives of the MICROS program and cut into the profits of the micro-enterprises it sought to help.

Background

Jaime Carvajal was the President of the Carvajal Foundation, a private nonprofit foundation in Cali, Colombia, funded in part by the Carvajal Company, one of the largest private enterprises in Colombia. The Carvajal Foundation was run by a Board of Directors comprised of the Archbishop of Cali, four members of the Carvajal family, a President, and an Executive Director chosen by the Board. Since 1961 it had supported a variety of programs aimed at improving the lives of the urban poor ranging from cultural and educational training to self-help housing programs.

The MICROS micro-enterprise program was founded in 1977 as a response to unemployment and uneven income distribution problems in Cali. It was composed of a series of administrative training courses designed by Carvajal to be geared towards micro-enterprises, technical assistance visits that complement the training, and credit provided through a financial intermediary. (See Exhibit 1 for a brief program description.)

Jaime Carvajal believed that the focus on quality was well worth the effort and the expense, and considered the MICROS program to be very successful. Like other Carvajal Foundation programs, the MICROS program had been a pioneer effort. The Carvajal Foundation had departed from existing models of credit-based micro-enterprise assistance and developed its own training methodology and training materials. Because the Foundation was fortunate to have the financial stability of the Carvajal company behind it, the Foundation Directors were able to spend years developing their program, without the pressures faced by some other programs of producing high loan repayment rates at very low cost in a short period of time. The Foundation had concentrated more effort on developing a methodology to meet the long-term needs of micro-entrepreneurs than it did on recovering the costs of its program. The resulting micro-enterprise model developed by the Carvajal Foundation seemed relatively expensive and promised to rely on substantial Foundation support unless ways could be found to cut costs or develop other sources of funding.

Why Reduce Program Costs?

By 1980, reducing the program costs became an issue for several reasons. First, several foundation directors in other cities and towns had heard Jaime Carvajal speak about his program and were impressed. Mr. Carvajal felt that the program's features and results would make other private foundations enthusiastic about replicating the program. However, since most other Colombian foundations were much smaller than Carvajal, they had fewer financial resources and probably could not afford to support a costly program. Aside from financial constraints, some of these foundations were in more rural areas, where local educational level, transportation, banks, and staff were all likely to cause more difficulty than they had in Cali.

Jaime Carvajal was delighted by other foundations' interest in micro-enterprise assistance. As far as he was concerned, there were more than enough micro-entrepreneurs in Colombia for all the foundations to become involved. He also believed that it was wise to cooperate with other foundations so that together they could build on the existing knowledge of micro-enterprise assistance and learn from one another. As it had always been the goal of the Carvajal Foundation to disseminate its programs to other organizations, it was more than willing to devise ways to reduce its program costs and do whatever else it could to make it feasible for other foundations to adopt the program.

Second, Mr. Carvajal was concerned about making the Foundation less dependent on the Carvajal Company's dividends to carry out its programs. If the Foundation could reduce its costs and become more financially self-sufficient, it could continue to carry on its programs regardless of the financial success of the company. Since the MICROS program had become the Foundation's largest project, reducing the Foundation's expenditure on the program would reduce this reliance and allow the Foundation to serve more clients.

Another reason that cost reduction was a concern at this time was that the Inter-American Development Bank (IDB) had raised the possibility of providing support for a micro-enterprise credit fund to expand the Carvajal program to other areas of the country. The IDB was impressed with the impact the MICROS program seemed to have on its clients and was willing to consider funding its replication in other cities by the Carvajal Foundation and by other foundations as well. But the IDB, which promotes financial self-sufficiency in its investment projects, might be reluctant to fund the replication of MICROS given the program's perceived high cost and its current financial dependency on the Carvajal Foundation. It was therefore very important for the Carvajal Foundation to assist smaller foundations in replicating the program to show the IDB that the program *could be* replicated—so as not to miss out on an opportunity to involve the IDB in this venture. The Bank's support was not assured, but it provided the hope that a much wider scale program would be possible. Consequently, Jaime Carvajal made the issues of cost reduction and replication priorities.

Current MICROS Financing

The Foundation was originally established by the Carvajal family with a grant of 40 percent of Carvajal Company shares of stock. Because the Carvajal Company is one of the largest companies in the country, dividends on the shares represented a considerable amount of reliable income for the Foundation. The Foundation had also received support in the form of consultants and advice from international donors.

In addition to stock dividends, the Foundation derived income from user fees and interest charged to participants in its programs. Although the Carvajal Foundation did not lend money directly to its clients, it played a key role in determining the interest rates charged by the Bank of

Bogota and the Foundation for Higher Education (FES),[1] its financial intermediaries. The Bank of Bogota charged Carvajal clients 24 percent interest on loans: The Bank earned 3 percent; 8 percent was reinvested in the Carvajal loan fund; 12 percent went to cover some of Carvajal's costs of training and monitoring clients; and 1 percent went back to the Inter-American Development Bank that had provided the Bank with the low interest loan for this purpose.

All of the Carvajal Foundation's programs charged fees to participants, but because the fees were scaled to take into account the low incomes of Carvajal program participants, they did not always cover the cost of its programs. In the case of the MICROS program, the cost of providing courses and counseling to a micro-enterprise client for a period of two years was roughly U.S.$250–$300. However, Carvajal program participants were only charged half of this cost. Another 20 percent of the cost was covered by a portion of the interest fees (received from clients who borrowed funds for their businesses), which were paid to the Carvajal Foundation by the financial intermediary that handled loans to micro-enterprises in its programs. The remaining 30 percent was subsidized by the Carvajal Foundation.

Options to Decrease Program Costs

The ways in which the Carvajal Foundation could reduce its program costs included the following:

Use Student Advisors. Advisors were trained staff members who worked one-on-one with micro-enterprise clients at their place of business. They complemented and reinforced skills taught by trainers in group sessions. Because these visits were seen as routine and usually did not involve technical business advice, it did not seem necessary for advisors to be professionals, but possibly students with a background in business skills. If an agreement could be reached with a local university, the Carvajal Foundation might be able to arrange to pay students a fraction of an advisor's salary.

Eliminate a Program Component. By trimming down the scope of the program from providing training, technical assistance, and credit to perhaps just training and credit, the program could save a considerable amount of money. Of the three components of the MICROS program, providing technical assistance was the most labor intensive, and therefore the most costly to provide.

Require Less Training Courses. The MICROS program required that qualified clients pass through six training courses before they would be eligible for credit. By requiring less courses, training costs and training time could be reduced.

Increase the Class Size. By increasing the number of students per class, per unit costs of training each student would be reduced. The courses are held in a large room that can hold about fifty people.

Options to Increase Income

Increase Course Fees. Fees currently covered half of the cost of the Carvajal Foundation's training and technical assistance. The Foundation believed that participants in their programs would value them more if they paid a fee for the services. Training courses were also educational, a social good that Mr. Carvajal thought was worth subsidizing. So far this principle had worked well. But if the fees per course were increased, what might the results be? Already, it was sometimes difficult to explain to some poor business people the benefits of training. Many clients at first believed they should *receive* money from a large foundation, not *pay* money to it. Only after the training concepts had positive effects and the business owners made more money (usually after the first or second course) did the entrepreneurs realize how valuable the training was to them.

Increase Interest Rates. Although MICROS did not lend directly, it was involved in negotiating interest rates because it did a considerable amount of work to prepare clients for creditworthiness. The Foundation for Higher Education (FES), a nonprofit foundation that lent the money, distributed a certain percentage of the interest back to the Foundation for its work. Perhaps the percentage could be increased through a redistribution of the existing interest rates or an interest rate hike. Although it did not seem right to raise interest to the poor, their loans were inherently more risky and therefore cost more. (Many of the clients who received loans through the MICROS program had been borrowing money at rates up to 10 or 15 percent each month from moneylenders.) So it might be necessary for clients to pay more for their loans to subsidize the training component.

Increasing the Number of Loans. If more loans were disbursed, then more interest would be earned because of the increased size of outstanding portfolio. This could cover the cost of some of the training.

Increase Loan Size. By increasing the size of loans, more interest could be earned on each loan transaction. For the same size of portfolio, fewer transactions would be required. This would facilitate the work of the financial intermediary and require less monitoring on the part of the Foundation staff.

Charge Late Fees. If a client does not repay his or her loan on time (and does not have an acceptable excuse), the Foundation could charge a late fee. Because loans are guaranteed to the financial intermediary by a guarantee fund, the Foundation carries the cost of delinquent payments through lost interest and collection costs. The program could earn more money by increasing these penalties.

Find New Sources of Funding. If the program as it stood was always going to require a subsidy, one way to allow MICROS to continue to grow was to find other funding sources. The Colombian government was one potential source of assistance. Perhaps there were nonfinancial ways they could help as well, like removing some of the barriers typically confronted by small businesses all over Colombia. Any assistance from the government had its risks as well. Would links with the government endanger the autonomy of the Foundation? How could this be controlled? Were there other funders that might be interested in funding a successful micro-enterprise assistance program designed and managed by an indigenous organization?

To make the program attractive to other foundations, Jaime Carvajal was compelled to reduce the amount of the subsidy. As he weighed various options to do this, he also wondered if there were yet other possibilities that should be considered.

Note

1. FES, a private nonprofit institution, was set up in 1964 to administer funds donated by individuals and companies to the University of the Cauca Valley. Today, FES not only administers funds for a wide variety of other organizations, but acts both as a foundation that supports its own development projects, and as a financial institution that lends and invests funds much like a bank. It is accepted widely as a reliable financial intermediary for a number of notable organizations. "A number of Colombian institutions have found it advantageous to use FES as a broker because of its skills and contacts. It has the advantage over conventional consulting and banking services of being non-profit. Furthermore, it provides a linkage between the Colombian private sector, government, and outside funding agencies ... It handles the funds for all the programs in Colombia of UNICEF, UNESCO, the Technical Cooperation Agency, the World Health Organization, the Pan American Health Organization, as well as a number of Colombian government agencies." (Thomas G. Sanders, "Promoting Social Development: Private Sector Initiatives in Cali, Colombia," *UFSI Reports*, No. 21, South America, 1983, p. 3.)

Exhibit 1
BRIEF DESCRIPTION OF THE CARVAJAL FOUNDATION MODEL

The Carvajal Foundation Model

The Carvajal Foundation was the first foundation in Colombia to become involved in micro-enterprise projects. Foundation staff had closely studied a micro-enterprise assistance model in Brazil that had been developed with the technical assistance of ACCION International, a U.S. based private organization. However, the Carvajal Foundation decided not to adopt ACCION's credit-based design and instead to focus its program on administrative assistance, which it believed was a more crucial need for poor entrepreneurs in Colombia. It took several years to develop the Carvajal model and the accompanying training materials.

Training

MICROS clients are required to enroll in six administrative courses designed to teach micro-entrepreneurs how to manage their business and best to use the credit provided later on. They include sessions on accounting, cost calculations, investment projects, and so forth. The training courses were developed gradually, with the feedback and participation of clients. Each class is facilitated by a trainer and optimally has fifteen to twenty participants engaged in active discussion about their own businesses as they work through the training books. (See Exhibit 2 for information on courses offered.)

Administrative Assistance

At the end of the fifteen hour-long courses, technical advisors visit the client's place of business to reaffirm the concepts taught in the training courses and to assure that the concepts can be practically applied to the participant's business. The advisor monitors the client's progress and explains any course concepts that are not clear. In these sessions, those with less academic background can catch up with the rest of the class. The technical assistance visits are seen as a necessary compliment to the courses offered by the Foundation and course participants must agree to work with the technical advisors.

The cost of technical assistance is included in the training fees because the two are designed to go hand-in-hand. Although Carvajal has not calculated the costs of running this component of its program, technical assistance is usually one of the most costly elements of assistance because it is so individualized and requires transportation to and from the businesses.

Credit

The MICROS program does not provide credit directly to its clients. Rather, it works with a financial intermediary, FES, the Foundation for Higher Education. FES administers funds received from external donors and lenders, and conducts the loan transactions with MICROS clients. Once clients have passed through the required number of courses and Carvajal has established that the enterprise is operating at a net gain, clients can be recommended to receive FES credit. Although all money transactions occur between FES and the clients, Carvajal advisors are involved in providing credit in that they help establish the level of loans required and they follow up on delinquent loans.

The interest rates charged by FES are also agreed upon by development banks that lend funds for micro-enterprise loans and by the Carvajal Foundation. Interest charges have been on par with government small industry loans, but since development banks have lent funds to FES at very low interest, the remaining interest can be split between FES and the Foundation to cover their costs. The amount earned by each is negotiated. Therefore, if the costs of the program increase and interest rates are increased, the Foundation might be able to negotiate a greater percentage of earnings for itself.

Exhibit 2
EVALUATION OF CLIENT SATISFACTION
WITH CARVAJAL PROGRAM

Training[a]

Course Title	Course Objectives	Participation[b] in Course (%)	% of Participants who Applied Skills
Accounting Principles	Train participant to summarize, organize, and record information.	100	66
Costs	Classify, calculate, and carry out a cost study.	100	84
Marketing	Develop a marketing strategy.	86	70
Investment Projects	Recognize factors that determine an investment project. Identify, define, and analyze project.	88	57
Management Principles	Know basic management principles. Identify modern management tools.	62	61
Financial Analysis	Analyze and interpret the financial state of a business.	60	53
Personnel Management	Apply personnel selection, training, evaluation, and motivation techniques.	20	30
Production Principles	Provide the necessary tools to improve the production management of the business.	14	86
Quality Control	Provide necessary tools to carry out quality control in the business.	18	56

Source: Translation from "Programa MICROS-Cali: 10 Años al Servicio del Sector Micro Empresarial," *Impulsamos Microempresarios*, Fundacion Impulsamos, S.A., Cali, Colombia, 1987, Vol. 7, p. 13.

[a] The results in these columns were obtained in a survey conducted by students of the University of Buenaventura of Carvajal clients, three years after participating in the Carvajal courses. The study population consisted of 155 clients who had completed more than four courses in 1984. Seventy-six percent of those clients interviewed had not received credit through MICROS and their views reflect the benefits they received from the training courses and technical assistance alone.

The first six courses were considered prerequisites to qualify for credit. All courses are twelve hours long except financial analysis which is ten.

[b] Courses build on previous skills and are usually taken in sequence.

Exhibit 2 (cont'd)

Technical Assistance

Seventy percent of those surveyed received technical assistance. Although technical assistance is a mandatory complement to training for those who wish to qualify for credit, some business owners who participate in the training courses may not qualify for credit, may not be micro-enterprises, or for some reason do not want technical assistance. Eighty percent of those who received technical assistance were satisfied with the support they received. Those who were not satisfied with the technical assistance thought it was superficial; those who liked it cited the clarity and patience of the advisors as most desirable features.

Credit

Although 44 percent of the micro-enterprises applied for credit, only 55 percent of those applicants received financing. Problems with the credit component of the program included:

- Lack of a guarantee due to small size of business (30%).
- Client perceived that administrative procedures were too burdensome (30%).
- Client had to work with too many advisors; lack of continuity (10%).
- Business too disorganized (10%).
- Loan amount approved was less than client wanted (10%).
- Clients did not complete courses, so did not qualify (56%).

Exhibit 3
EXAMPLE OF AN AFFILIATE PROGRAM RUN
BY ANOTHER FOUNDATION IN A SMALLER CITY

The program described below was started in April 1986. It is run by the Chamber of Commerce of a mid-sized Colombian city and receives program funding from the Inter-American Development Bank. The Carvajal Foundation provided initial assistance in starting up the program and training staff. A Carvajal advisor specializing in programs of this size now visits the affiliate program regularly to monitor the program for the IDB and to provide additional assistance.

Training Report: Cumulative Number of Persons Attending April 1986–March 1987

SECTOR	Industry	Commerce	Service	No Business	Total	Percent Desertion
COURSE						
Accounting	105	31	36	32	204	2.4
Costing	102	30	36	31	199	5.9
Marketing and Sales	90	22	32	29	173	11.5
Financial Analysis	86	22	30	27	165	11.5
Investment Projects	87	21	31	27	166	8.4
Administrative Principles	83	21	30	25	159	5.0
Quality Control	10	1	2	1	14	na

Approved Credit April 1986–March 1987
(amounts in Colombian pesos; 1 U.S. dollar = 245 pesos)

	Sector	Number of Loans	Amount of Loans
Regular Credit	Industry	13	2,150,000
	Commerce	3	410,000
	Services	1	180,000
	Totals	17	2,740,000
Rotating Credit Fund[a]	Industry	9	1,330,00
	Commerce	1	100,000
	Services	0	0
	Totals	10	1,430,000

[a] This fund was a credit line that allowed clients to cash client checks at a discounted rate before the date written on the check. Post-dating checks is common practice in Colombia and often leaves small business people short of cash.

Case 9

FUCODES:
Working with Solidarity Groups vs.
Individual Clients

This case was written by Margaret Bowman, in collaboration with
Merilee Grindle. It is intended as a basis for class discussion rather than
as an illustration of either effective or ineffective handling of an administrative situation. The collaboration and support of the Executive Director of FUCODES and his staff are gratefully acknowledged.

Julio Gonzalez sat in his office preparing a presentation for the next
meeting of the FUCODES (Costa Rican Development Foundation) Board
of Directors. In the coming months of 1987, the Board members wanted
to develop a more explicit policy regarding the Foundation's target
clients and the type of loans it offered, and they wanted Julio to outline
that strategy and present his recommendations for the organization's future. Julio was confident that he would have little difficulty in convincing
the Board to continue to move the Foundation in the direction he had
charted since taking over as Executive Director. Since that time he had
made several changes, but the greatest had been the decision to move
from lending exclusively to solidarity groups[1] of farmers and fishermen
in rural areas, to lending primarily to individual micro-entrepreneurs[2] in
and around San Jose. Julio believed that this focus had been primarily responsible for the dramatic improvement in the organization's efficiency
and financial success in recent years. As Julio was thinking back proudly
over how far the organization had come during his administration, he
received a call from the President of the Board of Directors. "Julio, after
careful consideration, I think that our future program strategy should
target farmers in the rural areas of Costa Rica—they are really the ones
who can use our help the most. I propose that we discuss a plan for
reaching these farmers using a group lending strategy, and think about
shifting the program's emphasis toward this target group. I hope you can
incorporate these ideas into your presentation." Perplexed, Julio contem-
plated how to approach the up-coming Board meeting and how to prevent the organization from repeating its past mistakes.

Background

FUCODES, the Costa Rican Development Foundation, was established as a nonprofit organization in 1973 by a group of seventeen Costa Rican businessmen with the assistance of the Pan American Development Foundation (PADF). The organization was also supported by local chapters of the Kiwanis Club, the Lions Club, and the Rotary Club. The objectives of the organization centered around improving the lives of the most needy sectors of Costa Rican society by offering credit, training, and technical assistance to clients who satisfied its eligibility requirements. (See Exhibit 1 for a description of the organization's objectives.) The FUCODES loan fund was financed by international donations and loans. (See Exhibits 2 and 3 for detail of donors.) Although FUCODES was not founded with the goal of achieving self-sufficiency, interest from the loan fund and local private sector donations were expected to cover a portion of its administrative costs.

Julio Gonzalez was a young man with a background in economics and agriculture. When Julio became the executive director in 1982, FUCODES was nine years old and had six years of experience with its micro-enterprise credit program. Although the FUCODES micro-enterprise program experienced satisfactory results during the first three to four years of operation and gained the support of national and international donors, its financial health subsequently declined, and in 1980 and 1981 the organization suffered such low levels of loan repayment and staff morale that the program's viability was threatened.

Julio had been hired with the explicit goal of bringing FUCODES out of its financial and administrative crisis. Consequently, his foremost concern was improving the low rates of loan repayment and controlling the operational costs of the program. However, he was not only charged with improving the organization's internal affairs, but was also expected to improve the organization's public image. To that end, he explored ways to develop relations with other development organizations and strengthen ties with the local business community.

Soon after arriving, Julio conducted his own analysis of the situation by looking through old records, interviewing staff members, and talking with other organizations to understand the factors that led to FUCODES' problem with group loans. His analysis of the situation led him to make changes in the organization and to adopt a strategy of making loans almost exclusively to individual urban micro-enterprise clients. Although the President of the Board favored targeting agricultural areas, he agreed that FUCODES had to be more selective in its choice of clients and consider lower risk loans in order to improve the financial performance of the organization in the short run. He was therefore willing to go along with the targeting strategy.[3]

Much of the pressure for change came from the Foundation's international donors, who were alarmed by the low repayment rates. (See Exhibit 4 for data on loan repayment and donations.) PACT,[4] the organization that had been underwriting the bulk of FUCODES' administrative expenses, began to reconsider the value of its assistance not only because the low repayment rates were a clear sign that some aspect of the program was not functioning properly, but also because it believed that by funding FUCODES' expenses, it could have been inadvertently allowing FUCODES to delay administrative decisions that might have made it more efficient. As a result of these concerns, in 1983 PACT temporarily suspended disbursement of funds to FUCODES that it had previously approved. At the same time, Solidarios, another international donor that had assisted FUCODES by providing low interest loans, also withheld disbursement of funds until organizational changes were made. Julio made these changes and funding was soon after reinstated.

As Julio was thinking about how to address the President's desire to incorporate more groups into the FUCODES program, he thought about the reasons he had decided to emphasize individual loans over solidarity group loans back in 1984. As he reviewed the changes he had made, he wondered whether the Foundation was sufficiently strong in terms of its human and financial resources to make a successful shift back to group lending.

History of FUCODES Prior to 1982

FUCODES' Original Approach

Originally, FUCODES worked with solidarity groups consisting almost exclusively of low-income farmers and fishermen, although a small number of groups were urban-based and engaged in activities such as shoe repair and tailoring. To ensure that it targeted the "poorest of the poor," FUCODES required that all clients had to meet financial eligibility criteria. In addition to the financial restrictions, the FUCODES board also specified several noneconomic guidelines, such as a preference for projects with a high economic and social impact on the local community. (See Exhibit 5 for a more detailed description of loan requirements and characteristics.)

FUCODES believed the provision of credit alone was insufficient and had to be accompanied by technical assistance and training. And it insisted that all groups receive group training and agree to accept technical assistance before they could qualify for a loan, even though many solidarity groups did not see the need for the policy. (See Exhibit 6 for a more detailed description of the methods FUCODES used to assist its group clients.)

Julio Rethinks the Group Strategy

Although the concept of group lending seemed sound to Julio in theory, the program statistics in 1980 and 1981 showed otherwise. Julio realized that group lending enabled FUCODES to target poorer clients and fostered notions of solidarity and group responsibility, but the strategy was not working for FUCODES in financial terms. And perhaps more pertinent from his perspective, he realized that his performance as Director would be judged largely on the basis of program statistics such as repayment rates, number of clients served, administrative costs, and the amount of loans FUCODES disbursed to clients.

FUCODES' original decision to pursue a group lending strategy was influenced by a number of factors. The Costa Rican government's development strategy promoted the formation of cooperatives and groups as a means of providing assistance more effectively. (See Exhibit 7 for outline of government policy.) FUCODES' major donors—Solidarios, IAF, PACT, and USAID—also supported group development and encouraged FUCODES to pursue a group lending strategy. In addition, PADF provided FUCODES with an advisor whose experience was with groups, to help set up the program. (See Exhibit 2 for description of organizations that supported FUCODES.) Not surprisingly, the emphasis of outside donors on group-oriented development also had the effect of attracting Board members who were in favor of a group lending strategy. Both the President and the Vice-President of the Board, who had been in office since the organization's inception, firmly supported the Foundation's group-oriented approach.[5] (See Exhibit 8 for list of Board members.)

Despite support for a group lending strategy from the top, statements by promoters suggested deficiencies and client dissatisfaction with the group methodology. One of the promoters who had been with the organization since 1977 thought that the main problem FUCODES had with groups stemmed from the fact that the criteria for group size had been inflexible. As he commented:

> At first, groups had to have a minimum of fifteen members. In some sparsely populated rural areas, there were not enough local residents to make up an entire group, so members from elsewhere would be recruited to join who, because of their distance from the project, were not as involved as the other members. They were really tokens, filling in spaces so the group could qualify. The fact that some members did not feel closely connected had a lot to do with loan repayment problems. If group members were friends or had to see each other daily, they would make sure to come up with their portion of the payments.

Another problem was access by group members to equipment or materials purchased that all members were supposed to share. As another promoter commented:

> In the typical case of a group of 15 fishermen who purchased a boat, it was physically impossible for all of them to share it. Usually, several members became the primary users of the boat while the others who did not use it did not feel they had an obligation to repay. In other instances, members were recruited to meet the size requirement and never intended to be a part of the group. They thought that their signature was more of a reference for the other members rather than an obligation.

Another major problem was that farmers and fishermen were subject to conditions that made it difficult for them to repay loans. A promoter noted:

> A three or five year loan period seemed like a long time to those who had not had loans before. Most clients were not used to saving just to repay a loan, and consequently often did not have the money when payments were due. Remember, they get money when they sell their harvest and it goes pretty quickly after that. The situation is different for fishermen since they can sell their catch once a week or so, but fishermen are not well-known for saving their money for very long either. Besides, the earnings of both groups are largely determined by weather conditions in a given year and therefore fluctuate considerably.

Julio thought that these problems should have been detected by the advisors and actions taken to address the deficiencies. The fact that corrective actions were not taken indicated flaws in the communication system between the main office and field advisors. Julio believed that another possible cause of the low repayment rate was that the Foundation did not offer other positive incentives to group members to strengthen the motivation of the solidarity pledge.[6]

Julio's Program Changes

Within his first several months, these comments and other observations made by the advisors convinced Julio that major strategic changes and reforms in the lending procedures were necessary to improve the low loan repayment rates. (See Exhibit 4 for detailed account of repayment rates.) Julio also thought that the organization's administrative costs were excessive and a further drain on loan funds.

Julio made these observations to the FUCODES Board of Directors and convinced them that a number of changes were necessary to prevent the organization from falling into financial ruin. First, in order to reduce

FUCODES' operational costs, he reduced the promotional role of advisors by making an agreement with several communications associations to donate radio and television time to FUCODES to announce its services. Since Costa Rican communications systems are quite modern and extensive, and many rural clients have radios and telephones (or access to them), the media announcements did reach clients who could then call for more information. Julio also reinforced the understanding between FUCODES and the government organizations who provided technical assistance. (See Exhibit 2 for government organizations that support FUCODES.) As a result, FUCODES was able to increase its services and promotion considerably without hiring more staff members.[7]

A second change Julio made in 1982 was to revise the loan requirements. Client suggestions reflected that a smaller group size might be helpful, so Julio reduced the required group size from fifteen to twelve people per group. This change made it easier for promoters to form and work with groups, and also increased the likelihood that the group members knew and liked each other. In an experimental attempt to find an optimal group size, Julio continued to lower the number of clients per group. Over time, he reduced the required number of group members to ten, then eight, and finally to five. At five members per group, the promoters reported that groups were easy to work with, yet large enough to derive the psychological and financial benefits of working as a group.

Although FUCODES had considered lending to individuals before 1984, it was hesitant to do so because it thought individual clients would require more expensive and time consuming technical assistance than groups. It also thought that by lending to individuals it would lose the economies of scale it had previously enjoyed. The idea also seemed to be counter to FUCODES' original philosophy of group development. Over time, however, as more urban micro-enterprise clients approached its office for loans, it decided that it made more sense to adapt its program to their needs.

Accordingly, in 1984, Julio convinced the board to accept a new program aimed at individual micro-enterprises in San Jose. FUCODES thought that loans to individuals would require more work than group loans because of the increased number of transactions per beneficiary. However, in many ways, the urban micro-entrepreneurs proved easier to work with. First, urban entrepreneurs were more likely to have heard the radio announcements, live close to a bank, and be situated closer to other government advisory services. Second, training and technical assistance were not more complicated or costly to provide. Training sessions continued to be provided to groups of individuals. And third, because individuals were not required to undergo group cohesiveness training,[8] the organizing process was shorter allowing clients to qualify for loans in a much shorter period of time. Since FUCODES' technical assistance was provided mostly by outside organizations with the capacity to attend to many individual clients, this change did not overburden FUCODES. As a result of these changes, both repayment rates and interest earnings increased. (See Exhibit 5 for individual loan requirements.) FUCODES also found that the new individual client interactions were less expensive and more manageable than working with groups had been. As a result, FUCODES gradually adopted a policy of lending almost exclusively to individuals in a wide variety of productive activities. It continued to lend to some well-established groups but in 1987 was no longer promoting group loans.

In an effort to increase income and enhance the organization's image, Julio also developed a program of business "associate members" who contributed to FUCODES. Previously, the only assistance FUCODES received from the business community was from the original seventeen founding members who donated some of their time or administrative skills. However, by talking to friends and large business owners, Julio and the Board were able to attract other "associates" to contribute to FUCODES for philanthropic reasons and also for tax purposes. The philosophy of the organization had always been one of businesses helping other businesses, but Julio emphasized this aspect of the program much more than his predecessor. As he noted:

> In our country, larger businesses are more anxious to help out an upcoming business sector because they relate to them more than they do to farmers. Also, businesses see their micro-enterprise support as insurance for a more stable free-market economy. What we try to do is to graduate small businessmen to a higher level so that they can one day have the opportunity to participate as associates themselves.

FUCODES created an environment that attracted associates to join other prominent business leaders in helping small businesses. To ensure that the associate program would appeal to the local businessmen, associates were invited to discuss plans to assist FUCODES at social gatherings and meetings in prestigious hotels where they met other businessmen. They occasionally visited client workshops where they would offer advice. These activities were very popular and resulted in an increase in the number of business associates from 26 in 1980 to 290 in 1986, and an increase in local donations from U.S.$1,163 in 1980 to U.S.$141,966 in 1986.

Since Julio had come to FUCODES, the organization had changed markedly in terms of its clients, the methodologies it used, and its sources of funding. The changes were necessary as the Foundation needed to regain its image as a successful development organization, and micro-enterprise loans seemed a certain way of increasing the number of clients, decreasing the late payment rates, and attracting more international loans and donations. The urban micro-enterprises also had shorter production cycles than farmers[9] and could therefore repay their loans more quickly, allowing FUCODES to recycle its loan funds more often. Overall, the changes that Julio instituted in the FUCODES loan program improved the repayment rates and succeeded in regaining donor confidence in the program. Under Julio's stewardship, the organization had resolved its prior problems and earned a reputation that the USAID Mission described as "high-ranking for effectiveness, competence, and fiscal responsibility." In June 1985, USAID evaluators also had this to say about the administration of FUCODES:

> Internal operating procedures, including pre- and post-credit evaluation, are well organized and the quality of human resources available to the foundation, both on staff, from affiliated members, and from cooperating institutions is quite satisfactory ... Field visits to beneficiaries indicated that the financing of working capital and machinery was having a very direct impact on employment generation, and only $400 to $800 of capital was required per new employee among those visited.

Situation Facing the Executive Director

Julio was proud of how far FUCODES had come since 1981 and he was not enthusiastic about reliving negative experiences with groups. Therefore, the phone call he had just received from the President of the Board was unsettling. The Board of Directors realized that many of the changes in the FUCODES program had been necessary and, at the time changes were made, had been very supportive of the measures. Julio understood the perspective of the President and Vice-President: They wanted to reach the very poor clients who had the least access to other assistance. Certainly the fishermen and farmers in the rural areas could use more help, but he wondered whether FUCODES was the most appropriate vehicle for such assistance given its limited resources and past experience. Julio thought that it would be easier for him to accommodate the President's wishes if the organization's funds were not as constrained or if he had a larger staff, but these were not immediate possibilities.

Julio was also not sure whether a "better" group lending strategy, or a mix of groups and micro-enterprise clients, might offer a potential solution. In the past year, one of the original groups of thirteen coffee growers reapplied for a loan, but they requested individual loan amounts based on the size of each man's plot of land. FUCODES accepted this arrangement, but required guarantees of land or a house from each group member instead of the usual solidarity pledge. It was too early to tell, but Julio thought that this novel lending method might offer a solution to his dilemma.

Julio wanted to be able to present a recommendation to the board as to how FUCODES might incorporate group lending programs without endangering FUCODES' financial position, but also wanted to present the *pros* and *cons* of other options to the Board. As he sat down to outline his presentation to the Board, he was aware that he would have to carefully analyze the organization's past results to be able to defend his position.

Notes

1. Solidarity group members borrow money together; their loan guarantee is a "solidarity" pledge of collective responsibility by all members to repay the group's debt.

2. FUCODES defines micro-enterprises as those that have up to ten employees and annual sales of less than U.S.$59,000 (3.5 million colones).

3. In the President's mind, he had always intended to return to working with groups of farmers since this was his major development concern. In his view, the targeting of individual urban businesses was a temporary measure to stabilize the foundation's credit program. It was not clear that he ever communicated this opinion to the Director.

4. See Exhibit 2 for a description of Private Agencies Collaborating Together (PACT).

5. Both the President and the Vice-President of the FUCODES Board had been on the Board of Directors of Solidarios for years. In 1987, the President of FUCODES was elected to be the President of the Solidarios Board of Directors as well.

6. In other solidarity group programs, timely repayment of a first loan would qualify members for a larger loan later.

7. It was not necessary for him to reduce the staff size since the Board had fired many of the advisors shortly before Julio took over as a director. (The donation of mass media advertising time continues to work well for FUCODES in 1987 and has made FUCODES well known in Costa Rica.)

8. While FUCODES increased the number of transactions per beneficiary (mostly main office transactions), it reduced the need for lengthy group interactions.

9. Micro-enterprise production cycles were roughly three to six months from the purchase of raw materials to income generation whereas agricultural crops usually had a yearly production cycle. Therefore, farmers had a greater possibility of not being able to repay in the year as opposed merely to falling behind in payments by several months.

Exhibit 1
FUCODES OBJECTIVES

FUCODES Objectives, 1976

The FUCODES objectives have changed over the years. As could be expected, the objectives reflect the influences of advisors and donors. The Board of Directors established the following objectives for FUCODES in 1976:

1. To stimulate marginalized sectors of the country so that they can generate and design their own development strategy.
2. To improve the cultural, social, economic, and political level of low-income people.
3. To encourage the integration of marginalized groups into the socioeconomic life of the country.
4. To encourage groups of fishermen, artisans, farmers, and so forth, to form small community enterprises.
5. To stimulate small industry.
6. To stimulate agricultural production and fishing.
7. To use credit as a means of educating and orienting clients toward the private sector.
8. To interest and stimulate the private sector about its civic responsibilities to help develop the country.

FUCODES Objectives, 1986

By 1986, the FUCODES objectives included individual enterprises in urban areas. According to Julio, FUCODES now promotes a "formula for social responsibility whereby medium and large businesses extend a hand to small businesses through timely and flexible credit, training, and technical assistance." The objectives of the organization as stated in 1986 reflect a change in philosophy to one of "businesses helping other businesses." FUCODES did not emphasize group development, but mentioned "small productive enterprises" as the target of financing. The stated objectives at that time were:

1. To improve the living conditions of beneficiaries by supplying them with timely credit, technical assistance, and training.
2. To make socioeconomic development of micro-enterprises possible to increase the production and productivity of our country.
3. To stimulate micro-entrepreneurs to adopt new techniques and methods that improve the production and profitability of their businesses through agreements with CUP, INA, and ITCR. (See Exhibit 4 for detail.)
4. To facilitate the adequate and timely supply of resources to productive activities.
5. To increase investment in small industries and arts and crafts enterprises to generate employment in urban as well as rural areas.
6. To attend to the continuous needs of micro-entrepreneurs who have been marginalized from traditional sources of training and credit.

Source: FUCODES annual reports and program descriptions.

Exhibit 2
AFFILIATION WITH OTHER ORGANIZATIONS

PADF (Pan-American Development Foundation) was organized in 1962 by officials of the Organization of American States and prominent business people to mobilize U.S. and Latin American business people to participate in a social development network. Their goal was to provide incentives for local business people to organize national development foundations to support grassroots development among the poor—and "put philanthropy on a business-like basis." PADF was crucial in obtaining financing for FUCODES from USAID, IAF, and IDB.

Solidarios (Council of American Development Foundations) is a private, non-profit organization that provides financial assistance, funding, and training to its affiliate foundations in Latin America. Solidarios was founded in 1972 by fourteen of the Latin American development foundations (organized by PADF) to represent the national development foundations. PADF and Solidarios tried to divide their respective tasks in dealing with development organizations, but they ended up more or less as competitors as Solidarios tried to develop its independence. This relationship created some tension between PADF and Solidarios.

Solidarios believes that development foundations should emphasize group lending rather than loans to individuals, based on the idea that credit can promote cohesion among the rural poor so that they can actively change their environment for their own betterment. Most of Solidarios' donations to FUCODES are therefore earmarked for group development efforts in rural areas. Solidarios obtained support from USAID, PACT (Private Agencies Coordinating Together), IDB, and the European Economic Community and their emphasis on group lending closely paralleled USAID and PADF rural development policies during the 1960s and 1970s. Solidarios also believes in a learn-by-doing method of extending credit. FUCODES has received credit and training from Solidarios since 1973 and is an active member of the organization.

USAID (United States Agency for International Development) contributes money to PACT, which is then distributed to FUCODES. USAID generally does not contribute money directly to private organizations in Costa Rica, but does so through a local agency called ACORDE (formerly a division of CINDE). The guidelines for this money are essentially USAID guidelines, however. USAID supported a group rural lending policy throughout the 1960s and 1970s, but switched to an emphasis on urban-based micro-enterprises after 1979. USAID continues to be a major funder of FUCODES through ACORDE.

ACORDE (Association for Costa Rican Development Organizations) is a private, nonprofit Costa Rican organization dedicated to strengthening private voluntary organizations institutionally. ACORDE receives its funding from USAID and provides financial assistance to private voluntary organizations (PVO) that have credit, training, and technical assistance projects. The assistance is expected to improve the efficiency and efficacy of PVOs and to ensure a positive impact on the quality of life of the underprivileged (ACORDE grew out of the PVO department of CINDE, Costa Rican Coalition of Development Initiatives).

PACT (Private Agencies Collaborating Together) is a U.S.-based nonprofit organization funded by USAID to distribute money and provide technical assistance to a variety of development projects. PACT provided seed money to start FUCODES and continued to be a major funder until USAID moneys were distributed through CINDE and ACORDE.

INA (National Apprenticeship Institute) is a government organization that provides basic training courses to micro-entrepreneurs in the areas of small industry and arts and crafts.

CUP (University School of Puntarenas) graduates advise groups of FUCODES clients in agriculture, fishing, and beekeeping.

ITCR (Technological Institute of Costa Rica) donates technical assistance to FUCODES beneficiaries.

CANAPI (National Chamber of Arts and Small Industry) coordinates FUCODES loans to arts and small industries, especially ceramics.

APTAMAI (Association of Small Industrial Maintenance Workshop Owners) coordinates FUCODES credit and technical assistance to its members.

CANARA and *CANAMECC* (Chamber of Radio and Chamber of Collective Communications Media) strengthen the national membership of FUCODES by donating mass media spots to promote the program.

Costa Rican Chambers of Commerce, helps strengthen the membership of business associates who donate to FUCODES.

Others. Additionally, FUCODES has the support of the government of Costa Rica, the Solidarity Unions, the Cooperative Movement, the Catholic church, and many private businesses.

Exhibit 3
ECONOMIC AND FINANCIAL EVOLUTION OF FUCODES

	1976	1977	1978	1979	1980	1981	1982	1983	1984	1985	1986
Exchange Rates colones/dollars	6.00	8.76	8.92	19.06	8.60	42.00	40.00	43.65	48.70	50.35	59.00
Economic Results											
INCOME											
Donations by Affiliate											
Donations, Cash	0	0	0	0	[a]	[a]	[a]	11,821	19,489	26,854	46,671
Donations, In-Kind	0	0	0	0	[a]	[a]	[a]	9,261	44,524	127,818	95,295
Total Affiliate Donations	0	0	0	0	1,163	310	4,850	21,082	64,013	154,672	141,966
International Donations											
USAID/ACORDE	26,375[a]	500,000[a]	[a]	[a]	[a]	[a]	[a]	0	[a]	[a]	0
PACT	[a]	[a]	72,886[a]	[a]	[a]	[a]	[a]	0	16,414	[a]	0
Solidarios	[a]	[a]	15,000[a]	37,110	[a]	[a]	[a]	0	48,585	[a]	0
Other (PADF, IAF)	[a]	[a]	[a]	[a]	[a]	[a]	[a]	0	[a]	[a]	0
Total International Donations	[a]	[a]	[a]	[a]	172,326	26,429	110,900	0	182,236	108,239	0
Total Donations	[a]	[a]	[a]	[a]	173,488	26,738	115,750	21,082	246,249	262,911	141,966
Interest Income	[a]	[a]	[a]	[a]	9,535	3,249	17,900	28,683	29,133	19,662	67,312
International Loans	[a]	[a]	40,000[a]	[a]	19,651	4,024	19,200	17,503	9,893	95,452	0
Other Income	[a]	[a]	[a]	[a]	40,581	8,405	13,250	7,967	6,121	21,761	10,628
INCOME TOTAL	[a]	[a]	[a]	[a]	243,256	42,595	166,100	75,235	291,396	356,264	219,907

Exhibit 3 (cont'd)

	1976	*1977*	*1978*	*1979*	*1980*	*1981*	*1982*	*1983*	*1984*	*1985*	*1986*
EXPENSES											
Personnel	[a]	[a]	[a]	[a]	43,605	12,381	17,275	26,644	50,287	[a]	[a]
Operations[b]	[a]	[a]	[a]	[a]	165,465	45,405	14,700	30,809	112,653	228,533	190,926
Financial[b]	[a]	[a]	[a]	[a]	0	0	0	0	0	26,004	9,829
EXPENSES TOTAL	[a]	[a]	[a]	[a]	209,070	57,786	31,975	57,453	162,940	254,537	200,755
NET SURPLUS (DEFICIT)	[a]	[a]	[a]	[a]	34,186	(15,189)	134,125	17,782	128,456	101,727	19,151
Financial Results											
ASSETS	[a]	41,500	[a]	248,000	313,953	58,738	173,025	193,795	339,986	553,704	553,337
LIABILITIES	[a]	[a]	[a]	[a]	128,721	31,667	23,950	66,075	97,054	248,240	240,807
FUND BALANCE	[a]	[a]	[a]	[a]	185,232	27,071	149,075	127,720	242,931	305,464	312,530

Source: Compiled from FUCODES annual reports and Solidarios, "FUCODES—Un Esfuerzo de la Empresa Privada Hacia la Comunidad Rural," July 1985.

[a] Financial data were not available for the first four years. International donations only are listed; indicates complete information not available to the casewriter.

[b] Includes currency fluctuations, devaluation, transactions costs, and interest.

( ) Indicates negative cashflow.

Exhibit 4
FUCODES CREDIT PROGRAM STATISTICS

	1976	1977	1978	1979	1980	1981	1982	1983	1984	1985	1986
Exchange Rates: colones/dollars	6.00	8.76	8.92	19.06	8.60	42.00	40.00	43.65	48.70	50.35	59.00
CLIENT LOANS IN PORTFOLIO											
Small Industry											
Number	2	5	9	9	a	a	a	6	28	51	55
Amount	2,000	9,000	20,700	31,250	3,256	762	8,025	19,908	112,127	201,589	171,864
Percent	100	31	28	25	2	2	5	10	38	55	47
Agriculture											
Number	0	4	6	8	a	a	a	3	5	7	17
Amount	0	15,150	22,750	28,950	87,907	19,571	109,025	110,515	84,324	35,154	52,034
Percent	0	52	31	22	45	51	71	54	29	10	14
Services											
Number	0	0	0	0	0	0	a	0	5	7	15
Amount	0	0	0	0	0	0	1,850	0	20,695	26,614	63,559
Percent	0	0	0	0	0	0	1	0	7	7	18
Arts and Crafts											
Number	0	0	0	0	a	a	a	3	7	8	5
Amount	0	0	0	0	6,279	690	3,700	15,006	34,825	26,812	7,797
Percent	0	0	0	0	3	2	2	7	12	7	2
Fishing											
Number	0	2	5	9	a	a	a	12	5	2	4
Amount	0	5,100	30,900	65,800	98,256	17,214	31,600	59,748	22,917	61,996	46,102
Percent	0	17	42	53	50	45	21	29	8	17	13

Exhibit 4 (cont'd)

	1976	1977	1978	1979	1980	1981	1982	1983	1984	1985	1986
Agro-industry											
Number	0	0	0	0	0	0	0	0	3	2	4
Amount	0	0	0	0	0	0	0	0	18,397	16,485	21,186
Percent	0	0	0	0	0	0	0	0	6	5	6
TOTAL LOANS											
Total Amount in Portfolio	2,000	29,250	74,350	126,000	195,698	38,237	154,200	205,177	293,285	368,650	362,542
Amount Loaned in Year	2,000	27,500	45,100	40,100	197,209	16,118	130,676	64,730	201,508	184,333	113,861
Total Loans in Portfolio	2	11	20	26	30	37	49	na	53	77	100
Group Loans	2	11	20	26	30	37	49	na	25	13	7
Individual Loans	0	0	0	0	0	0	0	0	28	64	93
OTHER STATISTICS											
Late Payment Rate (loans over 90 days late)[b] in Percent	[a]	[a]	[a]	[a]	18	32	na	3	8	7	11
Number of Employees	22	23	25	25	28	5	6	9	11	11	11
Number of Associate Members	17	17	17	17	26	32	58	148	200	255	290
Number of Beneficiary Families/Year	20	80	96	130	144	167	275	735[c]	422	539	400

[a] Indicates complete information not available to the casewriter.
[b] FUCODES considers a loan default rate of 10% or less to be acceptable.
[c] Of these beneficiaries 680 belong to an artisan association and do not get loans directly. The funds are used for marketing, training, and overhead for a tourist shop.

Exhibit 5

FUCODES LOAN GUIDELINES AND CRITERIA

Conditions	Micro-Enterprises Characteristics	Groups
General Requirements	Business is personally administered by owner and contributes significantly to his or her income.	Activity personally administered by and contributes significantly to each participant's income. Groups do not have to be legally registered to qualify.
Client Limitations	Ten or fewer employees, annual sales < 3.5 million colones (U.S.$56,700), assets < 128,000 colones (U.S.$ 2,100). Experience in project area and willing to accept FUCODES advice and training.	Each group member must fit within the financial guidelines established for individuals. Clients must have experience in project area and be willing to accept advice and training.
Minimum Participants per Loan	One person, dedicated full-time to the activity.	Groups must consist of at least five active members. (Has changed over time.)
Geographic Area	National level; rural or urban.	National level; rural.
Loan Amount	Up to 300,000 colones (U.S.$4,900).	Up to 1.5 million colones (U.S.$24,300) for group.
Use of Loan	Farming, Small Industry, Arts and Crafts, Agro-industry, and Services.	Farming, Small Industry, Arts and Crafts, Agro-industry, and Services.
Real Interest Rate[a]	15% Farming; 18% Other Activities.	15% Farming; 18% Other Activities.
Terms	Up to three years for working capital. Up to five years for machinery, equipment, and capital improvements.	Up to three years for working capital. Up to five years for machinery, equipment, and capital improvements
Grace Period	Up to six months.	Up to six months.
Form of Payment	Monthly installments or according to the activity.	Monthly installments or according to the activity.
Loan Disbursement	Up to five disbursements.	Up to five disbursements.
Loan Guarantees	Moral, fiduciary, mortgage. Owner responsible for loan.	Moral, fiduciary, mortgage. All group members responsible for loan.

Source: PRODEME: Condiciones Generales de los Creditos, FUCODES document. Supplemented by recent FUCODES documents.
[a] Set by Board of Director, equal to or less than bank rates established by government for each sector.

Exhibit 6
DESCRIPTION AND EVALUATION OF FUCODES GROUP STRATEGY

To determine how best to make its resources available, FUCODES conducted diagnostic studies of the regions it planned to work in. It also contacted and exchanged information with other authorities and local leaders working in those areas. FUCODES promoters personally visited potential clients to inform them about the organization's training and credit program, and to explain that assistance would be available only to people who agreed to work in groups. They encouraged potential clients to band together with others engaged in the same economic activities to form groups of fifteen to thirty people. This one-on-one promotion required a promotional staff of ten, which was large in relation to the thirty loans FUCODES had outstanding in 1980.

After establishing contact with a group, the same promoter continued to work with the group members to organize and train them to cooperate together on a productive project. In the process they facilitated group decision making, helped to elect group leaders, and assured that projects remained within FUCODES' guidelines. Once a group decided upon a project, the entire group would submit a single investment plan to purchase materials or equipment to be used on a shared basis.[1] Clients identified their own projects, resources, investment needs, technical assistance requirements, and so forth. Every member of the group was informed of loan obligations and signed a promissory note indicating his or her "solidarity" pledge to repay the loan on time. In the event that one member was unable to repay his quota, the other members would make up the difference. This solidarity mechanism replaced the need for physical loan guarantees and allowed poorer beneficiaries, who typically did not own sufficient assets (to use as a loan guarantee), to qualify for credit.

Training

FUCODES offered groups two kinds of training: group training to teach members how to work together productively; and administrative training to improve the efficiency of projects. Because the object was to get group members working together cooperatively, FUCODES required that all client groups receive some training as a group before they received a loan. Group training helped clients to analyze their problems and to seek solutions that would promote group cohesiveness. The training usually was given at the clients' place of business. Because group members assumed a joint obligation, FUCODES believed it was important for training sessions to be participatory so as to include all the member's views.

Before a group was eligible for credit, it was also required to put together a basic accounting system that allowed it to keep track of its project. It also had to convince the promoters that it was able to work together. These skills were taught in training sessions, but both processes were time consuming if the members had not had previous experience working in groups. Consequently, the start-up phase

---

[1] Promoters filled out a credit application according to the plans discussed by the group and submitted first loan requests to the Development Department for revision. Subsequent projects were prepared entirely by the promoters.

of the project took as long as six months before an agreement could be reached over the use of the loan and to formulate an investment plan.

Administrative training sessions were aimed at improving the efficiency of client businesses, and helped groups to make investment decisions and to set up bookkeeping systems. The FUCODES advisors held administrative training sessions regularly in the main San Jose office, using specially designed teaching materials to impart administrative skills. Training was also sometimes conducted by outside organizations at the client's business place. Unlike the group training, administrative training was not a prerequisite to receiving credit, but it was strongly recommended.

Technical Assistance

Assistance was originally provided to groups needing managerial or technical advice by the FUCODES advisors. Because the groups were located all over Costa Rica, FUCODES maintained a relatively large staff of promoters to attend to them. When administrative costs became more of an issue in 1980, FUCODES looked for other alternatives to provide assistance more efficiently.

In 1981, FUCODES formalized agreements with a number of government-sponsored organizations to provide specialized technical assistance to FUCODES clients. Although many of the FUCODES promoters had agricultural and economic backgrounds, the foundation found it useful to draw on the expertise of organizations like the National Institute of Apprentices (INA) and the University School of Puntarenas (CUP) whose students specialized in agriculture, fishing, small industry, and arts and crafts. This arrangement allowed FUCODES promoters to assist a greater number of clients, and for clients to receive specialized assistance and advice. And because many of the advisors provided by outside organizations were students or recently trained individuals, FUCODES was often required to cover only their travel and meal expenses as their work for FUCODES was considered part of their training. (See Exhibit 2 for a further description of organizations that provided assistance to FUCODES.)

Technical assistance was designed to improve production methods, apply concepts learned in training, or to discuss new business decisions. When FUCODES' staff did not provide the technical assistance, they acted as an intermediary in this process by recommending certain types of assistance to clients and coordinating the other advisors who worked with FUCODES clients. In addition, advisors from the FUCODES Development Department were responsible for following up on credit projects. They tried to visit groups once each month to provide technical assistance to the various projects and to monitor the interactions among group members. If personal visits were not possible, the advisors would offer assistance over the telephone. Advisors were also responsible for submitting status reports on the projects and for recommending additional actions for FUCODES and for the groups themselves.

Credit

In order to receive credit, clients applied directly to the FUCODES office in San Jose because the promoters did not have the authority to approve loans. Once a loan was approved by the Board's Credit Committee, the loan check was disbursed to a representative of the group. Loans terms and interest rates were also established by the Board of Directors, but varied according to the type of business activity and the risks involved. Likewise, loan periods varied from one to four years. (See Exhibit 6 for a description of FUCODES' group loans.)

A FUCODES advisor would check to see that the loan money was invested in the investment project specified by the group and see that the group members understood they had to pay the group representative before each loan payment was due to FUCODES. Agricultural loan payments were due every six months, whereas fishing payments might be due every month. If one member could not pay his or her share, the others would have to cover that portion to meet their collective obligation, and the group could later work out reimbursement of that money among themselves.

Most of the program's financial transactions occurred in the main office. A group representative could either make loan payments to a local branch of FUCODES' bank, or deliver the payment directly to the office in San José, but most of the groups delivered their payments to the office. They did so because many rural areas did not have a bank branch, and also perhaps because the clients did not feel comfortable doing business with banks. In the event that a group could not present a payment on time, the group representative would contact the advisor to explain, or alternatively, the advisor would contact the group to see why repayment had not occurred and to remind it of its obligations. Depending on the reasons, FUCODES could either consider the loan late and continue to charge interest on the loan, or refinance the loan and change the due date.

Evaluation of FUCODES Program by Solidarios

FUCODES grew very rapidly in 1978 and 1979. It was able to attract more international donations, which increased its assets from U.S.$41,500 in 1977 to U.S.$248,000 in 1979. It introduced new programs, strengthened its fishing and social promotion projects, and tripled its staff in a few years. Between January and July 1980, when many of FUCODES' first loans were due, the combination of nonrepayment of loans and increased administrative costs of the expanded program resulted in a program deficit of U.S.$70,000. In an effort to identify the causes of the deficit, consultants from Solidarios, one of FUCODES' supporters, conducted an evaluation of the program. In the evaluation, Solidarios identified several main problems within FUCODES at that time:

- lack of an institutional strategy and methodology to execute and supervise promotional and credit programs, recuperation of funds, and administration of resources;
- lack of supervisory, training, and technical assistance follow-up on group loans;
- lack of a recruitment and selection policy for administrative and technical personnel;
- inability to provide their internal contribution as agreed upon with USAID;
- lack of promotional policies and strategies to attract private local funding;
- lack of a general working plan that specified short- and medium-term goals that took into consideration available human and financial resources.

Although Costa Rica was undergoing hard times economically (the exchange rate increased from 8.6 colones/dollar to 42 colones/dollar in one year), the situation was aggravated by a default rate of up to 80 percent in 1981. Many of these loans, especially those extended to fishermen, were never recovered.

Exhibit 7
OUTLINE OF COSTA RICAN DEVELOPMENT PLAN

The following general goals are included in the "Return to the Land" (Volvemos a la Tierra) government strategy of the 1982–86 National Development Plan:

Political Objectives
- Strengthen democracy.
- Protect ethnic and cultural values.

Economic and Social Objectives
- Improve income and wealth distribution by increasing incomes of the poor in urban and rural areas.
- Increase employment in the country.
- Increase economic growth.
- Improve the efficiency of productive sectors of the economy.
- Lessen the economic differences among regions and increase participation in development planning.
- Improve capacity to export goods and develop internal capacity to substitute national products for those previously imported to improve the Costa Rican Balance of Payments.

The Costa Rican government supports the development of cooperatives through INFOCOOP. INFOCOOP, the National Institute of Cooperative Promotion, is an autonomous government agency that is charged with supervising all the cooperatives in Costa Rica. In 1986 there were 545 cooperatives with 270,000 members in the country, accounting for about 30 percent of the economically active population. INFOCOOP supervises the administration of the cooperatives, provides training and technical assistance, and provides loans for productive projects designed by the cooperatives. (Most of its services are provided free of charge.) The institution had strong political support from the previous government and is financially well off. A number of the cooperatives are very large and politically significant.

Exhibit 8
FUCODES ORGANIZATIONAL CHART, 1987

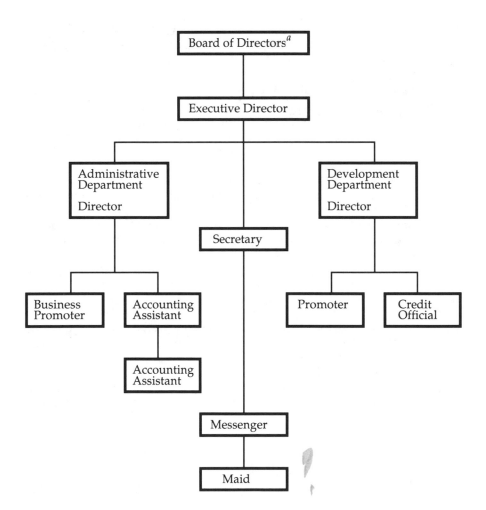

---

[a] Directors represent a wide range of successful private sector businesses.

The Grameen Bank Project (A): Who Are the Poor and How Can They Best be Helped?

This case was written by Dr. Kay Calavan and Professor H. I. Latifee in collaboration with Dr. Muhammad Yunus. It is intended as a basis for class discussion rather than as an illustration of either effective or ineffective handling of an administrative situation. The collaboration and support of the Executive Director of the Grameen Bank and his staff are gratefully acknowledged.

In 1972 Dr. Muhammad Yunus returned to Bangladesh from the United States. He had spent seven years there completing his doctoral degree in Economics at Vanderbilt University, teaching at Tennessee State University, and mobilizing support in the United States for the 1971 Bangladesh War of Liberation. On his return to Bangladesh, he found a war-ravaged, newly born country with multiple national problems. These included a long-term stagnating economy, serious social-economic-political disruptions, a rapidly increasing population on an overcrowded landbase, high unemployment and underemployment, and low agricultural productivity (see Exhibit 1). Along with other foreign-educated Bangladeshis who were returning, he wanted to use his skills in the rehabilitation of his newly independent country. At the urging of a former professor, Dr. Yunus first joined the newly created Planning Commission as Deputy Chief of the General Economics Division. But he quickly realized that this was not his kind of work. After two months he resigned and went home to Chittagong in the Southern region of the country.

In December 1972 he joined the Department of Economics, Chittagong University, as Department Head. He desired to work in a university setting where he and interested colleagues and students could conduct action research and learn first hand about economic conditions in the villages. At that time there were few field data describing the 90 percent of the country that was village-based. He introduced new courses, tried to give a problem-solving orientation to the courses taught in the Department, and set up an informal program called the Rural Studies Project. As a part of this orientation, he wanted to help solve the problems in the village adjacent to the University campus. He made it known that "a University is a reservoir of knowledge for the whole world and if that knowledge does not spill over the nearest land, then it is useless." Soon after he took the teaching position, rural living conditions in Bangladesh worsened considerably because of the devastating 1974 flood and resulting widespread famine.

"Three Shares Farming" in Jobra

Famine made Dr. Yunus, like many concerned people in Bangladesh, look very seriously at the food self-sufficiency issue. Early in 1973 he was surprised to see that the agricultural land around the University campus remained unused during the winter season. This was the season when the country could grow a flood-free and high-yielding variety (HYV) of rice. In fact, several areas in Chittagong played a leading role in producing HYV winter *(boro)* rice. He found it unacceptable that land next to the campus should remain fallow during this potentially very productive season.

Dr. Yunus wanted to understand why people did not utilize their land to grow *boro* rice. He began by visiting nearby villages, talking with the villagers, and making careful observations about their situations and activities. To deepen his understanding, Dr. Yunus began, with the help of a colleague and several students, to conduct a socioeconomic survey of Jobra, the village next to the University campus. They found that most of the villagers (52 percent) were landless people who did not own any cultivable land. There were no large landlords in Jobra, only small and marginal farmers. Also, the village had a food deficit—producing just enough rice to feed the village population for only ten months in a year—in spite of the fact that it contained fertile fields, a perennial *chora* stream source of water, a deep tubewell, at least two nominal agricultural cooperatives, and a large number of unemployed persons who could provide agricultural labor.

The deep tubewell was virtually unutilized—sixteen acres were irrigated during the 1973–74 winter season and only twenty acres in the 1974–75 season (see Exhibit 2)—mainly because there was no effective local irrigation organization to manage water for a large command area. In the 1974–75 season, the few participating farmers spent more time fighting with each other over bad money management of the tubewell than growing rice. At the beginning of the next winter season nobody came forward to use the deep tubewell. Dr. Yunus reasoned with the villagers to organize themselves to grow the irrigated crop. Some of them replied that they would rather go hungry than eat "bitter rice."

When Dr. Yunus failed to persuade the farmers, he requested that they convene a meeting of all farmers where he would try to help them find a solution. At the evening meeting villagers shouted at each other. About midnight, when they had exhausted themselves, Dr. Yunus offered them a plan for a local system that he called the "Three Shares Farm" or *Nabajug Tebagha Khamar* (NTK). This system would be run as follows:

1. A Management Committee would be set up to run, for a *boro* season, the deep tubewell and supply water, HYV seed, fertilizer, and insecticides for Three Shares Farm, which included land cultivated by participating farmers. The Management Committee would borrow from a local commercial bank branch to supply all inputs for the *boro* season for participating farmers. Dr. Yunus would head the Management Committee.

2. The members had to abide by the rules and regulations framed by the Management Committee. There would be weekly meetings for participants and the Management Committee to talk about problems and arrangements.

3. The farmer, whether owner or tenant, would remain responsible for all preharvest operations.

4. At the time of harvest, each plot of land would be divided in three equal parts with the harvest from the parts going to the Three Shares Farm Management Committee, the farmer, and the owner of the land. If the Farm Management Committee had a surplus over its expenditures, the surplus would belong to the participating farmers. If the farm had a deficit, Dr. Yunus would personally cover this deficit.

It was a long and difficult process for Dr. Yunus to convince the villagers, especially the landowners, that this was a reasonable proposal. They were particularly suspicious that this was a trick by Dr. Yunus to socialize landholdings. Also, the landlords insisted on their usual one-half of the crop. However, at a meeting arranged by Dr. Yunus one week later, the Jobra farmers agreed to try this local management system as an experiment for the 1975–76 *boro* season.

It was the responsibility of Dr. Yunus to convince the Janata Bank Branch located outside the University gate to provide a preseason loan to the NTK organization. This was a novel undertaking for any commercial bank at this time because they were not yet initiated to agricultural lending. Furthermore, Dr. Yunus was told that the branch located in the campus had never given loans, let alone to villagers. This branch saw itself, like other rural branches of commercial banks, as an outlet for collecting deposits for the bank head office, which would then be used for loans to urban businesses (see Exhibit 3). In addition, any agricultural lending programs required land collateral for loans. But Dr. Yunus made it clear that for this loan he could not offer such collateral. Instead he offered to act as personal guarantor of the Tk 45,000 loan, and the bank accepted the alternative.

Three Shares Farm (NTK) was very successful in terms of increasing village agricultural productivity and yearly incomes of participants (see Exhibit 2). The acreage under *boro* cultivation increased to 85 acres, and the per acre yield increased from 11 maunds to 29 maunds (1 maund = 40 kgs.). The village became a food surplus village. However, unexpected problems for the Management Committee included cheating on the Management's share and Management paddy storage and marketing problems. Consequently, Management was short Tk 13,000 for repaying the loan. Dr. Yunus repaid this from his own pocket.

The next year the farmers approached Dr. Yunus and asked him to again take a loan and organize the NTK system. However, he clearly told them that he had demonstrated the benefits of the system and now it was their turn to organize and manage the system. At the beginning of the *boro* season, the Jobra farmers finally called a meeting and decided to undertake the NTK cultivation. Under Dr. Yunus' patronage, the Management Committee took a loan from the local bank that they successfully repaid. (The locally managed Three Share Farm (NTK system) in Jobra has continued in operation until the present day and significantly expanded the cultivated acreage.)

The Other Jobra

After the successful 1975–76 *boro* season experiment, several events caused Dr. Yunus to focus his attention and that of his research colleagues elsewhere in Jobra. Dr. Yunus came away from the Three Shares Farm experiment confident about his ideas. He had proved that the necessary ingredients for development were there in the village all along; the only thing needed was some local organizational framework that people could work with, and some institutional arrangements to support the program. With this newly gained confidence he presented his thesis in a paper titled "Institutional Framework for Self-Reliant Bangladesh" in the 1976 annual convention of the Bangladesh Economic Association in Dhaka. He argued in his paper that it is essential to set up a government at the village level (*gram sarkar*) to organize people and resources to solve their own problems. He argued that this village government should be made up of representatives from all sections of village people (for example, a farmer group and a women's group), including representation from the landless people through their own association. Many in his audience criticized the *gram sarkar* concept. A key criticism was that the landless can't form their own strong organization because they have no assets ("zero plus zero = zero") and because they are subservient to rich villagers who won't allow them to organize. Dr. Yunus argued that "We can't assume each landless person equals zero and we are overlooking the strength of landless numbers." Dr. Yunus made a final comment that the present discussion was speculation until one of them made the attempt to organize the landless and came back with the experience.

As he returned to Chittagong, Dr. Yunus was intrigued by the question of whether an effective landless association could be formed. From his past village experiment, he saw that his early NTK efforts had directly aided local landowners and tenant farmers and caused an increase in the demand for agricultural labor in the *boro* season. But the NTK program provided only marginal benefit, mainly a few days of post-harvest threshing work, to the majority of the villagers who were landless and to the poor households in which women were sole or important wage earners. He remembered at the previous Jobra *boro* harvest season the many women who came to husk paddy with their feet. They fought for locations to do this work early in the mornings. He remembered thinking "How many women can find an income from this activity?"

On his return to Chittagong, Dr. Yunus started paying more attention to the poverty issue. Why should one remain poor? What was keeping them from moving out of poverty? Dr. Yunus was trying to discover his own economics rather than take it from the textbooks with which he was disenchanted. He made a habit of visiting people at their homes in Jobra and talking about how they earned a living and survived and what their daily lives were like. It was not easy for Dr. Yunus and his male associates to talk with poor Jobra women because of the strict *purdah* rules in the conservative Chittagong area. However, they worked out a method of sitting outside a house and talking through a girl go-between or through the house wall to the women inside. He also assigned some students, including two women students, to prepare some case studies and to collect other data.

One woman Dr. Yunus talked with revealed that she earned only Tk 0.50 (two U.S. pennies) by making a bamboo stool. It was difficult to believe anyone would work for so little. She made so little because she had no money to buy bamboo to make the stool. So she borrowed the money from the trader who bought the final product. The trader could not miss the opportunity of pushing his margin to the extreme and virtually eliminating the return for the craft woman. This was a stunning experience for Dr. Yunus. He decided to find out how many more people in the village were borrowing from the traders to carry on their work. He, with the help of a student, came up with a list of forty-two persons borrowing a total amount of Tk 856 (U.S.$57). Dr. Yunus later recalled that at that time he felt ashamed of himself for belonging to a society that could not provide a meager $57 as loans to forty-two able, skilled human beings who were trying to make a living.

Dr. Yunus and his research students also found that in Jobra one important occupation of landless males was rickshaw pulling in and around the Chittagong University area. They did not own rickshaws since they had no money. They had to rent rickshaws from well-to-do rickshaw owners who charged Tk 8 per day as rent, leaving them very little profit. Dr. Yunus began to think about how they could be helped to pull their own rickshaws and enjoy their income. Women who husked paddy for other people all day earned a pound of rice plus one meal of leftovers. If they could purchase paddy and husk it at their own homes, they could make a profit of Tk 20 *and* keep broken rice and chaff. People who wove cloth all day on someone else's loom got a low wage of Tk 25. Although the same amount of labor on one's own loom brought an income of Tk 45, the poor weavers did not take this opportunity because they could not get capital at reasonable cost to purchase yarn.

The data revealed that the poor, including many women from poor households, were engaged in a wide variety of nonagricultural earning activities but received minimal profit from these activities. They already possessed "survival skills" in processing agricultural products, home manufacturing of locally used goods, storage of agricultural produce, marketing goods, and providing maintenance and transport services. However, they did not have access to credit with reasonable terms to purchase necessary raw materials and tools for profitable use of their labor. Their only source of capital was from middlemen and moneylenders with usurious rates of interest. There were many types of moneylending for the disadvantaged. All of these were highly oppressive but socially accepted contracts in Bangladesh. The normal rate of interest was 10 percent per month, but the rate could reach 10 percent per day. There were also in-kind loans such as borrowing a maund of paddy at the beginning of the planting season and repaying it with two and a half to three maunds of paddy at harvest. A number of forms of land securities for loans allowed the creditor to use the land until full repayment or often the right to purchase the land at a predetermined price at the end of an agreed period. Another form of loan security was obligatory supply of agricultural labor on creditors' land. The researchers collected data indicating a vicious cycle for the disadvantaged households of increasing alienation of land and profit from labor eaten up by middlemen and moneylenders and neighboring elite household employers.

Dr. Yunus and his associates had completed an analysis of the problem of village poverty in Bangladesh. Now he needed to work out a possible solution to the problem and test his hypotheses.

Exhibit 1
BANGLADESH COUNTRY CONTEXT: MID-1970s

General Factors[a]
- Estimated population of 77 million (1974).
- Nearly 90% of population lives in the rural areas.
- Population is about 85% Muslim; the remainder are Hindus, Buddhists, and Christians.
- Estimated national income distribution (1974):
  - Highest Quintile—42%
  - Lowest Quintile—7%
- In 1975–76 the exchange rate was about Tk 15 = U.S.$1

Distribution of Total Owned Land in Bangladesh, 1977[b]

Acres	Total Households (%)	Total Agricultural Land (%)
0.00	32.8	—
0.01–1.00	29.1[c]	9.6
1.01–3.00	23.4	28.1
3.01–5.00	8.0	20.5
5.01–7.00	3.0	11.7
7.01 and above	3.7	30.0

Estimated Incidence of Rural Poverty in Bangladesh: 1963–64 and 1975[d]

Year	Absolutely Poor[e] (% of households)	Extremely Poor[f] (% of households)
1963–64	51.7	9.8
1975	70.3	50.5

[a] *Source:* Bangladesh Bureau of Statistics, *Statistical Year Book of Bangladesh*, Dhaka, 1980.

[b] *Source:* USAID, 1977, "Report on the Hierarchy of Interests in Land in Bangladesh," Dhaka and Washington.

[c] In 1977 the percentage of households which were estimated to be "functionally landless" with less than 0.4 acre of land was around 50%.

[d] *Source:* A.R. Khan, "Poverty and Inequality in Rural Bangladesh," ILO (WEP) Working Paper, Geneva, 1976.

[e] Per capita monthly income of Tk 23.61 or less corresponding to per capita calorie intake by the family of 1,935 Kcal, that is, 90% or less of the recommended intake.

[f] Per capita monthly income of Tk 17.02 or less corresponding to per capita intake by the family of 1,720 Kcal, that is, 80% or less of the recommended intake.

Exhibit 2
BORO CULTIVATION IN JOBRA
BEFORE AND AFTER THE THREE SHARES FARM SYSTEM

Season	Cultivated Area (acres)	No. of Farmers	Yield/Acre (maunds of rice)[a]
1972–73	6	—	10.0
1973–74	16	—	13.0
1974–75	20	—	14.0
———— Three Shares Farm Started ————			
1975–76	85	156	29.0
1976–77	79	135	34.0
1977–78	103	185	31.5
1978–79	160	217	31.0
1979–80	181	257	31.7
1980–81	180	255	35.0
1981–82	181	257	35.0

Source: Latifee, H. I., "Report on Nabajug Tebhaga Khamar," Department of Economics, Chittagong University, Bangladesh, 1983.
[a] 1 maund = 88 pounds.

Exhibit 3
BANK DEPOSITS AND LOANS
IN URBAN AND RURAL AREAS IN BANGLADESH: 1972–1983
(taka in crores)[a]

Year	Deposits			Loans		
	Urban	Rural	% Rural	Urban	Rural	% Rural
1972–73	616.21	96.17	13.5	572.59	47.70	7.7
1973–74	791.83	123.58	13.5	727.53	60.61	7.7
1974–75	880.73	137.46	13.5	749.83	62.47	7.7
1975–76	1,002.85	156.51	13.5	856.68	72.12	7.7
1976–77	1,290.08	155.18	10.7	1,087.36	66.57	5.8
1977–78	1,516.07	231.62	13.3	1,353.11	136.69	9.2
1978–79	1,939.14	354.05	15.4	1,665.33	181.05	8.8
1979–80	2,402.84	404.18	14.4	2,402.68	277.34	10.4
1980–81	2,963.68	559.89	15.9	2,963.68	412.55	12.2
1981–82	3,256.31	593.79	15.4	6,77.48	560.12	13.2
1982–83	4,243.65	854.35	16.8	4,086.92	439.67	9.7

Source: Bangladesh Bank. Latifee, H. I., "Role of Nationalized Banks in Bangladesh," Department of Economics, Chittagong University.
[a] 1 crore = 10 million.

Case 11

The Grameen Bank Project (B): An Experimental "Grameen" Branch Bank

This case was written by Dr. Kay Calavan and Professor H. I. Latifee in collaboration with Dr. Muhammad Yunus. It is intended as a basis for class discussion rather than as an illustration of either effective or ineffective handling of an administrative situation. The collaboration and support of the Executive Director of the Grameen Bank and his staff are gratefully acknowledged.

Through the action research of the Rural Studies Project at the Chittagong University, Dr. Yunus discovered one big reason for poverty: people did not receive fair return for their work. More often it was not lack of work that made people poor, it was work with little profit that made them poor. He saw an immediate opportunity to intervene to improve the situation. He took money from his own pocket and asked a student to make it available as loans to the listed persons, so that they did not have to borrow from the traders, and would not be obligated to sell their products to him at his price. He soon decided, however, that personal charity was not the best response. Proper institutional arrangements were needed to take care of the credit needs of the poor at reasonable interest rates. To work out these arrangements he went to the manager of the bank from which he had borrowed for the Three Share Farm. The bank manager told him that the rules of the bank did not permit him to lend any money to poor people. An individual must offer collateral before he can borrow, and a poor person cannot offer the collateral. Dr. Yunus did not give up hope because he thought his idea was too important to give up. With the advice of the branch manager he met a senior official in the bank's hierarchy. This official first suggested that each poor loan applicant could find a well-to-do person as a guarantor. However, Dr. Yunus knew that with this arrangement the poor would be exploited by the well-to-do. Finally, he negotiated a deal with this official by offering himself as the guarantor for the loans in *lieu* of individual collateral.

Having an agreement in principle, Dr. Yunus tried to work out the operational procedures. He did not want to repeat the experience of other Bangladesh credit programs, such as cooperatives, where the loans did not get repaid. He wanted to make sure that all his loans were repaid on time without fail. To come up with ideas he started having meetings in groups with the potential borrowers in Jobra. He decided that these loans would be made available only to landless people, that is, people not owning any cultivable land at all. He wanted to familiarize himself with them and their economic activities and check out their reactions regarding the rules he was about to finalize. Several such sessions took place before a set of rules were announced. Based upon his discussions with the landless about what they thought would work, Dr. Yunus decided that groups would be formed according to the activities for which loans would be taken. If one borrowed for a milk cow, he or she would belong to the milk cow group. If one borrowed to purchase a rickshaw, he would belong to the rickshaw pullers group. Not all the members of the group would receive loans at the same time. If something went wrong with repayment of the first loans, waiting members would not be able to receive loans. Group responsibility for repayment of loans was substituted for the usual requirement of land collateral to insure loans. Most loans and interest (at bank rate of 16 percent) were to be repaid in weekly installments at compulsory weekly group meetings. However, rickshaw loans would be repaid in daily installments to a local shopkeeper.

After all these arrangements had been established, the first loans for seven borrowers, totaling Tk 16,050, were disbursed on January 4, 1977 (see Exhibit 1). Repayment arrangements were quite cumbersome. Receiving daily repayments and keeping the records straight were not easy, particularly if one was depending on a volunteer shopkeeper to do all this. Dr. Yunus, a colleague who enjoyed working with him, and a couple of student volunteers were responsible for conducting the weekly meetings, collecting installments, and doing the record keeping. As the amount of work increased, Dr. Yunus sanctioned Tk 50 (U.S.$3.00) monthly allowance for each of the student volunteers from the Chittagong University Rural Economics Programme, a Ford Foundation-supported program of which he was the Director.

More loans were requested in the months of March, June, and August from the bank (see Exhibit 1). But as the amounts of the loans started increasing, record keeping at the branch was also increasing and there were noticeable delays in sanctioning and disbursing loans. The Janata Bank Head Office, which had not foreseen an ongoing series of loans to poor villagers, started asking many questions about each loan and declined to lend money in some cases. With uncertainty and delays in loan disbursements, the confidence of the potential borrowers as well as of the current borrowers in the program started to decline. There was irregular attendance at the weekly meetings and occasional erratic repayment behavior. In one case, a man who had bought a cow for fattening sold it early and stopped attending meetings and making loan repayments. The group organizers had to work hard to regain group confidence and discipline. In this case, the group went to the man's home and took one cow from his cowherd, sold it, and repaid his loan.

In June 1977, Dr. Yunus had a chance meeting with Mr. A.M. Anisuzzaman, at that time the Managing Director of the Bangladesh Krishi Bank (the National Agricultural Bank), in his Dhaka office. Upon meeting Dr. Yunus, Mr. Anisuzzaman took the opportunity to accuse the academicians of being removed from reality and not being useful in solving practical problems. He asked Dr. Yunus to help him clear up the mess his bank had created for itself over the past years. Dr. Yunus responded by arguing that it would be better for him to use his time making a fresh beginning. He argued that the banking system was working under wrong premises, and someone should set them right. Dr. Yunus explained what he was doing in Jobra and challenged Mr. Anisuzzaman to set up an experimental branch in Jobra and hand it over to Dr. Yunus, who would design its rules and operate it. Dr. Yunus was quite surprised when the BKB Managing Director promptly accepted this proposal.

As a result of this conversation in June 1977, an experimental branch of BKB was set up in Jobra in March 1978 and was handed over to Dr. Yunus. This branch was formally named the "Experimental Grameen Branch," and the project itself was named by Dr. Yunus as the Grameen Bank Project (Village Bank Project). Dr. Yunus selected its staff, and BKB paid the salaries. Problems showing up at Janata Bank now were resolved by shifting the lending from Janata Bank to the Grameen Branch of BKB. With Janata Bank, Dr. Yunus had to stand as guarantor for every single loan. With the Grameen Branch, this was not required. It was much easier now to expand the project because he was making all the rules for this new credit system. At the Grameen Branch a full-time project coordinator, called a "Field Manager," was appointed to run the project. Several of Dr. Yunus' students were appointed as "bankworkers" to attend centre meetings, collect installments, keep loan records, and monitor the loan utilization.

Based on the early loan experiences, Dr. Yunus introduced many changes in the working procedures to make things run more efficiently and avoid the risk of default. The activity-based groups were not stable bodies but increased or decreased in size according to types of loans. Also, borrowers had to move from one group to another if they borrowed for a different purpose the next time. Dr. Yunus abandoned the idea of groups organized according to activity and opted instead for multiactivity mutual support groups with five to ten members of their choosing. Group members had to be from the same village and be "like-minded" to encourage trust and cooperation. Each group was to elect a chairman and a secretary. Although Dr. Yunus' first idea was that both men and women would participate in the same groups, experience indicated that this was operationally difficult for women. They could not comfortably sit in the same meetings with men and were consequently left out on some decisions. Based upon this finding, Dr. Yunus decided to have separate women's groups.

All loans were to be repaid in weekly installments at the required weekly meetings. A Group Fund was introduced to mobilize personal savings; each member was required to save one taka each week. Later a 5 percent group tax was introduced to help boost the savings. An Emergency Fund was introduced as a contingency/insurance fund to cover default, accidents, theft, or death. It required a borrower to pay the equivalent of 50 percent of the amount paid as interest on the loan.

The definition of a "landless person" was revised upward to include a person who comes from a household owning less than 0.4 acre of cultivable land. (A local unit, the *kani*, was adopted as the highest land ownership that the project would accept, and this unit happened to be equivalent to 0.4 acre. A few years later this ceiling was refixed at 0.5 acre when the project expanded in other districts where the local unit did not make any sense.)

To make the weekly meetings more organized the concept of a "centre" was introduced. Several groups were to make up a centre and hold their weekly meetings in a convenient location around their homes. All centres in one village were to federate into a Village Landless Association (*Bhumiheen Samiti*) and later a Village Women's Association (*Mohila Samiti*) was added. Each centre was to elect its centre-chief, and deputy centre-chief. Each Association was to elect its own chief and deputy chief.

Because of the evolution of the project, different groups were subjected to different rules depending on when they joined the Grameen Bank Project. Dr. Yunus decided to sort out all the rules and make them applicable for all groups. These approved rules were printed in a booklet containing the bylaws. (To this date these rules remain the basic principles of the Grameen Bank.)

Project activity soon attracted the attention of people in villages adjacent to Jobra. There was demand for expansion to neighboring villages. As the credit project expanded, the Grameen Branch provided those loans. At this time the Managing Director of the Sonali Bank also became interested in the Grameen Bank Project and requested Dr. Yunus to include the Sonali Bank branch in a neighboring union (*Hathazari*).

By the end of 1978 the experiment had developed into a promising credit program (see Exhibit 2). Dr. Yunus and other staff in the GBP felt they had successfully demonstrated that: (1) a system could be developed for extending banking facilities to the poor; (2) given a support institution, the poor could effectively participate in a credit program and create their own employment; (3) the poor could repay the loans with commercial interest in a timely fashion; and (4) the poor could increase their incomes through their own activities.

Through papers presented at conferences by Professor Yunus, the project was capturing the attention of Government officials and influential members of the banking community. The banking community was working with the Government and donor organizations to provide more effective credit programs for rural development. However, the experience of the banking community in dispensing rural credit was an unhappy one. Could the Grameen Bank Project serve as a model of how to provide credit to the poor on a national scale or would the project be dismissed as a one-professor, one-village type of experiment with a limited lifespan?

Exhibit 1

GRAMEEN BANK PROJECT LOANS IN 1977

Loan No.	Amount (Tk)	Processing	No. of Loanees	Activities
1	16,050	1 day	7	Rickshaw Cow Fattening Snack Selling
2	25,300	44 days	10	Rickshaw Cow Fattening Rickshaw Mechanic Tailor
3	39,000	60 days	25	Rickshaw Milk Cow Goat Fattening Trading
4	55,500 (received Tk 31,000)	76 days	33	Rickshaw Milk Cow Cow Fattening Goat Fattening Poultry Raising Cattle Trading Rice Trading Tea Stall Old Cloth Selling Grocery Stall Timber Trading

Source: Asaduzzaman Khan, "Report on the Jobhra Bumiheen Samiti," Rural Studies Project, Department of Economics, Chittagong University, 1978.

Exhibit 2

GRAMEEN BANK PROJECT REPORT—1978

Organization	Began	Groups	Loanees	Loans (Tk)	Default (%)
Jobra Bhumiheen Samiti	December 1976	26	154	247,350	0.005
Fatehpur Bhumiheen Samiti	February 1978	58	194	305,650	Nil
Bhabanipur Bhumiheen Samiti	May 1978	4	8	13,500	Nil
Jobra Mohila Samiti	February 1978	10	56	16,150	Nil
Fatehpur Mohila Samiti	March 1978	14	51	22,300	Nil
Totals		112	463[a]	604,950	

Source: Muhammad Yunus, "Bhumiheen Samiti (Landless Association) and Mohila Samiti (Women's Association) in Jobra and Other Villages," Grameen Bank Project, Dhaka, 1978.
[a] The total membership was 641 with some members waiting to apply for loans.

Case 12

The Grameen Bank Project (C): Choices for Nationwide Banking for the Poor

This case was written by Dr. Kay Calavan and Professor H. I. Latifee in collaboration with Dr. Muhammad Yunus. It is intended as a basis for class discussion rather than as an illustration of either effective or ineffective handling of an administrative situation. The collaboration and support of the Executive Director of the Grameen Bank and his staff are gratefully acknowledged.

Mr. Saleh Ahmed, a Senior Deputy Director of the Bangladesh Bank, the central bank of the country, pulled out the file on the Grameen Bank Project (GBP) and began to ponder the issue before him. He was in charge of overseeing this project, which was sponsored by the Bangladesh Bank. For several months beginning March 30, 1982, Dr. Muhammad Yunus, the GBP Project Director, had been distributing versions of a proposal to the key members of the banking community. This proposal made a strong request that his experimental credit project for the rural poor, jointly implemented with the six nationalized commercial banks (NCBs) and the Bangladesh Krishi Bank (BKB), the national agricultural bank, be converted into a new and separate banking institution. The proposal requested that the bank Managing Directors who had cooperated in setting up the experiment now join in deciding on a permanent institutional structure. Mr. Saleh Ahmed was not a key decision maker in this case, but he had been an enthusiastic supporter of the project at the Bangladesh Bank and had closely followed the experiment. At the firm request of Dr. Yunus he had been appointed to his present responsibility.

The Bangladesh Bank (BB) had sponsored and largely funded the GBP experiment to test the Grameen Bank Project and see if it could be integrated into the operations of the seven Government controlled banks. By December 1984, the GBP was supposed to develop a system in the banks whereby they would be able to manage effectively the special credit program for the landless and other rural poor as a routine part of their banking business. After two and one half years of the collaborative experiment, Dr. Yunus had raised the questions of whether the nationalized banks would actually adopt the program and more critically whether they could adequately implement this specialized program. There were many more institutional incompatibilities (that is, objectives and mode of operation) between the GBP and the banks than anticipated at the beginning of the experiment. After managing the GBP experiment for two and one half years, Dr. Yunus argued that only a specialized bank or other type of credit institution focused on rural poverty would be able to expand operations and effectively achieve the objectives. Bank officials argued that given time they could adequately implement this credit program as part of their portfolios. Also, they were convinced that a specialized bank with a parallel banking system for the rural poor managed by nonbankers would not be a viable financial institution.

The Grameen Bank Project was developed during 1976–79 by Dr. Yunus through an action-research program conducted in the village of Jobra adjacent to Chittagong University and in other nearby villages. This was one activity carried out by the University Rural Economic Programme headed by Dr. Yunus. He was trying to set up a system for providing bank credit on reasonable terms to the greater portion of the rural population (rural landless/near landless and poor rural women) who had never been reached by other bank rural credit programs. An underlying assumption of his project was that the rural poor had skills to carry out productive activities but lacked access to capital at reasonable rates to purchase stock, raw materials, or simple tools to create self-employment opportunities and generate a reasonable return on their labor. He also argued that because the landless and poor rural women were generally not farmers and had no land collateral, they were not reached by other agricultural and rural credit programs. In the past rural credit programs targeted for small farmers were dominated by village elites. He argued that the agricultural labor market could absorb only a small portion of the under- and unutilized, but growing, labor resource of rural poor.

The Grameen Bank Project consisted of GBP units that worked with participating rural bank branches to implement a closely supervised credit program (see Exhibit 1). The GBP staff were funded by the participating banks with concessionary credit for loan funds from the Bangladesh Bank. The staff were recruited, trained, and managed by the GBP Office during the experiment but were supposed to be absorbed as specialized bank staff. The GBP staff lived and worked in the villages, locating village clientele and helping them organize into small credit groups; training them in the required disciplines of this credit program (that is, appropriate use of loan funds, weekly meetings, and weekly loan repayments and contributions to the Group Fund and Emergency Fund); and disbursing loans and collecting repayments.

Mr. Saleh Ahmed recalled the three previous meetings of the bank Managing Directors in which they uniformly rejected the proposals submitted by Dr. Yunus requesting a separate bank or other type of credit institution. However, the newly appointed Finance Minister, Mr. A.M.A. Muhith, saw some merit in Dr. Yunus' proposal, and decided to call another meeting of the bank Managing Directors in his office. This special meeting was set for the next day, December 28, 1982. To prepare for the meeting, Mr. Saleh Ahmed had set aside the afternoon and evening to review the Grameen Bank file. He slipped the proposal to the bottom of the file and began reviewing the other documents.

Grameen Bank Project—Initial Phase

The first memo in the file, dated February 3, 1979, was from the former Deputy Governor of the Bangladesh Bank, A.K. Gangopadhyay, stating his interest and that of the Managing Directors of the commercial banks and the BKB in the model evolved near the Chittagong University campus by Professor Yunus to provide credit to the rural poor. Mr. Gangopadhyay also noted:

> ... since the Bangladesh Bank in collaboration with the Krishi Bank and commercial banks were trying to evolve a viable credit mechanism for the benefit of the rural poor, the proposed extension of the experiment should be taken up as a credit project of the Bangladesh Bank.

Leaning back in his chair, Mr. Saleh Ahmed recalled that since Liberation from Pakistan (1971) and the nationalization of the Bangladesh banking sector, the banks were under pressure from the Government to participate vigorously in the country's development process. The country was suffering severe food and deficit conditions as a result of increasing population pressure on an overcrowded landbase, long-term stagnation of the rural economy, the effects of the war, and very immediately the 1974 famine (see Exhibit 2). The bankers were cooperating with the Government and donor-initiated programs to set up rural bank branches and increase rural credit and rural development efforts (see Exhibit 3).

In October 1978, the Bangladesh Bank, with the support of USAID, sponsored a conference on "Problems and Issues of Agricultural Credit and Rural Finance." Some researchers presented papers demonstrating that current institutional credit programs were not adequately reaching small farmers or the landless and there were high default rates. Dr. Yunus argued in his paper that his Grameen Bank Project near Chittagong University was successfully providing credit to the landless and had excellent repayment rates. Skeptical bank participants at the conference challenged Dr. Yunus to demonstrate that his model could be replicated elsewhere in Bangladesh where Professor Yunus was not as well known and where he did not have available eager student workers.

Dr. Yunus promptly accepted the challenge. He told the audience, "If the bankers are willing to support such a project, I am willing to expand it over a whole district." Later the Bangladesh Bank requested that Professor Yunus take a two-year leave from the University to be engaged full-time as Project Director of the experiment. The proposed project would be located at Tangail District and would also continue the limited activities near Chittagong University.

By June 27, 1979, Mr. Gangopadhyay, Deputy Governor of the Bangladesh Bank, had sent out a cover letter for "Notes on Arrangements for the Grameen Bank Project" prepared by Dr. Yunus. At that early date it was understood that the GBP would accomplish the following:

1. It will endeavor to strengthen the existing banking system in terms of service facilities, mode of operation, personnel, and its socioeconomic role in the rural communities it serves.

2. It will help each bank branch in the Project area to take up the responsibility of becoming an integral part of the development process of the area it serves. The Project will endeavor to transform the bank from a passive institution waiting for people to come and try to persuade it about the soundness of a proposal, to an active organization which will be persuading people to do things and making its financing available for all those things. It will generate income for people not having an income, create new economic activities, provide special assistance to the economically disadvantaged groups, and mobilize savings. Its operation will not be office based. Clients will not go to the bank, but the bank will go to the client. It will develop a new system of supervised loaning rather than continue the present security-oriented system. The crucial test for this project would be to demonstrate that the bank is as easily accessible to the poor as is the moneylender.

The Notes also emphasized:

It will be appreciated that success of the Project depends totally on active support and cooperation of all the participating banks.

In addition, the Notes set out the organizational structure for this joint GBP-Bangladesh Bank experiment, basic work procedures for GBP staff and bank branch staff, and the budget (see Exhibits 1 and 4). On reflection, Mr. Ahmed noted that this initial plan had been followed throughout the Project.

All field staff would be recruited by the Project office in collaboration with the participating banks. The Field Managers and Bank Workers (GBP staff) were placed under the administrative control of the Project Office but were deemed employees of the banks that they served and that paid their salaries. It was planned that three to four branches from each of the six nationalized commercial banks and the BKB would be brought under the Project during this first year of its operation.

The next document picked up by Mr. Ahmed was the Minutes of a Banker's meeting held on June 18, 1980, eight months after GBP field operations started. One decision at this meeting was that all participating banks would use simplified loan documentation forms as suggested by the GBP Office. A second decision designed to reduce a communication gap in the Project was that Head Offices of the participating banks should circulate all papers/documents relating to the policy decisions on GBP to their Regional Managers' Offices and their branches to guide their actions with GBP units. Mr. Ahmed then read a Bangladesh Bank Circular Letter announcing simplified approximation procedures suggested by Dr. Yunus for the bank branches to use in calculating interest for the large number of GBP loans.

GBP Expansion Plan—IFAD Support

After calling for some tea, Mr. Saleh Ahmed returned to the file. He recalled that after one year of the GBP experiment an IFAD (International Fund for Agricultural Development) Project Identification Mission arrived to request that the Bangladesh Bank identify agricultural credit projects they could fund. Among other projects, the Bank suggested they talk with Dr. Yunus to see about financing the GBP. The first reaction of the Mission was that what the GBP was doing was not banking and was not agricultural. A few days later the IFAD Mission changed its mind and asked to share support of the GBP with the Bangladesh Bank.

A following document, a "Note for Consideration in the Managing Directors' Meeting on GBP," drawn up by Dr. Yunus noted some achievements of the year-old Project (see Exhibit 5) and then moved to the main agenda—a proposal for a joint IFAD/Bangladesh Bank–funded GBP Programme Expansion (1981–84). Major elements of this expansion were coverage of four districts in different regions and a target of 100 participating bank branches by the end of 1982 with each bank providing four branches in each district. Funding for the Project was to be done in the following manner (amounts in crores of Tk):

	Bangladesh Bank	IFAD	Total
Loan Fund	5.00	5.00	10.00
Training	0.15	0.15	0.30
Administration	1.30	0.00	1.30
TOTAL	6.45	5.15	11.60

The Bangladesh Bank charged 3 percent interest for IFAD funds and 6 percent (later 8.5 percent) for its own funds.

Dr. Yunus' Note then listed actions needed to prepare for the Expansion Programme:

1. Selection of the Field Managers and Bank Workers can be done by the participating banks themselves or [can] follow the same procedure as before.

2. Local [bank branch] Managers will arrange the office space in consultation with the Project Office. We propose that the regional offices be empowered to make advances up to Tk 35,000 to the potential landlord to construct the office housing.

3. From the past experience it appears that it would avoid a lot of delays and misunderstandings if we can simply place the following budgeted amount (Tk 28,000) per branch at the disposal of the project office and entrust them to spend the amount against the budget items under the supervision of a committee of the Local [Managers] headed by the Project Director.

4. Project Office will arrange the training.

5. In the context of the expansion programme, we propose that the AGM level [bank] officers be designated as GBP officers at the head offices and sent to the project office for a month to work in the field to gain experience.

6. We propose that in all districts local [bank managers] be empowered to sanction GBP loans at the recommendations of the Project Director/Assistant Project Director.

7. At the present, local [bank managers] are empowered to sanction individual loans up to Tk 5,000 each. We propose that this limit be enhanced to Tk 10,000 in each individual loan case. This is required because many loanees are paying back the first loan and asking for increased amount as their next loans.

After ordering another cup of tea and standing up to stretch his legs, Mr. Ahmed began reading the next major document, an IFAD nine-month review of the numerous projects they funded (including the GBP) in the Bangladesh Small Farmers Agricultural Credit Project (see Exhibit 5). Mr. Ahmed recalled how positive the IFAD Team's conclusions were about the GBP:

1. The low ranking of agriculture [loan activities] is quite understandable, because most loanees are landless and they are not even in a position to hire/purchase land to start cultivation. Therefore, petty nonagricultural activities are the only means through which they could raise their income. This also clearly

showed that a pure agricultural lending scheme cannot touch this group in rural Bangladesh. Available evidence suggests that under the Government's on-going Tk 1,000 million Special Agricultural Credit Programme, the landless group has been virtually left out.

2. This margin [between 5.75 percent effective bank refinancing rate and 13 percent rate to borrowers] seems to be adequate for the GBP to break even at the end of the second year and earn a profit from the third year. As for the potential borrowers, the alternative rate from the money lender would be 10 percent per month. [They] find that with the lower cost of the GBP loan, their profit margin has increased.

3. The loan repayment performance is excellent. This record of loan repayment is due to effective supervision by the CC [Centre Chief] and BW [Bankworker] of loan utilization and subsequent behavior of the loanees. Weekly installments are collected by the BW at the weekly center meeting where attendance is compulsory. The CC is also expected to maintain close personal touch with individual members, advise and help them out if necessary in case of difficulty. This role of the CC is vital in the case of female members who may need continuous encouragement and sometimes intermediation in matters of conflict and tension within the household. The female groups could potentially emerge as a strong influence on the society in effecting an improvement in the social status of the poor women who are otherwise relegated to a very marginal existence.

4. From an organizational and personal commitment viewpoint, the most sensitive aspect of the GBP is its relationship with participating banks. The response of officials of participating banks varies widely. At the policy level, the concept of the GBP has been accepted in principle and the banks are in the process of making adjustments to their conventional banking rules and procedures to accommodate the requirements of the GBP. This attitude, however, is not necessarily reflected among all local branch officials who are in daily contact with the field operation of GBP Units. A close understanding and smooth cooperation between GBP personnel (particularly the Field Manager) and local Branch Manager, Cashier, and other officers is absolutely vital for successful implementation of the project. It is somewhat ironical that this question should assume such as a dimension. All GBP Unit personnel are as much bank employees as the local branch officials are. Therefore, one would have expected that the

existing branch officials would consider the GBP as an integral part of their own operation (expanded though).

5. The attitude of the local branch bank officials to GBP operations ranges between benign tolerance and suppressed hostility, often giving way to open noncooperation. What the bank officials complain about is the "additional" workload involved in completing the accounting records of all finance transactions of the GBP which are large in number but each one is small in amount. They feel that either they should have extra help or the record-keeping work should be done by the GBP personnel. The workload that the bank officials refer to is a debatable point. In recent years, bank branches have multiplied greatly in number reaching down to the Union level. This is how the policy makers and the banking community felt that they would be able to reach the rural clientele at all levels. As a matter of fact this expectation was not realized and the capacities of many bank branches remained underutilized.

6. The noncooperation of local branch officials works in subtle ways. Bank Workers sometimes return late in the day from Centre meetings with the day's collection (by foot) to find that the Bank Manager is unwilling to accept the cash for safe-keeping on the plea that the bank transactions/working hours are over, although he is fully aware that the GBP premises are not very secure. In many cases the Project Director had to personally intervene to sort things out. Again, the Bank Managers are supposed to countersign all transactions recorded in various passbooks but so far this has not been followed through regularly because of the reluctance of bank officials to cooperate.

7. The Group Fund is to be operated by the group and it should be able to make withdrawals from the bank where the money is deposited as they wish, with the only stipulation being that the Group Chairman and Secretary should go to the bank branch personally to make the withdrawal. Some of the bank officials are imposing an additional requirement that the group would have to make a formal written application to the Manager for making any withdrawal from the Group Fund. This results in intimidating the group members. Withdrawal difficulties have historically been an important disincentive for potential small savers to make use of formal institutions like rural banks, post office savings banks or commercial banks.

8. In order to understand the GBP one must also understand the role played by its founder and Project Director, Professor M. Yunus. He has single-handedly evolved the concept of the GBP,

persuaded the conservative banking community to participate in the scheme, developed its rules and procedures, personally supervised the opening of branches, and is now about to undertake the responsibility of expanding the programme in four new districts. [He and other policy makers] ... are now relying on the strategy of developing a well-trained and motivated cadre of Bank Workers. Among others, the underlying assumption is that given the existing glut of educated unemployed in Bangladesh, the BWs will easily develop a stake in job security which could only come if the GBP functioned properly and expanded.

GBP Expansion Phase—Other Donor Support

Mr. Ahmed remembered that other donors (that is, UNICEF and Ford Foundation) had also wanted to support the GBP. UNICEF provided funds for training women trainers in 1981. The Ford Foundation funding was divided into: a grant for training, research, and evaluation; an emergency fund to meet "unforeseen problems" such as unexpected delays in Commercial Bank Branches in providing needed work aids; and a loan guarantee fund (which was never used). The rationale for this Ford Foundation support was to help the GBP address the criticisms of the staff of the banks (for example, the Project is too costly and risky; requires a degree of flexibility beyond the means of commercial banks and extra work without incentive; and is not as attractive as other lending opportunities).

The Ford Foundation Proposal also noted:

> Project staff are concerned therefore that commercial banks may not participate fully or for a long enough period to allow for an adequate test of the Project. Time is important as far as the Project Officers are concerned, for they believe that: (1) the costs of the Project will decline as the size of loans increases (i.e., incidence of group borrowing increases), and as supervision becomes less intensive as borrowers become better acquainted with procedures and groups become well established; (2) that returns to commercial banks will be adequate once the Project is well established; and (3) that banks will participate more actively when it can be demonstrated conclusively that default rates are low.

GBP Restructuring Proposal

With few interruptions Mr. Ahmed was able to reach the final set of documents in the GBP folder. These proposals laid out the issues of the current decision facing the banking community and the Government. The top document was the one that had raised the whole issue in the first place—the issue of what to do with the pilot GBP started in 1979 by the request of the Bangladesh Bank and the Bank Directors. With renewed concentration, Mr. Saleh Ahmed bent to reread certain key sections of the proposal. Dr. Yunus argued:

> Based on the experience of GBP over the last two and a half years one can afford to be optimistic about the impact of a GBP type banking operation in reducing the poverty of the poorest segment of the population of Bangladesh and generating employment for the vast majority at a speed faster than any other known methods. [See Exhibits 5 and 6.]

Dr. Yunus then listed difficulties in operating within the present organizational framework with the GBP as one small credit program in the "omnibus programmes" of the NCBs and the BKB:

1. The banks' traditional urban orientation and focus on the needs of the economically fortunate class rather than the concept of bank employees going out to the villages.

2. GBP staff lack job security and are leaving because they are not being absorbed as permanent bank employees as originally agreed. In addition, there is a lengthy and complicated bank recruitment process involving too many departments and significantly slowing the replacement process and Project expansion.

3. At the bank branch level there is often an uncooperative, even unfriendly, attitude of the regular bank staff directed toward the GBP units. There are several reasons for this such as unclear lines of authority and particularly the extra workload created by the GBP without any monetary compensation for the regular bank staff.

4. The fact that each bank had to release funds for each branch separately resulting in complex GBP follow-up procedures for dealing with delays.

5. Bank restrictions on the GBP providing loans to a broad range of income-generating activities (e.g., shallow tubewells) because of traditional collateral requirements and conflict with other bank programs with these specific targetted activities.

6. Lack of bank agreement on the authority of the Project Director to frame all GBP procedures.

7. Reluctance of some banks to pass on the refinanced amount to the branches at the agreed concessional interest rate.

Mr. Saleh Ahmed knew Dr. Yunus believed that in order for the Grameen Bank program to be effective and expand it had to be organized as an institution separate from the complicated bank bureaucracies. At first Dr. Yunus discussed several alternative structures for this specialized institution: Government-sponsored specialized bank, Government corporation, private specialized bank, private specialized bank owned by the landless group-members themselves, nonprofit NGO specialized bank, and joint venture specialized bank with nonprofit NGO and landless group member support. Dr. Yunus preferred setting up a private bank, the Grameen Bank Limited, owned by the landless members. For the first time, the Government was allowing private banks to be established with 30 million taka capital required. The GBP group members had saved 10 million taka in their Group Fund and Emergency Fund accounts. Dr. Yunus thought the Government might give special permission to start the bank with this amount.

During the months following the submission of Dr. Yunus's restructuring proposal, the Bangladesh Bank had invited the BKB and the NCBs to comment on the proposal. There were also three bankers' meetings at which the proposal was discussed. Mr. Saleh Ahmed had seen that the banking community was adamantly against a separate banking institution. He leaned back and reviewed some of their arguments against the Grameen Bank Ltd:

1. The decision should be deferred until the existing experimental project is completed [1984] and a comprehensive evaluation is made. No study had yet established that the proposed Grameen Bank would be more effective than say the BKB for achieving the objectives of rural credit.

2. There were no real shortcomings or failures on the part of the NCBs/BKB in carrying out the GBP. The proposal was an overreaction to minor staff and procedural problems that could be worked out without justifying the establishment of a separate institution.

3. All the banks argued that GBP loans are more highly supervised and hence more costly than NCB/BKB lending and could never be financially viable without extreme concessional rates and grant support. If the NCBs/BKB could get funds at such low rates, they would have a better performance in rural credit, particularly because they had an established banking organisation down to the village level.

4. The banks were apprehensive about the financial viability of a bank operating solely in a weaker sector because Grameen Bank would be unable to achieve a sound deposit base, which is essential for a bank.

5. The project proposal did not make it clear how manpower requirements for a Grameen Bank would be met. Wouldn't the

proposed bank be "as much handicapped by manpower constraints as the NCBs/BKB in carrying out the objectives of
grameen [e.g., village] banking?"

6. Nationalised Commercial Banks were created to promote socioeconomic objectives as well as do commercial banking. They must
be able to perform both types of jobs or otherwise the purpose of
the nationalisation would be defeated.

7. History and experience of the unsuccessful Bangladesh cooperative banks which were created as specialized banking institutions
should be kept in mind in this decision. Banks should be managed by professional bankers.

8. The GBP success was mainly due to the ability of the present
GBP Project Director, Dr. Yunus, to motivate project officers to be
committed workers in rural areas. Therefore, the solution to the
problem of the banks' being unable to provide enough devoted
officers who are willing to work in villages was not the creation
of a new banking institution, but the creation of a separate agricultural banking cadre of workers who would expand rural
credit through the NCBs.

9. The proposed Grameen Bank would not be able to observe the
provisions of the Banking Companies Ordinance, 1962, and
would thus create problems for the Banking Control Department. Any new credit institution for the rural poor should not be
a bank but could be a nondeposit-taking institution restricted to
lending to the rural poor.

Following the first two meetings of the bank Managing Directors, Dr.
Yunus contacted the newly appointed Finance Minister under the recently declared Martial Law Government, Mr. A.M.A. Muhith. He had
previously shown a personal interest in the GBP and had had a couple of
discussions with Dr. Yunus about the Project. After attending the third
bankers' meeting, Minister Muhith had called a meeting in his office for
December 28 with the idea that his presence and that of the Secretary of
Finance might move the bankers to give more consideration to this proposal. In addition, he asked Dr. Yunus to prepare a special proposal for
the proposed bank with 40 percent of shares held by the Government
and 60 percent of shares held by the group members. Minister Muhith
was hopeful that the bankers would be more responsive to this proposal
which included partial government shareholding. This was the proposal
to be discussed at the next day's meeting. Glancing at his watch, Mr.
Saleh Ahmed quickly put the file in order on his desk. As he left his office, Mr. Saleh Ahmed pondered how these policy makers would decide
to institutionalize the GBP credit program for the poor.

Exhibit 1
GRAMEEN BANK PROJECT ORGANIZATIONAL CHART

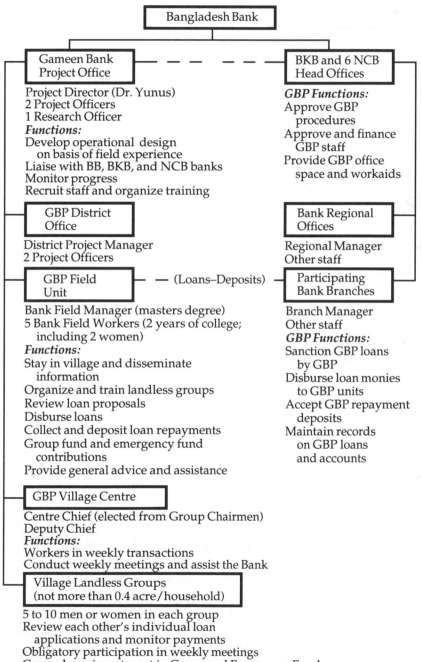

Bangladesh Bank

| Gameen Bank Project Office | BKB and 6 NCB Head Offices |

Project Director (Dr. Yunus)
2 Project Officers
1 Research Officer
Functions:
Develop operational design
  on basis of field experience
Liaise with BB, BKB, and NCB banks
Monitor progress
Recruit staff and organize training

GBP Functions:
Approve GBP
  procedures
Approve and finance
  GBP staff
Provide GBP office
  space and workaids

GBP District Office

District Project Manager
2 Project Officers

Bank Regional Offices

Regional Manager
Other staff

GBP Field Unit — — (Loans–Deposits) — Participating Bank Branches

Bank Field Manager (masters degree)
5 Bank Field Workers (2 years of college;
  including 2 women)
Functions:
Stay in village and disseminate
  information
Organize and train landless groups
Review loan proposals
Disburse loans
Collect and deposit loan repayments
Group fund and emergency fund
  contributions
Provide general advice and assistance

Branch Manager
Other staff
GBP Functions:
Sanction GBP loans
  by GBP
Disburse loan monies
  to GBP units
Accept GBP repayment
  deposits
Maintain records
  on GBP loans
  and accounts

GBP Village Centre

Centre Chief (elected from Group Chairmen)
Deputy Chief
Functions:
Workers in weekly transactions
Conduct weekly meetings and assist the Bank

Village Landless Groups
(not more than 0.4 acre/household)

5 to 10 men or women in each group
Review each other's individual loan
  applications and monitor payments
Obligatory participation in weekly meetings
Compulsory investment in Group and Emergency Funds

Exhibit 2
BANGLADESH COUNTRY CONTEXT, 1981

Population Factors
- Estimated population of 90 million.
- Population expanding at rate of about 2.8% per year.
- Average density per square mile—over 1,886 persons. World's most densely populated area except for certain urban areas.
- Average household size is 5.89 people.
- About 20% overall literacy with female literacy about 13%.
- Average life expectancy at birth is 46 years.
- Population is about 85% Muslim; the remainder are Hindus, Buddhists, and Christians.

Economic Factors
- Nearly 90% of population lives in the rural areas.
- Over one-half of the rural families are "functionally landless" having less than 0.4 hectare of land. The percent of rural landless households has increased from 16% to over 50% in the last 15 years.
- Many of the landless are also "functionally unemployed" since wage employment other than part-time work on farms is nearly nonexistent. Foreign-donor supported food-for-work programs and Government rural works programs provide seasonal income.
- Average annual income is about U.S.$140 per capita.
- In 1981 the exchange rate was about Tk 17 = U.S.$1.

Political Factors
- 1971 Independence from Pakistan following War of Liberation.
- Martial Law Government.
- Administrative structure includes 20 Districts, 71 Subdistricts, and 4,472 Unions overlying about 68,000 villages.

Banking Institutions
- After Independence, the Central Government Bank was called the Bangladesh Bank.
- The Bangladesh Krishi Bank is the specialized bank for agriculture and rural development. It had 334 rural branches in 1980.
- After Liberation, a Presidential Order nationalized the private banks creating six Nationalized Commercial Banks (Janata, Agrani, Sonali, Rupali, Uttara, and Pubali).
- In 1973, the Government requested that the NCB's set up sections to provide agricultural credit.
- All banks require collateral for credit, in effect excluding the landless and near landless from formal credit sources.

Source: Bangladesh Bureau of Statistics, 1982, *Statistical Yearbook of Bangladesh,* Dhaka, December 1983.

Exhibit 3

MAJOR BANGLADESH RURAL CREDIT PROGRAMS: BANK PARTICIPATION, 1980–82

Name of Program	Target Population	Participating Banks
1. Taka 100 Crores Special Agricricultural Credit Program (multiple programs including intensive crop production programs)	Farmers	BKB/Agrani/Sonali/Janata/Uttara/Rupali/Pubali
2. Special Credit Scheme for Small Farmers (IFAD; multiple programs)	Small farmers (< 3 acres)	BKB/Agrani/Sonali/Janata/Uttara/Rupali/Pubali
3. Rural Finance Experimental Project (USAID; multiple subprojects)	Small farmers	BKB/Agrani/Sonali/Janata/Uttara/Rupali/Pubali
4. Grameen Bank Project	Landless (< 0.4 acre)	BKB/Agrani/Sonali/Janata/Uttara/Rupali/Pubali
5. Pilot Scheme for Small Farmers (IFAD)	Small farmers	BKB
6. Swanirvar Programme	Small farmers/landless women/youth	Sonali/Janata/Agrani/Rupali
7. Irrigation Equipment to Rural Landless and Marginal Farmers (BRAC/Proshika/Ford Foundation)	Landless/marginal farmers	BKB
8. Deep Tube-Well Irrigation and Credit Program	Small farmers	BKB (with CARE and BADC)
9. Rural Agricultural Branch Programs (Krishi Shaka)	Small farmers	Sonali
10. Asian Survey on Agricultural Reform and Rural Development (FAO/UNDP)	Small farmers/landless laborers	Janata

Exhibit 3 (cont'd)

Name of Program	Target Population	Participating Banks
11. Bangladesh Rural Development Board Credit Program	Farmer coops/women coops	Sonali
12. Small Farmers Service Centers	Small farmers	Agrani
13. Joint Farming Program in collaboration with Bangladesh Agricultural University	Farmers	Agrani/Janata
14. Hand-Pump Tubewell (MOSTI)	Small farmers	BKB
15. Save the Children Agricultural Project	Small farmers	BKB
16. Financing Landless People of Chittagong Hill Tracts	Landless	BKB
17. Christian Reformed World Relief Committee: Crop Inputs Project	Small and marginal farmers	BKB
18. Mennonite Central Committee Project		Janata
19. Financing Sugar Cane Growers Through Sugar Mills	Sugar cane growers	Janata
20. Scheme of Muktanagar Association (OXFAM)	Farmers	Janata
21. Post-Harvest Technology, Storage, and Marketing Credit	Small/medium farmers	Agrani
22. Blacksmith & Pottery Development Scheme—Rajshahi		Janata

BKB = Bangladesh Krishi Bank (National Agricultural Credit Bank)
Sonali, Agrani, Janata, Uttara, Rupali, and Pubali = nationalized commercial banks

Exhibit 4
GRAMEEN BANK PROJECT BUDGET, 1981
(1981 exchange rate: Tk 17 = U.S.$1)

Yearly Expenditures for Single GBP Unit (paid by the participating bank)		*Income for Single GBP Unit*
Salary		13% Interest on outstanding
Field Manager	15,000	loans of typical GBP Unit =
Bankworkers (4)	24,000	Tk 132,252[a]
Assistant Bank- worker (1)	4,200	
Peon-*cum*-guard (1)	6,000	
Subtotal	Tk 49,200	
Maintenance of Workaids and *Depreciation of Furniture*	Tk 1,267	
Other Overhead Expenses		
Office Rent	4,800	
Office Stationery	3,864	
Conveyance	1,376	
Miscellaneous	1,906	
Subtotal	Tk 11,946	
Cost of Loan Funds at *4.5% Interest Rate* (typical loan fund of Tk 1,017,323)[a]	Tk 45,759	
		Net profit of typical GBP Unit =
Total Costs	Tk 108,172	Tk 24,080[a]

[a] These estimates represent a position achieved by typical GBP Units in the second year of Unit operation provided the Unit can organize groups with at least a total of 678 loanees and an average loan size of Tk 1,500.

Notes: The Bangladesh Bank provided Tk 740,250 the first year of operation for capital expenses and salary expenses of the Head Project Office in Tangail and a suboffice in Hathazari. This money was provided by a project development fund at the BB. For succeeding years, the BB provided salaries and operating funds for these project offices.

The managers of participating bank branches reported that about 40% of their staff time was spent on routine work on GBP loans (Mahabub Hossain, *Credit for the Rural Poor: The Grameen Bank in Bangladesh*, Bangladesh Institute of Development Studies, 1984). If this proportion of bank staff salaries is added to the estimate, the typical GBP unit was running at a loss. However, the GBP Director and staff argued that this routine work could be handled much more efficiently.

Exhibit 5

PROGRESS OF THE GRAMEEN BANK PROJECT, 1980–83

Indicators	1980	1981	1982	1983
Number of GBP Branches	25	25	54	86
Number of Villages Covered	363	433	745	1,249
Number of Groups	2,935	4,818	6,242	11,667
Number of Members	14,830	24,128	30,146	58,320
Male/Female Membership Ratio	2.15/1	1.57/1	1.58/1	1.18/1
Number of Loanees	11,644	21,704	24,177	46,428
Cumulative Amount Disbursed				
(Taka '000)	21,046	53,673	95,578	194,920
Amount Repaid (Taka '000)	7,295	32,701	64,181	123,153
Savings: Group/Emergency Funds				
(Taka '000)	1,602	4,772	9,586	19,361
Loans by Sectors:				
Agriculture/Forestry	3	1	2	1.5
Livestock/Fisheries	25	23	23	2.9
Processing/Manufacturing	20	27	24	26.0
Trade/Shopkeeping	37	42	44	37.7
Transport Services	15	7	5	5.9
Joint Enterprises	—	—	2	2.7

Sources: (1) Grameen Bank Annual Reports, 1980, 1981, 1982, 1983; (2) Dr. Kamal Siddiqui, *An Evaluation of the Grameen Bank Operation*, July 1984, Grameen Bank.

Exhibit 6

SUMMARY OF THREE SURVEY RESULTS ON GBP IMPACT ON LOANEE INCOMES

Survey Sponsored by	Sample	Period	Income Before Loan (Tk)	Income After Loan (Tk)	Percent Increase
Bangladesh Institute of Bank Management	50 women in Silimpur, Tangail	1980–81	428 per month per family	740	+ 73
Bangladesh Bank	175 members, 90 men and 85 women, drawn from 5 branches in Tangail and 4 branches in Chittagong	1981–82	5,806 per year per family	9,166	+ 58
Bangladesh Institute of Development Studies	600 randomly selected members	1980–81	1,037 per capita per year (before 1980)	1,740 (1982)	+ 68

Source: The titles of the studies are cited in the text. Table taken from: Dharam Ghai, *An Evaluation of the Impact of the Grameen Bank Project*, March 1984, Grameen Bank.

Case 13

IIRR (A):
Participative Management for
the IIRR Rural Credit Program

This case was written by Rebecca F. Catalla and Francisco Roman. It is intended as a basis for class discussion rather than as an illustration of either effective or ineffective handling of an administrative situation. The collaboration and support of the President of IIRR and his staff are gratefully acknowledged.

The Issue

In 1986, the field staff of the International Institute of Rural Reconstruction (IIRR) was reviewing the results of a question it had asked itself and the IIRR top management two years before: How can the Institute's community partners become more involved in the management of IIRR's rural credit program? The question aimed at the core of IIRR's tenets of "release, not relief; outsiders can help but insiders must do the job." That is, IIRR prided itself on its focus on training, research, and education programs that would mobilize and develop the rural communities to a stage where they could solve their own problems and design their own uplift programs.

Up until 1984, IIRR's approach to its credit program consisted of a combination of a lending scheme, and training programs and technical advice to organize the people's organizations (POs) to a point where they were deemed capable of managing the loans themselves. In addition, IIRR also assisted their client POs in joining together to carry out such activities as cattle upgrading or a feasibility study for a rice mill, which involved dealing with both government and nongovernment agencies to obtain other, external funds and resources.[1]

The above financial policies were consistent with the IIRR principles. But the field staff pointed out that these policies were little different from the policies and procedures of traditional, formal lending institutions. Thus, decision making rested on a four-person IIRR Credit Committee, which highlighted an approach of "management by authority figures and by technical experts," both of whom lacked the actual experience in the realities of village-level dynamics.[2]

In addition, the requirements of the credit program appeared to emphasize the economic aspects of projects and thus gave the impression of running counter to the "village-level evocative processes" of community involvement in social and not merely economic development, processes that the field staff were utilizing in their work.[3]

The credit program was initiated in 1978 and represented IIRR's first major effort to put together a rural financing strategy. The strategy was still being examined in 1984, when the field staff raised the question of PO participation in the control and administration of the credit program. Other questions raised in the course of responding to the issue were: (1) How should the POs be involved in the management of the credit program? (2) How should IIRR involve the POs? and (3) When should the POs become involved?

The International Institute of Rural Reconstruction

Mission

The IIRR is a private, nonprofit rural development organization with its headquarters based in the Philippines, in Silang, the province of Cavite, located forty kilometers outside of the major metropolitan area, Manila. IIRR has six affiliated national rural reconstruction movements and two alumni networks located in the Philippines, India, Thailand, Ghana, Colombia, and Guatemala. IIRR was established in 1967 as a world research and training center by Dr. Y. C. James Yen, a Chinese-born, Western-educated reformer. IIRR is an outgrowth of Dr. Yen's Chinese Mass Education Movement, which he established in China in the 1920s.

IIRR's mission is " ... to generate and share with others experiences and lessons on how best to enable the rural people of developing countries in Asia, Africa, and Latin America to improve their lives." IIRR utilizes three major programs to meet the mission objective: field operational research (FOR), international training (IT), and international extension (IE); IT and IE represents a "sharing mission," while FOR is the "generating knowledge and learning" component (see Exhibit 1).

FOR undertakes field research projects and activities on the needs and problems of rural communities based on four key areas identified by IIRR: livelihood, self-government, health, and education. IIRR espouses a set of "people-centered rural reconstruction principles of going to, living among, and learning from the peasant people ... planning and working with them ... " IIRR therefore uses an "action-research" mode where lessons and insights are drawn from field experiences and used (1) for refining and improving program strategies, such as the credit program; and (2) for sharing the activities internally, with the national rural reconstruction movements and alumni networks, and externally, with governments and NGOs.

IIRR runs, on its own, through its field workers, as well as with practitioners from other institutions, biannual international training programs, as well as regular outreach programs throughout the year in Cavite. The training programs also are aimed at influencing individuals and organizations " ... to help them become more effective in releasing the innate potentials of peasant peoples in developing countries."[4]

IE's original thrust of "encouraging the emergence of indigenous, private, rural reconstruction efforts in developing countries"[5] has expanded to include strengthening the national rural reconstruction movements and alumni networks. Training programs, technical support, and consultancy are used to create "centers of learning and support for development workers."

IIRR Organization

The basic IIRR organization consists of senior specialists, program experts, the rural reconstruction facilitators (RRFs), and the support staff. The senior specialists are the executive officers of IIRR and/or its unit heads. The program experts, who could include senior specialists, are experts in specific areas, such as fish culture, livestock raising, regenerative agriculture, credit, and literacy. The RRFs are the field workers, and the support staff consist of researchers, and finance, communications, and administrative staff. IIRR's organization has evolved over time, as the institute attempted to integrate its activities (see Exhibits 2 and 3).

Control and authority reside in the executives and senior officers of IIRR. However, their decisions, particularly those relating to FOR activities, which are the core of IIRR, are a function of lessons learned in the field. Programs and projects are formulated, refined, or terminated based on the continuing dialogue with the field staff through the Field Program Committee (FPC) and the Field Forum; both venues serve to assess the strengths and weaknesses of IIRR programs or projects. The FPC consists of the Field Director, the Project Team Leaders, and representatives from Research and Communications; the Field Forum is a larger gathering of the FPC members and the RRFs. The two venues were used in IIRR's search for a participative management approach to its credit program.

IIRR'S Rural Credit Program

Beginnings

IIRR's rural credit program began in 1978 as part of a strategy in the area of Self-Government aimed at involving women in development through organizing economic activities under women's leadership. With an initial amount of RP Pesos 132, 885 (U.S.$1.00 = RP P 7.50) for loans, IIRR assisted informal women's groups to enter various income-generating activities such as growing ornamental plants, swine raising, and organizing consumer and credit cooperatives. The "women's section" of the Self-Government group were provided with project management training, technical assistance, and small loans ranging from RP P 350–600, for the ornamental plant projects, and from RP P 1,000–2,000 for the piggery projects.

Between 1979 and 1980, the Livelihood group, as part of FOR, initiated a financing support program among its client-farmers. At the time, IIRR perceived that the field program, perhaps unconsciously, was neglecting its basic principles and was not integrated with IIRR's other activities. The farmers' financing program therefore both examined the process and assisted the farm communities to solve their livelihood problems. One result was a requisite, prior to a loan extension, for the formation of POs by the proposed beneficiaries; the latter were supplemented by training in rapport building and basic management tools. The Livelihood Group was then under the leadership of an economist, and he established guidelines for administering program funds of RP P 956,540.

At this time, an ad hoc body called the Production Loan Fund Committee (PLFC) was formed. It was a four-person team composed of the IIRR Vice-President, and the heads of the Livelihood program, administrative support, and field operations. In 1980, the PLFC approved its first loan for rice production activities for a PO that the Livelihood group had helped to establish,[6] and took over the credit programs for the womens' groups and for the farmers, as well as the loan support for other projects.

The Credit Program by 1984

IIRR's experience between 1978–80 in rural financing was recognized by one of its credit specialists as " … at best limited and unsatisfactory."[7] However, the credit specialist also decried the current financial system using the figure portrayed in Exhibit 4 to clarify his points.

The credit specialist noted that it was only in 1981 that IIRR's credit program began to reach out to the Exhibit's C and D portions of the rural population, and he claimed that they were " … unlikely to ever become part of the institutionalized credit system." He also used Exhibit 4 to summarize his view of the situation, as follows:

> The major existing rural credit programs, either directly or indirectly administered by rural banks and bilateral and multilateral aid agencies are, perhaps, often well-intentioned but typically almost all end up by benefitting the large or medium-sized farmers who represent the rural elite. As a result, both the marginalized farmers and the rural landless poor are almost totally excluded from the scope of major existing rural credit programs.

The exclusion of the marginalized farmer and landless poor from existing programs is particularly serious because technical assistance provided by governments and aid agencies often goes hand in hand with their financial assistance. Exclusion from one program automatically implies the exclusion from the other.

In this situation, the only credit recourse that these two categories (C and D) of the rural poor have is the traditional moneylender or middleman (E). The latter relies on social relationships, is flexible in his requirements, does not require paperwork, and does not ask for collateral. It is, therefore, easy for him to keep the marginalized farmers and rural landless laborers in his grip. His debilitating impact on borrowers is due largely to the fact that he does not explicitly charge an interest rate. The farmer is instead tied to the moneylender for sources of supply and markets, which often results in effective interest rates in excess of 100 per cent per annum, even though they are not explicitly stated. It is ironic that often, governments and international aid agencies are the most vocal critics of the money-lending system, when in fact, their policies and the implementation thereof are largely responsible for its existence and pervasiveness in most Third World countries, especially the rural areas.[8]

IIRR's Staff Capabilities in Credit Management

The dissatisfaction with IIRR's credit management revolved around the issue of participation. IIRR had "satisfactory" performance in other aspects, such as repayments, although it could still not match the collection performance of the commercial banking system. Part of the reason was IIRR's previous experience in credit management. Some of the early staff were recruited from the Philippine Rural Reconstruction Movement (PRRM). The latter predated IIRR and is now an institute affiliate. PRRM ran a financing program with credit unions as early as 1954. When IIRR started fifteen years later, it created a guarantee loan fund of RP P 20,000 (U.S.$1.00 = RP P 4.00). Later on, in 1978, for instance, two of the IIRR credit program staff had supervised the credit program among the beneficiaries of the agency where they were previously employed. Most of the Livelihood staff who served as loan monitors for the 1980 farmer financial support program had prior experience with PRRM's credit unions and credit cooperatives. Other program experts who joined IIRR were familiar with the credit programs of their own banks and government and other NGO financial assistance schemes. The variety of experiences were used to develop a responsive credit program for the "bank outcasts" with whom IIRR worked.

Consolidating the Credit Program Experiences

IIRR in 1983 put together in writing its previously unwritten guidelines, and rural reconstruction and credit experiences at the field level. The written guidelines included the following purposes: "To stimulate not only livelihood-related income generating activities, but also projects and activities in non-livelihood areas (i.e., social, cultural and political); To develop responsible community leaders and members; To mobilize savings of the rural population and to generate new capital." The purposes embody the basic IIRR premise that credit of itself is of secondary importance, and the focus is on the transfer process to the "poorest of the poor." The objective is not necessarily to eliminate the moneylender but to increase alternative credit sources and the volume of money available to the rural poor.

IIRR defined a two-stage development, with four interlocking components, in its credit approach (see Exhibit 5).

According to IIRR, organization is essential to identify and target the beneficiary, who in turn can increase his or her access to financial and other resources through a PO, and thereby increase income and savings. Capitalization in turn should be the "natural result" of increased savings. Without increased capitalization, "an organization and its members are doomed to perpetual dependency and the goal of participatory and self-sustaining growth is likely to remain an unattainable dream for both."

IIRR applied the above model as follows: The 1980 PLFC was renamed the Project Loan Fund Committee, absorbed the credit specialist in the PLFC, and replaced the head of the administrative support unit with the Finance Director, who became the new committee's overall manager and action officer.

The beneficiaries were required to have a minimum level of individual and group capitalization before approving a loan request, which the RRFs were in the best position to monitor; the action officer therefore also supervised IIRR's eleven RRFs. The RRFs also collected amortizations and assisted in carrying out loan audits. They were IIRR's "front-line" staff and had other tasks—providing training on topics such as loan management, accounting, and bookkeeping, and preparing simple feasibility studies, as well as guidelines on managing meetings and the role of board members. They also provided technical assistance to the POs.

One successful example of IIRR's approach to credit was the Tartaria Farmers' Association, organized by IIRR from the landless farmers in a 370-hectare rice-growing, upland village in Silang. The group was originally formed in 1980 with twelve members, some of whom had trained at IIRR on a cattle fattening project. The group went through a training period before and after acquiring the loan. The Association with IIRR's assistance undertook several income-generating projects. The Association now has fifty-eight members recruited from the disadvantaged persons of their villages, and it has borrowed amounts ranging from RP P 48,000 to RP P 114,000 (U.S.$1.00 = RP P 20.00) eleven times without repayment default; it has branched out into other activities that include coffee and rice trading, and calf production; and it is assisting IIRR in organizing other farmers' associations in neighboring villages.[9]

The Credit Program in 1984 and 1985

From 1980 through 1984, IIRR carried out its credit program with the basic approach that it had developed: providing credit to POs that it had helped form and had strengthened through training. The new PLFC met monthly to process loan applications, to refine the accounting and management financial systems, to assess the status of the POs' loans and projects, and to discuss credit related matters such as the establishment of a "people's bank" and a proposed review of the Philippine rural financial system. The action officer also made it a point to meet the loan applicants personally. The RRFs trained and guided the POs, and helped them to link up with other technical and credit institutions, and with government agencies.

In 1984, feedback from the RRFs was subject to the regular review by the Field Program Committee. It appeared to the RRFs that the procedures for managing the credit program did not adequately reflect a participative element. Although the program overall strengthened POs and skillfully provided needed services, the decisions on the approval, release, and management of the loans emanated and rested with the Project Loan Fund Committee. Requirements such as the feasibility study tended to "turn off" both the POs and the RRFs. Some of the requirements in the loan agreements seemed very legalistic to the PO-beneficiaries; the harshest criticism directed at the committee was that it had become "like the IMF or World Bank" and had lost the quality of *damayan* (a local word connoting spontaneous, informal, and active mutual assistance).

IIRR's first response was to stipulate that, in addition to the four PLFC members, there would be:

> ... one representative from the people's organizations in the municipalities being covered by IIRR, on a rotating basis and to be chosen by the beneficiaries themselves. In addition, the Institute's program experts in Self-Government and Livelihood may be made either regular PLFC members or be on call for specific meetings ... The Committee also exercises the option to invite other IIRR field staff and even outsiders to the Institute to attend special meetings if they feel that this will enhance the quality and content of the discussions held therein ... [10]

However, despite an effort to put the plan in practice between the second quarter of 1984 and the first quarter of 1985, dissatisfaction was still evident among the RRFs and the POs.[11] Consequently, in a meeting of the FPC, IIRR's Field Operations Director designated two staff members to draw up further implementation guidelines. One month later, the two IIRR staff submitted a three-phased timetable: (1) to form a loan committee in each PO in 1985; (2) to form a federation of the loan committees by 1986; and (3) to include a representative of the POs in the PLFC by 1987.

Some staff reactions to the proposal were: (1) the PO representatives should be able to sit in the PLFC within a shorter period; (2) some of the fourteen existing POs already have capable representatives; and (3) the PLFC's role had to be explained to the POs prior to the formation of a federation.

In response, the two IIRR staff members came up with additional suggestions:

1. Federations could be formed at different levels: interest groups such as farmer or women groups at the lowest level, followed by community and then municipality groups.

2. Lending and loan management should be the first activity of the groups.

3. Within one year at most, PO representatives would be integrated with the PLFC and would participate in the deliberations on loan applications.

4. The POs would need additional "strengthening" in order to actively participate in IIRR deliberations on its other field programs.

However, implementation slowed down by mid-1985, because of the two staff members' increased regular workload, and the inability of other staff to take the lead due to work pressures.

The Credit Program in 1986

IIRR regarded the issue as important and it renewed its efforts to increase PO participation in the credit program in early 1986. The Field Director created a five-person PLFC Task Force in April 1986. The Task Force's job was to consolidate all previous suggestions and then to work out a plan of action. The Task Force conducted meetings to review the previous suggestions on criteria for selecting PO representatives to the PLFC, the number of representatives, the required training or preparation for the PO representatives, their roles and responsibilities, benefits or compensation, terms of office, and so forth. By mid-1986, the Task Force members began a round of consultations at the village level. In late 1986, IIRR then held two one-day workshops involving IIRR and the POs. With respect to participation, three options emerged (see Exhibit 6 drawn by one of the IIRR field staff).

In the discussion with the POs, the latter continued to regard the PLFC as the key body to formulate and execute credit policies, and to process and approve loans. The main interest of the POs was in becoming part of the process through the PLFC.

The divisions or groupings of the POs were made at two levels. The POs were organized into a general committee composed of three categories of POs; each category would send their representatives to the PLFC. As noted, the maximum number of PLFC members was fixed by IIRR at eleven, and IIRR retained a permanent five-person membership.

Models I and II were similar, and used Cavite as the prototype. One group was organized at the municipal level; the two others consisted of either village or *sitio* (a smaller subdivision of a village) groups located in the upland and the lowland areas of Silang. Model I opted for equal representation, while Model III considered the magnitude of municipal projects, such as feedmilling and marketing, and suggested giving that group four representatives. Model II, on the other hand, emphasized the fact that there were POs not directly engaged in agriculture, and addressed the issue of providing initial guidance by including IIRR staff (RRFs) within the groups.

Conclusion

The workshops brought out other suggestions and criticisms that reflected still unresolved issues. For example, it was suggested that the three divisions as a whole could make recommendations to the PLFC, but new projects and "large" or municipal level loans should be left entirely to the PLFC. Criticism focused on the possible imbalance if groups were to be distributed in the three divisions. In the proposed trial area, there were only four municipal-wide organizations while there were seventeen village- and *sitio*-based groups. The latter might be difficult to organize, according to both the POs and the RRFs. Model III, while perhaps practical from the project financing standpoint, created an imbalance by leaving numerous village-level concerns to only two representatives. The POs, at the end of the workshops, were leaning toward Model II.

Notes

1. IIRR Project Progress Report on the Participatory Approach to Rural Economic Development Program for the quarter ending December 31, 1982.

2. Memorandum to the Field Director, May 18, 1984.

3. Minutes of the meeting of the Project Loan Fund Committee, January 25, 1984.

4. IIRR IT Program, 25th IT Handout, October 1986.

5. Kamal Malhotra, "The International Extension Program: A Brief Overview," mimeographed paper, July 1985.

6. Thomas M. Olson and V. H. Olander, "Acquisition Systems in Action," *Rural Reconstruction Review*, Vol. 4, 1982.

7. Kamal Malhotra, "Financing People's Organizations: The IIRR Experience," IIRR Occasional Paper No. 6, October 1983.

8. *Ibid.*

9. Ken Powelson, H. Anarna, and L. Capistrano, "Credit as a Tool for Self-Sustained Development," *International Sharing*, Vol. 2, No. 2, August 1987.

10. Kamal Malhotra, "Project Loan Fund Policy and Procedures Document," May 1984, mimeographed paper.

11. Henry Mercaida, "Task Force Report on PO Participation in the PLF Management," August 9, 1986.

Exhibit 1
IIRR'S MISSIONS AND PROGRAMS

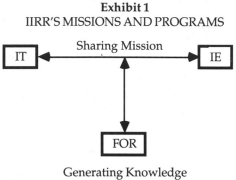

Generating Knowledge
and Learning Mission

Exhibit 2
IIRR'S ORGANIZATIONAL CHART
(circa 1978)

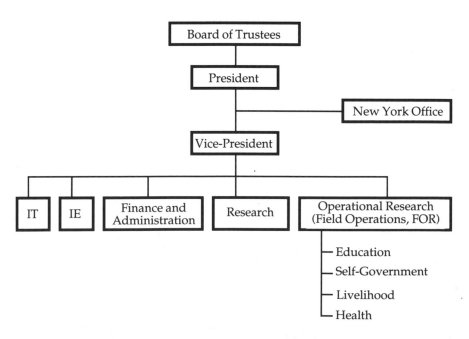

Exhibit 3
IIRR'S ORGANIZATIONAL CHART [a]
(circa December 1986)

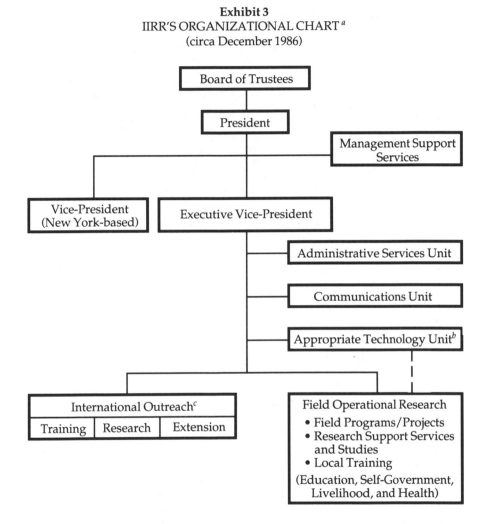

[a] IIRR was currently reviewing the structure portrayed here.

[b] Most program experts, especially in livelihood projects, were in the Appropriate Technology Unit. However, health and credit specialists were not necessarily in this unit.

[c] Research as a component of the sharing and international outreach mission was still in an incipient stage, and had no description at the time.

Exhibit 4
A CONCEPTUALIZATION OF THE RURAL CREDIT SYSTEM

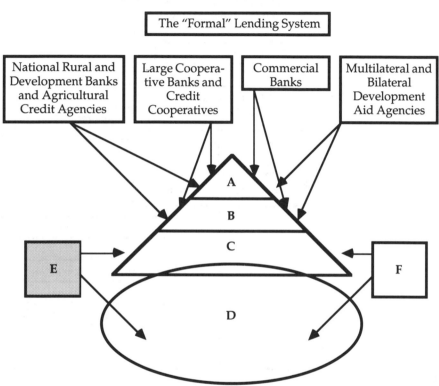

Notes: The farm **pyramid** represents all the farmers in rural areas. The typical farm pyramid is made up of three distinguishable subgroups: large-, medium-, and small- or marginal-sized farmers. Segment **A** denotes the large-sized farmers, who might comprise around 5 percent of the farm population in the typical less developed country (LDC). The medium-sized farmers are in segment **B**, and may comprise around 15 percent of the farm population in the typical LDC. The "formal" lending agencies service the large- and medium-sized farmers. Segment **C** represents the bulk (80 percent) of the LDC farmers.

Oval **D** depicts the rural landless poor, who are unorganized or loosely organized. They might comprise as much as 25 percent of the **total** rural (including farmers) LDC population.

Box **E** represents the middlemen and merchants who are the primary credit recourse for groups C and D. The box indicates the existence of a money-lending system, although the fund sources are generally independent of one another, as represented by the individual dots in the box. Box **F** includes IIRR and other NGOs who compete directly with the money-lending system.

Exhibit 5
THE FOUR COMPONENTS OF IIRR'S CREDIT PROGRAM

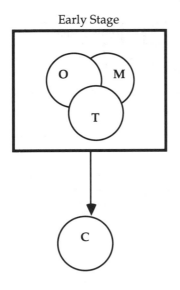

Early Stage

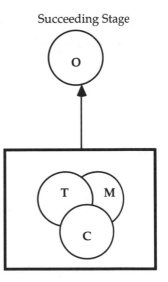

Succeeding Stage

Notes: **O** = Organization
          M = Management
          T = Technical Inputs
          C = Capitalization

Exhibit 6
THREE MODELS FOR PEOPLE'S ORGANIZATION PARTICIPATION

PLFC Model I

(5 PO Members in each of the 3 PO Divisions—no IIRR staff)

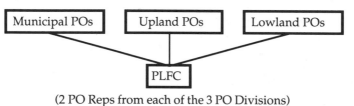

(2 PO Reps from each of the 3 PO Divisions)

PLFC Model II

(Each PO Division consists of 7 PO Members and 2 IIRR Staff)

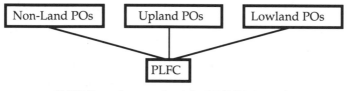

(2 PO Reps from each of the 3 PO Divisions)

PLFC Model III

(5 PO Members in each of the 3 PO Divisions—no IIRR staff)

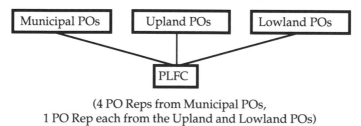

(4 PO Reps from Municipal POs,
1 PO Rep each from the Upland and Lowland POs)

Notes: PLFC = 11 members, 5 from IIRR + 6 from People's Organizations (POs).

Case 14

IIRR (B):
The Relationship with the
Integrated Agricultural Cooperative

This case was written by Marissa B. Espineli and Francisco Roman. It is
intended as a basis for class discussion rather than as an illustration of
either effective or ineffective handling of an administrative situation.
IAC is a disguised name; otherwise, the case is an authentic representation of the experiences of IIRR. The collaboration and support of the
President of IIRR and his staff are gratefully acknowledged.

Part I: Summary of the Situation

IAC is a cooperative of farmers organized in 1976. It produces, processes,
and markets livestock feeds on behalf of its members. Most of the livestock raisers of IAC were scholars trained in the International Institute of
Rural Reconstruction's (IIRR) People's School. IAC grew to become one
of IIRR's larger, more sophisticated, and more successful cooperatives,
and generally had a special relationship with IIRR.

In 1986, IAC pursued an ambitious two-stage expansion program
that included the purchase of land for the project, and the construction of
a warehouse, concrete fence, employees' living quarters, a tool shed, and
two poultry houses. IAC also bought a hammer mill—an apparatus for
milling corn—and incurred additional expenses to air condition its administrative office and to hire new employees for its permanent staff.
IIRR financed the IAC expansion. In that same year, several members
withdrew their share capital, totaling U.S.$8,000[1] from the cooperative.

Furthermore, the Ministry of Agriculture issued a directive prohibit-
ing the importation of corn, based on its initial statistics, which indicated
that the country might have a sufficient supply of this feedstuff. Around
the same time, the National Food Authority (NFA), the agency in charge
of regulating the importation of food grains, permitted the private sector
to deal in soya bean meal. The NFA also indicated that it would no
longer replenish its own warehouse with soya bean meal once it had exhausted its existing stocks.

IAC estimated that it needed 100,000 kilos of yellow corn, priced at U.S.$0.20/kg, and 40,000 kilos of soybean meal at U.S.$0.27/kg, for an approximate total of U.S.$31,000, in order to sustain its inventories for its regular operations. IAC planned to buy the soybean meal from the NFA, and to pay farmers in advance for their yellow corn output, in order to ensure its supply, since IAC forecasted an increase in the price of corn and soy feedstuffs in the coming months.

The cooperative's liquidity was already impaired by the expansion projects and the withdrawal of capital shares. IAC's Board therefore passed a resolution requesting a production loan from IIRR's Project Loan Fund Committee (PLFC) for U.S.$31,300. On February 9, 1987, the cooperative's General Manager filed a loan for that amount to the PLFC-IIRR.

The loan went through the PLFC's application process, and on February 18 the Finance Manager of the Committee provided his comments on the IAC loan proposal in a memorandum to the PLFC executives. In it, he indicated that IAC's loan request was justified given its reduced 1986 cash flow; the memo also indicated that the cooperative had a favorable repayment record. On the other hand, he noted delays and misunderstanding in meeting the demands of its loan contract with IIRR for its second-stage expansion; he also raised the issue of the strong profit orientation of the cooperative and its leadership, and noted the existence within IAC of a group of larger and more successful members. At the same time, he informed the PLFC of his own efforts to link IAC with the agricultural extension of one of the Philippines' larger and stable commercial banks, the Bank of the Philippine Islands-Agribank. The Finance Manager concluded by recommending approval of the loan application, based on a referral by IIRR to BPI-Agribank, on a six-month term, with a commercial interest rate.[2]

At the IAC Board meeting on March 14, the General Manager reported that PLFC-IIRR had denied the loan application, but instead had referred IAC to the BPI-Agribank.

One of the IIRR staff was also a Rural Reconstruction Facilitator (RRF) of IIRR for IAC; he was concurrently a member of IAC. One of his tasks was to promote IIRR's rural development approaches to the cooperative. He was present at that meeting and he attempted to "soften the blow" of what appeared to be a denial of a justifiable loan application. He also noted the "special relationship" between IIRR and IAC; in particular, he informed the group that a representative of the German Freedom From Hunger Campaign (GFFHC) would be visiting IAC on March 17; the GFFHC was one of IIRR's largest donors, and IAC, through IIRR, had obtained a loan at favorable terms, from the GFFHC, for its first-stage expansion; the loan was under the supervision of the PLFC. The

Board subsequently decided to begin negotiations with BPI-Agribank while renegotiating its production loan application with the PLFC.

The IAC Board and the PLFC executives met on March 16 at IIRR. IAC requested the approval of its production loan, which it had reduced to U.S.$10,000. The PLFC replied that the application would be reconsidered but that the interest rate would be increased to keep it in line with the prevailing market rate; however, the specific rate was not yet decided upon.

On March 23, the Finance Manager recommended approval of the U.S.$10,000 loan, and prepared an agreement for IAC with the following terms and conditions: an interest rate of 17 percent, which reflected the prevailing bank rate on short-term loans, payment in four equal monthly installments of principal and interest starting May 31, and subject to the proviso that IAC ought to pursue a loan application on its own with BPI-Agribank. With respect to the latter, the loan contract also stipulated that if IAC could obtain a loan from BPI-Agribank at more favorable interest rates, IIRR would refund IAC the difference. IIRR released a check for U.S.$10,000 for IAC on that same day. In making this decision to charge IAC 17 percent on its loan, instead of the usual 12 percent,[3] the Field Operations Director of IIRR made the following points:

> It is IIRR's long standing plan to eventually link all of the of the People's Organizations (POs) that it is assisting to the regular financing institutions [that is, banks] in order to minimize their dependence on IIRR. As a step in this direction, it was agreed by the PLFC, IIRR's loan fund's policy-making body, long before the IAC loan was submitted, that IIRR will gradually increase its interest rate slowly to approximate that of the banks. In this way, the POs will also be able to adjust gradually to the terms and conditions of the banks, thus making it less difficult for them to make the transition from borrowing from IIRR to borrowing from the banks. The PLFC also decided to apply the increased interest rate first to those POs whose financial situations can bear the higher rate without too much difficulty. IAC was a natural choice in this regard because it is the most financially stable of all the POs.

On March 24, the IAC General Manager returned the check to the Finance Manager, together with a letter in which IAC stated that (1) the BPI prevailing interest rate was only 13 percent, and (2) IAC had reviewed its cash flow and had decided not to borrow from either IIRR or BPI-Agribank, and would finance the operations internally instead.

The Finance Manager informed the PLFC of the situation, and indicated that the results, while unexpected, might prove to be good for all concerned. However, he also made the point that it was almost impossible for the IAC Board to hold a meeting, within less than twenty-four hours, the time between the release and the return of the check; he raised the possibility that the General Manager had acted on his own without any formal approval from the IAC board.

The Field Operations Director noted that, unlike the other smaller organizations IIRR dealt with in the area, relations with IAC were generally rather formal, with written communications prevailing on all problems and decisions. This was partly a result of IAC's growing size, and also because of other factors. As the Field Operations Director explained:

> Our relationship is formal, yet cordial; businesslike, yet accommodating. The formality of the relationship stemmed principally from the style of the IAC Board Chairman at the time. He is a police officer who was formal in his dealings with just about everybody. He is also a relative newcomer to the IAC Board; the previous chairmen tended to be much less formal in their official dealings with IIRR.

Part II: Three Interviews

Interview with the Director of the Field Operations Division, IIRR

Q: How would you describe the relationship between IAC and IIRR?

A: Our relationship with IAC is one of those special relationships, because it is one of our largest borrowers—loans are in the millions [of pesos]. IIRR negotiated separately with one of its large donors, the German Freedom From Hunger Campaign, to provide IAC with a loan for its expansion project. IAC repays this loan to IIRR.

Aside from this special loan, other large loans were made available to them from the IIRR general loan fund at a 12 percent interest rate. In terms of repayment performance, they are considered the best. Though from a financial point of view, the cooperative may be considered the best, we believe that they should not be accorded similar concessions given to small people's organizations [POs]. We find IAC financially stable and there is no point in subsidizing their operations. Besides, we suspect that most of the benefits of the cooperative may go to its better-off members.

Q: Why did you say that benefits go to better-off members?

A: The original intention behind organizing the cooperative was to serve the interest of both livestock growers and feedgrain producers. Livestock growers referred to are those who grow livestock in the backyard, and feed-grain producers are small farmers who grow corn. It is a cooperative with a symbiotic relationship between the two. But IAC has been selling its feeds to big dealers, and most of them are members of the cooperative. The small livestock growers buy their feeds from these dealers. Thus the patronage refund goes to the dealers and not to the small farmers.

Besides, IAC is a big organization composed of more than five- hundred members. In terms of decision making, it is not possible for it to call a general assembly and so participation in decision making is quite poor.

Because of these points, we motivated them to make some effort for the leadership to become more participative. In fact, in some of their previous loans, it is stipulated in the contract that loans are awarded provided that they organize chapters in strategic areas of Cavite, so that their services can be made available to small farmers and livestock growers. But they do not seem to be very keen on this, and so, because of this, we feel that IAC's interest in IIRR is purely business, that is, of an institution that serves to provide them with loans. So we started to deal with them formally, in a business-like manner, very much different from other POs. If we want a meeting with them, we send them a letter. If we have visitors who want to see the place, we request them formally, very much unlike other POs, where we just send word that we're waiting for them or that we're meeting with them.

Q: What is IIRR doing about these developments that you recounted?

A: As I said, we made some effort to motivate the board to be receptive to its original purpose, like stipulating some of those things in the contract when we award them a loan. In fact, we are inviting them to a meeting where IIRR senior staff will sit and discuss the agenda. Only last week, when the IIRR President was available, they confirmed their availability, but one day before the meeting, when I was giving instructions to prepare for it, I was informed that they cancelled the meeting because not all members of the Board could be present.

One week before, when they agreed to the meeting, I think that they already knew that not all Board members would be available, and I don't see it as the real reason for cancelling the meeting. I think that the agenda that we prepared had something to do with it. I know that they're not prepared to answer some of the issues listed in the agenda, like the land titles that we're asking concerning the project expansion, and the organization of chapters.

Besides, I think that IAC has the feeling that they don't need our money anymore. I said this because we are now organizing the People's Organizations Loan Fund Committee [POLFC]—it's a federation of POs that will eventually manage IIRR's credit program. Almost all the POs, no matter how small, are represented here, but IAC didn't send anyone.

Q: When and how did this relationship problem that you described start?

A: The last Chairman of the Audit/Inventory Committee was our accountant. This committee made a critical report [in 1986] on the status of IAC and its overall operation and general management. As our employee, of course, IAC thinks that it is IIRR speaking, and they think that we are critical of what they are doing. Of course, we ourselves are critical, and this is met by them with hostility. They sent word through the RRF that they won't honor any communication coming from IIRR unless it is signed by our President, which could be the reason why our last invitation for a meeting was not honored.

Q: What was your reaction when you learned that the check was returned?

A: I'm not too concerned. If they don't want the loan, this only shows that they don't need our money. But I still hope that they join the POLFC because I don't know how they would react if the concept of a people's bank is implemented.

Q: How was the idea of increasing the interest rate decided on?

A: It was suggested, recommended by the Finance Manager, and everyone [in the PLFC] agreed to this suggestion because we found his reasons for doing so valid. Besides, even before the Finance Manager recommended it, we already had this feeling that they should be charged the prevailing business rate.

Interview with the Finance Manager, IIRR

Q: How would you describe the relationship between IAC and IIRR?

A: It is compared to a parent and child relationship. As parents, we want our children to do what we think is best for them. When the child grows and begins to decide for himself, we have this mixed feeling of joy and indifference. It is true with IIRR and IAC. Its relationship is at the stage when the child has grown up and the parent is challenging whether he can be on his own.

Q: There was the decision to increase the interest rate to IAC. How did this evolve?

A: Even before that decision to increase the interest rate, we already have this feeling of not granting them any loan. They cannot be compared to other People's Organizations. They earn millions. We want them to go to the banks because we know that they can afford what the banks offer. Besides, there are other pressures from the donor agencies to charge them the prevailing interest rate in the market.

Q: How was it decided?

A: This, as I said, is a feeling that every member [of the PLFC] shares. In a meeting among PLFC members, we agreed on the increase. By how much? This we really hadn't decided among ourselves then.

Q: Why was the interest rate set at 17 percent? What was your basis for this?

A: Actually, the idea came from me. I suggested it. What I had in mind was to align the interest rate to be charged to IAC to what was prevailing in the market. Interest rate then was from 17 to 19 percent, or higher.

Q: You made some effort to link them to BPI-Agribank. Why were they unable to get the loan from the bank?

A: You know how banks operate. It really takes too long; it's too slow.

Q: Were they informed of the increased rate?

A: Yes, there was this meeting. The IAC Board called on us, the PLFC members, and in this meeting the Executive Vice-President kept on emphasizing that the interest rate that will be charged on this new loan shall be in line with the prevailing market rate. So I think they expected it. Besides, when we released the check, the General Manager signed the agreement and voucher, which means he agreed to it.

Q: What was your reaction to their decision to return the check?

A: It's a mix of good and bad feelings; I think it's good because we are really also in need of our cash, and it's good because this gives us some clues that they can really be on their own. Somehow it's offensive, because you went through the entire process, and here they are returning the check. I find some of the Board now are a bit cocky. In the past, the Board members would think twice before they would do anything like that.

Interview with the Rural Reconstruction Facilitator (RRF), Field Operations Division (FOD), IIRR

Q: As both an IAC member and the RRF in charge of the cooperative, how would you describe the IIRR-IAC relationship?

A: IAC is an independent organization. It is only one of the many that we [IIRR] support. We have no right to press demands, but some of our senior staff here think that we have the proprietary right over them because we loaned them some money. If our motive is that these POs whom we support be self-reliant, we should know our role well. Sometimes we tend to be very critical, we misunderstand them. I don't know if this is the result of being very protective of our investments.

We have a tendency to look at organizations from an ideal point of view. We give suggestions on how the cooperative could improve as an organization from our own point of view. Like this participatory thing, we want them to encourage participation but we forget that our own culture discourages this—in our own family, not everyone really participates in the decision making process. The relationship of some of our senior staff with them is that of being overcritical. Sometimes, I find myself sandwiched between two differing views when I have to stay neutral.

But I have to protect myself—to avoid trouble I suggested that every communication be done in black and white.

Q: You mentioned something about demands. How does this occur?

A: When they [PLFC] release loans, they stipulate some demands in the contract. I find it puts some constraints on the relationship. I have consulted a lawyer about this, and even from the legal point of view, these demands cannot be imposed even if they are written in the contract. One problem about us [IIRR]: we create pressure on ourselves. Whatever the donor says, we do.

Q: Was it the donor who made the decision to increase the interest rate and to make these demands?

A: That is what they [PLFC] said. But what I am saying is—it's all right, but we also have to look at how it affects the beneficiaries. Let us go back to IAC's first expansion loan. A feasibility study was prepared, and through IIRR, they [IAC] were able to get a loan from the German Freedom From Hunger Campaign. The loan was approved and attached to it were some demands, like putting up the poultry house, and setting aside 250,000 pesos for the production capital. The 250,000 was deposited with IIRR. The amount intended for the construction was used up, and there was still a lot to be done. You know how prices went up in those days. They [IAC] tried to borrow from that portion of the loan that was set aside, but instead they were sent to the banks. But it took them several negotiations, and they still were not able to get a loan from the bank.

Q: Why could they not get loans from banks?

A: You know how banks are. They require so much from the creditor. They [IAC] have enough collateral, but there are so many requirements that they [IAC] find difficult to produce on a moment's notice. And so they looked to IIRR as a friend who can help them. When they were awarded the loan, but at an increased interest rate, they were very much surprised. Look, there are other POs who can't pay their loans for five years, and here's one whose repayment performance is outstanding, and we were giving them a high interest rate.

Q: Why do you think that there was an increase in the interest rate for the IAC loan?

A: The problem with us [IIRR], we are comparing ourselves with banks and financing businesses. The financing business is different; they have to have high interest because of their losses. Thus, they require that their borrowers be insured. In the same manner, we require IAC to insure their properties. We made some demands in our contract. This created a rift and I think it's IIRR who created it, and it gives me some problems in my dealing with them [IAC] because I am with the Institute. In fact, their attitude toward me has changed a lot. They used to call me in my house for consultations on some problems. Now they don't do it anymore.

Anyway, I can still help them in my own private way as a member of the cooperative.

Q: How do you see IAC's financial stability?

A: It is very stable and has financial capability. It has overshot its own capital requirements by one million pesos. This was a result of a capital build-up system that I introduced, that is, a savings fund of one peso for every bag of feed sold. Its reserve fund is liquid; it has some problems on loan collections from some members, but I think they can manage without us. They have their own internal and external auditors.

Q: What of its leadership?

A: The leadership is quite elitist. The Board members are a good mix of professionals, farmers and women. Their teamwork is good but it has a tendency to be elitist when not balanced. But this is not how they are perceived by the majority of the members. They trust this group very much. There is no personal animosity among the Board. Sometimes they are critical of one another, but I don't think it was meant to put each other down.

Let us take the case of its past President [who was running for reelection]. In the last general assembly, this past President dominated throughout and this was something the rest of the members did not like. An election was scheduled that day, but the time was eaten up by the discussion that took place during the open forum. The election was rescheduled for another meeting, and this past President lost in the election.

Q: What about their decision-making process?

A: They discuss among themselves the whole day. They are given honoraria for this. Since the Board has seven members, it is easy to get a quorum. They calendar their meetings to ensure that everybody will be present in the meeting. In cases where there is a very dominant member during the meeting, the group makes a decision when he is not present.

Q: Let us go back to the 1986 Audit/Inventory Committee report. How did you react to it?

A: I think there were some mistakes there. You see, if you belong to a group, you show respect to one another by discussing it, and you ask the feelings of the person involved about it before presenting it to a big group. If we become overcritical about the person, I don't think it is the person who is placed in an embarrassing situation; I think the organization is much more embarrassed. Besides, I don't think it was fair; if you see the evaluation, it is focused not on performance but on personalities.

Q: How did the person concerned react?

A: The Chairman of the Board [of IAC] was hurt and I think it is just normal.

Q: How was the report perceived by those present in the general assembly?

A: It was something that they thought was good, and it was accepted by everyone. Some expressed negative attitudes about it. I don't know, I just feel that the people were still affected by the EDSA [E. de los Santos Avenue] revolution [which overthrew Marcos]. It was just three days after that, and you know how people are. It was quite noisy, and there were unruly groups around, then.

Q: What do you think of the PLFC decision to increase the interest rate to IAC?

A: Just as I said, I think they compared our operations to that of a bank. They found IAC to have this capability to pay, they charged them the business rate, but it was not presented to the cooperative very clearly. The way they [IAC] were informed about it was rather absurd. They [IAC] were not even prepared for it.

Q: What about the requirements stipulated in the contract, such as forming a chapter group, land titles, and so forth?

A: It would take time for IAC to have the land titles of the area covered by the expansion loan ready. You see, land titles are issued to persons, not to a group or to an organization. Even the former owner of the land may not have the land title—what he has are other documents of ownership.

As for the chapter groups, I think IAC is exerting some efforts to do this. They have local chapters in two of their areas.

Q: They [IAC] were invited to a meeting on October 27, with the senior staff of IIRR. Why was this cancelled?

A: They really could not come up with a decision about it, because when it was presented to the [Board] members, not everyone would be available, but they agreed to the meeting. When IIRR followed it up and was informed by the General Manager that the Board had no decision about it yet, it was really the truth. I was assigned to follow this up a day or two before the meeting. I was told [by IAC] that the meeting has to be cancelled. Anyway, they agreed on another date, but the [IIRR] President and EVP were not around then so they all finally agreed to meet on December 12.

Brief Bio-data of the Field Operations Director

Age 43, he is Assistant to the President and Director of the Field Operations Division; he has been with IIRR for seven years. Prior to joining IIRR, he was Director of the Presidential Task Force on Youth and Sports Development, Managing Director of the Cardona Development Foundation, Inc., and a consultant to UNESCO.

He graduated from the University of the Philippines, A.B. Political Science, and attended special continuing education courses at the East-West Center in Hawaii, and at the School of Management Studies, Polytechnic of Central London.

Brief Bio-data of the Finance Manager

Age 45, he is IIRR's Comptroller, and the Project Loan Fund Manager of the Credit Program; he has been with IIRR for six years. As Comptroller, he manages the finances and controls funding of IIRR's farm operation systems; as Fund Manager, he is responsible for monitoring IIRR's credit and financial management training programs for the village organizations.

His previous work experience was as Comptroller of the Puerto Azul Beach Hotel in Cavite, and the Manila Peninsula Hotel; he was also Senior Auditor for Coopers and Lybrand, and C.P.A. for a large Philippine accounting firm.

He holds a B.S. in Commerce, major in Accounting, and a local M.B.A.

Brief Bio-data of the RRF

He is single, age 53, and a livestock and poultry specialist. He was a rural reconstruction worker for two years, before he joined IIRR in 1959 as the person in charge of the IIRR Campus. He was then promoted to Plant Superintendent and became responsible for the development of the 54-hectare IIRR campus in Cavite. He has been a Rural Reconstruction Facilitator for fifteen years, and reports to the Director of Field Operations.

He finished his B.S. Agriculture and specialized in Animal Husbandry. He obtained his M.A. in Agriculture at North Carolina State University in the United States, and has attended several study tours abroad.

He is one of the founding fathers of IAC. He has been an advisor to the Board and to the IAC management staff since 1976, and plans out projects with IAC. As RRF, he conducts training for the management and staff of IAC.

Part III: Postscript

The Field Operations Director indicated that an on-going, working relationship between IIRR and a cooperating PO is a critical component to IIRR's success. However, he also noted that the relationship among IIRR staff is equally important to IIRR's success, if not more so. The IAC issue involves both elements, and the Field Operations Director explained the difference of opinion between the PLFC and the RRF in the following manner:

> This has to be seen in relation to two factors. One is the policy of IIRR to allow its staff to express whatever opinion they may have on any decision, whether for or against, provided that once a decision is

affirmed, they are duty bound to carry it out. On the issue of the higher interest rate, the RRF thought that it was not yet a final decision since there was an appeal from IAC for the PLFC to reconsider the decision. The second factor is the RRF's relationship, and feelings toward, IAC. As the IIRR staff member most involved with IAC, he has developed a somewhat "paternalistic" attitude toward it, and he tends to defend IAC whenever there are decisions or reactions that he perceives to be against IAC. He also tends to be overprotective of the cooperative, to the point of not wanting it to lose whatever advantage it may already have, e.g., a lower interest rate than what comparable cooperatives may have to pay when borrowing from banks and other regular financial institutions, even if it is natural for it to lose some of the advantages in the course of time. The RRF is also very sensitive to the implications of the situation, e.g., IAC " ... used to call me in my house for consultations on some problems. Now they don't do it anymore." The unsaid part of this statement is the RRF's feeling that the reason IAC is no longer as close to him as before, per his perception, is that IIRR no longer treats IAC in a "special" way; therefore, they see no reason to also continue treating IIRR, and its staff, including the RRF himself, in a "special" way.

Notes

1. The 1987 exchange rate fluctuated around U.S.$1.00 = RP Peso 20.00.

2. Under this arrangement, it is the BPI-Agribank which actually makes the loan.

3. Economic conditions were making it increasingly difficult for PVOs to sustain a relatively low interest rate. As of April 1, 1988, IIRR added a 3 percent service fee to the standard 12 percent interest rate on all POs, regardless of age, size, or financial situation.

Case 15

Indonesian Rattan Basket Exporting Company: Business Goals vs. Development Goals

This case was written by Dr. Ross Edgar Bigelow. It is intended as a basis for class discussion rather than as an illustration of either effective or ineffective handling of an administrative situation. The case draws on field work done in Indonesia in 1987. Some of the names have been changed. The permission from Dr. Bigelow and the representative of the CJEDP Project to include the case in this book is gratefully acknowledged.

Wawwam Makes Baskets in His Village

Wawwam was awakened by rain falling in his face through his leaky roof in the small village of Suruh. But he was happy at the prospect of collecting payment for the eleven baskets he and his wife had made for the basket export company during the week. A tidy sum of 22,500 Rupiah (U.S.$14) would help him repair the roof. As a farmer of cassava and irrigated rice, he would welcome the extra income from basket weaving.

Wawwam had gone from his village to the Indonesian Rattan Basket Exporting (IRBE) Company in Ungaran, ten kilometers away, on the previous Wednesday and collected 18 kilograms of raw material. That is all that his bicycle could carry. He was returning today, Saturday, ten days later to collect his money. He planned to go on to get some new roofing materials while he was in town. The Company had held a training program for Suruh producers to teach them how to make rattan baskets last year. Wawwam had not known anything about basket production before that, nor did his wife. If they had had children who were old enough, they would have been able to aid in the basket making and increase the income of the family. Some of Wawwam's neighbors with large families were producing for IRBE almost twice as much as his family for each ten-day period.

Wawwam was able to gain a marketable skill. The training had lasted for two weeks, from eight in the morning until four in the afternoon with an hour for lunch each day. Saturday training was only half a day. Because all the training was practical hands-on activity, the improvement in technique came quickly. In only eighty hours of instruction at the Company in Ungaran, Wawwam was able to gain a valuable skill. Wawwam had never imagined he would be making baskets, but farming does not take all of his time and the extra off-farm income helps a lot.

AID/Jakarta Promotes Small Business Development

David Beyers, the Agency for International Development (AID) Enterprise Specialist based in Jakarta, had only five days to make an important go/no-go decision about additional funding for an Agency employment generation project in Central Java. He had heard wonderful reports from the American contractor running the project about its promotion of small business activities. But Jim Cellers, the contractor's small enterprise specialist based in Central Java, had also told David that he questioned whether Project employment goals were really being achieved. A week before, he had visited the Indonesian Rattan Basket Exporting Company which the Project helps, and he suggested to David that he stop in to see if he thought the firm was having the kind of development impact that was desired by AID/Jakarta. The budget was in the final stage of preparation and the level of funding for the Enterprise Development Project of Central Java hung in the balance. David had a morning to visit one or two firms assisted by the AID funds and decide for himself whether AID goals were being met by such firms.

Indonesian Rattan Basket Exporting Company

Until recently, there had been no company to employ Wawwam. The Indonesian Rattan Basket Exporting Company, which began operations in 1980 and fell into bankruptcy, only reopened in 1985 on a limited scale. The owner's nephew, an economics student in his final year at the university, was made General Manager. At first, IRBE produced only for local seasonal consumption—New Year's, Christmas, and *Id Il Fitr*, the Moslem holiday at the end of Ramadan. Production then was estimated at a mere 200,000 Rupiah (U.S.$125) for the year.

When David visited the Company and saw its operation, he told the Company staff that, "the main reason for the Company's resurgence must be attributed to its new business relationship with the Central Java Enterprise Development Project (CJEDP)." An activity funded by AID and run under an agreement with Development Alternatives, Inc., CJEDP is trying to help businesses develop in Central Java for the express reason of employment generation. Small business is viewed by AID as an engine for rural jobs and a foundation for a strong economy over the longer term.

In late 1985, CJEDP took interest in the production potential of IRBE and began to contact foreign basket buyers on their behalf. When the young manager first took over, he was not successful in locating export markets. Several prospective international buyers approached IRBE but no one placed orders. A buyer told CJEDP staff, "Basket quality is questionable and I am uncertain the manager understands what we want."

Market explorations by CJEDP staff landed an order for one 20-foot container to Australia in November 1985. Indonesian Rattan Basket Export was reenergized. Slowly buyers were contacted and orders began to come in. By mid-1986 the Company's sales averaged four to five-and-a-half million Rupiah (U.S.$2,500–3,500) per month. By early 1987 they had grown to over 27 million Rupiah (U.S.$17,000) per month. Three major buyers from Connecticut, Australia, and Hawaii (for the U.S. West Coast market) had brought IRBE to financial viability. Prospects for continued expansion were good.

With CJEDP's help, the Company had trained and was working with seventy village workers with some four beneficiaries per worker. In addition, there were twenty on-site employees by early 1987. Against the firm's revenues of U.S.$17,000 per month, monthly costs were $13,500. Annual outside funding was $31,000—all from CJEDP—for technical assistance, transportation, communications, marketing, and personnel.

In 1987 one of the major buyers asked the Company to increase its order to two containers of baskets per month. The buyer also offered to help it with worldwide marketing assistance and quality control advice in exchange for exclusive rights to certain specific basket designs. This seemed at first to be a seller's dream come true. Here was a great opportunity for expansion. However, the General Manager worried that there were downsides: production capacity using the village industry approach was limited, quality would have to be improved, and other established customers might have to be dropped to fill the big buyer's order. Clearly there were risks involved.

The challenge was to balance supply and demand. To increase export potential required, on the one hand, that IRBE expand the quality and quantity of its production, and on the other hand, that it attract buyers and keep them happy. One cannot afford to build excess capacity; yet just as bad would be to have orders that cannot be filled. What if the big buyer lost interest or did not like the quality of their product? The bubble might burst!

Despite the risks, IRBE management decided it needed to change gears and increase its productive capacity. To do this would require a fivefold increase. It would also require an assembly line operation, they believed, rather than the cottage industry approach with its "bicycle brigade." The company explored purchasing rattan fiber splitting machinery to increase output per worker. The Company believed that by using improved technology and an assembly line, the quintupling of production could be achieved without an increase in the number of workers. Village producers could move to town and continue their basketmaking, but since they were farmers it seemed unlikely that they would choose to do so. With short-term, inexpensive training available, new in-town workers could replace them. Would the recently employed village workers, like Wawwam, now be employed?

Economic Outlook

Indonesia controls the world rattan market. Kalimantan (the Indonesian portion of the island of Borneo) is the only remaining major source of rattan, providing about 95 percent of the world total. Borneo lies a short distance across the Java Sea from Semarang in Central Java where the company is located. Historically, mostly Chinese companies exploited rattan from rainforests in Kalimantan, then trans-shipped the raw material to Taiwan, Singapore, Hong Kong, and elsewhere for manufacture into quality furniture and baskets. The only major difference between high quality rattan goods and lower quality items lies in the skill of the craftsman. Basket quality is calculated on a point system well known to buyers and sellers around the world. The best quality products come from the Philippines, Japan, and Taiwan. Even though Indonesian artisans had only recently started to produce export-quality goods, they were increasingly successful in export markets against strong international competition.

In October 1986 the Government of Indonesia passed laws that restricted to domestic firms the export of rattan as a raw material. Because Indonesia controls the source of supply, when the new regulation took full effect in 1989 Indonesian producers took over control of the industry. Already, by the end of 1987, market prospects for rattan in the richer nations looked excellent. Little businesses like IRBE should have an excellent future, all other things being equal.

The Role of CJEDP

According to Central Java Government officials, the Central Java Enterprise Development Project had played a critical role in helping IRBE rise from the ashes. Marketing, management assistance, and quality control had been provided. Jim told David that the CJEDP Export Specialist, an Indonesian with U.N. Industrial Development Organization (UNIDO) experience and twenty-seven years in the Government of Indonesia's

Department of Trade, had assisted the IRBE management with many key organizational and export decisions. CJEDP business specialists had advised the firm. With the help of a Filipino expert in rattan production who had operated a very successful business of his own back in the Philippines, the Project had provided quality training to Indonesian artisans, like Wawwam. David believed that CJEDP specialists had clearly become important factors in the company's expansion.

David had been informed that CJEDP filled all kinds of business gaps in Central Java in rattan products, metalworking, and shrimp production. It helped a variety of small entrepreneurs like those of IRBE and it worked collaboratively with—but independently of—the government and AID. David had heard from Company staff that "CJEDP identified business opportunities, found markets for goods, lured potential buyers, provided information on market and technology, determined lowest-cost improvements of products for producers, and helped small Indonesian firms consummate deals."

"The credibility of CJEDP among potential and actual buyers was, perhaps, just as important as to the Company," Jim had said. CJEDP staff had the ability to communicate in English and could overcome barriers to trust. International buyers apparently saw CJEDP as an honest intermediary and First World business broker.

David Faces a Decision

David had to decide whether the Agency's employment goals were served by CJEDP as reflected in its work with the little Company in Ungaran. He also needed to determine what the long-term prospects would be for a firm after outside assistance came to an end. He looked over his notes and began to consider what he would put in his report.

Exhibit 1
BENEFIT TO COST RATIO

As one point of reference in his evaluation, David Beyers thought about using the framework below to calculate the benefit to cost ratio for the project.

Line 1   Number of Participants
(Workers and Beneficiaries)   _____

Line 2   Annual Revenues   _____

Line 3   Annual Operating Costs   _____

Line 4   Outside Funding   _____

Line 5   Annual Revenues per Participant
(Line 2 divided by Line 1)   _____

Line 6   Annual Operating Costs per Participant
(Line 3 divided by Line 1)   _____

Line 7   Net Annual Benefits
(Line 5 minus by Line 6)   _____

Line 8   Total Outside Funding per Participant
(Line 4 divided by Line 1)   _____

Line 9   Benefits to Costs
(Line 7 divided by Line 8)   _____

Source: Robert R. Nathan Associates, 1986, *The Cost Effectiveness Field Manual,* PACT, New York.

Case 16

PRODEME:
Program Design Issues

This case was written by Margaret Bowman. It is intended as a basis for classroom discussion rather than as an illustration of either effective or ineffective handling of an administrative situation. The collaboration and support of the Executive Director of PRODEME and his staff are gratefully acknowledged.

The Dominican Development Foundation (DDF) established the Program for the Development of Micro-Enterprises (PRODEME), a loan program, to provide credit and managerial assistance to "micro-enterprises" operated by the poor in Santo Domingo, Dominican Republic. The program was designed and managed by Steve Gross, a full-time outside consultant to the DDF. During the first two years of PRODEME's existence, Steve Gross expanded the size of the program significantly and, in the process, became more familiar with the problems inherent in lending to small businesses.

Steve was convinced that the program's objective of providing credit and technical assistance to micro-enterprises had the potential to increase the welfare of the poor. However, after two years' experience, he questioned some of the program features he himself had designed. Steve had recently received a copy of an evaluation of the program by external evaluators that indicated that the loan default rates in the program were starting to climb above an acceptable level and that the program was increasingly unable to cover its administrative costs. The evaluation's conclusions merely reinforced what he already knew—that the program design needed to be adapted to suit better the needs of the clients. As things stood, clients either were not repaying their loans or would be unable to do so in the future.

It had taken two years for the program's design flaws to be reflected in the default statistics and Steve realized that if those problems were not corrected, the program would soon be in financial difficulty and could even collapse altogether. Although Steve could foresee the pending financial crisis, as a foreign consultant he realized he had little power to alter the program without the support and consent of the Dominican Development Foundation's directors. And while he knew that he could have little effect on the bureaucratic administrative processes that kept the lending costs so high, he thought he could probably change the program design to improve repayment rates. He relayed his findings and suggestions for change to the President and Executive Director of the DDF and, on several occasions, tried to convince the DDF Board of Directors that the program should be altered. He went as far as presenting to them specific solutions to the problems that he had identified. But because PRODEME was riding on a wave of political success, the Foundation's Directors were reluctant to change anything in the program. Steve's dilemma was to try to resolve some of these problems before his contract with the DDF expired in two months.

Small Business in Santo Domingo

Although the Dominican economy was growing at roughly 5 percent per year in 1982, the distribution of the income generated was quite skewed, with most going to the small percentage of affluent families. The poorer half of the population received only 13 percent of the country's total income while the richest 6 percent received about 43 percent. According to the Dominican Planning Office, 75 percent of Dominicans lived below the poverty line. And many of those people had migrated to Santo Domingo in search of employment because of the limited job opportunities in the countryside. In fact, 20 percent of the entire population lived in the capital. Naturally, this urban migration exacerbated the already limited income and employment opportunities in the city.

In 1981, the unemployment rate was roughly 24 percent and the underemployment rate was as high as 50 percent of the potential labor force. Of those employed, roughly half were estimated to be employed by informal sector businesses—the tiny enterprises started and run by the poor that engaged in a broad range of activities in the manufacturing, commerce, and service sectors.[1] Although those micro-businesses represented a important part of the economy, most were not receiving any kind of support from the government or from private organizations. (See Exhibit 1 for more information about the Dominican Republic.)

The Dominican Development Foundation[2]

The Dominican Development Foundation (DDF) was a private, nonprofit community service organization located in Santo Domingo. It was established in 1965 by leading Dominican businessmen and professionals to provide services and assistance to poor farmers who did not receive development or support services. The Foundation was supported financially by donations and a small amount of government assistance.

The DDF had an eighteen-member Board of Directors, elected annually, that established budgets, determined program direction, and participated in fundraising efforts. The Foundation, headed by an Executive Director, was divided into two main departments: the Program Department (credit, technical assistance, and training programs) and the Finance/Administration Department (responsible for budgetary, personnel, and program development functions). Through the Program Department's Rural Development Program, the DDF promoted social organization and collective problem solving with farmers and also offered credit and technical assistance. By 1980 the DDF's Rural Development Program operations had worked with community leaders and businesspeople to assist more than 2,700 farmer associations (60,000 farmers).

In addition to its credit programs, the DDF also offered several other programs that either complemented the credit assistance it provided or generated revenue for the organization. PLANARTE, the Artisan Development Plan, for example, provided technical assistance and credit to rural artisan groups and also established a marketing outlet through which the crafts were sold. PLANARTE also conducted two managerial and administrative training programs through which DDF offered seminars and workshops for beneficiaries. To raise revenue, the Foundation also sold donated collectors' items and agricultural and medical equipment. The DDF had an annual budget of almost U.S.$1.5 million and a staff of more than 100. (See Exhibit 2, DDF Organizational Chart.)

ACCION International

ACCION International, an independent, nonprofit organization founded in 1961 and located in Cambridge, Massachusetts, has supported and provided technical assistance to micro-enterprise and agricultural credit projects in Latin America since 1973. ACCION does not fund projects directly, but instead receives grants from USAID and the Inter-American Development Bank. The bulk of those funds support revolving loan funds and a staff of field consultants who work in close conjunction with local credit organizations. ACCION provides assistance to a variety of programs and has the institutional capacity to share experiences among the programs it works with through the technical advice of its consultants. The Cambridge office provides backup support to the local institutions it works with and continues to monitor the progress of its programs. And although ACCION prefers to work with established organizations, it has on several occasions helped local leaders to form credit institutions that lend to low income clients. In doing so, it has increased the incomes and created employment opportunities for large numbers of the poor throughout the region.

Steve Gross

Steve Gross was ACCION's consultant to the DDF in Santo Domingo and had been working with the organization since 1978 on a rural credit program. As part of that role, he consulted in program design and training, and provided technical assistance in program development of the DDF's credit programs for groups of small farmers *(campesinos)*. He believed that a true test of a program's success was the reaction of clients themselves, and consequently he emphasized meeting clients' stated needs.

Steve's Vision of a Micro-Enterprise Assistance Program

In 1980, Steve was given a contract by USAID to conduct a feasibility study of the potential for urban micro-enterprise support in Santo Domingo and to assess what forms of intervention would be most effective in providing such support. In his survey, Steve discovered that the primary need expressed by micro-enterprise owners was credit. He also estimated a large demand for such assistance. See Exhibit 3 for results of feasibility study, and Exhibits 4 and 5 for a breakdown of the informal sector activities and unemployment in Santo Domingo.

The feasibility study suggested that Santo Domingo was a good place to establish a micro-enterprise credit program, and Steve thought that the DDF was an appropriate institution to implement the program because the DDF had a good reputation with donors and had the support of local businessmen. Furthermore, those groups seemed very interested in the idea of assisting micro-enterprises.

Especially since the Reagan administration had taken office, support for small enterprise projects had become very popular at USAID. As an ACCION representative and an expert in credit program development, Steve had close ties with the USAID office in the Dominican Republic. Steve had spoken to several USAID officials about the prospects of starting a micro-enterprise assistance program and they seemed very interested in funding such a program, as they thought that small informal sector micro-enterprises[3] seemed to offer a promising solution to the income and employment problems of Santo Domingo.[4]

Steve had also developed good relations with some of the DDF Directors and prominent business people in Santo Domingo who were very interested in assisting small enterprises. Camilo Lluberes, the treasurer of the DDF and a prominent businessman with political aspirations, was particularly interested in helping the urban informal sector. Steve met with Camilo several times to discuss their ideas for a micro-enterprise credit program in Santo Domingo. Camilo knew other businessmen who also would be interested in supporting an urban enterprise program, and Steve met with some of them to discuss his ideas and to gauge their support. Because the Dominican government had limited resources, there had been a history of private sector involvement in development activities in the Dominican Republic. According to Steve, "Business leaders were generally very interested and excited about the prospects for a credit program to help poor businesses."

Although the DDF's credit experience had mainly been with agricultural credit, Steve believed the organization would be capable of providing urban business credit as well.[5] The infrastructure for providing credit already existed in the DDF, and administering the new program might actually be easier since the clients would be located closer to the main office and to the technical advisors than the farmer clients were.

Therefore, when the DDF *campesino* training project neared its end, Steve presented his idea for a micro-enterprise credit program to the DDF Directors. This suggestion made sense to Steve since there was support for such a program, but initially some Directors were not receptive to the idea. The DDF's Board believed it should continue to work with needy rural farmers, especially since all their lending experience was with farmers. The executive director claimed that the DDF "once lent money at the urban level and it didn't work—the program was not successful." Although he did not elaborate on the DDF's previous experience, it was clear that any attempts to work with urban entrepreneurs occurred before the DDF had developed the institutional capacity to administer a large loan program. Steve was persistent, and he eventually convinced the DDF Board to implement an urban micro-enterprise credit program with his assistance.

PRODEME: Origins

Until 1981, the DDF focused its entire resources—an annual budget of U.S.$1.5 million—on rural areas where the majority of poor Dominicans live. With Steve's help, in May 1981 the DDF created PRODEME and extended its programs to urban areas, where it provided technical assistance and credit to small informal sector businesses. PRODEME was initially funded by grants totaling U.S.$845,000 from USAID, the Inter-American Foundation, and Appropriate Technology International for the first three years of its operation. USAID funds also covered technical assistance to the DDF from ACCION International. Based on a feasibility study he had conducted of the informal sector of Santo Domingo, Steve established three major objectives for the PRODEME program: (1) creation of employment; (2) enhancement of income; and (3) the provision of credit and management assistance to micro-entrepreneurs at low cost.

PRODEME Program Components[6]

PRODEME had two components designed to reach two different levels of beneficiaries: the micro-enterprise component and the solidarity group component. Both programs involved credit and technical assistance to help the business owners to use their credit productively. (See Exhibit 6 for a comparison of program components.) The micro-enterprise loans were extended to individual entrepreneurs who employed up to six employees and whose investment was no larger than U.S.$10,000. This group was comprised of shoemakers, carpenters, printers, mechanics, seamstresses, food vendors, and craftsmen. The businesses of micro-enterprise owners were larger than those of the solidarity groups. According to an evaluation of the program by Jeff Ashe, "In contrast to the solidarity group beneficiaries, members of this group tended to be among the upper strata of the poor. It is the increased employment opportunities offered to the truly poor that justifies this type of project on social grounds."[7] The objectives of the micro-enterprise component were stated in term of increased income and employment. Technical assistance for micro-enterprises focused on providing management advice to improve enterprise efficiency, productivity, and growth.

Micro-enterprise participants promoted the program among other businesses owners they knew; Foundation coordinators were not responsible for recruiting clients. After a business owner made an initial phone call or a visit to the Foundation, a coordinator was assigned. The coordinator visited the business several times, often weekly, to help start a simple bookkeeping system and to prepare the client's loan application. Loans were usually made for U.S.$1,000 to be repaid in monthly installments over a year. After the loan was approved, the coordinator continued the weekly visits to help detect problems, check on loan repayment, and provide further technical assistance in bookkeeping, marketing, and effective management of employees.

Solidarity Group Component[8]

The solidarity group component reached the smaller enterprises that had almost no capital and no collateral and that did not have a fixed place of business. "Solidarity groups" consisted of small groups of five to eight members who are all responsible for repayment of the group's loans. One group member is elected as a representative and is responsible for collecting payments. Solidarity group members represented an extremely high credit risk, and individually would not have met the requirements for the micro-enterprise loan program. According to Steve, "In a group, the peer pressure exerted on other members of the groups would be sufficient incentive for group members to repay loans without having to rely on material guarantees." The solidarity group component, while including these goals, also had the more intangible aim of "empowerment." Through the experience of working in groups, the solidarity group members were supposed to develop mutual support and leadership. The advice given to groups centered on working together as a group but included business advice to improve the efficiency of client businesses.

The solidarity group method was supposed to cut administrative costs of the program because groups of five to seven clients could be served at one time, with one loan. The clients themselves had the major responsibility for promotion, selection, and group formation. These groups were also expected to exchange management information among themselves to strengthen the business skills they possessed and eventually to form grassroots advocacy organizations. Although PRODEME did not directly promote the formation of spin-off groups to address other common problems faced by the poor, the DDF assumed that the group participants would see some of the benefits of working collectively and they would find other ways to work together.

The largest group of solidarity group participants in PRODEME were the *tricicleros* of Santo Domingo. They rode three-wheeled *triciclos* with large carts on the front, delivering fruit and vegetables from the market to surrounding neighborhoods. The *tricicleros* rented their vehicles for one fifth of their daily wage, and had to pay even more to store them at night. The solidarity group loans to *tricicleros* allowed them to purchase their *triciclos*. Each group member received a loan of U.S.$300 (enough to purchase the triciclo) and also received an additional U.S.$25 loaned for working capital. Loans were repaid in weekly installments, over a year.

To become eligible, solidarity group members attended a two-part, four-hour course on the program emphasizing the solidarity group concept and their responsibility to repay loans. At the end of the course, members selected group presidents. The group members also attended weekly *barrio*-level meetings for one to two months before the credit request was submitted to the program. Later, the group would get together with a PRODEME coordinator to repay the loan. When a member was eight weeks late in repaying his or her loan, the possibility of repossession of assets or some other measure was discussed.

Loan Disbursal

Loan disbursal decisions were made by a committee and were similar for both program components. A long-standing DDF method of disbursing loans to marginal clients was through the purchase order system. This system was designed to minimize abuse of the credit, and required that each client go to a store approved by the DDF to receive a quote on the cost of what she or he wanted to buy. The loan recipient received the merchandise directly and the merchant was paid in cash or by check by DDF. Under this system, money never passed through the hands of the loan client, and merchandise had to be bought in stores approved by the DDF. The Credit Department felt that this ensured that the money paid out in loans was actually going for business purposes. Loans for the purchase of a major piece of capital equipment used a similar method. When a purchase order was not possible, loans were disbursed to clients by checks from the DDF directly to the client. The negative side of the purchase order system was that the business owner was restricted to the number of stores from which to choose and the store owner had to wait a long time for the deal to be closed. Therefore prices paid by DDF clients for inputs tended to be considerably higher than those paying with cash.

An analysis by DDF program staff indicated that clients lost roughly 10 percent of the value of their loans from having to use the purchase order, and that was considered a very conservative estimate. Nevertheless the DDF believed that purchase orders were justified because they guaranteed the use of credit for authorized uses only.

Credit Lending[9]

PRODEME's credit lending system, based on DDF's rural lending procedures, was primarily designed to ensure adequate control of funds and careful accounting of loan expenditures. The loan review process consisted of eight separate review steps and involved up to nine or ten DDF staff from the Program Department and the Finance/Administration Department. The process took up to six months from loan application to disbursement. (See Exhibit 7, DDF Loan Review Process.)

Position of PRODEME within the DDF

According to an evaluation of the program by Otero and Blayney, the position of the PRODEME program within DDF had been a problem:

> Although the DDF enthusiastically embraced this new urban program, its initial institutional response was to anchor it under the existing Rural Development Program, rather than to create a separate department. Only in July 1982, fifteen months into the program, did the DDF implement major organizational changes, which raised PRODEME to the status of a department parallel to the Rural Development Program. At this time, DDF also created mid-level management positions for PRODEME, assigning a director for each of the program components. While this new stature solidified PRODEME, and afforded it added credibility and leverage within DDF, the program now also had to adhere rigorously to DDF's established *modus operandi*, thereby sacrificing some of its capacity for innovation and flexibility.[10]

Popularity of the Program

PRODEME received considerable attention in the Dominican Republic. According to Steve Gross, "… before people barely knew what the term micro-business meant. It got attention because it was the first micro-enterprise program in Santo Domingo and it was the first to use solidarity groups." Not only did PRODEME address the needs of some of the poorest people through solidarity group loans, but since it promoted free enterprise, it had the financial backing of prominent business leaders.

Because the poor in the informal sector were a political issue, several political figures, including the President of the country, also backed the PRODEME program. The Mayor of Santo Domingo was particularly interested in the program and had appeared in newspaper photographs with DDF staff supporting PRODEME. Steve Gross felt that the visibility of the program in Santo Domingo and among international donors made the DDF directors reluctant to alter the program from its original design.

Problems with PRODEME

By September 1982, problems were beginning to emerge in the PRODEME program. Until early 1982, virtually all loan payments had been made on time. By April 1982, the repayment rate had decreased from almost 100 percent repayment to 80 percent and by September 1982, the repayment rate was down to 67 percent. Steve talked to some clients to discover the reasons for default. According to the clients, they were unable to pay back their loans because they had spent the money and did not have enough to repay their loans. Steve knew that the only previous borrowing experience had been with moneylenders who offered very short-term loans. Clients were not used to saving money to repay it at the end of the year. Steve understood that the temptation for them to spend the money was very great given their pressing needs for food, clothing, and other household goods.

Steve Gross knew what could happen if clients failed to repay loans. First of all, if the DDF did not make visible efforts to recoup the money, word would spread to the other clients that they too might not have to pay. If clients could not repay loans over a prolonged period of time, PRODEME would be in financial trouble because the program had developed high recurrent administrative costs. Since mid-1982, when the default rates rose, the coordinators estimated they spent half of their time collecting loans and dealing with repayment problems rather than providing assistance or finding new clients.

The *tricicleros* were having difficulties as well. In one third of the groups it had been necessary to remove a group member or to repossess a *triciclos*. Forty percent of the *tricicleros* and 13 percent of the working capital recipients had used up their loans and had returned to informal credit sources.[11] (See Exhibits 9 and 10 for more information on the state of the program to date.)

Steve's Dilemma

Steve's contract with the DDF would soon expire and he was concerned that he would have to leave the country without leaving behind a fairly solid micro-enterprise program. He had strong encouragement from his home organization, ACCION, to continue his work supporting micro-enterprises, but even ACCION did not have any means of influencing the decisions of a private local foundation. Steve's main concern was to meet the needs of the urban poor, who were not receiving assistance from any other organizations and who stood to benefit from such a program. Since PRODEME was the only program lending to such small but vital enterprises, the program's failure would undo three years of hard development work and leave the business owners without recourse to other sources of credit. Therefore, Steve wanted to work quickly to save the program before he returned to the United States.

Notes

1. Informal sector businesses operate outside of the economic mainstream; they are not registered with the government, do not pay taxes, and are not subject to health and safety regulations.

2. Maria Otero and Robert Blayney, "An Evaluation of the Dominican Development Foundation's Program for the Development of Micro-Enterprises (PRODEME)," prepared for USAID Dominican Republic, Washington, November 1984.

3. Defined here as businesses with fewer than six employees and less than U.S.$10,000 in assets.

4. Despite their appeal to the USAID staff, those businesses are considered very risky business investments by banks because they are small and do not follow established business practices. Consequently, their credit options are very limited. Micro-enterprise owners typically obtain loan funds from moneylenders who charge interest rates of up to 20 percent per day on loans and who tend to lend on a very short-term basis—often limiting the loan period to several weeks. Naturally, the high cost and short-term nature of such credit limit its usefulness for business investment purposes, especially for small entrepreneurs with few resources.

5. As an ACCION representative, part of Steve's role in the country was to find appropriate conduits for ACCION programs in existing organizations. The DDF seemed to him a likely candidate.

6. Otero and Blayney, *op. cit.*

7. Jeffrey Ashe, *The PISCES II Experience: Local Efforts in Micro-Enterprise Development*, USAID, Washington, Vol. 1, 1985, p. 9.

8. Susan Sawyer and Catherine Overholt, "Dominican Republic: Program for Development of Microenterprises."

9. Otero and Blayney, *op. cit.*, p. v.

10. *Ibid*, p. ii.

11. Sawyer and Overholt, *op. cit.*

Exhibit 1
DOMINICAN REPUBLIC
(Republica Dominicana)

Currency
Peso = 100 centavos

Structure
the economy is still predominantly agricultural, with this sector accounting for 18% of GDP; however, a growing manufacturing sector already represents 16% of GDP, other industries 12%, and services 54%

Main industries
sugar milling, bauxite mining, nickel mining, gold mining, textiles

Main crops
sugar cane, coffee, cocoa, tobacco, rice, maize

Main exports (share of total)
sugar 45%, coffee 7%, cocoa 5%, ferronickel 9%, gold 11%, chemicals 5%

Main trading partners (share of total)
exports—U.S. 72%, U.S.S.R. 5%, Cuba 3%
imports—U.S. 44%, Venezuela 15%, Mexico 11%, Spain 5%

External debt (public)
in 1982 stood at U.S.$1,620 million; debt servicing in that year equalled 18.7% of the country's export earnings

Energy
the country's energy imports equal 24% of its total export earnings

Main mineral resources
nickel, bauxite, gold, silver

Main imports
foodstuffs, oil, raw materials, and capital goods for industry

Foreign investment
net inflow of direct private investment in 1980 was U.S.$13 million

External debt (private)
U.S.$287 million in mid-1984

Exhibit 1 (cont'd)

Key Economic Indicators

Economic Indicators	Unit	Period	1979	1980	1981	1982	1983
Population	million	mid-year	5.30	5.44	5.58	5.74	5.87
Exchange Rate	Pesos/U.S.$	end-year	1.00	1.00	1.00	1.00	1.00
International Reserves[a]	million U.S.$	end-year	238.6	208.14	225.2	129.0	171.3
Money Supply	million Pesos	end-year	643.3	579.6	660.5	731.5	781.4
Consumer Price Index	1980 = 100		85.7	100.0	107.5	115.8	—
Product (GDP)	million Pesos	year	5,496	6,649	7,227	7,877	—
Exports (FOB)	million U.S.$	year	866.1	972.4	1,188.0	767.7	781.7
Sugar	million U.S.$	year	200.9	309.5	533.9	287.6	276.4
Ferronickel	million U.S.$	year	123.4	101.9	110.6	24.2	80.3
Coffee	million U.S.$	year	157.7	76.8	76.8	95.6	76.4
Cocoa	million U.S.$	year	78.5	51.1	55.8	59.0	60.9
Imports (FOB)	million U.S.$	year	1,057.8	1,425.7	1,450.2	1,255.8	1,271.2
Production							
Sugar	'000 tons	year	1,300	1,090	1,285	1,219	1,160
Cocoa	'000 tons	year	27	39	40	(est) 40	(est) 39
Coffee	'000 tons	year	61	67	51	66	48
Bauxite	'000 tons	year	540	510	405	—	—

Source: From *South Magazine.*
[a] Minus gold.

Exhibit 2
DOMINICAN DEVELOPMENT FOUNDATION
PARTIAL ORGANIZATIONAL CHART, 1983

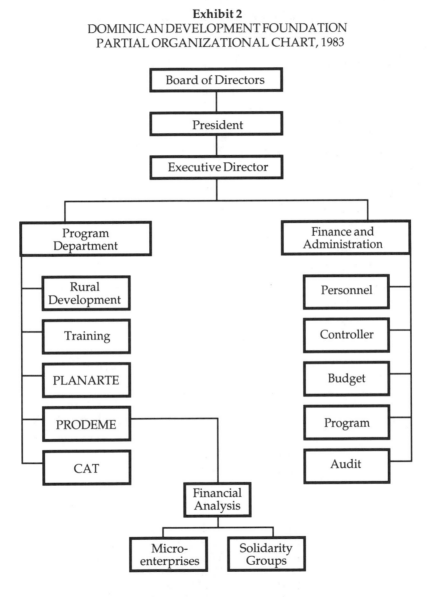

Source: Maria Otero and Robert Blayney, "An Evaluation of the Dominican Development Foundation's Program for the Development of Micro-Enterprises (PRODEME)," prepared for USAID Dominican Republic, Washington, November 1984.

Exhibit 3
A SURVEY OF BUSINESS OWNERS IN THE INFORMAL SECTOR

The following information was extracted from a feasibility study conducted by Steve Gross in 1980. The data refer to a survey of informal sector business owners in Santo Domingo and in six surrounding cities.

Problems in Establishing a Business

None	61.9%
Lack of capital	21.8%
Lack of clientele	8.5%
Lack of a place of business	5.9%
Lack of knowledge	1.9%

Principal Problems at the Time of Survey

Lack of money	33.3%
None	31.4%
Lack of clients/market	14.1%
Lack of equipment/machines	10.1%
General economic situation; high cost of materials	6.6%
Lack of adequate business place	2.9%
Lack of electricity	1.3%
Lack of transportation	0.3%

Source: Steve Gross, "Estudio de Factibilidad Programa de Micro-Empresas," Dominican Development Foundation, 1980.

Exhibit 4
UNEMPLOYMENT LEVELS FOR THE
ECONOMICALLY ACTIVE URBAN POPULATION
(based on the 1970 Population Census)

	Men		Women	
Age Groups	Unemployed	Rates	Unemployed	Rates
Total	75,264	22.7	40,047	26.7
10–14	5,029	34.8	3,289	31.9
15–19	12,281	34.7	7,590	30.7
20–24	11,993	23.8	7,190	26.3
25–29	9,146	20.7	4,723	23.0
30–34	7,248	17.6	3,628	21.9
35–39	6,476	17.2	3,243	21.4
40–44	6,248	19.9	2,505	21.8
45–49	3,945	17.8	1,861	22.6
50–54	4,085	22.2	1,784	28.3
55–59	2,434	18.6	1,127	8.1
60–64	2,308	18.5	1,296	8.9
65–69	1,531	20.5	603	6.9
70–74	1,235	20.2	409	6.4
75+	1,304	19.0	718	6.9

Source: N. Ramirez, A. Tatis, and D. German, *Población y Mano de Obra en la Republica Dominicana*, Instituto de Estudios de Población y Desarrollo, January 1983.

Exhibit 5

A TYPOLOGY OF INFORMAL SECTOR ACTIVITIES IN SANTO DOMINGO

Activity	Gender	Level of Investment and Earnings
Retail of charcoal; neighborhood markets; fixed location for storage; occasional delivery	female dominated	very low to low
Bottle and cardboard retail on foot	male dominated	very low to low
Bottle and cardboard retail on tricycle	male dominated	low, but profitable in quantity
Coffee stand; neighborhood route to work; semifixed location	female dominated	low, may expand to sale of food
Fritura—stands selling hot, prepared foods; semifixed location	female dominated	low, but slightly expandable
Stand selling ices or fruit; semifixed location	male dominated	low to medium
Tricicleros—selling fresh fruit, vegetables; nonfixed	male dominated	low to medium
Street-corner stands selling chewing gum, candy, cigarettes; semifixed location	female dominated	medium
Ventorillo—streetside window selling candy, cigarettes; fixed location	female dominated	medium
Fantasia—bigger, streetfront store selling beauty items, toys, clothing, etc.; fixed location	female dominated	medium to high
Buhoneros—enclosed stands on side of street selling sundries, semiprocessed foods, etc.	mixed	medium to high
Neighborhood foodstands selling fruits, vegetables, chicken, etc.	mixed	medium to high
Neighborhood home beauty parlors, fixed location	female dominated	medium to high
Tricicleros—selling ice cream or packaged ices, nonfixed packaged ices, nonfixed location	male dominated	high
Neighborhood butcher shops, fixed location	male dominated	high
Neighborhood seamstresses, fixed location	male dominated	high

Source: Susan M. Sawyer, Report prepared for ACCION International, Santo Domingo, February–March 1983 (unpublished).

Exhibit 6
PRODEME COMPONENTS

Solidarity Groups	Micro-enterprise

Promotion

Word of mouth—informal conversation among friends, relatives and workmates. Meetings to explain how programs are set up and run by beneficiaries.	Word of mouth—informal conversation between project participants and micro-business owners. Response to announcements in newspapers.

Selection

Consensual selection of group members who will share responsibility for loan payment.	Suitability of client is determined by the project staff through an economic analysis of the business. Loans are further guaranteed by property, inventory, or cosigner.

Mechanism

Clients form their own credit program of from five to eight business owners. Group process is reinforced by regular meetings of the solidarity groups, in barrio-level meetings or through the Association.	One-on-one assistance to individual clients.

Assuring Loan Payback

Group structure ensures that those who do not repay will be pressured by other group members. If this fails, program coordinators can, as a last resort, repossess property purchased through the loan.	Coordinators are advised of late payments and visits are made to the business. If this is not sufficient, legal procedures are carried out.

Management Assistance

Exchange of ideas about improving business practices occurs informally through conversations with group members and more formally in meetings with the Association.	Program personnel teach clients how to improve their businesses in one-on-one sessions or in formal courses.

Exhibit 6 (cont'd)

Solidarity Groups	Micro-enterprise

Beneficiaries' Role in the Program

Clients can assume increasingly important roles in meeting program goals:

- membership
- informing others about the program
- taking an active role in the solidarity group
- becoming a solidarity group president
- participating more actively in the Association
- assuming Association leadership.

Aside from the clients' activity in program promotion and the courses, their role is limited.

Most Appropriate Client Population

Very smallest businesses.
May be appropriate for larger businesses, but this needs to be explored.

Larger shops of two employees or more.
Probably not suited for the smallest businesses as cost per beneficiary is higher and the supportive structure of the group is absent.

Comparison of solidarity groups

Tricicleros	Working Capital Loan Recipients

Is working as a vendor principally of fruits and vegetables or as a collector of bottles, cardboard or metal.

Is working as a sidewalk vendor, a market stand holder or a cottage artisan, most likely a seamstress.

Is male head of household (there are no female tricicleros): 88% are heads of households averaging five six members.

Is a female head of household: three-fourths of the working capital loans are to women business owners. Of these, 58% are heads of household and 15% are wives; the rest are other adults living in the house hold. Of the men, 75% are heads of households. Households average between six and seven members.

Exhibit 6 (cont'd)

Tricicleros	Working Capital Loan Recipients
Average age 30: virtually none are over 50; pedaling a heavily laden *triciclo* through the streets of Santo Domingo is work for the young.	*Average age 38*: three-quarters are between 21 and 50.
Is poorly educated: average 4 years.	*Is poorly educated*: average 4 years.
Is an immigrant to Santo Domingo: only 4% were born in Santo Domingo.	*Is an immigrant to Santo Domingo*: only 5% were born in Santo Domingo.
Is a long-term urban resident: average 9.6 years. Only 18% have been in Santo Domingo 3 years or less.	*Is a long-term urban resident*: average 14 years. Only 2% have been in Santo Domingo 3 years or less.
Has lived in the barrio for several years: average 5.5 years.	*Has lived in the barrio for several years*: average 6.5 years.
Works long hours and is experienced: workweek averages 48 hours, 6 eight-hour days. They have been *tricicleros* for an average of 5.3 years.	*Works long hours and is experienced*: workweek averages 47 hours over 6 days; worked at their current occupation for 8.7 years.
Percentage of Family Income Derived from Business: 87 percent of *tricicleros*; business is 75 to 100 percent of family income; for the remaining *triciclos* owners, their business was at least 25 percent of family income.	*Percentage of Family Income Derived from Business*: 42 percent of working capital recipients' business is 75 to 100 percent to family income; 25 percent of the recipients reported that their business was less than 25 percent family income.

Source: Jeffrey Ashe, *Assisting the Survival Economy: The Micro-Enterprise and Solidarity Groups Projects of the Dominican Development Foundation*, Vol. 1, ACCION International/AITEC, Cambridge, Mass., 1984.

Exhibit 7

CHANGES IN DDF LOAN REVIEW PROCESS

Staff	Responsibilities	Procedural Revisions in Place
Program Department		
1. Coordinator	A. Make first contact with client.	A. No. of visits decreased from average of 16 prior to loan disbursement to 4–5
	B. Complete loan application form with beneficiary.	B. Form reduced from 13 to 9 pages (microenterprises) and 10 to 4 pages (solidarity groups).
	C. Complete financial analysis of microenterprise.	C. Break-even point, depreciation, and others dropped as requirements to loan application; considered of little use for assessing microenterprises.
2. Program Manager	A. Reviews application.	A. Remains unchanged.
	B. Approves/Disapproves.	
3. Financial Analyst	A. Reviews application for loan.	A. Closer coordination with field staff to lower loan rejection at this stage of review.
	B. Approves/Disapproves.	
4. Program Director	A. Reviews application.	A. Remains unchanged.
	B. Approves/Disapproves.	
5. Loan Committee	A. Review applications.	A. Composition changed from high involvement by Board members (three persons) to committees made up of top level staff. Loans grouped by size and distributed to three loan committees. More frequent loan committee meetings.
	B. Approves/Disapproves.	

Exhibit 7 (cont'd)

Staff	Responsibilities	Procedural Revisions in Place
Finance Department		
6. Controller's office	A. Reviews approved loan.	A–C. Remain unchanged.
	B. Processes contract.	
	C. Conducts spot audit of the microenterprise.	
	D. Issues purchase orders and check. to client.	D. More checks issued directly to clients, but purchase order system still predominant.
Program Department		
7. Coordinator	A. Delivers check to client.	

Source: Maria Otero and Robert Blayney, "An Evaluation of the Dominican Development Foundation's Program for the Development of Micro-Enterprises (PRODEME)," prepared for USAID Dominican Republic, Washington, November 1984.

Exhibit 8
DOMINICAN DEVELOPMENT FOUNDATION
PRODEME BALANCE SHEET

	FY 1981	*FY 1982*	*FY 1983*
Assets			
Cash	14,967.78	231,602.19	220,267.97
Loans (net)	5,989.68	262,786.10	349,426.26
Approved Loans to Award	—	5,944.00	75,054.70
Accounts Receivable	—	999.67	2,726.22
Equipment	—	—	3,654.44
Allocated Funds	—	—	79.50
Fixed Assets (net)	—	17,947.33	18,685.61
Promisory Notes	—	—	3,806.83
Totals	20,957.46	519,279.29	673,701.53
Liabilities			
Accounts Payable	100.85	4,197.12	10,452.61
Deferred Income	—	40,713.88	36,597.56
Retained Earnings	—	2,330.64	13,939.24
Totals	100.85	47,241.64	60,989.41
Net Worth			
Accumulated Income	—	25,056.61	507,037.65
Results of Period	20,856.61	446,981.04	105,574.47
Totals	20,856.61	472,037.65	612,612.12
Totals, Liabilities and Net Worth	20,957.46	519,279.29	673,601.53

Source: Maria Otero and Robert Blayney, "An Evaluation of the Dominican Development Foundation's Program for the Development of Micro-Enterprises (PRODEME)," prepared for USAID Dominican Republic, Washington, November 1984.

Exhibit 9
DOMINICAN DEVELOPMENT FOUNDATION
PRODEME INCOME STATEMENT

	FY 1981	FY 1982	FY 1983
Income			
Interest Income	39.68	21,337.32	59,721.33
Donations for Operations	22,904.00	481,013.64	162,689.00
Other Income	—	551.20	1,487.33
Totals	22,943.68	502,902.16	223,897.66
Expenses			
Services Purchased	—	3,399.19	623.73
Maintenance and Repair	—	277.34	556.01
Travel and per Diem	230.15	8,857.64	17,398.67
Publicity and Promotion	—	158.90	316.70
Fixed Costs	—	1,916.46	4,540.36
Other Costs	—	1,522.21	22,268.53
Personnel Services	14.10	33,213.02	59,299.10
Fringe Benefits	1,833.00	5,733.53	13,054.51
Miscellaneous	9.50	842.83	265.58
Totals	2,086.75	55,921.12	118,323.19
Results of the Period	20,856.93	446,981.04	105,574.47

Source: Maria Otero and Robert Blayney, "An Evaluation of the Dominican Development Foundation's Program for the Development of Micro-Enterprises (PRODEME)," prepared for USAID Dominican Republic, Washington, November 1984.

Exhibit 10

PRODEME'S ACCOMPLISHMENTS

Date	Micro-enterprises			(Annual Summary)		No. of Loans	Solidarity Groups			
	No. of Loans	Loan Amt.	Average Loan Amt.	No. of Loans	Loan Amt.		No. of Clients	Total Amt.	Average Amt.	Average per Member
July–Dec. 1981	49	$91,788	$1,873	63	$119,146	64	418	$100,160	$1,565	$240
Jan.–June 1982	14	27,358	1,954	—	—	40	236	56,341	1,409	239
July–Dec. 1982	38	74,877	1,970	92	175,256	54	324	72,486	1,342	224
Jan.–June 1983	54	100,379	1,859	—	—	99	546	130,117	1,314	238
July–Dec. 1983	56	88,959	1,589	92	145,920	86	474	106,455	1,238	225
Jan.–June 1984	36	56,961	1,582	—	—	30	169	46,365	1,546	274
Totals	247	$440,322	$1,783	247	440,322	373	2,167	511,924	1,372	236
Targets	250	500,000	2,000	Combined Actual: 952,246 Target: 1,058,000		310	1,860	558,000	1,800	—

Employment Generation Summaries

	Micro-enterprises			Solidarity Groups	
	Target	Actual		Target	Actual
New Jobs	500	370	Jobs Strengthened	1,860	2,240
Indirect Beneficiaries	1,500	1,480	Indirect Beneficiaries	11,160	13,400

Source: Maria Otero and Robert Blayney, "An Evaluation of the Dominican Development Foundation's Program for the Development of Micro-Enterprises (PRODEME)," prepared for USAID Dominican Republic, Washington, November 1984.

Exhibit 11
PARTICIPANT'S EVALUATION OF PRODEME

Both the loan recipients and a control group were asked to evaluate the microenterprise component of PRODEME: What did they most like? What aspect of the program caused them the most problems? What would they like changed?

What did they like best about the program?
- (40%)   The loan
- (30%)   The courses
  "You learn to control your business," "Management assistance is what guarantees that a business will progress."
- (25%)   "The loan terms are comfortable"
  The loan terms "permit a person to pay according to his ability without so many requirements." "The program is better than the moneylenders."

What do they like least about the program?
- (46%)   The purchase order
- (21%)   The terms of the loan
- (15%)   Liked everything about the program
- (14%)   The slowness of receiving the loan.
  "With the purchase order, they won't let you buy where you know you can get your supplies at a lower price. And you have to buy everything at once. So, if sales aren't good you don't have anything left to try something else and your business can go under."
  "Taking so long to get money affects my ability to get a good price."
  "The purchase order shows the program doesn't have confidence in the micro-entrepreneurs."

What changes are desired by the participants?
- (38%)   Abolish the purchase order system
  "You should eliminate the purchase orders and have faith in loan guarantees. If you don't trust in the guarantees, why do you ask for them?"
- (21%)   The loan terms
  "The loan quotas should be smaller and the loans should be given for a longer period of time."
- (14%)   PRODEME takes too long to get loans into the hands of beneficiaries.

Source: Jeffrey Ashe, *Assisting the Survival Economy: The Micro-Enterprise and Solidarity Group Projects of the Dominican Development Foundation,* Vol. 1, ACCION International/AITEC, Cambridge, Mass., 1984.

Exhibit 12
EXCERPTS FROM A MEMO TO THE EXECUTIVE DIRECTOR
OF THE DOMINICAN DEVELOPMENT FOUNDATION
(translated from Spanish)

TO: Bolivar Baez Ortiz
         Executive Director, DDF
FROM: Stephen H. Gross
         Associate Director, ACCION International/AITEC
RE: Micro-enterprise Program Report

Two months have passed in the third and last year of the AID donation that covers the operational costs of the program. In other words, the program has ten months to reach self-sufficiency; that is, at the end of three years the income (interest) of the Program should cover the operational costs and the "overhead."

To arrive at this equilibrium point, in my opinion, two things are necessary: (1) increase the number of loans, and (2) remove the subsidies on the interest rate that is being charged and recover the real cost of money and services loaned.

If, for example, the operational expenses of the program are U.S.$100,000 per year and if we assume that the Solidarity Group loans will cover 60 percent of the program's costs (because we are currently charging them a higher interest rate to cover the added risk they represent) and individual micro-enterprise loans cover 40 percent of the program's expenses, then:

X = the amount the program must loan to cover expenses
Loans to Solidarity Groups
    $0.24X = \$60,000$ (60% of the program's expenses)
    $X = \$250,000$ (amount program would have to lend)
Loans to Micro-enterprises
    $0.12X = \$40,000$ (40% of the program's expenses)
    $X = \$333,333$ (amount program would have to lend)

PRODEME currently has six micro-enterprise advisors and five solidarity group advisors. Therefore, to arrive at the equilibrium point, each micro-enterprise advisor would have to maintain a portfolio of U.S.$55,555—in other words, only 22.2 active loans of U.S.$2,500 each. For solidarity groups, the advisors would have to maintain a portfolio of U.S.$50,000—or only twenty-five active loans of U.S.$2,000 each.

Conclusions
Without a doubt PRODEME has had a great impact, not only on the program participants, but, through other organizations, at the international level as well. At the national level, the Foundation, through the pioneer PRODEME program, has initiated that which can be classified as an entire support movement toward the informal sector of the economy much the same as it has done in the rural areas of the country.

Case 17

Save the Children: Sustainability and the Community-Based Lending Model

This case was written by Elizabeth Campbell. It is intended as a basis for class discussion rather than as an illustration of either effective or ineffective handling of an administrative situation. Some of the names have been changed. The permission from Ms. Campbell and the Save the Children Federation to include the case in this book is gratefully acknowledged.

As the plane descended through the clouds, Jane shuffled her papers into a folder and thought about the assignment she was taking on in Honduras. Several weeks ago Save the Children's Latin American regional office had received a request from the field that Jane come to Honduras on a technical assistance visit in support of their community credit program.

Six months earlier the Field Office had abruptly decentralized the credit program management from the Field Office in Tegucigalpa to "impact areas." The program was operating in three impact areas, which is the term Save the Children uses to define discrete geographic areas made up of ten to fifteen communities. Under the new credit system, field staff and community committees controlled all funds and administrative processes. There were reports that the credit program was functioning well in the La Esperanza impact area, while it was not performing as well as it could in the other two areas.

The acting Field Office Director was concerned about how the credit program decentralization process was being managed and wanted Jane to evaluate the feasibility of this change as well as to review the credit program as a whole. Just how Save the Children's Community-Based Lending Model was functioning in La Esperanza would be the focus of her attention over the next two weeks.

As the plane landed, Jane was contemplating the challenge of this assignment and how best to support the credit program decentralization process so that the communities can responsibly manage their own funds. With a jolt she was in Tegucigalpa and her mind turned to customs formalities and preparing to meet the Field Office staff.

The Scope of Work

That evening, Jane had dinner with the Deputy Director, Carmen, who was leaving the next day for a vacation. Over dinner, they discussed Jane's scope of work for the technical visit.

My objective for your time here is to establish clear, uniform policies and procedures for the credit programs so we can help the field staff monitor the program and guard the loan fund from de-capitalization. We've been doing credit for two years here and now we want to put it closer to the model of community management that we originally envisioned. We send the money out to the impact areas, but I'm not sure how it's being used. You'll have a week in La Esperanza to visit borrowers and talk with community credit committees and then we're bringing the whole staff—from all three impact areas—to Tegucigalpa for a credit workshop. I'll be busy with other things while you're here, so it's all up to you.

Save the Children's Community-Based Lending Model

Save the Children was founded in 1932 as a private, nonprofit, nonsectarian organization to assist impoverished people in Appalachia. Save the Children now conducts self-help community development programs in forty three countries including the United States. With this fifty years of experience, Save the Children has developed and promoted a community-based integrated rural development strategy (CBIRD). This integrated strategy promotes community development through projects in the health, food production, water, housing, and small enterprise development sectors. Save the Children uses a methodology of active community participation and organizing to develop strategies for defining and addressing development problems. The agency believes that small enterprise and credit programs are an important component of this integrated approach, helping create the resource base needed to guide the community development process toward self-reliance and sustainability.

To support the implementation of credit programs, Save the Children articulated the "Community-Based Lending Model" based on the agency's field experience. Three principles represent the core of the model:

1. Low income borrowers can be *a good credit risk* if the funded activity is viable and profitable and an effective community loan guarantee system to secure loans is in place.

2. *A well-designed credit program* can raise borrower income levels, improve the quality of life for borrower's families, and contribute to the development of the economic resource base of a poor community.

3. Credit programs are co-managed with *community credit com-mittees* to select responsible borrowers and create the sense of so-cial responsibility necessary to ensure loan repayment. These community credit committees will ultimately become fully re-sponsible for the loan fund, having both managerial and finan-cial control over the credit program.

The Honduras Credit Program

Objectives

Since 1985, the Honduras Field Office has been managing a credit pro-gram with a variety of objectives. First, the Save the Children field staff uses the credit program as a mechanism to support educational and con-sciousness raising efforts. The staff believes that participation in a com-munity credit scheme will promote the responsibility, honesty, and dis-cipline needed to help beneficiaries develop a basis for self-help. In addi-tion, the educational objectives of the program include skills transfer to increase technical and administrative capabilities.

The Honduras credit program also reflects major economic develop-ment objectives including increasing agricultural production, raising in-comes, and improving the overall quality of life of beneficiaries' families. The capitalization of borrower enterprises, as they save or invest in-creased earnings, is also an important economic objective. Finally, the Save the Children field staff in Honduras wishes to promote the creation and consolidation of community institutions that are permanent, sus-tainable, and profitable. They believe that they can accomplish this through the gradual transfer of program management and ownership to the community committees organized and trained for that purpose.

Policies

The credit program beneficiaries are primarily small farmers who grow potatoes, corn, beans, fruits, and vegetables. Loans are given to groups and to individuals, although the majority are given to groups. Solidarity group loans are granted to Agricultural Committees with six to fifteen members. Loans have also gone to a number of small industries. None of the borrowers in this program have access to commercial credit due to their lack of collateral and limited knowledge of banking procedures.

The program now has eighty-four outstanding loans. Only twenty-six of these loans were granted under the new decentralized system. The remaining fifty-eight loans were disbursed when control of the credit program was based in the central Tegucigalpa Field Office. The interest rate is 15 percent, although a number of groups have requested that it be lowered to 11 percent (the government rate for basic grains lending). The average group loan size is U.S.$1,723. The loan size and term are determined according to the nature of the activity and the size of the Agricultural Committee or solidarity group. The loan fund is maintained in a commercial bank savings account in the name of each impact area's community Regional Credit Committees. The Save the Children accountant holds the passbook.

Administration

The credit program has four levels of control: the Agricultural Committees, the Local Credit Commissions, the Regional Credit Committee, and the supervision and support of the Save the Children field staff. In the lending process, these groups have varying responsibilities.

Agricultural Committees. These are the borrower groups that form for the purpose of applying for a loan. The majority of these loans are secured through a solidarity guarantee whereby one member of the group provides a plot of land, a pair of oxen, or other item as collateral for the group's loan. Some of the members do not have any form of collateral, requiring the trust of their group members in order that they may be party to the loan. In this way a social control mechanism is put into action that should support high repayment rates.

Local Credit Commissions. These local groups are formed in each village to review the applications and approve them to be passed on the Regional Credit Committee. They are also charged with verifying the guarantees and receiving the loan repayments. The Local Commissions take the first action should a problem arise and if it is not resolved, report it to the Regional Credit Committee.

Regional Credit Committee. This Regional Committee is composed of five members elected from among the Local Credit Commissions to form a Board of Directors for the impact area. They receive the applications from Local Credit Commissions for the final review. If they approve the loan, the process continues on to the disbursement stage. The Regional Credit Committee has the credit program bank account under its name and its President must sign the withdrawal forms. It is customary that they meet every fifteen days in the Save the Children impact area office where the files are kept.

Save the Children Field Staff. They have a very important role in all stages of the lending process. They do not have a vote on the Regional Credit Committee.

Credit Program Portfolio

There are no certain figures on the actual financial situation of the loan fund. According to one informal source, delinquency in repayments may be as high as 38 percent. These figures refer primarily to the loans granted under the previous system which located the majority of the control in the Tegucigalpa office. Although this situation has not been studied in depth, it is likely that the high delinquency rates can be attributed to technical problems (droughts, insect plagues, and so forth) and the lack of clear administrative controls.

Field Visit Highlights

En Route to La Esperanza

The next morning, Amilcar, the Impact Area Coordinator, arrived to take Jane to La Esperanza. He put her bag in the back of the jeep and headed out from Tegucigalpa. They discussed the credit program at length as they drove. The roads turned from pavement to flat dirt and finally to steep and muddy trails as they left the central valley for the isolated mountain communities to the east. Amilcar commented:

> We really feel that the primary responsibility of the field staff is to educate the people so they can make their own decisions. I see all of our programs as a small but important step toward promoting social change and empowering the people.
>
> This credit program is very important because it gives people opportunities to grow more food, but we're also trying to instill a sense of responsibility and discipline along with technical skills. We see the credit program as supporting the community organization process and giving the community committees a resource base. With access to credit the people can control more of the production process.

Jane recognized this would be a tremendous opportunity to see just how the community-based lending notion functions on the ground. She asked, "What is the community's role in the credit program now?"

> Well, those who serve on the Local Credit Commissions of each community and the Regional Credit Committee take their responsibility very seriously. The Local Commissions receive applications from Agricultural Committees or other borrower groups, review them, and send them to the Regional Committee for a final decision. They're doing it all. We don't even have a vote on the loan applications. The decision to decentralize the program out of the Field Office in Tegucigalpa to the impact areas and the communities themselves has really brought us closer to our goal of developing community management capability. You'll see. Fortunately the La Esperanza Regional Credit Committee has a meeting scheduled this week to review loan applications.

They arrived, six hours later, in La Esperanza. Amilcar left Jane at a small *pension* and agreed to meet her the next morning to introduce her to the staff and begin their visits. As he drove off down the narrow dusty street, laughing children and squealing animals jumped out of his way.

The Accountant

The next morning, Jane worked first with the accountant, Herman, to gather basic information on the status of the loan fund and learn about the systems they had in place.

"How many loans do you have outstanding?" she asked.

"About eighty-four," he replied, pulling open a file drawer full of folders. "Just recently the Field Office finance officer came out from Tegucigalpa to help us figure that out," he added.

Herman showed her a large spreadsheet which listed loans approved, the amounts, date disbursed, and the funded activity. Almost all were farmer group loans for basic grains and potatoes. Some were for fruit trees and there were two small enterprises, carpentry and weaving.

Jane studied the sheet and then looked at a few of the loan folders, "What is the program's repayment rate?"

Herman shuffled through the papers, explaining that the system had not functioned well from Tegucigalpa and that many of the loans made before the funds were put in the hands of the communities were not being repaid.

"We're not holding the community credit committees responsible for those outstanding loans," Herman added. "The loans made since the communities were given more responsibility are just coming due. With these new loans, we will be able to track the new repayment rates. We expect a much better performance."

A Repayment

Just as he was speaking, a man tapped softly at the door and asked if he could come in. Manuel Rivas, a Honduran peasant, removed his hat as he entered the room.

"I have a matter to discuss with the accountant; it's about my loan repayment." said Manuel. "I have most of the money here with me. I've just come from the market and prices were not good today. I will finish the harvest next week and will pay the rest at my Local Credit Committee meeting."

Accepting the payment, Herman thanked Manuel, who quickly ran off to catch a ride with a government health worker who was heading toward his village for an immunization campaign. Jane and Herman finished their review just as Jose, the agronomist, arrived to take Jane to visit some of the borrowers. Herman headed off to the bank to deposit Manuel's payment. Jane helped Jose load some bags of fertilizer into the jeep and they started off.

The Agronomist

"I need to take these bags of fertilizer to San Jeronimo. It's on our way to Azahualpa where the Azahualpa Local Credit Commission will be meeting at ten o'clock," said Jose as he checked the list of the inputs he had agreed to bring up to San Jeronimo. "We'd better get moving; the roads are pretty bad this time of the year."

Leaving the little town of La Esperanza behind, they set off in the jeep to visit some of the communities where Save the Children is working. As they climbed slowly through the mountainous terrain, Jose pointed out the various fields where the credit program has helped the people to buy the inputs required to raise the yields of their crops.

> The important thing here is that they get the inputs on time. We've really committed ourselves to increasing food production, and the credit program is the key. It gives the farmers the money up-front so they can get the fertilizer they need. We don't actually disburse cash for the fertilizer. We buy it in bulk and distribute it to the farmers according to the value of the loan. It is difficult to get the applications together though and it takes me a long time to do all the technical calculations to get the right size loan for each plot.

As they arrived in San Jeronimo, a group of ten farmers was waiting. They thanked Jose for the fertilizer and told Jane how much the credit program had helped them. As one of the group expressed it: "Before we had these loans, we had to go looking for work in the *haciendas* with our *sombreros* in our hands. Now we wear our *sombreros* on our heads and work on our own plots."

Jose recorded the fertilizer transaction in his notebook and they bid *adios*. Jane and Jose had to hurry to reach the Azahualpa Local Credit Committee in time for its weekly meeting.

The Local Credit Committee Meeting at Azahualpa

At the base of a steep hill, Jose parked the jeep and pointed to a trail. "The community house where the meeting is being held is at the top of the bluff."

When they reached the top, they found the meeting room empty; no one had yet arrived. Jane sat on the step while Jose pointed out other communities in the distance and talked about the area. Save the Children was working in twenty-four communities in La Esperanza province.

Finally, some Committee members began to trickle in. Although the president, Juan, had not arrived and only half the members were present, Jose decided to begin the meeting. He knew he could speak to the others in the fields later where they were probably working hard to get the harvest in.

"This meeting is to discuss how the next group of loan applications should be filled out," he began. He continued on to explain how the form must be completed. Most of those present asked his help in filling it out. He asked them to turn the completed forms in to the Local Credit Commission secretary to be reviewed, before being sent on to the Regional Credit Committee with Juan the president.

At this point, several people objected: "Juan's children have been sick and he is very busy with his harvest. He will not have time and we must get these applications in."

Two farmers asked if they could get new loans for their groups to cover the losses that some of their members have suffered with this crop. One had put up the guarantee for his group and was concerned that he not risk losing his two cows.

"We can make an arrangement with the delinquent borrowers that won't affect your guarantee," responded Jose.

Jose agreed to take the loan applications and to speak with Herman and Amilcar to see how they could refinance the concerned group's loan. The two farmers looked relieved at his decision and moved to leave the meeting.

Knowing that Jane wanted to meet more people, Jose suggested that they visit a field where he knew there would be many people harvesting potatoes.

The Farmers of San Juan de Dios

After driving across several ridges and into another valley, Jose and Jane arrived at the communal plot at San Juan de Dios. Twenty farmers worked busily on the sloping plot, digging up potatoes and bagging them to be weighed. They arrived together with several women and children bringing the midday meal in pails. The farmers sat at the edge of the field to eat their beans and rice, which they invited Jose and Jane to share. A friendly conversation ensued.

"What have been the major successes of the credit program for the farmer groups?" Jane asked.

"We have been able to produce more food for our families and have received training to grow healthier crops," answered one man.

"The best thing is to have access to credit, which we never had in the commercial bank before," responded another.

A number of them commented that the Committee had helped them to organize other activities for the community.

"What are the biggest problems that you have had?"

"Well, we really don't have any insurance system in case our crops fail: prices are unpredictable; we have trouble planning the planting and input schedules; most people don't understand the procedures for loans, and often attendance is poor at meetings."

"In the years when there are frosts or droughts, we are really in trouble and even in good times some people don't understand why they must pay back their loans," added another.

Jane scribbled in her pad, trying to sort credit issues from agriculture issues, "Where does this system need to be improved?" she wondered.

While Jane spoke with the group, Jose reviewed with the community's agriculture volunteer the soil improvement treatment that they were planning to do after the harvest. The volunteer network had made attending to the many communities more feasible. Jane and Jose finished their tour of the area and started back for La Esperanza. It had been a long day and tomorrow was the Regional Credit Committee meeting that would provide still more insight into the program.

The Regional Credit Committee Meeting

Early the following morning, the Regional Credit Committee members began arriving at the Save the Children office in La Esperanza for the meeting. Jane, Amilcar, Jose, and Herman sat at the back of the room to observe the proceedings.

The president opened the meeting and asked the secretary to read the minutes of the last meeting. They were approved by the other members of the Regional Credit Committee, the vice-president, the treasurer, and the three representatives of local Credit Commissions. All had been elected from the Local Credit Commissions membership the previous year.

After the old business was reviewed and the guests were presented, new business was brought up. Several Agricultural Committee basic grains loan applications were presented. Jose added another three including those which he had brought from the Azahualpa Local Credit Commission. All were pretty routine and generated little discussion.

"Are the necessary forms in order?" asked the vice-president.

The secretary paged through the documents, "Yes, the application, the technical diagnostic of the fertilizer mix needed and the amount of seed to buy, and the group's guarantee papers. It all appears to be in order." The loans were approved.

The second set of loan applications were from two women's groups that wanted to establish poultry businesses. Questions were raised about where they were going to get the chickens and where they planned to sell them. Both groups had already ordered their chicks and were looking forward to the Christmas season to provide a good market. The treasurer said they only had enough funds to approve one of the projects. After some discussion, Dona Juta's loan was approved.

As there was little other business at hand, the meeting was ended and Dona Mercedes arrived with large trays of *yucca*, chicken, rice, bread, and Coca Cola for lunch.

Case 18

Senegal Community and Enterprise Development Project (A): Defending Viability

This case was written by S. Lael Brainard. It is intended as the basis for class discussion rather than as an illustration of either effective or ineffective handling of an administrative situation. Some of the names have been changed. The cooperation and support of the many individuals who served as resource people for the development of this case are gratefully acknowledged, particularly the personnel of the CEDP.

John threw down his pen and stood up to resume his pacing. He was to submit the strategy document for approval in one week, and he expected considerable controversy on several of its central features. In particular, he would have to strengthen the argument for establishing financial viability as the primary goal of the Project. He also would have to convince several of the organizations involved that this approach was consistent with the emphasis of the original Project paper on strengthening the agricultural sector through support to small-scale entrepreneurs.

John McKenzie had recently been appointed Small Business Advisor of the Community and Enterprise Development Project (CEDP) in the Sine-Saloum region of Senegal. He was charged with developing a program of support for small-scale entrepreneurs, and was in the midst of formulating a strategy for the SSE Program. John had just returned from consultations at Management Systems International (MSI), his home office, where work was completed on a strategy paper. This finalized strategy document would be reviewed by several organizations including USAID, the main funding agency; New TransCentury Foundation (NTF) and MSI, the contracting and subcontracting agencies respectively; the National Project Committee (NPC), consisting of representatives from nine ministries of the Senegalese government; and the Management Unit of the CEDP. (See Exhibit 1.)

There were few specific guidelines for designing the program, other than the original Project paper. John found the paper difficult to work with; it had been written a full two years earlier (in 1983), and was overly theoretical, providing little guidance for implementation.

In addition, the Project paper set forth multiple, not necessarily consistent objectives. The Project paper provided for two programs within the CEDP: an agricultural assistance program targeting village organizations (VOs) through private voluntary organizations (PVOs), and the SSE Program. The goal of the CEDP overall was to promote the development of the agricultural sector in accordance with the recent structural adjustment policies of the Government of Senegal. These policies included the privatization of activities formerly undertaken by parastatals, including the supply of agricultural inputs and the processing, marketing, and distribution of output. The SSE Program was to assist in this process through support to small-scale entrepreneurs engaged in these activities.

Another objective stated in the Project paper was to offer training, advisory services, and loans to small-scale entrepreneurs who would not otherwise have access to the formal credit market, in order to enhance their management effectiveness and their access to bank credit. And lastly, the program was to be institutionalized at the end of the five-year grant period, which John took to mean that the loan fund cover its costs.

John's first concern upon arriving in Kaolack two months earlier had been to get to know his future clientele. To this end, he and Dr. Malcolm Harper—a former professor of his and consultant to the Project through much of the strategy formulation phase—designed and conducted a four-week survey. With the help of ten researchers, they surveyed 310 small enterprises and 86 market vendors in the one large city, Kaolack, and four large towns in the region, and in 36 smaller towns and villages. The results of the survey, along with extensive visits to potential clients, gave John a good indication of who his clients would be, where they were located, and what their needs were. They also confirmed John and Malcolm's prior belief that the main constraint encountered by SSEs was access to credit, and that they had less interest in or need for formal training programs in literacy and numeracy.

John's view of the role of credit in small enterprise support had developed over the course of nine years working with small enterprises in developing countries, first as the manager of a match factory in Sierra Leone, later as the proprietor of a yachting business in the West Indies, then as the director of a distributorship for appropriate technology equipment, and most recently in directing an income-generating project in Beirut. His view took on theoretical foundations in studying and later working with Malcolm at the Cranfield School of Management in the United Kingdom. John and Malcolm's views on credit were fully consonant with what came to be known as the minimalist approach. As John readily admitted, "I didn't come here, Malcolm didn't come here, with a completely open mind about credit."

The minimalist approach stresses the primacy of credit in supporting small entrepreneurs, and the need to minimize nonessential services such as unsolicited advice and training in order to achieve cost-effectiveness. The objective of the minimalist approach is to provide lower cost assistance to entrepreneurs based on their needs. According to the minimalist approach, small businesses in developing countries are hampered most by a lack of ready credit. It strives for cost-effectiveness by concentrating first on credit as the primary need. Auxiliary services should be provided only when needed to make the credit fully effective, as evidenced by demand from the clientele for such services, and, in certain circumstances, by their willingness to pay a nominal fee for them. In this sense it is "demand driven."

The minimalist approach can be contrasted with the more integrated approach to small enterprise support commonly associated in Africa with the Partnership for Productivity model. The integrated approach emphasizes integrated training and advisory services in SSE support programs. It makes the provision of credit to small enterprises secondary to and conditional on such primary support services, on the premise that these services can be effective only in combination.

Malcolm had compiled a report of the survey findings, the reception of which had been mixed. In particular, the NPC members strongly contested the design and findings of the survey. The survey findings together with the strategy document would serve as the basis for the SSE Program strategy. John knew it would be difficult to convince the various audiences that the program he proposed was true to the original intent of the Project, since it differed markedly from the original Project document in following the minimalist strategy and in stressing viability as the primary objective. The proposed approach and objective had controversial implications for the choice of target client groups and the services offered, which John would have to defend.

Defending Viability

The Project paper stated that the Project should be institutionalized at the end of the grant term, but was vague on how this was to be done. Referring to the high expected cost per entrepreneur in the first few years, it stated, "the only way such an investment in assistance can be justified is for it to start an SSE growth and improvement momentum which will be self-sustaining after the life of the Project."

Larry Cooley, President of MSI, and John believed that institutionalization should be the dominant consideration in the strategy design; they thought that the Project would make a lasting impact only if it could sustain itself. As John saw it, "the loan fund is going to be institutionalized. If the loan fund doesn't pay for itself, if it eats itself up, then what are we doing here in the first place?" This in turn implied making financial viability the primary goal. The focus on viability appealed to John and Larry because it would provide a clear set of criteria for evaluation.

Kate Randall, who was then the director of the CEDP and John's immediate boss within the Management Unit, disagreed strongly with defining viability as the primary objective. Following conversations she had at USAID, Kate wrote to John: "[USAID officer] emphasized that we are not to create an institution, but to get help to the level of the economy which is not served by financial assistance at present … In short, creating a self-sustaining loan program is not the primary objective of the Project. The SSE component … is to assist those who manufacture or distribute [agricultural] factors of production and those who commercialize the products of agriculture."

Client Selection

Eligibility: Agricultural or Broad

The target industry groups specified in the Project paper were narrowly delimited to those supplying agricultural inputs and those processing, distributing, or marketing agricultural output, in line with the objective of strengthening the agricultural sector. "The Project's SSE development component intends to strengthen Sine Saloum SSE output of implements and services used in primary sector agricultural production." The Project paper estimated there were 1,500 such SSEs in Sine Saloum using a complicated procedure extrapolating from doctoral research on the amount of employment in the trades (see Exhibit 2).

From the perspective of viability, restricting the activities eligible for credit to those directly upstream and downstream from agricultural production was undesirable. The survey results indicated that the number of SSEs falling into these categories covered only a small portion of the total pool of SSEs lacking access to the formal credit market and would generate limited demand. The survey indicated that only 3 percent of agricultural production was sold to and only 6 percent of agricultural inputs were purchased from private traders, the rest going through parastatals or cooperatives (see Exhibit 3). Discussions with entrepreneurs suggested they were reluctant to enter these businesses because of the riskiness associated with agricultural production and because they expected the government to continue to intervene in these activities. Malcolm's survey report concluded that, "the privatization of agricultural marketing and inputs supply is at a very early stage. This is not an immediately attractive business opportunity for new or existing enterprises."

In addition, the categorization of businesses was not straightforward. First, as the center of the peanut basin, the entire regional economy revolves around agriculture, so that it is arguable that almost all types of small-scale businesses serve the agricultural sector, at least indirectly.

Moreover, many entrepreneurs, particularly merchants, change their activities as different opportunities arise over the course of the agricultural cycle. Thus, for example, a blacksmith might specialize in mending hoes during the rainy season and in construction equipment during the dry.

There was strong feeling both within the Management Unit and within USAID that the target SSEs should be narrowly delimited to those directly involved in "the support and commercialization of the agricultural sector." Kate challenged the conclusion that this sector was too small to sustain the credit fund: "I believe that there is more activity in this area than meets the eye. The study [survey] was a rapid reconnaissance based on visual identification of enterprises with permanent premises. It did not look for the home-based or farm-based enterprises and I believe has overlooked an important area of activity. I think there will be enough clients for us to make an impact on the economy of the area."

Ousmane Thiam, the director of the PVO Program, maintained that the overall purpose of the Project as stated in the Project paper was to strengthen the agricultural sector, in support of the Government's new agricultural policies. As such, a central contribution of the Project would be to promote the integrated development of agricultural production and commercial activities in rural areas. "One of the principal innovations of the Project is that it addresses the agricultural producers and the entrepreneurs of a rural area simultaneously and thereby promotes the mutual reinforcement and integration of these two sectors of rural development activity ... The integration of the rural economy will be more easily realizable if the SSE component activities are limited to ... the provision of inputs and the transformation/commercialization of output," rather than diluting the focus to include nonagricultural enterprises.

In essence, both Kate and Ousmane envisaged that the SSE and PVO programs would work toward the same goal through different intermediaries. SSE would promote agricultural development by providing support to artisans making farm implements, seed and fertilizer merchants, and farm produce transporters and processors. "You might have to take on more risk perhaps," Ousmane conceded, but there were important opportunities in these areas. "It would make it easier for my PVOs and VOs if they didn't have to go to Dakar to buy seeds and implements."

At USAID there was also some concern that the program support the government's policy of privatizing the agricultural sector. Overall, however, John got mixed signals from USAID over how narrowly to focus.

Focus on Towns or Villages

There was some sentiment within the Management Unit that the SSE Program should concentrate on rural entrepreneurs, again in line with the agricultural emphasis of the Project. Kate, in particular, thought that the commercialization of agricultural production would be best served by targeting rural entrepreneurs. In contrast, Larry was quite clear that this should not be the primary emphasis. "Development of enterprises should be focused on those entrepreneurs, enterprises, and localities most likely to succeed and to generate employment. This may well favor 'urban' (e.g. in Kaolack and large towns) activities and require considerable flexibility in interpreting (or possibly even abandoning) the initial suggestion that all enterprises be agriculturally related." The Project paper provided little guidance on this point.

Survey findings suggested that targeting rural enterprises alone would not be cost effective. The survey indicated that farmers make the bulk of their purchases in large towns, of which there are four in the region in addition to Kaolack. The transport system in the region is cheap and reliable, so that villagers have easy access to market towns.

The survey found businesses in the smaller communities were smaller, more seasonal in nature, less active, and "less likely to respond to assistance" than those in the towns (see Exhibit 4). This last observation was based on discussions with rural entrepreneurs that suggested they did not have well-formulated investment ideas, a clear notion of how much money they wanted to borrow, or a real understanding of repaying loans out of investment proceeds. Indeed, only 14 percent had new business ideas, compared with 71 percent of the urban entrepreneurs surveyed, who had "specific, if not necessarily realistic ideas for new products, new premises, new equipment or other improvements that they would like to introduce." In addition, the literacy and numeracy levels of rural entrepreneurs were less advanced. Malcolm further noted that businesses in urban areas had been established more recently and their owners were younger. Only a small percentage of rural enterprises had been opened in the last two years, which Malcolm thought suggested that "the village economies are stagnant or declining, while new business formations are taking place in the urban areas."

The choice of whether to concentrate on towns or villages would have important implications for the size and location of the field network, and thus for costs, as well as for the client groups emphasized.

Agricultural Loans to Individual Producers

No provision had been made in the original Project design for loans to individual farmers, and already this clientele group was showing strong interest in obtaining loans for market gardening and animal fattening projects. It was arguable that the Project should serve this group, since they were directly involved in agricultural production. Many of the loan proposals were quite attractive, having been submitted by civil servants who had worked in the agricultural sector and, moreover, were able to secure the loans with their salaries.

There was, however, considerable disagreement over whether and how to serve this group. The PVO Program was considered inappropriate for this function, since it was set up to handle group projects. In addition, its staff had little commercial expertise, although it did have the technical expertise needed to evaluate these projects.

Kate believed that the Project was ill-suited to serve individual agricultural producers, and should either exclude this group or create a third program exclusively to serve it. She reasoned that agricultural loans are extremely risky, and the SSE side did not have the expertise to evaluate them. "This is a very risky area for our Project to get into in that we have absolutely no expertise in agriculture or in agricultural loans. Senegal has a very bad history with credit, and most, if not all, credit programs, even those managed by agricultural experts, have failed. I cannot see where our Project, with expertise in the development of small enterprises, can hope to succeed." Her argument rested on the assumption that these would be large loans with a maturity of several seasons and no collateral to secure them. "The credit would be spent, in almost every case, on consumables: fertilizer, seeds, fodder, medicines, etc. Once the money is spent and the harvest sold, there would be nothing to reclaim except the money which may very well have been spent on things difficult to repossess ..."

The CEDP's Credit Specialist disagreed strongly, arguing that the CEDP should serve this group because "to do otherwise would be to exclude a major part of the available market to which the Project could make loans. Further, the Project would be excluding the rural agricultural producers it is meant to serve." He pointed out that the loan proposals were for dry season projects with generally high returns and short maturities—six months or less. He cited similar projects that had successfully made loans of this sort with repayment rates of over 93 percent. These loan programs relied on the moral commitment of the villagers for security, along with the threat that support would be discontinued in the event of nonrepayment.

John saw no reason not to consider these project proposals, as he saw them essentially as commercial activities. "I don't know about gardening, but a pound of beans is a pound of beans, and I know a lot about marketing ... And I know as much about animal fattening as about printing [that is, but very little, but enough to judge the soundness of an investment]."

Microenterprises—Women

Kate had been encouraging John to devise special measures to serve market vendors. She believed that this group warranted attention because it comprised mostly women, in marked contrast to the small-scale entrepreneurs. Fifty-seven percent of the market vendors in the survey were female, as compared to only 2 percent of the small business owners.

The vendors generally had no access to credit other than through their suppliers (mostly men), and were in a very weak bargaining position.

Preliminary survey results indicated that this group's needs are for a high volume of very small loans, and that the group would be difficult to serve, having no capital and no fixed premises. One quarter of the survey respondents reported a daily turnover of under U.S.$3.50, and fully 43 percent reported daily earnings of under U.S.$1.50, suggesting the need for very small loans and the riskiness of the clientele. On the other hand, nearly 90 percent frequented the same market every day, which would make them less difficult to serve. And their reported need for finance was high: 50 percent were able to purchase only with cash from suppliers, 72 percent stated that a lack of finance rather than storage, spoilage, or low demand kept them from buying more produce, and 84 percent reported finance as their major problem (see Exhibit 5).

Kate was dissatisfied with the findings. She contended that the survey had given the market vendors superficial treatment and "it turned up practically no sound information on the dynamics of this sector."

John was concerned that trying to serve the vendor population would prove both costly and risky, and distract considerable attention from what he saw as his main task, thus undermining the potential for institutionalization. "We're already wacky enough from a commercial bank's perspective, lending to SSEs. God knows how they would perceive market vendors." It wasn't clear to him why Kate was stressing this group, as there was no reference to this group or to women specifically in the Project paper. In addition, he saw no basis for believing that serving this group would have a more significant development impact than serving other small enterprises.

Nonetheless, he was willing to test a market vendor program, as long as it would be evaluated separately from the SSE loan fund. He and Malcolm thus included in their recommendations a proposal for a market vendor program based on the solidarity group model used by ACCION. It provided for a pilot program that, if successful, would be followed by the development of a market vendor program serving fifty vendors in each field office (see Exhibit 6).

In preselling the proposed program to the NPC members, however, John encountered significant opposition over the market vendor program. He argued for the program in terms of promoting a more equal distribution of wealth and increasing the bargaining power of market vendors vis-à-vis wholesalers. The NPC members objected for two reasons. They argued that market vendors are enmeshed in a delicately balanced set of family-based relationships that might be adversely affected by any intervention. In addition, their main concern was with development, which they identified with technology transfer and commercialization of agriculture, and not at all with strengthening market vendors.

Range of Services

The Project paper had proposed an integrated program offering technical assistance, training, advisory services, and credit. "The first task of the Project's Small Business Advisory Unit will be to train the working proprietors of artisanal production and service enterprises to perceive themselves as entrepreneurs. Once this step has been accomplished, the SBA Unit will provide the initial thrust required to stimulate self-generating development. The SBA Unit will address itself to removing and overcoming constraints." In concrete terms, this would imply, "during the life of the Project, approximately 675 SSEs will receive up to two years of intensive assistance (at least one consultative visit every ten days), one training seminar every quarter, and one year of less intensive follow-up assistance (one visit per month and one seminar every six months)."

John, Malcolm, and Larry were dead set against this approach on the grounds that it was prohibitively costly and ineffective. In line with the minimalist approach John determined that "because it is expensive to provide training [and] consultancy, we will not use these unless we see bottlenecks in the effective use of credit."

Defining training narrowly as business literacy and numeracy training, Malcolm and John included questions about educational levels, literacy, and bookkeeping in the surveys, as well as questions about the entrepreneurs' most pressing needs (see Exhibit 7). The entrepreneurs uniformly identified credit as the main constraint on their businesses, and only a small proportion showed interest in literacy and numeracy training. John interpreted the answers as: "No, I don't do books. No, I don't want to do accounting. No, I don't want any training. I haven't got time." There appeared to be little need for technical assistance, since about two-thirds of the entrepreneurs had been apprenticed. On the other hand, literacy and numeracy levels were found to be poor. In Kaolack and the three large towns, 17 percent of the entrepreneurs were illiterate and 47 percent kept no written records. These numbers were 38 percent and 70 percent for the smaller communities.

John envisaged a lengthy up-front application process that would substitute for more formal training and advisory services as well as analyze the viability of the proposed investments. The prospective client would engage in an application/*cum* planning process with a business advisor, which would include several visits to the business premises, construction of financial statements for the existing activity and *pro formas* for the proposed investment, and estimation of cash flow and working capital needs. Formal business literacy and numeracy training would be organized if demanded by a sufficient number of clients.

Exhibit 1
SENEGAL COMMUNITY AND ENTERPRISE DEVELOPMENT PROJECT
STYLIZED ORGANIZATIONAL CHART[a]

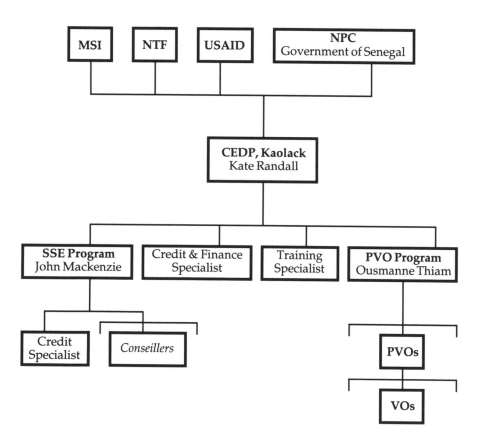

[a] The chart reflects the structure of the organization at time of project implementation. For simplicity some positions are not shown. Some names have been changed.

Exhibit 2
PROJECT PAPER ESTIMATES OF NUMBER OF SSEs
IN SINE SALOUM REGION

The figure of 1,500 agri-related SSEs in Sine Saloum eligible for Project assistance was estimated as follows:
(a) 16,383 persons in Sine Saloum are employed using trade skills. Of these, approximately 5,000 are employed using potentially agri-related trade skills (L'Organisation de L'Artisanat, Ph. Belhomme OIT, Annex D).
(b) Dividing 5,000 persons by an estimated average of 2.5 persons per SSE suggest the existence of 2,000 agri-related SSEs.
(c) Subtracting from 2,000 SSEs an estimated 500 owned by foreigners of absentee elites, and therefore not eligible for Project assistance, leaves 1,500 agri-related SSEs.

Exhibit 3
SURVEY RESULTS: AGRICULTURAL INPUT SUPPLY
AND OUTPUT DISTRIBUTION CHANNELS

The following table gives information obtained from twenty-eight of thirty-six of the smaller communities where interviews were undertaken during the investigation.

	Parastatal Corporations	Cooperatives	Private Traders
Customer for main agricultural produce	50%	47%	3% (1 case)
Supplier of major agricultural inputs	70%	24%	6% (2 cases)

This information confirms comments by several informed observers who suggest that the privatization of agricultural marketing and inputs supply is at a very early stage. This is not an immediately attractive business opportunity for new or existing enterprises.

Exhibit 4
SURVEY RESULTS: SIZE, EMPLOYMENT, AND BUSINESS SKILLS
OF RURAL AND URBAN ENTERPRISES

The data that demonstrate the significant differences between the small enterprises in Kaolack and the three larger towns, and the smaller communities, can be conveniently discussed under scale, business skills, and apparent future potential.

	Kaolack and Three Large Towns	Smaller Communities
Scale		
Annual turnover under		
1 million cfa (U.S.$2,500)	20%	38%
Annual turnover more than		
5 million cfa (U.S.$12,500)	34%	18%
Employment		
No employees (excluding owner)	19%	48%
1 to 5 employees (excluding owner)	48%	36%
6 to 10 employees (excluding owner)	20%	12%
11+ employees (excluding owner)	13%	4%
Seasonality		
12-month operation per annum	97%	75%
Business Skills		
Owner illiterate	17%	38%
Literate in Arabic/Wolof	35%	37%
Literate in French	33%	17%
No written records of any kind	47%	70%
Further Potential		
Owner's age over 50	26%	35%
Business less than 2 years old	31%	12%
Owner has ideas for future development	71%	14%

Exhibit 5
SURVEY RESULTS: MARKET VENDORS

The salient findings from eighty-six market vendors from all four locations were as follows:

Sex	male 43%	female 57%
Attendance	7 days/week 87%	< 7 days/week 13%
Products sold	perishables 72%	nonperishables 28%
Estimated daily sales	under 1,000 cfa 24%	over 1,000 cfa 76%
Estimated daily earnings	under 500 cfa 43%	over 500 cfa 57%
Supplier terms	cash only 50%	credit 50%
Membership in *tontines*	yes 34%	no 66%

Reason for not buying more produce	lack of finance	72%
	lack of demand	22%
	lack of storage	5%
	goods would spoil	1%
Perceived major problem	finance	84%
	demand	8%
	other	8%

Exhibit 6
PRO FORMA MARKET VENDOR PROGRAM

The target financial statement for one extension worker *(conseiller)* after three and a half years, would appear as follows:

Total portfolio	
10 groups of 5 vendors at 10,000 cfa	500,000 cfa
Income	
1% fee for 50 weeks = 50% of portfolio	250,000 cfa
Direct expenses	
Defaults at 10% of portfolio	50,000 cfa
Cost of funds at 10%	50,000 cfa
Extension worker bonus	25,000 cfa
Default penalty	–500 cfa
Net bonus	24,500 cfa
Total direct expenses	124,500 cfa
Net contribution per annum	125,500 cfa

Exhibit 7
SSE SURVEY QUESTIONNAIRE
(Translated from French)

1. Establishment name
2. Establishment address
3. Proprietor name and age
4. Manager name and age
5. Year business was founded
6. Type of business
7. Number of employees who are family members and paid, family members and unpaid, family members and apprenticed, paid outsiders, unpaid outsiders, apprenticed outsiders.
8. How many months of the year is the business in operation? During which season?
9. What are your annual revenues?
10. What is the main constraint on increasing your revenues?
11. Are you officially registered?
12. How many times in the last month did you go to Kaolack? To Dakar?
13. Have you ever borrowed money? How much? From whom? Under what terms?
14. Do you keep business records? If so, who maintains them? What type of records? Could you tell me of a decision you made using the figures from these records?
15. How did you decide on the unit price of your products?
16. What changes in your products or your establishment have you made in the last year?
17. What changes do you want to make in the future?
18. Do you know how to read and write in French? In Arabic? In Wolof? In any other language?
19. For how many years did you attend school?
20. Did you serve an apprenticeship in this trade? For how long?
21. How many years have you been practicing this trade? Other trades?
22. Have you received any technical training?

Instructions to the questionnaire taker:
23. How many clients did you see while you were at the establishment?
24. Glance around at the inventory of the business. Identify the two most numerous types of primary materials or finished goods. Ask the entrepreneur the amount of each good that she or he sells or uses in the course of one month. Calculate if the inventory is less than that needed for one month, exceeds that needed for three months.

Case 19

Senegal Community and Enterprise Development Project (B): Achieving Viability

This case was written by S. Lael Brainard. It is intended as the basis for class discussion rather than as an illustration of either effective or ineffective handling of an administrative situation. Some of the names have been changed. The cooperation and support of the many individuals who served as resource people for the development of this case are gratefully acknowledged, particularly the personnel of the CEDP.

Through a series of working sessions—first with Management Unit members, NTF, and MSI, and later with individual NPC members and USAID—John worked out a compromise proposal that seemed likely to win acceptance. The primary objective of the SSE Program would be viability with a view to eventual institutionalization, and the program's design would be explicitly in line with the minimalist approach.

Eligibility would be restricted during a pilot phase of six months to those enterprises engaged in the production and supply of agricultural inputs and the commercialization and processing of agricultural output. At the end of the pilot phase, eligibility would be reviewed and possibly expanded to include most small enterprises if demand from the narrower group proved insufficient (see Exhibit 1). John planned to accept applications from all types of businesses during the pilot phase nonetheless. He believed that it would be necessary to expand eligibility to ensure adequate demand, and having a large number of sound loan proposals in hand would strengthen his argument at the end of the pilot phase.

There would be no program specifically targeted to market vendors initially, in order not to distract management attention from the main task of establishing a self-sustaining small enterprise credit fund. The establishment of a market vendor program would be reevaluated once the credit fund was firmly established.

Both rural and urban enterprises would be eligible for loans, but initial marketing efforts and the location of field staff would be concentrated in Kaolack and the four largest towns. This plan was consistent with the minimalist emphasis on achieving maximum impact with min-

353

imal resources and with the survey findings indicating that urban entrepreneurs were more dynamic.

Credit was to be the sole form of assistance initially, supplemented by the informal training given during the loan application process. All loan applicants would be asked if they desired business skills training, however, and training programs would be designed as the program evolved if there were sufficient demand.

Taking these elements as the basis for the SSE Program strategy, John now had to design measures to implement the strategy. The key considerations in program design would be reaching the clientele, covering costs, and achieving repayment.

Business Advisor Network

Configuration

The central element in reaching the small-scale entrepreneur would be a network of business advisors *(conseillers)* who would serve as the link between the client and the Management Unit. The Project paper specified that there should be four business extension agents "intensively trained to deliver training, consultation, and other forms of assistance to SSE's" in line with the comprehensive nature of the support envisaged. Their salary was estimated at 135,000 cfa (U.S.$450) a month, which was comparable to a middle-ranking civil servant.

John's main concern in configuring the field network was to achieve adequate outreach at minimum cost. This implied getting the *conseillers* out in the field so as to be close to their clients and well away from the head office. Field offices would ideally be located so as to provide access to a large concentration of clients, so that the *conseillers* could stay in their offices as much as possible, minimizing travel time and costs. The survey identified four towns in the region large enough to sustain a field office and sufficiently spread out to afford access to most villages. Also, given the disproportionate concentration of SSEs in Kaolack, John favored locating two offices there.

In order to emphasize outreach and to maintain a lean organization, John wanted to push as much responsibility out to the field as possible, and thus proposed making each field office an accounting unit. While in a comparable commercial organization this would mean making each office a profit center, John feared that this would be too complicated initially.

In line with the commercial focus of the Project, John conceived of the field staff more as loan officers than as the advisors envisaged in the Project paper. The *conseillers* would have several responsibilities. They would be responsible for making potential clients aware of the program.

They would perform an enabling function in helping their clients to think through and present sound business projects and in informally teaching them to plan. At the same time, they would be responsible for analyzing the business proposals and evaluating their profitability. On the back end, they would be monitoring repayment, receiving monthly payments, and tracking any problems closely.

Qualifications and Compensation

In order to hold costs down with an expanded network of advisors, John decided to recruit less experienced, lower paid staff than those suggested in the Project paper. In recruiting researchers for the survey, John had come across no applicants with the education and extensive small enterprise experience envisaged in the Project paper. He also preferred not to hire university graduates, fearing that a university education was not sufficiently practical, and that university graduates would be averse to spending most of their time out in the field. Also, hiring staff with little formal education would enable John to hold costs down with an expanded network of advisors.

Local pay scales supplied by the Bureau de Travail suggested that 82,000 cfa (U.S.$275) a month was the low end of the salary scale for the qualifications John was seeking. He had already identified six promising candidates among the ten people who had conducted the survey who he believed would be willing to work at this salary level.

John also wanted to make compensation partially incentive-based. This plan suggested a compensation system that would reflect each *conseiller's* overall contribution to the viability of the Project. John favored some mixture of bonuses to reward the generation of sound loans and penalties to reflect the losses to the Project from nonrepayment.

John was concerned that the system be both simple for the *conseillers* to understand and accurate in reflecting the relative financial impact of interest income and loan losses and the extent of the *conseillers'* control over repayment. Malcolm's report recommended a bonus of 10 percent of interest income generated and a penalty of 1 percent of any nonrepaid principal. This system of compensation would entail a lag of approximately 12 months, however, because the rewards would begin to accumulate only after the principal had been repaid. Also, the correct mix of rewards and penalties to cover costs varied greatly depending on how the bonus was calculated and on assumptions about the default rate, the spread on funds, and the *conseiller's* loan portfolio. Under certain assumptions, the *conseillers* would stand to increase their income from 50 to 75 percent (see Exhibit 2).

In conversations with NPC members, however, it became apparent that several of them were strongly opposed to the bonus system. John found their concerns to be ill-defined, and he suspected that the main problem was that a successful *conseiller* could expect to earn an income comparable to a mid-level civil servant (before perquisites, which are considerable in the civil service). In truth, the NPC members had little experience with the use of incentive-based compensation, as this is not a common practice in the formal sector in Senegal.

Loan Approval Criteria

In line with the objective of viability, Malcolm and John proposed establishing a loan qualification process that would focus on the estimated profitability of the proposed investment. This would be unusual for a development project, but in John's words, "We see superviability as a proxy for development impact." He reasoned that financing an investment with a high return stimulates development by creating economic value. And the program would be promoting development simply by virtue of serving a high-risk clientele that would otherwise be denied access to formal sector financing.

In addition, the criterion would in no way be applied heartlessly. If a proposal were to be rejected as commercially unsound, "instead of just playing the role of banker I would then like to really understand the situation and propose how we might go into some partnership with the entrepreneur."

On the other hand, the proposed philosophy sounded more like Adam Smith than the usual emphasis of USAID on serving disadvantaged groups. "We want to go with winners. The people we are looking at are potential winners and we want to give them the means to haul themselves up by their bootstraps. This is not a welfare program." As such, it sat uncomfortably with those judging the Project in strict social welfare terms.

More concretely, John was considering imposing requirements for first-time loan proposals of a ceiling of the lesser of U.S.$10,000 or one third of the business' annual turnover, a maximum term of twelve months, and a hurdle rate of 100 percent return on investment (ROI). The first two requirements were intended to minimize risk and establish a track record for the borrowers and for the Project. John calculated the maximum loan size based on an estimate of cash flow relative to the average turnover of survey respondents and their equity investment.

John believed that the high ROI hurdle would be a good idea for two reasons. The survey and field visits had revealed that accounting data were very unreliable or nonexistent so that estimating profitability was very imprecise. "You have to leave a lot of leeway for error." In addition, since most of the entrepreneurs tended to move capital between their businesses and their family budget freely depending on need, and assuming that the existing level of business activity was just meeting family needs, a high ROI would ensure that repayment would not be made at the expense of family consumption. In talking with entrepreneurs, John got the impression that there were a lot of potentially high return projects in need of financing, and that the ROI hurdle would not be prohibitive (see Exhibit 3).

Interest Rate

The main considerations in calculating the interest rate were viability, affordability, and legal requirements. John and Malcolm arrived at the figure 24 percent through a rough calculation making several assumptions about default rates, average loan size, and field costs (see Exhibit 4). This also happened to be the legal maximum usury rate, and just covered the economic rate of return on small commercial activities as estimated in the Project paper. On a declining balance basis the rate would work out to 13.5 percent (simple interest) of the original loan value.

The legal maximum for commercial banks is 15.5 percent (some banks interpret this as simple interest and others as declining balance). Banks also impose fees and notarization requirements that add significantly to the cost of borrowing, making them unattractive or inaccessible sources of finance to small-scale entrepreneurs. These include a 17 percent value added tax on the interest charges, a loan application fee ranging from U.S.$40 to U.S.$170, a collateral registration procedure costing a minimum of U.S.$500, and a requirement that borrowers have a bank account for at least six months prior to applying for a loan. Finance companies, which extend credit for the purchase of specific goods, are subject to a legal maximum of 24 percent, but are reputed to make more than that by raising the prices of goods sold on credit relative to those paid for in cash. The survey findings indicated that informal market rates vary between 50 and 500 percent.

The Project paper proposed charging "normal commercial market rates" on the grounds that "in this Project, a primary function of the interest rate is educative. It has to make clear to borrowers that money is a scarce resource that one has to pay for." The market rate was estimated as the Central Bank commercial discount rate plus 1.5 percent, or 12 percent in 1983. John faced considerable opposition to the proposed 24 percent from the NPC. Several NPC members were opposed on moral grounds. They argued that "the Project is supposed to help people, not rob them."

Ousmane and some of the NPC members were concerned about the 24 percent interest rate because of its ramifications for the PVO side of the Project. Ousmane contended that since people switch freely between commercial activities and agricultural production as opportunities arise in the rural areas, different interest rates for the two programs could divert resources from one set of activities to the other. "In the limit we could assist in the destructuration [sic] of the rural economy .... Thus, assuming that both programs would offer a uniform interest rate, Ousmane argued that 24 percent would be unsustainable given the economic rate of return on agricultural production (see Exhibit 5). However, John reworked his numbers he did not see how the loan fund could charge less than 24 percent and still cover costs. Indeed, even with a 24 percent interest rate the Project would be making losses the first few years.

Collateral

A key element in achieving viability would be ensuring repayment, as the loss from one bad loan could swamp the interest income from several good ones. This was particularly important since the region in which the program was operating has the worst credit record in the country, and the history of agricultural credit in Senegal overall is one of cycles of heavy borrowing, massive default, and wholesale forgiveness. In addition, the traditional Senegalese concept of lending and borrowing blurs the distinction between gifts and loans.

In view of this, John knew that it was essential to design a loan qualification process that would minimize the risk that an investment project would go bad or that an entrepreneur would be tempted to renege on his contract. The second line of defense would be ensuring that in the case of default the Project would have legal claim to valuable assets and an ability to capitalize on that claim, and communicating to clients that the Project would lay claim to those assets. In John's words, "What is credit? Credit comes from *credare*, which is confidence. When you lend someone money you must be confident that you will get it back. If you lend without strings here, you can be very confident you won't get it back."

On the other hand, the collateral requirement is a primary obstacle for small-scale entrepreneurs in obtaining formal sector financing. Banks require that collateral be notarized by an expert so that in the case of default there is no question as to the Bank's right to seize the assets. Without such a notarization, a court must first determine that the lender has a right to the assets, which is a time-consuming and somewhat risky procedure. The notarization is prohibitively expensive for small borrowers, costing from 5 to 10 percent of the loan value.

In addition, certain borrowers, particularly those in the villages, have no assets acceptable to banks. Banks accept valuables, property in land or houses, capital equipment, or a guaranteed income as collateral. In considering this problem, the SSE Credit Specialist stated, "we must take into account that no title to property or capital can be given by the borrower in the villages because such titles frequently have no value and also are located in geographically isolated places." The only security in these circumstances is "their given word, their honor, their dignity, their character which risks being humiliated." John thus needed to design a collateral requirement that would ensure the Project's financial solidity and yet be sufficiently flexible to be able to serve those excluded from bank credit.

John knew that the success of the SSE Program would depend not only on the design of each of these measures individually, but also on how effectively they would operate in combination. Thus, for instance, ensuring repayment would depend not only on the effectiveness and motivation of the *conseillers* in collecting payments, but also on screening proposed investments rigorously in the first place, on communicating the concept of credit and the importance of repayment to the borrower, on setting an interest rate high enough to cover operating costs and expected losses without being prohibitive, and on making collateral requirements sufficiently stringent to discourage default but sufficiently flexible to include borrowers who would otherwise have no access to formal sector financing. John sat back down at his desk and picked up his pen.

Exhibit 1
SSE CATEGORIES

Category I
Enterprises related to the provision of agricultural inputs
  • Manufacture and supply of agrochemicals
  • Manufacture and supply of seed and animal feed
  • Manufacture and supply of tools
  • Service enterprises supporting the above activities

Category II
Enterprises related to the direct handling of agricultural outputs
  • Transportation
  • Marketing (wholesale/retail) of crops and livestock
  • Food processing
  • Service enterprises supporting the above activities

Category III
Enterprises related to the provision of goods and services to the agricultural community
  • Transportation (for example, taxi, bus)
  • Wholesale/retail (for example, clothes, hardware, medicine)
  • Manufacturing (for example, carpenters, metalworkers, manufacturing domestic goods)
  • Services (for example, mechanics, tailors)

Exhibit 2
CONSEILLER PORTFOLIO PROFITABILITY WORKSHEET

6 Agents	Salary	80,000 cfa	5% Default
	Office	20,000 cfa	100% Funds Loaned
	Travel	10,000 cfa	
20 Loans @ 1,500,000 cfa			30,000,000 cfa
Interest/Income @ 24%			7,200,000 cfa
Expenses			
Defaults @ 5%			1,500,000 cfa
Cost of Funds @ 10%			3,000,000 cfa
Business Agent Bonus			685,000 cfa
	Total		5,185,000 cfa
	Income less Expenses		2,015,000 cfa
	Fixed Cost		1,320,000 cfa
	Contribution		695,000 cfa

Sensitivity Analysis on:
Default Rate
Number of Loans per *Conseiller*
Bonus Basis

Exhibit 3
HARPER REPORT: THREE CLIENT PROFILES

M. Seck and His Charrettes

Seck felt ashamed of the charrettes he made; he knew he could make far better ones, and sell more of them, if he could only improve the material. But he did not see how he could solve the problem.

He made and sold about four charrettes every months; he sold them for 40,000 cfa, and the angle iron and other materials cost about 15,000 cfa for each charrette. Seck could not afford to buy this material himself; he had to wait until a customer could pay an advance of 15,000 cfa so he could buy the material and then make the charrette. When he finished, the customer would pay the balance of 25,000 and take it away.

The problem was that none of his customers was willing to give him enough money to buy new material. With 15,000 cfa Seck could buy only scrap steel, which had to be joined and repaired before it could be used, so the charrettes were never of very high quality.

Seck knew that charrettes made from new material sold for 60,000 cfa; the material cost 20,000 cfa rather than 15,000 cfa for scrap, and he would have to buy enough for five charrettes at one time. The actual manufacturing would cost no more for a charrette made with new material, and might cost less because it was not necessary to repair the steel before assembling it.

Seck was not fully occupied all the time; if he worked really hard, he could have made as many as ten charrettes a month, but he sold only an average of four at the moment. He had plenty of young apprentices who were willing to help him, for little or no reward, because they could then learn how to make charrettes themselves, but Seck's own domestic expenses used up every franc he owned. He wondered how he could ever afford the better material, so that he could increase his income and make charrettes he would be proud of.

Mbaye the Carpenter

Mbaye had a successful carpentry business, but he wanted to improve it still more. He had worked with combined spindle molder and planing machines when he was in Paris some years before, and he estimated that if he had such a machine, he could earn an additional 150,000 cfa each month, after paying for all the timber, electricity, and so on that would be used.

Mbaye obtained a price list from an Italian manufacturer, which stated that the machine he wanted would cost 1.2 million cfa. He was very happy, because this happened to be exactly the same amount of money he had saved in the bank. He decided to order the machine.

He was surprised, however, when he wrote to the manufacturer, and they replied telling him that it would cost a further 400,000 cfa to pack the machine and deliver it to Dakar. Nevertheless, he went to the bank, and it agreed to lend him the necessary money. The interest charge would be 24 percent a year, but it still seemed worth doing. Mbaye made further inquiries, however, and was very disappointed to find that it would cost another 1 million cfa for import duty and other costs. The bank said it would lend him this money as well, on the same terms, but Mbaye decided not to buy the machine. It was ridiculous, he thought, to pay more for freight and duty than for the machine itself, and the interest charges would make the situation still worse. Maybe he would buy himself a car with his savings instead.

Diop the Mechanic

It was very difficult for Diop even to get into his workshop, because so many cars were parked around the front, out into the street and up against the walls. His friends used to congratulate him on having so much business, but Diop himself knew very well that all the cars were the cause of his difficulties, not a sign of his success.

Most of the cars were finished, waiting for the owners to collect them, and some had been there for over a year. One or two, on the other hand, had been brought in only recently. Their owners had asked Diop to repair them, and he had said he would, but he had not yet started. How could he, when he had not got enough money to feed his family, without even starting to buy any paint or parts for the cars?

Most of his customers paid some deposit, but it was usually not enough for the parts that were needed. Although Diop tried to estimate what parts would be needed and their cost when his customers brought their cars in, once he started to work on the cars he often found that more parts were necessary, and the customers were often not even able to pay for what he estimated would be necessary at the beginning. As a result, he had used up all his money paying for parts, and buying food for his apprentices and his family. Now his business was at a standstill.

Diop looked sadly at all the cars; one or two of them were quite new and nearly all of them were repaired and ready to run. It was ironic, he thought, that he should have so many valuable cars in his business, and yet have no money of his own at all.

Exhibit 4
HARPER *PRO FORMA* INCOME STATEMENT
(cfa)

Small Enterprise Loans		
Total portfolio, 20 loans at 1,500,000 each		30,000,000
Income		
Fees and Interest at 24%		7,200,000
Direct Expenses		
Default at 5% of Portfolio		1,500,000
Cost of Funds at 10%		3,000,000
Extension Worker Bonus	72,000	
Less Default Penalty	15,000	
Net Bonus		57,000
Total Direct Expenses		4,557,000
Net Contribution P/A		2,643,000
Total Contribution per Extension Worker P/A		
125,000 + 2,643,000		2,768,500
Fixed Costs per Extension Worker		
Salary and Benefits at 80,000 per month		960,000
Office Rental at 20,000 per month		240,000
Travel Costs at 10,000 per month		120,000
Total Fixed Costs P/A		1,320,000
Net Contribution per Extension Worker		
P/A = 2,768,500 – 1,320,000		1,448,500
Total Contribution of 6 Workers		
P/A = 6 x 1,448,500		8,691,000
Loan Fund = U.S.$450,000		
equivalent at current exchange rate to		179,100,000
Total Portfolio		
Small Enterprise Loans (6 x 30,000,000)		180,000,000
Micro Credit (6 x 500,000)		3,000,000
		183,000,000

Exhibit 5
SELECTED PROJECT ESTIMATES OF
INTERNAL RATES OF RETURN AND SENSITIVITY ANALYSIS

	Base Case	10% Less Production	20% Less Production	10% Increase in Costs	20% Increase in Costs	10% Less Production and 10% Increase in Costs
Vegetable and Fruit Production	31%	—	18	20	—	19
Livestock Fattening	20	10	—	11	—	—
Village Woodlot	2	—	—	—	—	—
Fishing Production	51	40	—	—	—	—
Small Rural Enterprise	23	—	7	—	10	—
Overall IRR	25	—	—	—	—	—

(—): IRR was not calculated for these cases.

Case 20

Tototo Home Industries: Assistance Strategies for the Future

This case was written by Dr. Martin Walsh. It is intended as a basis for class discussion rather than as an illustration of either effective or ineffective handling of an administrative situation. The collaboration and support of the Executive Director of Tototo Home Industries and her staff are gratefully acknowledged.

Mrs. Elvina Mutua sat down with her staff to discuss plans for the forthcoming field visits. In a month's time, in July 1988, Tototo Home Industries would be hosting a week-long workshop in Mombasa for PVOs and donors on the theme of "Partnership in Development." One day had been set aside to show the participants some of the women's groups on the Kenyan coast trained and assisted by Tototo. Mrs. Mutua was clear about the purpose of these visits: they were to highlight the importance of partnership at grassroots level and the role of indigenous PVOs like Tototo in being able to understand and respond effectively to local needs and problems. She suggested taking the visitors to see groups that illustrated specific problems and the different assistance strategies developed by Tototo in response to these. One trip, for example, might focus upon the integration of welfare and income generation projects; another, Tototo's business training program; and a third, its rapidly growing savings club scheme.

After some discussion, six visits were agreed upon, each with a different theme. Only one staff member expressed some reservation: "If we show the visitors such diverse examples of Tototo's work, isn't there a danger that they'll be left wondering just exactly what our approach is?" It was an important point to consider, and one with much wider implications. In essence it reflected one of the most difficult decisions facing Mrs. Mutua in her position as the Director of Tototo. Which assistance strategy or strategies should Tototo pursue? In answering this question she had to review Tototo's relationship with both its rural clients and its various external partners. There were different arguments on both sides, and the coming workshop, to which all of Tototo's donors had been invited, put increasing pressure upon Mrs. Mutua to make up her mind.

History of the Rural Development Program

Tototo Home Industries was started in 1963 by a Christian Aid (U.K.) volunteer working with the National Christian Council of Kenya (NCCK). It began as a small project marketing handicrafts produced by low-income women in Mombasa town. Mrs. Mutua, who had a background in administration and voluntary work for different women's organizations, joined Tototo in 1968. Under her direction Tototo's urban programs expanded and staff also began to work closely with handicraft producers outside of Mombasa, many of them members of organized women's groups. Mrs. Mutua was impressed by their repeated requests for other forms of assistance, though at first she lacked the means to respond. Her opportunity finally came in 1977, when World Education Inc., a PVO based in the United States, approached Tototo with a proposal to set up a two-year pilot project for six women's groups in Coast Province. This was the beginning of a long fruitful collaboration between the two organizations. Its outcome was a fully operational rural development program based primarily upon the training of women's groups. See Exhibit 1 for an account of the overall expansion and organization of Tototo. Exhibit 2 provides some general information on women's groups in Kenya and on the coast.

Nonformal Education and Integrated Development

The pilot project, which was funded by USAID, began in 1978. It was designed as an experiment in World Education's special field of expertise, nonformal education:

> The purpose of the project was to test a nonformal education methodology by providing training to women which did not require literacy; where the content of the training was determined by the women participants themselves; and where the educational methods fostered participation of all members of the group through discussion, analysis, decision-making, and collective action. The broad outcomes of the experiment were expected to include the improved health and nutrition of both women and their families, increased income, and greater participation in the life and affairs of their communities.[1]

From the outset Mrs. Mutua was enthusiastic about World Education's participatory approach. It echoed her own development priorities and provided Tototo with a training methodology that was well suited to working with rural women's groups with a predominantly nonliterate membership. The training was not tied to a fixed set of objectives, but promoted an open, integrated, approach to women's development that gave priority to the participants' own assessment of their needs. Not only was this an attractive idea, but it also seemed to work in practice. When the pilot project came to an end in 1980 it had produced a number of positive results, not least in terms of the wide range of development activities in which the six groups were engaged and the growing confidence of their members. This confidence also extended to Mrs. Mutua and her staff, who together with their World Education counterparts judged the experiment to have been a success.

Finding funds to develop the project further was difficult at first. Neither Tototo nor World Education had adequate financial resources of its own. Mrs. Mutua, who was comparatively new to the fund-raising process, had to rely upon the experience of her sister organization. In 1981 World Education secured a two-year matching grant from USAID to cover, among other things, the costs of Tototo's new training program. Through 1983 World Education struggled to keep the program alive with a series of relatively small donations raised from a variety of sources including World Education's annual appeal. Efforts were redoubled to find a more secure funding base for Tototo's program and these paid off in 1984 when both the Ford Foundation and Lutheran World Relief made the first of a series of major grants to Tototo. In the same year World Education won a large grant from the USAID mission in Nairobi to set up the Kenya Rural Enterprise Programme (REP). In 1987 REP, which provides assistance to PVOs throughout Kenya, became Tototo's third major financial donor.

The pilot project evolved, albeit in somewhat piecemeal fashion, into a comprehensive training program. By 1985 Tototo was working with 45 groups (including two men's groups) in locations scattered across Kenya's Coast Province. The training was based upon a model that the pilot project had established. Groups were selected for training with the assistance of local government officials and extension agents, often in response to direct requests from the groups themselves. Literate coordinators chosen by each group were then trained by Tototo staff in a variety of nonformal techniques designed to help group members to assess their collective needs and plan activities around them. The coordinators used these techniques in weekly group meetings and kept records for Tototo field staff who paid regular visits to monitor group activities and help iron out any difficulties that might have arisen. As the program developed it became evident that overreliance upon coordinators created a number of problems and as a result elected group leaders were drawn into the training process. On-site training sessions for groups were also introduced. The basic methodology, however, remained the same. Ideally training and intensive follow-up covered a period of two years, after which groups were expected to have become largely self-sufficient in planning their activities.

None of the groups, with the exception of five that Tototo had trained for the YWCA,[2] graduated from the program after completing training. One reason for this was that the program had expanded to include a number of sub-programs that were not linked directly to the training cycle, though they were a product of its integrated approach. The development of these sub-programs also reflected Mrs. Mutua's strong commitment to the needs of her clients, not just as groups but also as individuals and members of wider communities.

The sub-programs covered three main areas: health and family planning, savings, and credit. Each of them involved collaboration between Tototo and other agencies. Tototo worked closely with the Family Planning Association of Kenya (FPAK) and the Center for Development of Population Activities (CEDPA) in setting up health and family planning projects for a number of its groups. A savings club scheme for both group and nongroup members was introduced by Mrs. Mutua in 1984 following a visit to the Savings Development Movement in Zimbabwe sponsored by the Ford Foundation. Meanwhile Tototo was active in helping its groups to obtain grants from the government and different donor agencies, both local and (with the help of World Education) international. Tototo also administered a program of small grants funded by Trickle Up, Inc. (U.S.A.). In 1983 Tototo secured funding from Bread for the World (West Germany) to set up a small revolving loan fund. With further inputs from the Ford Foundation, Lutheran World Relief and REP, the revolving loan fund became another important component of Tototo's program.

Business Training and Consultancy

While the rural development program continued to develop along lines determined by the objectives of the pilot project, a new set of directions for Tototo was beginning to emerge. In 1984, with Mrs. Mutua's approval, World Education submitted a grant proposal to PACT (Private Agencies Collaborating Together, United States) for a new three-year collaborative project. Its purpose was twofold: to upgrade the business skills component of the training program, and to develop Tototo's capacity to market its training services to other organizations so that the program could become at least partly self-financing. To some extent this proposal reflected changes in the donor environment and World Education's understanding of the implications of these for itself and Tototo. Nonformal education was no longer in vogue; women's income generation, especially if called small enterprise development, was. Also, the international donor community was showing increased interest in programs that enhanced the independence and interdependence of southern PVOs, especially programs that were replicable in such a context.

World Education had, in fact, already begun to promote Tototo's training skills elsewhere. In 1982 Tototo staff had traveled to Zimbabwe to assist the Adult Literacy Organization of Zimbabwe (ALOZ) in the design and implementation of income generation programs. In 1984 World Education hired Tototo to work with the Maseno South Small Enterprise Development Project in western Kenya. Mrs. Mutua and her staff enjoyed this work, and were more than willing to take on more.

The main impetus for subsequent developments in Tototo's small business project came, however, from anthropological research within the rural development program. In 1982 World Education had secured a grant from AID to conduct this research with Tototo on the groups within its program. The full results of the case study (as it was called) began to emerge in 1985. World Education staff were both disturbed and fascinated by its detailed account of the constraints operating upon groups and their enterprises. The case study made clear that the content of Tototo's nonformal training program was not meeting the needs of the women's groups' businesses, particularly as those needs had changed over time. While the program had helped many groups to set up welfare and income generation projects, the degree of success of these projects had more to do with direct interventions like the provision of credit and regular advice from Tototo field staff, than any intrinsic effects of the training itself. However, the training process was invaluable in a number of ways, not least in the confidence and encouragement it prompted within the women's groups. But the researcher found that the training did not affect their internal decision-making procedures to the degree that Tototo and World Education had intended. Moreover, the training as originally designed did not address either the business skills the women needed or the contextual constraints they would have to overcome if they were to free themselves of dependency on the advice and assistance of Tototo. Indeed, the technical skills and financial assistance that Tototo did provide were found to be insufficient to ensure success in the income generation projects. Most of the businesses initiated by Tototo's groups were struggling hard to survive.

These findings provided an important stimulus to the work which was to follow. Although she was less critical of the original methodology, Mrs. Mutua had been dissatisfied for some time with the income generation component of Tototo's program. She was equally dissatisfied with the overtechnical methods employed by other Kenyan PVOs: their interventions—the introduction of complex bookkeeping systems was one example—had invariably failed when applied to groups with which Tototo worked. In consultation with World Education she agreed that they should develop their own training methodology adapted to the needs and requirements of the existing program. A consultant was hired in 1986 to carry out this task, along with others covered by the PACT grant.

The business consultant, Kevin Kane, worked intensively with Tototo staff both in Mombasa and in the field. Eight of the women's groups already in Tototo's program were chosen to take part in the project. Over a period of four months Tototo staff were trained in a variety of business skills, and together with Kevin they designed a set of management interventions to address the specific business needs of groups. Finally, a nonformal education specialist sent by World Education helped turn these into training exercises that could be used to impart business knowledge to rural women. The results were impressive. The groups involved showed significant improvements in business performance, not least in increased revenues, capacity to reinvest, and the provision of regular returns in the form of dividends and wages to their members. (See Exhibit 3 for further information on the business training program, its methodology and subsequent performance.)

Tototo's training program was revitalized. In 1987 eight more groups went through the new business training and World Education sent Kevin back to Mombasa at Mrs. Mutua's request to follow up on his earlier work. One of his jobs was to outline a consultancy strategy for Tototo based primarily upon the business training: "The Tototo Way" as it was dubbed. Tototo and World Education also discussed plans to produce a training kit or manual to help Tototo market its services to other organizations. Mrs. Mutua was keen that this should include elements of the original training program, in particular, exercises designed to foster group confidence, participation, and organizational coherence. Under the heading of "leadership training" she considered these an essential part of Tototo's work. In late 1987 a Tototo-World Education team traveled to Swaziland to conduct the first of three training workshops for Home Economics Officers working with rural women's groups. The second workshop, on introductory business skills, took place in October 1988. This was only the first of a number of joint ventures that World Education hoped to be able to undertake with Tototo on the basis of the new training content.

1988 was a busy year for Tototo in its new role as a consultancy organization focusing on training. In addition to the Swaziland contract Mrs. Mutua and the staff of the rural development program were working (or about to work) on a series of consultancies negotiated independently by Tototo. These included training for an ILO project in Tanzania and work for different organizations in Kenya: the YWCA, the Kenya Business and Professional Women's Club, the Canadian High Commission, and UNICEF. This series was in addition to their (re)training more groups on the coast and running the various sub-programs within the rural development program. To cap it all, in July Tototo was hosting a

PVC/donor workshop to celebrate its ten-year partnership with World Education and share with other organizations working in Africa the lessons that it had learned in a decade of rural development.

Some Options for the Future

As the "Partnership in Development" workshop approached, Mrs. Mutua was under increasing pressure to clarify her position on the future of the rural development program and its different components. For one thing she would have to present a favorable image to the large number of workshop participants. More than fifty representatives from different organizations were expected to attend. Many of these were potential clients. Others represented Tototo's donors. Last but not least were Mrs. Mutua's colleagues from World Education.[3]

The Business Training Strategy

Over the past two years or so World Education staff and Mrs. Mutua mapped out their own vision of Tototo's future, though the full implications of this for the rural development program on the coast had not been worked out in any detail. This task had fallen to Kevin, who continued to assist and advise Mrs. Mutua and her field staff on an informal basis. He recommended that Tototo should expand its basic constituency of women's groups on the coast in order to demonstrate the effectiveness and replicability of the business training program. The success of this program would function as an advertisement for Tototo's training services, hence fostering its goal of self-reliance. It would also ensure the ongoing commitment of financial donors as and when funding was required. To date Tototo had failed to demonstrate that it possessed a replicable model for rural development: the groups that had been trained in the past remained dependent on Tototo and vice-versa. Too many of them showed too few signs of progress, and sooner or later Tototo's external partners would recognize this fact.

The business training provided an excellent opportunity to revitalize the Tototo model. Linked to existing credit mechanisms (the revolving loan fund) the training cycle should be developed and expanded by drawing new groups into the program and weaning them off when appropriate. This weaning process would also apply to groups already within the rural development program, especially those that had responded poorly to business training. Instead Tototo should concentrate upon groups that showed significant business potential and were likely to respond well to training. This focus on business training would require an overall rationalization of the rural development program and critical evaluation of its different components. As it was, a mosaic of loosely related and sometimes conflicting activities stretched and diluted

Tototo's organizational resources, including the time and skills of its personnel. Moreover, the existing situation ensured Tototo's continuing dependence on the whims of external donors. In the short term they might be queuing up to sponsor the program and/or particular initiatives within it, but there was no guarantee that they would continue to do so in the future. (Exhibit 3 provides a more detailed background to these arguments.)

A Grassroots Perspective

Mrs. Mutua was very much in favor of the business training and related consultancy work. She was less happy, though, with the prospect of pursuing this one strategy at the cost of others in Tototo's program. Some of her reasons for this came to the fore during her annual tour and review of Tototo groups in the months preceding the "Partnership in Development" workshop.

Over a period of weeks Mrs. Mutua had visited a number of the groups assisted by Tototo, including those she was thinking of showing to the workshop participants. The tour gave her ample opportunity to reflect on the history of the rural development program, the different interventions it encompassed, and what they had achieved over the years. Diversity and flexibility had always been key features of Tototo's work on the coast. Mrs. Mutua felt strongly that development should respond to the needs of those who needed it most, whatever these needs may be. This conviction had led her into working with rural women's groups, much as it had later led her to choose groups from some of the most marginal and economically undeveloped areas of the coast for inclusion in Tototo's program. It had also shaped her commitment to the participatory methodology and integrated goals of the pilot project, a commitment evident in her decision to retain leadership training in Tototo's new training of trainers package.

The positive results of this approach and the wide variety of interventions it had both demanded and inspired were apparent among the groups she visited. In some cases the results were obvious, and could be measured in terms of benefits not just to the group and its individual members but also to their families and the community as a whole. This was true of both welfare and income generation projects. Mkwiro women's group, based in a small island fishing community, was a case in point. Mkwiro's ferry boat business provided more than just a minor supplement (in the form of monthly dividends) to the income of group members. It also provided an important service for the whole community, not least by giving local women and their children regular access to the nearest mainland health clinic. Group members had in fact chosen to surrender their dividends to another project: the construction of a multi-purpose house (shop, meeting-place, nursery classroom). In the same spirit Mrs. Mutua had already begun to discuss with Lutheran World Relief the possibility of setting up an integrated development project in the area. This project would focus upon Mkwiro and two women's groups on the mainland; one of its priorities would be the provision of a local water supply and health care services for Mkwiro.

In other cases the results of Tototo's work were less tangible, but nonetheless real. A casual visitor to the Mazingira group, located in the semiarid region behind the coast, would find little to impress. Living in a difficult environment, group members faced almost insuperable odds in establishing a viable project. The group's goat trading enterprise, though improved after business training, was still only making a small profit. Mrs. Mutua knew, however, that Mazingira's progress over the years could not be measured just by looking at its accounts. The participation of women in long goat buying trips (lasting two days or more) was a sign of changes that the figures could never capture. If working with Mazingira was frustrating at times, it was also well worth the trouble. Mazingira and other groups like it posed a challenge. If organizations like Tototo were not willing to take up this challenge, then who would?

In some cases Tototo's commitment had paid off with surprising results. Mkoyo, one of the six groups in the 1978 pilot project, had been passed over as a candidate for business training. Its income generation record was weak and it was generally considered to be one of the more lacklustre groups in Tototo's program. This status changed when Tototo introduced its savings club scheme there toward the end of 1986. Much to everyone's surprise and delight by 1988 Mkoyo's savings club had deposited more money than any of the other clubs in the scheme, including ones that had been started two years earlier. Mkoyo's club was also the best organized, and its members had instituted new procedures that were already being taken up independently by other clubs in the scheme.

The savings club scheme epitomized Mrs. Mutua's approach. Since its introduction in 1984 it had proved one of the most popular interventions in Tototo's program. The clubs opened up savings to people who were otherwise unable to raise or maintain the minimum deposit demanded by the banks and building societies, leaving aside the question of their access to such institutions in the first place. The clubs were open to both group and nongroup members, women and men (who in some cases formed separate clubs). They were also relatively easy to run once their elected officials had been trained by Tototo. The original scheme had been adapted by Mrs. Mutua to suit the needs of Tototo's rural clients. Complex accounting procedures had been simplified and individual savings were recorded by a method that nonliterate club members could readily use and understand. Mrs. Mutua was justifiably proud of the result: by 1988 there were some fifty clubs in the scheme, with a membership much wider than that of Tototo's basic constituency of forty groups. She was also keen to develop the scheme further by using club deposits as security for loans to individual members, and was confident that she could win donor support to explore this proposal further.

This was only one of a number of ideas that Mrs. Mutua wanted to pursue. Another was the promotion of individual as well as group enterprises, adapting the business training for this purpose. The "Partnership in Development" workshop would provide her with a forum to present and discuss these ideas, particularly in the context of the field visits. In ten years of rural development Tototo had amassed considerable experience. At the same time it had not stopped learning. Most important of all, it was learning from the grassroots.

A Difficult Decision

Deciding which groups to show the workshop participants was relatively straightforward. Six groups had been chosen, illustrating different strategies employed by Tototo. (See Exhibit 4 for information on the field visits.) Deciding which of these strategies or combination of them Tototo should focus upon in future was considerably more difficult. Yet Mrs. Mutua knew that workshop participants would expect her to address this issue.

Notes

1. Quoted from a proposal written by World Education and Tototo for funding of the 1988 "Partnership in Development" workshop.

2 The Mombasa Branch of the Young Women's Christian Association has a small women's group program that has been fostered by Tototo's support and encouragement.

3. The workshop was funded by the Ford Foundation, Lutheran World Relief, and PACT.

Exhibit 1
EXPANSION AND ORGANIZATION OF TOTOTO

Since its inception in 1963 Tototo has expanded considerably. The organization currently employs some fifty personnel and operates four main programs:

1. *Handicraft marketing/retail shop.* Tototo began by marketing locally produced handicrafts through its own retail outlet in the center of Mombasa. This program was remodeled in the mid-1970s with the help of a Peace Corps volunteer/designer.[1] The shop now markets handicrafts produced by both individuals (men and women) and groups, including some of the groups in the rural development program. Tototo has had little success in developing an export market for their products. The shop also suffers from intense competition in the local tourist market. In recent years it has been subsidized by the rural development program and the donor funding which this has attracted.

2. *Vocational training.* This program was started in 1968 and became fully operational in 1971. Young women who have failed to qualify for higher (secondary) education are trained in tailoring, tie-dye, and other skills to help them secure employment or start small businesses of their own. The training school is in Mombasa and currently has some fifty students. The school is subsidized by the Ministry of Culture and Social Services as well as by Tototo's tie-dye program.

3. *Tie-dye production workshop.* The production workshop, also in Mombasa, was started in the mid-1970s with assistance from Bread for the World. At any one time the unit employs some thirty women, most of them referred to Tototo by social workers. They are given on-the-job training in the production of tie-dye fabrics and garments that are then marketed through Tototo's shop. This is the only one of Tototo's three urban programs that is not subsidized.

4. *The Rural Development Program (RDP).* Begun in 1978, this is Tototo's newest and most rapidly expanding program. RDP staff currently work directly with forty groups in four of the six administrative Districts that comprise Kenya's Coast Province. The most distant groups are some 200 kilometers away from Mombasa town. Others are situated within the urban perimeter, though not on the main island where Tototo and the RDP have their offices. The number of staff employed in the RDP has doubled since 1985. Twelve field supervisors work under the direction of Tototo's Assistant Director (a newly created position). They each have different responsibilities in the field. Four management supervisors and four accounts supervisors divide their work among the forty groups in the program, focusing in particular upon those groups engaged in business training. Two other supervisors are assigned to work with the fifty savings clubs (whose membership overlaps with that of the groups). Finally, two loans supervisors work with the groups in the revolving loan fund (in April 1988 there were seventeen outstanding loans). The loan fund is administered by Tototo's Accountant/Business advisor. All the above staff plus the Director collaborate in training and consultancy work, though smaller teams usually travel to undertake external consultancies.

Tototo's original objective was "to uplift the standard of living for women and girls in Mombasa, mainly the less fortunate." The expansion of Tototo's programs has since produced a broader formulation: "To assist and train low-income rural and urban adults in Coast Province of Kenya so that their quality of life is uplifted socially and economically."

Tototo is headed by a Management Committee comprising prominent members of the business and professional community in Mombasa. In practice most major policy decisions are and have been initiated by the Director, who acts as the Committee's Secretary. The Director is also responsible for the day-to-day running of Tototo and plays an active role in decision making at different levels within the organization. In terms of management style and ethos Tototo might be described as a maternalistic organization. In many ways this has worked in Tototo's favor. More than anything else Tototo owes its status as a development agency to the personal energy and vision of its Director. The staff, in particular those associated with the RDP, possess a remarkable collective spirit and enthusiasm. This is evident in their work as well as in the close relations Tototo has forged with different individual and institutional partners over the years. More recently, however, Tototo's external partners have expressed concern over the organization's capacity to cope with continued growth. World Education, Lutheran World Relief, and REP have all recommended reforms of one kind or another. Their recommendations have focused upon two main areas: first, the need for Tototo to strengthen the commercial side of its operations in order to provide the organization with a more solid financial base than it has at present; second, the need to rationalize the management of its different programs and reduce the heavy workload of the Director. Tototo has already begun to respond to these recommendations, though it has yet to allay all of its donors' concerns.

---

[1] The name *Tototo,* a Mijikenda term denoting superlative quality, was introduced at this time. The Mijikenda are a group of peoples who form the majority of Tototo's clients in the rural hinterland of Mombasa.

Exhibit 2
WOMEN'S GROUPS IN KENYA AND ON THE COAST

The women's group movement in Kenya traces a variety of origins, but its true history began in the mid-1960s with the formation of large numbers of groups in Kenya's Central Province. Broadly speaking these were formed in response to the increasing scarcity of land and male labor, against a background of political support for self-help initiatives (*harambee*) in building the newly independent state. While similar groups began to appear elsewhere in the country, the movement derived most of its later force from official recognition and encouragement. The Kenyan government first declared its commitment to a women's group program in 1966. In 1975, at the start of the International Decade for Women, it established a Women's Bureau to coordinate the activities of a nationwide program. Since then the number of registered women's groups in Kenya has increased sixfold. Latest (1988) estimates put the figure at some 1,000 groups with a total membership approaching three-quarters of a million women, over 10 percent of the adult female population.

The most developed areas of Kenya retain the largest share of women's groups. On the relatively underdeveloped coast there are proportionately fewer. In 1985 there were 958 registered women's groups in Coast Province with over 40,000 members. Most of the development agencies in Kenya are based in Nairobi and the women's groups on the coast receive comparatively little attention from them. Despite the fact that Mombasa is Kenya's main port and second largest urban center, Tototo is the only development agency based there.

Most women's groups receive little or no direct assistance except that provided by the government. They are required to register with the Department of Social Services and are subject to the various attentions of its extension agents, along with agricultural officers and local government chiefs. Women's groups are used in a number of ways to promote government development policies. They are eligible to receive grants toward their projects, though the demand for these is much greater than the supply. Groups are also encouraged to hold community fund-raising events (*harambees*) for the same purpose. Otherwise they typically raise subscriptions or shares from their members, and engage in a wide range of productive activities to gather seed-money for their projects. As a rule it is difficult for groups to obtain commercial credit or establish larger enterprises without external assistance. While most groups aim to develop community services or profitable enterprises, they also perform a variety of welfare and other functions for their own members (for example, by exchanging labor or by operating rotating credit associations).

Registered women's groups have to possess an elected chairwoman, treasurer, secretary, and committee. Within this framework actual distributions of authority and organizational procedures may vary considerably. Groups also differ considerably in size and composition, both from one another and as they develop over time. The largest group in Tototo's program has sixty-three members; others have an active membership of less than ten. Men may belong to women's groups, though in the majority of cases they are excluded. Groups with more than five male members have to register as self-help, not women's, groups. In general such groups, including those formed exclusively by men, are few and far between.

Exhibit 3
THE BUSINESS TRAINING PROGRAM

Methodology

The training program developed by Tototo's business consultant in 1986 took its cue from the findings of the USAID-funded case study of Tototo groups.[1] The case study indicated that whereas the original nonformal education training and the provision of credit had helped many groups to set up enterprises, these interventions had little effect upon their subsequent performance. Most groups experienced serious problems in operating their businesses. Few of them generated significant profits and even fewer provided regular returns in the form of dividends to their members. One reason for this was that groups ran their businesses like household enterprises, with very different forms of social and economic calculation in mind. As a result they competed poorly with the demands individual members' households and household enterprises made upon their time. This placed groups in a double bind. It also ensured their continuing dependence upon external assistance and finance (more often than not provided in the form of grants), interventions that treated the symptoms of the problem rather than its cause.

The business training set out to tackle these problems head-on. Whereas many training programs aim to provide clients with skills which they are assumed to lack, Tototo's program was designed to translate their existing knowledge of household enterprises into basic practices needed to run a successful group business. It did this by making use of Tototo's existing nonformal approach. The field staff, who by this time had become excellent participatory trainers and were adept in adapting formal lessons to the level of their clients (many of them having once been group members themselves), played an important part in this process. The result was a business training program that was unusually sensitive to the needs of groups and their members: first, because it was based upon a thorough understanding of the social and economic context in which groups and their enterprises operate; and second, because it directly acknowledged group members' own understanding of this context and addressed them in terms that they could readily recognize and apply.

Performance

Table 3.1 summarizes the performance of the eight groups that were trained in 1986. The business training began to take effect in the second half of the year. Prior to this, four of the groups were operating at a loss. By mid-1988 only one of them showed a deficit, occasioned by problems in the supply of chicks for its broiler project (up to this point it had registered increasing profits).

Table 3.2 summarizes the performance of the eight groups that were trained in 1987. In this case the training began to take effect in the first half of the year when six of the groups were in a state of decline and five of them registering deficits. One of the groups closed down its business when it emerged that one of its members had been misappropriating revenue. By the middle of 1988 all of the other groups were operating at a profit.

Most of the groups trained in 1986 and 1987 performed significantly better after training than they had before. There was, however, considerable variation within this overall picture. One group also accounted for 56 percent of the revenue generated by the 1986-trained groups in the first half of 1988. Another group, Mazingira, accounted for a mere 2 percent of the same figure. A number of similar low-potential groups were included by Tototo staff in the 1987 training program, though the business consultant had recommended that only groups with a significant potential for business growth be selected for training. A third batch of groups, chosen for training in 1988, did in fact meet this criterion.

To date the business training has largely been applied within the existing rural development program with its forty groups and different components. This specific use has resulted in a number of conflicts of interest. One of the groups trained in 1987—potentially the most profitable—fared disastrously when Tototo staff applied one of the principles of leadership training and intervened to reduce the power of its chairwoman (who had been managing the group's several businesses single-handed). In other cases the revolving loan fund has not been used as well as it might in conjunction with the training program. One donor provided a series of capital grants for group projects which cut right across the linkage between the revolving loan fund and business training. Staff have experienced difficulty in coping with their workload and in coordinating different sub-program requirements. While these might be described as teething problems, there are some indications that they will not disappear overnight, all the more so given that some of Tototo's financial donors have continued to sponsor interventions that conflict with the purpose of the business training program.

[1] The Ford Foundation funded a second phase of "action research" between 1986 and 1988 which allowed further elaboration of the case study findings and their direct application to questions raised during the development of the business training program.

Exhibit 3 (cont'd)

Table 3.1
GROUPS TRAINED IN 1986 [a]
(six-month periods)

		Jan.–June 1986	July–Dec. 1986	Jan.–June 1987	July–Dec. 1987	Jan.–June 1988
Total	REV [a]	143,200	158,000	321,300	337,900	358,100
for Eight	NCF	20,400	36,400	75,200	71,500	65,400
Groups	DIV	1,300	10,500	31,100	25,900	26,800

[a] *Key to the IES:*
REV = revenue
NCF = net cash flow (revenue minus expenses)
DIV = total dividend distribution to group members
n.a. = figure not available.
Figures are given in Kenyan shillings (rounded off to the nearest 100 shillings).
Over the period shown exchange rates varied between 16 and 17 Kenyan shillings
to 1 U.S. dollar.

Table 3.2
GROUPS TRAINED IN 1987
(six-month periods)

		Jan.–June 1986	July–Dec. 1986	Jan.–June 1987	July–Dec. 1987	Jan.–June 1988
Total	REV	n.a.	226,600	155,800	131,800	194,900
for Eight	NCF	n.a.	25,200	12,500	20,800	30,700
Groups	DIV	n.a.	n.a.	4,800	4,700	8,500

Note: See Table 3.1 for key.

Exhibit 4
THE "PARTNERSHIP IN DEVELOPMENT" WORKSHOP FIELD VISITS

Participants in the July 1988 workshop were given information packages introducing them to the six field visits that Tototo staff had planned. The following are edited versions of the descriptions included in this package:

Mamba
Integrating Community Welfare and Income-Generating Projects
Mamba Women's Group is based in a small trading center south of the Shimba hills. The group was formed in 1980 and has twenty-five members, many of them recent settlers in the area.

In the early years of its program, Tototo encouraged an integrated approach to development. Mamba, located in one of the most productive agricultural regions, was one of a number of groups that chose community welfare as its first priority. Assistance from CEDPA and UNICEF (mediated by Tototo) has helped the women move a long way toward their goal of improving health care in the community. Four group members were trained in mother/child health care, nutrition, and family planning, and organized monthly clinics in the village to promote this knowledge. Medicines were donated to the group and a small grant bought them a hand-operated grinding mill to be used in the preparation of weaning foods.

The women's devotion to this project was demonstrated when they pressed the Ministry of Health to be included on a schedule of mobile clinic visits so that village children could be immunized. After some resistance on the part of the Ministry, their wish was granted. In addition the group's coordinator was employed as a full-time mother/child health promoter in the village. Not all their aspirations have been satisfied, however, and the group has been unable to secure Ministry support for their plans to build a permanent health clinic in Mamba. In response the group began a small bakery enterprise, hoping that they could use the income generated by this to finance their project. To help establish the bakery Mamba received grants from The Pathfinder Fund and the Department of Social Services.

This development has led to a modification in Tototo's own priorities in dealing with the group. The introduction of a business training program has seen Tototo move away from an integrated approach. In line with this program, Tototo has generally encouraged groups to keep their business and community welfare interests separate. This policy was introduced because their integration can sometimes impose severe constraints upon the success of group enterprises. In this respect the situation at Mamba poses a problem to Tototo. What do you think Tototo should do about it, if anything?

Mazingira
The Challenge of Development in a Difficult Environment
Mazingira Group is located 8 km north of the Nairobi-Mombasa highway in the heart of the semiarid Taru desert. The group was formed in 1983 and has twenty-five members, six of them men.

The Taru desert presents a difficult environment to live and work in. Rainfall is scarce and many farmers move seasonally to the Taita area in order to cultivate crops. Women have to walk long distances through the bush to collect water, mindful of the threat from wild animals as they do so. The village—a collection of widely scattered homesteads—is remote from markets and lacks any obvious kind of infrastructure. Not surprisingly, many young people leave the area in search of better opportunities elsewhere. As a result, the group is primarily composed of older women. Most of them are nonliterate and the group has experienced considerable difficulty in finding a secretary and coordinator. Since the group was formed it has experimented with a variety of projects, most of which have met with little success.

Many of the groups that Tototo works with are in situations analogous to that of Mazingira. With few resources at their disposal, they have provided a constant challenge to Tototo's program. The problem is not merely one of devising interventions appropriate to a difficult environment, but also one of revising program expectations to take account of the local context. As Tototo has learned, development in a place like Mazingira has to be measured in a manner different from that in more favored locations.

The development of Mazingira's goat trading enterprise provides a good example of this. Measured on a balance sheet side by side with the accounts of group like Lukundo, it shows little to impress. Assessed in context, however, Mazingira's response to Tototo's training is no less significant. A simple fact like the participation of women on the long goat buying trips speaks volumes that the figures in an account book cannot. To a casual observer, the long-term commitment of women to marginally profitable (and often loss-making) groups can seem a puzzle. Long experience in the field has provided Tototo with a different perspective and a sensitivity to local context that donor agencies and PVOs promoting technical interventions often lack.

Mkwiro
Women Operating an Enterprise in a Traditionally Male Domain

Mkwiro Women's Group is located in a fishing village on an island off the south coast. The group was formed in 1979 and has sixty-three members, all of them women.

Mkwiro began as one of the many groups selling handicrafts to the Tototo shop. Their first project was to construct a multipurpose house in the village. Work on this project came to a standstill when the plot on which they were building was claimed by another villager. Advised by Tototo to choose a different project, the women faced a difficult decision. Some of them wanted to purchase a boat and operate a ferry service to the mainland, arguing that this would make it much easier for them to take their children to the clinic there. Others proposed that they should construct a water cistern to ease the village's water problems and reduce the expense and labor involved in having to buy and carry water brought from the mainland. The supporters of this project also argued that running a boat lay too far outside their experience: to operate and maintain the ferry enterprise they would be heavily dependent upon men. The sea was a man's domain, not woman's.

In the event, supporters of the water project were outnumbered and the ferry was chosen. Helped by a grant from MATCH International, the group bought a boat and an engine and their ferry service went into operation in late 1983. Almost immediately the enterprise began running into problems of the kind that some group members had predicted. A local man was employed to pilot the boat, purchase petrol, and supervise its maintenance. Income from the boat was divided every day into four equal portions following the practice of local fishermen: one portion for the pilot, one for purchasing petrol, one for the boat's maintenance, and one for the group itself. As a result the pilot was paid much more than if he had been a salaried employee, and the women effectively exploited their own labor by paying themselves a minimal sum for their turns working as the boat's conductor. The group's accounts were also thrown into disarray by this practice: only budgeted and not actual expenses were entered into their books.

Faced with a host of other problems, Mkwiro was not faring very well when Tototo introduced its business training program in 1987. The group's accounting system was relatively easy to remodel, but Tototo staff were unable to persuade the women to pay their pilot a monthly wage instead of a fixed proportion of boat revenue. The practice of dividing income into equal portions was too deeply rooted in the local economy. The result was a compromise between traditional practice and Tototo's advice. With a portion allotted to group dividends the women are now benefiting from their enterprise to an extent that they had previously not. At the same time business performance has improved considerably and the group has now revived its original building project.

Lukundo
Successful Group Enterprise and Business Training "The Tototo Way"

Lukundo Women's Group is located in a village on the southern slopes of Taita Hills. The group was formed in 1983 and now has forty-four members, all of them women.

Lukundo is, in conventional economic terms, the most successful group that Tototo assists. There are many reasons for this. The Taita Hills are one of the most fertile and developed areas in the whole of the Coast province. Cash crop production is well established and educational and literacy levels are comparatively high. When the women of Lukundo decided to invest in a maize grinding mill they made a particularly wise choice given the high level of maize production in the village area and the existing lack of such a service there. Once the machine had been purchased (with the help of a grant from MATCH) and installed they lost no time in organizing themselves into a duty roster to supervise its daily operations. For these and other reasons their maize milling enterprise got off to a very good start.

Starting a business, however, is one thing; maintaining and expanding it is another. This is a lesson that Tototo had learned from past experience with other groups and that helped prompt the decision to introduce a new business training program. Lukundo was one of the first groups to receive business training "The Tototo Way" when it was introduced in 1986. Indeed, and despite its good start, it was clear that Lukundo's enterprise was heading for difficulties. One of these stemmed from the fact that the women were declaring the monthly dividends in excess of their earnings. In effect they were decapitalizing their business: all the more serious a situation in view of the fact that they were about to start a second enterprise—a retail shop. In the absence of regular financial reports none of the group members had recognized this fact. Tototo's timely solution was to introduce their new system of pictorial financial statements and encourage the adoption of a new dividend policy. As a result of these other measures Lukundo's imminent difficulties dissolved. Their new shop was opened and the two enterprises now thrive side-by-side. The women now receive higher dividends than ever, making their temporary sacrifice when the business training was introduced more than worthwhile.

Ngamani
Promoting Individual Enterprise in a Group Context

Ngamani Women's Group is located in a village on the west mainland of Mombasa. The group was founded in 1975 and has thirty members, all women.

One of the observations made during the case study research of Tototo-assisted groups was the fact that women group members owe primary allegiance to the different households to which they belong. Households operate their own enterprises and have their own structures of control and decision making. Women's investment in group enterprises is very much conditioned by this fact and groups often suffer from the competing demands that households place upon their member's time, labor, and cash. This observation might be taken as a good reason for designing assistance strategies that promote individual enterprise: the constraints that operate upon group businesses are circumvented and the benefit to individuals and their household is more direct. It might be interpreted as an argument in favor of withdrawing assistance to group enterprises altogether.

The experience of Ngamani helps set these arguments in their proper context. Ngamani's main enterprise, poultry raising, has witnessed many ups and downs over the years. When group members started their own individual poultry projects with assistance from CEDPA and the NCCK, the women demonstrated an ability to run successful enterprises that had never been evident in their efforts as a group. At the same time their newly found commitment to these home-based projects was such that the group enterprise became even more run-down than ever, and was clearly on the verge of collapse.

Its sorry state, however, does not offer unqualified support for the argument to withdraw assistance. There are two main reasons for this. First, the individual projects did not develop in a vacuum. The group, effective or not as collective entrepreneur, was the means through which external assistance was channeled to the individual members. It functioned as a locus for training and provided the women with experience of a particular business that they subsequently transferred to their households. The group continues to play an important role in marketing individual members' produce.

Second, the development of individual business did not render the group enterprise beyond repair. Its potential viability was demonstrated when Tototo included the group in its new business training program. The group's broiler project has since performed much better than ever before. One result is that group members have begun to receive dividends from their enterprise, which they had not received in the past. If a group business can be developed to a level where it provides regular income distributions to its members, then it can draw labor commitments from them that they would otherwise give only to their households. In this way Ngamani has shown that both individual and group businesses can be developed side by side.

Mkoyo
Promoting Individual Savings and Credit in a Group Context

Mkoyo Women's Group is located in a village on the South Coast. The group was formed in 1977 and currently has forty-eight members.

Tototo has worked with Mkoyo since the start of its rural development program in 1978. Over the years Mkoyo has shown little income generation potential as a group. Its major projects, a nursery school and the construction of a house to rent out to local school teachers, indicate rather the importance of community concerns. The women's comparatively weak record in collective enterprise has, needless to say, a simple explanation. Living close to the coastal highway and easy access to markets, many of the group members are engaged in petty trading of different kinds. The women are not bereft of individual sources of income and have been happy to treat the group as a focus for social interaction and community welfare efforts rather than as a profit-making body.

This situation also provides part of the explanation for the phenomenal success of Mkoyo's savings club, which has deposited over 50,000 Ksh on behalf of its seventy-six members (ten of them men). This is more than any of the other fifty savings clubs in Tototo's programs—including many that have been in operation much longer.

The savings club scheme has been one of Tototo's most successful interventions. Its introduction from Zimbabwe and adaption by Tototo provides a model of partnership at different levels. The popularity of the clubs, whose membership is open to the wider community, arises from the fact they open up banking to many people who would not otherwise be able to afford a minimum deposit of 500 Ksh.

Tototo's experience with the clubs, and in particular with Mkoyo, has led Tototo to explore the possibility of a further innovation and one with potentially wide-reaching effects. The idea is deceptively simple: to use saving club deposits as collateral for bank loans to individual members. In this way the women of Mkoyo will be able to expand their individual enterprises and as a group will provide a valuable financial service to the community which otherwise it would have lacked.

Exhibit 5
BIOGRAPHICAL INFORMATION
ABOUT THE BUSINESS CONSULTANT

Kevin Kane

Mr. Kane has been involved with aspects of small business development since the 1960s when he promoted agricultural cooperatives in the southern United States. He applied business management skills to a plantation acquisition scheme in Papua New Guinea and set up a small enterprise funding system in Tonga as part of a national level rural development scheme. In the Caribbean Kevin worked for the OAS as a Regional Employment Promotion Specialist developing vocational skills training modules and managing a loan scheme that assisted trainees to set up small businesses. He has done extensive consulting for World Education, both with Tototo and the Rural Enterprise Program in Nairobi. Kevin lives currently in Nairobi where he is the Chief Technical Advisor for the ILO-funded Skills Development for Self Reliance Program. He holds a Masters in Public and International Affairs from the University of Pittsburgh and an M.B.A. from Clark University Graduate School of Management.

The UNO Project:
Learning from Feedback

This case was written by Jeffrey Ashe and Marjorie Lilly. It is intended as a basis for class discussion rather than as an illustration of either effective or ineffective handling of an administrative situation. The collaboration and support of the Executive Director of ACCION and his staff are gratefully acknowledged.

At the ACCION International/AITEC administrative offices in Cambridge, Massachusetts, Jeffrey Ashe, ACCION's Senior Associate Director, had just finished reading Judith Tendler's evaluation of the UNO microenterprise project in Brazil.[1] He swung his feet up on his desk amid the usual clutter of books and reports. The ten-year-old UNO project (Northeastern Union of Assistance to Small Businesses), initiated by ACCION, had been considered by most to be a model of success, but the report he held in his hands challenged many assumptions about the project.

The next day he was going to discuss his thoughts on the report with the other senior ACCION staff. The UNO project was still the basic model for ACCION's micro-enterprise projects throughout Latin America, even though the organization had not been directly involved with UNO since about 1978. He had to decide how seriously to take Tendler's criticisms, and what they might mean for ACCION's future policies.

Tendler's report actually reinforced some of Jeff's own concerns about cost and efficiency in micro-enterprise programs. As director of USAID's PISCES Project for Micro-enterprises (the forerunner of ARIES), he had been studying and implementing innovative techniques for addressing these concerns for several years. He had believed there was a need to educate and convince ACCION staff that its model needed some real changes beyond the usual tinkering that goes on in a project.

But Jeff's first reaction had been that much of what Tendler had said was overstated, although he recognized that it was part of an exceptionally well-executed and incisive analysis of the program. Most other evaluators had been dazzled by UNO's groundbreaking success in reaching the micro-enterprise sector and by its over 95 percent payback rates. They had hardly reached Tendler's conclusion that "[UNO's] style of operating does not seem worth copying because of the high costs per loan, the low productivity, and the insignificant portion of the target group reached." Jeff had to admit that Tendler's bold articulation of UNO's shortcomings unsettled some of his notions about what a micro-enterprise program ought to do and catalyzed his thinking into new directions.

Background: Description of UNO

UNO was established with the help of ACCION's staff person, Bruce Tippett, in 1972 in Recife, one of the poorest cities in Brazil, in the state of Pernambuco in the Northeast. ACCION had made the organizational decision to work with the micro-enterprise sector, because after about ten years' work in community development in Latin America it came to the conclusion that what the urban poor wanted most was help for their businesses.

In 1972 no one was working to a significant extent with micro-businesses, at least not in Latin America. In fact, UNO coined the word "micro-enterprise" to differentiate what it was doing—working with the tiny self-employment initiatives of the poor—from traditional small business projects. These traditional small business projects reached modern businesses with ten or more employees, well-established bookkeeping systems, and an established track record with banks. UNO was a pioneering effort because it proved to the development community, first of all, that micro-businesses could be reached and, secondly, that they could be trusted to pay back their loans.

The project was very cautious and single-minded in its approach, especially during its first six years. UNO limited itself for the most part to only two activities—lending to individual firms and training. It kept itself small, and took considerable pride in the fact that it maintained a "streamlined" administration with a small budget. Loan disbursal was actually carried out by the state development bank BANDEPE, which also provided some of the funding for the loans. Full-time staff salaries were low, and the part-time university students worked for only half the salary rate of the staff. People wanted to work for UNO because they thought the work was worthwhile.

UNO resisted the temptation of "upward drift" that is so common in this type of program—of extending credit to somewhat larger businesses—even though the interest charges on larger loans would have helped capitalize the project. UNO continued to focus on the unattended micro-business sector as they defined it: businesses whose owners have a maximum family income of U.S.$9,000 per year and who have no more than five employees in the case of commerces and services, and no more than ten employees in the case of industries. In reality most of the businesses UNO reached were much smaller; 73 percent of the clients had a family income of less than U.S.$3,240 per year and employees were usually family members.

UNO loaned predominately to retail businesses because lending to businesses that sold things was considered less risky than lending for manufacturing. Seventy-five percent of its loans went for short-term working capital rather than more risky long-term loans for fixed assets. Another important part of the methodology was that UNO kept its interest rates at 25 percent, through subsidies, even when rocketing inflation made that equivalent to negative 80 percent interest rate in real terms.

The retail stores that UNO assisted were mostly small grocery or hardware stores, with a fixed location. The grocery stores were often so small that they might perhaps sell one cigarette to a customer, a quarter of a cabbage, or two tablespoons of cooking oil. Most of the micro-industries made furniture, shoes, or iron grillwork. The service businesses were involved in auto mechanics, electrical repair, and photography. The UNO studies showed there were about 40,000 micro-enterprises in Recife, mostly in the newly settled poorer outskirts. Almost all of the owners were making more than the minimum monthly wage of U.S.$54; many were doing a lot better than that.

Problems with the Loan Process

Although UNO had made a lot of breakthroughs, there were still many problems with its credit disbursal system. The selection methodology was based on manuals sent by the U.S. Small Business Administration and involved four steps, each requiring a separate visit by the university student/worker:

1. a "census" to determine the number and characteristics of micro-businesses in a given neighborhood, as a learning experience for the program and as a means of making contact with possible clients;

2. a "selection" visit to the individual firm to see if it met UNO's criteria as to business size and to see if the owner was interested in receiving credit;

3. a "diagnosis," or financial analysis of a firm; and

4. an "account-building process" for the credit application.

Although the information collected in each visit overlapped to a certain extent with the previous one, the interviewer was required to "start from scratch" each time because of the triple digit inflation during this period. UNO completed loan proposals for 28 percent of the firms it initially identified; half dropped out after the "selection" visit, and 20 percent more left after the "diagnosis." Some prospective clients dropped out along the way because of business failure, and many more left because they grew exasperated by the complexity and repetitiveness of this whole process. Some more clients also dropped out between the last step and receipt of the loan because a certain piece of equipment they had wanted to purchase grew too expensive as a result of inflation or was no longer needed.

Because of the lack of vehicles, and inadequacy of public transportation, the student workers rarely met with more than one client during their half-day shifts. But the account-building stage was the most time-consuming. This process, which took one full working day, involved the construction of a complete set of accounts for the purpose of the loan application for the bank. It was not intended to teach the business owner how to keep accounts. Few of the micro-businesses kept any kind of records, and business and household accounts were often inextricably combined. In addition, there was a degree of exaggeration or underestimation on the part of loan applicants when they believed it was in their interest. Student workers became adept at getting at difficult data using various proxies, and at discovering inconsistencies resulting from client misrepresentations.

While the application was made out mainly to satisfy the banks, it also helped UNO calculate the amount of the loan. In many cases the loan was adjusted downward as the result of the account building. UNO almost never disqualified a client as a result of this process; it was usually other factors such as borrower loss of interest or inability to find a co-signer that caused people to drop out before getting a loan.[2] The complexity of this four-stage process and the delays caused by the banks that granted the loans meant that only about 200 loans were disbursed each year. The entire process from selection to issuing the checks took from a few weeks to six months, with an average of 100 days. So many clients were withdrawing that the situation finally reached a low point in 1978, when only half the credit proposals actually resulted in loans.

A Turning Point in the Program

In 1978 there were major changes in the program due to a number of factors, not least of which was that the World Bank developed great interest in UNO—partly because of UNO's growing reputation in the development community and partly because of World Bank President Robert MacNamara's big push to "reach the poorest." The project was funded for expansion to Caruaru, another city in the state of Pernambuco, and the central office was broken up into several branch offices, making it easier for promoters to visit the businesses. In 1980 an agreement was reached with the banks that required that credit be granted within 10 days of the loan application, as compared to an average of 100 days previously. About this time also the last three stages of the process for granting loans—selection, diagnosis, and account building—were collapsed into one visit.

Breaking these procedural bottlenecks made the program much more efficient. Unit costs dropped from an average in the 1974–79 period of U.S.$1,700 (or 82 percent of the loan value) to U.S.$733, or 46 percent of the loan, in 1981. As a result of both the increased funding and the streamlining of procedures, the number of loans given out each year more than doubled. The average loan size also went down a bit, from U.S.$2,000 in the early period to U.S.$1,604 in 1981.

The Presentation to the Staff

The day came for Jeff to discuss the Tendler report with the other directors—William Burrus, the Executive Director of ACCION, and Stephen Gross, another Associate Director visiting from the micro-enterprise project in the Dominican Republic.

> I've just finished reading Judith Tendler's evaluation of the UNO project, and there's a lot in it that has important implications for us. She's made some strong criticisms of some of the fundamental principles of UNO, despite many of the changes we have made since 1978.
>
> Perhaps her most important criticism is that program costs could still be greatly reduced. She thinks the program should be self-sufficient and compares UNO to banks that extend credit for a few cents on the dollar. The basic problem is low staff productivity, with only twenty-four loans being processed annually per staff member.
>
> Her second major criticism is that the number of clients reached should be greatly expanded. UNO only reached a negligible 0.3 percent of Recife's micro-business sector in 1981. She thinks UNO should be reaching poorer business owners, including a larger number of women entrepreneurs, who now make up only 15 percent of the program's clients.
>
> Her third major criticism is that UNO is not living up to its claims in regard to job creation, and feels that far fewer jobs are being created than UNO claims.
>
> Her fourth criticism is that the business training classes, which eat up 30 percent of the budget, should be eliminated, because they are seen as largely irrelevant to the business owners.

"On top of all this," Jeff added, "Tendler says that the UNO model is possibly not such a useful model in the first place. She recognized that

UNO was a pioneering project and that it has grown a great deal since the early days, but feels that the original model is outmoded."

Time and Money

William Burrus said to Jeff, "I'd be interested to know what Judith has to say about low staff productivity. What factor does she blame the most?"
Jeff responded:

> Well, one of the main areas she focuses on is what she calls the program's "extravagant" use of time, due to lack of vehicles and the requirement for repeated site visits, for example. The purpose of visits include the program's elaborate system of account building for proving credit-worthiness, which Tendler thinks has little intrinsic value either to the client or to the program. Account building does not play a major role in UNO's selection or rejection of clients, and the bank doesn't use it to make decisions, depending rather on UNO's judgment in almost all cases. She calls account-building "ritualistic," adding that "... because it looks like something that a respectable business would present in support of a credit application, it legitimates the applicant in the eyes of the bank."
>
> She also thinks the use of student workers, who carry out the account-building process, results in wastage and low productivity even though UNO felt that their low salary rate was one of the ways program costs were kept down. UNO also thought the learning experience the students were getting as a future generation of development workers was important. But Judith felt that their lack of business expertise cancelled out the benefits due to their cheap labor.

"What did the clients think of the students?" asked Stephen Gross.

> She says that the micro-business owners liked the students but that as often as not they received their advice somewhat skeptically, feeling that they had more experience than the students. Tendler thought the students' advice tended to be "formulaic" and almost always the same, boiling down to the same three recommendations to:
>
> 1. keep records;
> 2. diversify inventory; and
> 3. improve the appearance or cleanliness of the store.

"What about the training they got in the business courses UNO offered? Did the clients feel they got more professional instruction there?" asked Steve.

> Well, Tendler found that most of the clients who attended said they "could not put anything they learned into practice." One reason

for this is that the teaching lumped together information for all kinds of firms—retail, services, and manufacturing—and consequently was too general. Instruction on bookkeeping was often disregarded by clients because they were used to keeping accounts in their heads and found that adequate. Tendler sees UNO's training component as very expensive and as serving little purpose for the micro-entrepreneur.

Bill Burrus brought up another issue: "I would almost assume from her emphasis on self-sufficiency that Judith thinks interest rates should be raised."

"Yes, that's right," Jeff replied.

"By the way, what are the current commercial interest rates in Brazil?" interrupted Bill.

The current rate is at least 130 percent, and the micro-business owners are used to paying 200 to 400 percent a year for credit from moneylenders on the streets. UNO was only charging them the highly subsidized rate of 24 percent, which in real terms amounted to a negative rate due to inflation.

Burrus asked: "Did Tendler find out what the business owners thought about interest rates?"

Yes, when Tendler interviewed the clients, she found that the interest rate is of less importance to them than the *terms* of the loans. They preferred UNO's twelve- to fifteen-month repayment period over the banks' three-month period. Getting their loans quickly also seemed to be more important to them than paying a low interest rate.

Reaching the Poorer Level of Micro-Entrepreneurs

"I'd like to know what Judith had to say about the level of client reached by the program," said Steve. "What did she learn from the research she did?"

Jeff responded:

After wading though a welter of statistics about the poor in the areas where UNO works, she came to the conclusion that UNO business owners are "not only better off than most informal-sector workers, but also earn more than many formal-sector employees." For example, while the earnings of 51 percent of UNO clients were equivalent to more than two minimum wages before the loan, only 16 percent of the economically active population in metropolitan Recife fell into this category in 1979. Moreover, she noted that only 15 percent of UNO firms are headed by women, who generally make up the majority of poorer business owners.

Steve asked, "Did Judith give any examples of programs that have reached a higher percentage of women?"

> Yes, as a matter of fact, she mentions one program whose clients were 86 percent female—an urban micro-enterprise program in El Salvador that was described in the 1981 PISCES study.[3] She says that UNO lends predominantly to the retail sector, where only 22 percent of the firms are female-headed. In another section Judith suggests that UNO lend to more manufacturing and service firms because these sectors are more likely to produce new jobs. However, she did not hold out hope for the expansion of firms in any sector, because of the nature of micro-enterprises as she saw them.

"What did she say about job creation in general?" Steve asked. "You said she challenged UNO on this point." Jeff replied:

> Yes, she describes an ACCION ad in *Businessweek* in 1981, for example, as stressing that UNO created "3,000 new jobs" at the cost of $965 of credit per job. Although she does not have "robust statistical proof," she found from her own interviews with clients one or two years after loan disbursal that, of the jobs created by UNO, most were only temporary. In fact, another sample survey found that jobs had *decreased* by 5 percent. On the other hand, as Tendler points out in a footnote, statistics show that a matched sample from a non-UNO-assisted group showed a substantially greater decrease in employment [37 percent]. What UNO probably accomplished was the shoring up of many jobs that would probably have failed due to economic hard times if they hadn't been assisted by UNO.[4]

Further Considerations

The time had now come for Jeff to state his own judgments on Judith Tendler's criticisms and recommendations and what they meant for UNO and for ACCION's policy in general. In preparation, he had considered a wide range of questions. He noted that many of Tendler's suggestions paralleled the findings of the PISCES studies[5] and were actually already part of ACCION projects in the Dominican Republic and Colombia, but was it entirely clear yet that these policies worked? Was training superfluous in a micro-business program, or did it, as some argued, have a more lasting effect than the loan did? And what about the vast sector of street hawkers and vendors? Was it feasible to lend to them? How could the program lend to greater numbers? Would small loans to the poorest really result in increased income and job creation on a long-term basis or were the jobs created by such a strategy only ephemeral? Would the increased interest rates Tendler recommended be accepted by the clients, or would they discourage growth of the businesses? Could the student workers be abandoned in an effort to increase productivity? Jeff looked briefly over his notes and began his presentation of the implications of the Tendler report for UNO and for ACCION's methodology.

Notes

1. *Ventures in the Informal Sector, and How They Worked Out in Brazil*, AID Evaluation Special Study No. 12, March 1983, Office of Private and Voluntary Cooperation, U.S. Agency for International Development (AID Contract No. PDC-0100-S-00-2019-00).

2. The co-signer is usually a friend or relative of the borrower from the same neighborhood, not necessarily someone with greater assets than the borrower.

3. *The PISCES Studies: Assisting the Smallest Economic Activities of the Urban Poor*, edited by Michael Farbman, Office of Urban Development, U.S. Agency for International Development, September 1981.

4. *Ibid.*

5. *The PISCES Experience: Case Studies from Dominican Republic, Costa Rica, Kenya and Egypt*, Vol. II, U.S. Agency for International Development, December 1985.

Exhibit 1
EXCERPTS FROM JUDITH TENDLER'S REPORT ON UNO

Strengths and Weaknesses

I close this section [Introduction] with a list of UNO's most salient strengths and weaknesses, leaving the discussion of them for later. The achievements are the following:

1. UNO succeeded in reaching businesses that, in most part, would have had no access to institutional credit. Given the attraction of the highly subsidized interest rate to better-off borrowers, this is a significant achievement.

2. UNO attracted and built a staff that is highly dedicated to the organization's goals of getting credit to poor firms, and is highly sympathetic to the needs and problems of its client group.

3. UNO succeeded in becoming independent of its creator, AITEC, at a relatively early stage. The technical assistance relationship was ended only three years after UNO's creation, and AITEC funding terminated five years after creation, never having represented more than 3 percent of UNO funding in anything but the first year (when it was 19 percent). UNO entered its second decade of existence, moreover, with large, unprecedented increases in its public-sector funding.

4. UNO has earned an excellent reputation as a dedicated, competent organization from persons in both the private and public sectors.

5. Though UNO is a private voluntary organization, it succeeded obtaining a substantial share of its budget from the public sector from the start (33 percent in the first year). After eight years, moreover, UNO's good work and reputation resulted in its being noticed by the World Bank and included in three of its projects, bringing a major increase in its funding from the Brazilian public sector.

6. The creation of UNO was achieved with a fairly small commitment of funds from outside donors during the first four years—U.S.$23,600 from AITEC, and a total of U.S.$290,800 from others. After that point, large government contributions took over under the World Bank projects.

7. In addition to receiving public-sector funding, UNO has succeeded in warding off the political intervention that often afflicts government programs of subsidized credit.

8. UNO is a lean organization, with overhead costs of only 10 percent, only one vehicle (unusual for an entity that does so much field work), and much less of the hierarchy and rigidity that characterizes many public-sector entities in the credit and extension field.

9. Repayment rates on UNO lending, at 92 percent to 98 percent, are remarkably high.

10. UNO succeeded in avoiding various practices that have been associated with high delinquency in similar programs. Namely, (a) UNO has lent mainly for working capital instead of for investment; (b) it has stayed away from financing new firms; (c) it has financed only modest increments to a firm's fixed investment.

Along with its strengths, UNO has the following weaknesses:

1. UNO's operating costs have been quite high as a percentage of loan value— ranging from 50 percent to more than 100 percent, though falling to 46 percent in 1981; cost per loan is also high at U.S.$733 (Cr$66,900), though it has fallen from twice that level in the last few years.

2. Productivity is low, with loans made per student worker (full-time equiva-

lent) in Recife about twenty-four per year; if supervisory staff were included in the ratio, the productivity figure would be even lower.

3. UNO's Recife program hardly grew during its first nine years of operation, and reached only 0.3 percent of Recife's microfirms in 1981 (387 loans out of 120,000 firms). Even over the whole nine-year period, the total number of firms receiving UNO loans (1,219) was only 1 percent of the client population.[1]

4. Though private banks and the state bank contributed some funding for UNO credit in the early years, the banks did not sustain their financial commitment. Commitment of the state bank was never great enough until recently to resolve overwhelming problems of delay and requirements for documents, adding to average loan costs because of the number of discouraged borrowers who gave up after UNO prepared their loan applications.

5. UNO itself rejected the private banks' participation when interest-rate ceilings were removed in 1977, even though their processing of loan applications was smooth and rapid.

6. Financial support from the private sector, expected to be a mainstay of the program, never reached more than 29 percent of funding, and diminished to nothing after the first five years.

7. UNO has never been able to generate its own income, or to be as financially independent of the public sector as it was meant to be.

8. UNO spends 30 percent of its operating budget on courses for small-firm owners, courses that are of questionable value.

9. Only a minority of UNO borrowers seem to "graduate" from UNO credit to the formal banking system; that is, the rest must be permanently dependent on UNO for credit or revert back to their previous creditless state.

10. Though UNO has established itself as a reputable organization, its style of operating does not seem worth copying because of the high costs per loan, the low productivity, and the insignificant portion of the target group reached. As evidence for this, many of the features of the "model" are changing, it seems, as UNO rapidly grows to a more significant size under the World Bank project.

The above juxtaposition of UNO's strengths and weaknesses brings us back to the quandary posed at the beginning of this introduction—many of the weaknesses seem to be inextricably bound with the strengths. Does this mean that UNO's successes at surviving and becoming a praiseworthy organization were in any way a function of its weaknesses? Did the success require that UNO be a small, insignificant organization, with high costs and low productivity? Can the weaknesses be eliminated without undermining the strengths?

Growth as Unnatural

Small firms tend to expand to the point where family management and labor are exploited to the fullest, and then stop. Almost all the firm owners I interviewed had a sad tale to tell about a partner or an employee from "outside the family" who absconded with funds, or created a problem in the business in other ways. Thus owners often talked of expansion as an imprudent move, in that it would require taking on partners and employees who were "untrustworthy" by virtue of their being from outside the family.[2] The distrust was not without good reason. A study of failure rates among small firms in Brazil found that 89 percent of the failed firms were partnerships, while sole proprietorships accounted for only 11% of the failures.[3]

Another reason that small firms distrust new employees—and therefore avoid expansion—is the complaint that as soon as a worker is well trained, he will leave the job and start his own workshop. Peattie (1982)[4] reports this complaint in the shoe industry in Colombia, and cites the case of a shop owner who stopped training workers for this reason (n.d.:8). Because of this problem, she reports, ownership of a small workshop was considered "more desirable" than of a large one.

The difficulties of expansion are also revealed in the findings that small entrepreneurs will often create new firms when they are doing well, rather than expand their existing business. Kilby reports for Kenya that the small industry sector tends to expand "by replication" rather than by growth of existing firms, because easy entry creates competition and reduces profits to low levels, leaving no cushion for innovation and mistakes (1981:48). Marris and Somerset, also reporting on Kenya, find that when a businessman has spare resources to invest, he will start another small firm rather than expand his present business "beyond the critical limit of direct supervision" (1971:125). The evaluators of a small-business project in Upper Volta found that entrepreneurs "are reluctant to have any one economic activity become too large," because of fears of risk and of jealousy from neighbors (Goldmark et al. 1982:Chart IV-1). There is considerable evidence, in sum, that the management difficulties of expanding may put growth beyond reach for many small firms.

For service and manufacturing firms, the extreme seasonality of demand represented another major constraint to expansion. Firms could not handle the demand during peak seasons, and had no work in between. They had difficulty smoothing out the demand, even with UNO financing to buy inputs earlier, because customers bunched their requests during the peak period, giving little time to complete the order. Christmas, Carnival, and St. John's Feast are the major peaks; the customary payment of an additional months's salary to workers in December makes the Christmas peak the highest. These seasonally affected firms saw expansion as difficult, since they would be left with even more excess capacity in between the peaks.

[1] The 1,219 figure is obtained by subtracting 461 repeat loans from the total number of loans, 1,680, to obtain the total number of firms lent to in Recife.

[2] Marris and Somerset commented on the same phenomenon among African businessmen in Kenya (1971:124–125). This particular constraint to the expansion of small firms was the reason that AITEC/Rio de Janerio tried to set up a venture-capital affiliate to UNO in Bahia, MICROPAR. The effort failed, for various reasons, one of them being the reluctance of firm owners to allow an outside entity to have any part of their capital.

[3] Rattner (1978) as cited in Tyler (n.d.:159). In a study of the informal sector of the norteastern city of Salvador, Cavalcanti reports that it is rare to find partnerships except in manufacturing (1981:44).

[4] Lisa Peattie, "There's no business like shoe business. What is to be done with the informal sector: Case of the shoe business in Bogota," in Helen Safa (ed.), *Towards a Political Economy of Urbanization*, New Delhi: Oxford University Press, 1982.

Source: Ventures in the Informal Sector, and How They Worked Out in Brazil. AID Evaluation Special Study No. 12, pp. 5–8, 118–121. Washington, D.C.: U.S. Agency for International Development (USAID Contract No. PDC-0100-S-00-2019-00), March 1983.

Exhibit 2
LEVELS OF ENTERPRISE

From the PISCES Studies

Level I—Marginal

At Level I people do whatever they must to subsist. They do not perceive themselves as entrepreneurs, nor do they conceive of their money-making activities as "business opportunities." Their activities lack the systematic qualities of enterprises at other levels, especially planning and scheduling. Usually, the family of a person predominantly dependent on this sector cannot meet its survival needs with the income of the one marginal business, but must receive contributions from several micro-enterprises or income earners.

Activities are often extremely ephemeral—selling chewing gum or cigarettes on a corner, or colas and candies during parades. In many cases these marginal workers, who are frequently women or children, work on a day-basis as unsalaried distributors of large corporations.

Level II—Very Small

Level II entrepreneurs have a fundamental understanding of business practices and generally have either a viable going concern, or good business opportunities. After living in an urban area for a while, they can be expected to diversify or grow in the existing businesses, or might start more substantial businesses, albeit at a low level. Typically, Level II entrepreneurs will reinvest *whatever* resources are available—be it capital, raw materials, skills, effort, time, or ingenuity—into the business once it has been started. For example, a woman in Colombia began a tortilla business by making a few extra tortillas for a neighbor who spent her days at the market and who did not have enough time to make tortillas for her family. Before long the women discovered that many women in the *barrio* were willing to pay for fresh tortillas. She employed one daughter who was old enough to make tortillas correctly and had the other daughter wash the clothes and tend the baby so she could devote more time to the income-producing activity of making tortillas. Often, as one woman in a *barrio* begins to specialize in a business, another woman's time frees up her to specialize in an activity which can add an income to her family.

Level III—Small

At Level III people have better business skills, strong entrepreneurial drive, and generally a more substantial enterprise base off which to work. They understand the basic principles affecting their markets and are flexible enough to expand when the opportunity arieses.

Source: The PISCES Studies: Assisting the Smallest Economic Activities of the Urban Poor, edited by Michael Farbman, U.S. Agency for International Development, September 1981.

Exhibit 3

UNO: LOANS, LOAN VALUE, AND EXPENDITURES, 1973–82

(1981 constant U.S.$)[a]

Year	Total Costs[b] (U.S.$1,000)	Total Loan Value (U.S.$1,000)	Number of Loans[c]	Average Loan Value (U.S.$)	Average Cost per Loan (U.S.$)	Cost as a % of Loan Value (%)
1973	154.6	127.5	32	3,985	4,830	121.2
1974	254.1	491.2	174	2,823	1,461	51.7
1975	246.1	546.9	212	2,579	1,160	45.0
1976	273.4	259.0	147	1,762	1,861	105.6
1977	225.5	307.8	150	2,052	1,503	73.3
1978	318.9	255.0	138	1,847	2,311	125.1
1979	434.2	331.9	225	1,475	1,930	130.8
1980	545.1	696.3	470	1,481	1,160	78.3
1981	735.5	1,610.7	1,004	1,604	733	45.7
1982[d]	1,216.8	3,165.4	2,070	1,530	587	38.4

Source: Ventures in the Informal Sector, and How They Worked Out in Brazil. AID Evaluation Special Study No. 12, p. 144. Washington, D.C.: U.S. Agency for International Development (USAID Contract No. PDC-0100-S-00-2019-00), March 1983.

[a] Cruzeiro values were converted to 1981 constant cruzeiros using the general price index, and then converted to dollars at the 1981 average rate of Cr$91.265 to the dollar.

[b] Represents total UNO expenditures per year.

[c] Includes both Recife and Interior programs.

[d] UNO estimate.

Exhibit 4
EXCERPT FROM A MEMO SENT BY JEFFREY ASHE TO USAID STAFF
AFTER READING A DRAFT OF THE TENDLER STUDY

ACCION INTERNATIONAL / AITEC
TO: Thomas McKay, Austin Hymen, George Beloz, Judith Tendler
FROM: Jeffrey Ashe, Senior Associate Director
DATE: July 7, 1982

As you may know, I studied Judith Tendler's report in detail and spent a delightful day speaking with Judith and George Beloz on June 29. In general, the report is excellent and will be of great benefit to the AITEC staff. The many points she raised that I don't discuss here I am in general agreement with. There are several points, however, that were not considered in the analysis. Judith will incorporate many of the observations I made into her final version of the report, but I would like to sum up my points here:

A. *High Cost and Low Productivity*

1. It is not accurate to charge all project costs to the costs of packaging loans and monitoring them—that is, taking the entire budget and dividing this by the number of loans granted. There are other costs—for training, research and evaluation, educating other institutions, scrambling for next year's budget, and simply making costly errors and learning from them—that do not relate in their entirety to loan packaging and monitoring.

A more accurate measure of productivity requires a more detailed analysis of the UNO/Recife budget.

2. It is also unfair to consider as a cost of project administration what is really a problem of the *low productivity of the banks UNO works with*. Up until 1981 about one third of the loans prepared by UNO were never granted because of bank delays and red tape. Productivity would increase by at least one third if those costs were considered.

A related problem that increases costs is the extensive documentation required by banks. Once again this does not reflect so much on the "UNO model" as on the bureaucratic requirements of the banks UNO is working with.

3. It is also likely that part of the problem of "high cost and low productivity" is not the "model," but the low volume of loans granted in the program before 1981. According to the 1982 projections, total costs will be reduced to approximately 28 percent of the value of the loans granted. This figure is much more consistent with the costs of the AITEC-assisted programs in Bogota with the Fundación Compartir and in Santo Domingo with the Fundación Dominicana de Desarrollo. In both projects administrative costs are running about 25 percent of the value of the loans granted to reach a similar clientele. Because both the Cali and the Santo Domingo programs provide considerably more technical assistance than the Recife project, the costs for the Recife project could potentially be less than the 28 percent indicated in the 1982 projections.

4. Productivity has increased dramatically in 1981, not only because of increased loan volumes, but also because of cutting down the steps required in loan packaging from four steps to one. Fine-tuning the model resulted in a great increase in productivity. It also indicates that the UNO staff is not totally unconcerned about project costs.

Part III

The *AskARIES Knowledgebase*

Charles K. Mann

Part III

Introduction to
The *AskARIES Knowledgebase*

Introduction

Conceptually, *Seeking Solutions* is a three-part work—a comprehensive information resource for enterprise development. As the subtitle of this volume indicates, this book contains two of the three parts, the framework and the cases. The few pages that follow are not Part III of *Seeking Solutions*, but a conceptual overview of the true Part III: the *AskARIES Knowledgebase*.[1] Parts I and II lend themselves to publication and distribution using traditional medium of the printed book. Part III is far more usefully published and distributed as computer software, giving the user the power of the computer to help gain access to, analyze, extract, and share information useful in seeking solutions to particular problems. The goal is to deliver a wide range of information in the form in which it is most useful, the choice of the publication medium following that objective, rather than preceding it. Indeed, to an increasing extent, the book may not be the best medium for delivering large quantities of information to relatively remote or decentralized locations. Happily, Kumarian Press has shared the vision of *Seeking Solutions* as an integrated information resource, not simply as a book. Part III has thus been published as computer software, and Parts I and II as a book. Since *AskARIES* is an integral part of the work, it seems useful to introduce it here and to place it in the context of Parts I and II.

The Basic Idea of *AskARIES*

The literature of small enterprise development is large, uneven in quality, and often difficult to obtain. Yet many lessons and insights are available merely by looking to the appropriate sources. The *AskARIES Knowledgebase* was developed to put the knowledge contained in the core literature of enterprise development in the hands of managers, practitioners, and scholars. Designed for use with the widely used IBM-PC or compatible MS-DOS computer, *AskARIES* utilizes the organizing framework identified in Part I of this book, the "recurrent problems" facing enterprise development resource institutions (RIs). These problems are organized according to the four domains of capacity outlined in Part I: strategic, technical, administrative, and communications.

At first release, *AskARIES* summarizes and analyzes approximately 475 published and unpublished documents (books, articles, and papers) and includes a bibliography of about 1,700. It includes indexed summaries of relevant teaching cases, both those of Part II of this book and ones developed by other institutions such as the Asian Institute of Management and the Cranfield School of Management.

In developing the *Knowledgebase*, the ARIES research staff reviewed relevant documents for insights on one or more of the recurrent problems of the framework. Each entry is indexed under the appropriate class of problem. The particular problem is described along with its causes and approaches toward a solution reported. In many cases, the ARIES analyst has added in a separate section an independent commentary based on his or her own experience and study of the literature. Many of the documents have entries under more than one recurrent problem; and many of those dealing with multiple projects have been given multiple entries. The first record for each publication includes a general summary of it. Taken together, all of these first records represent the familiar annotated bibliography. However, this bibliography comprises only a subset of *AskARIES'* information and function. The innovation of the system—the "knowledgebase" dimension—is the additional *structured* information contained in the recurrent problem entries for the documents. (The recurrent problem structure is shown in Table I-4, p. 71.) These second, third, "nth" entries for each document carry the user well beyond traditional bibliographic sources. The schema in Table III–1 illustrates the relationship between the bibliographic and the problem oriented aspects of *AskARIES*. Thinking of *AskARIES only* as a bibliography will obscure the usefulness of the structured knowledge it contains, and the further contributions of the ARIES analysts.

Extensions of the Basic Idea

Like users of other software, my colleagues and I have discovered that the tools themselves help to define the task. More powerful tools lead to more ambitious analysis, as recent software history shows. The first important microcomputer business program took the spreadsheet as its metaphor, yet soon carried users far beyond the limitations of the pencil and paper spreadsheet.[2] While the metaphor gave new users an easy point of entry to the software, they soon discovered many altogether new applications for the computerized spreadsheet.

The database program underlying *AskARIES* was conceived by an academic scholar as a way to facilitate organizing and managing traditional notes, annotations, and bibliography.[3] Like the early users of

Table III-1
STRUCTURE OF A TYPICAL *AskARIES* RECORD

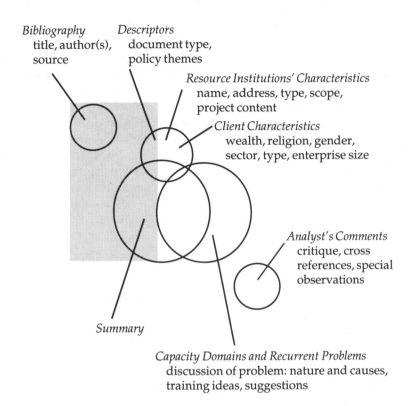

Bibliography
   title, author(s),
   source

Descriptors
   document type,
   policy themes

Resource Institutions' Characteristics
   name, address, type, scope,
   project content

Client Characteristics
   wealth, religion, gender,
   sector, type, enterprise size

Analyst's Comments
   critique, cross
   references, special
   observations

Summary

Capacity Domains and Recurrent Problems
   discussion of problem: nature and causes,
   training ideas, suggestions

Note: Shaded portion represents aspects of the *AskARIES Knowledgebase* that corresponds to information found in annotated bibliographic databases. The extensive addtional information, with its problem-solving orientation, is more in the spirit of the knowledgebase component of an expert system. The emphasis on this latter, analytical aspect makes *AskARIES* a unique resource for seeking solutions to small enterprise development problems.

spreadsheet programs, we discovered that we could push far beyond the bounds of the "notebook" metaphor. The combination of the program's large capacity for text and its ability to manipulate and cross-reference material in up to fifty "fields" (partitioned spaces) per "record" opened analytical possibilities not available with the notetaking methods the program had taken as its generational metaphor. Not only is it a system for filing and keeping track, but for content analysis.

The potential analytical capability of *AskARIES* derives from the fields containing information about characteristics of each RI itself, its clients, and the context in which it operates. This structure of the *AskARIES* combined with the power of the computer lest the user formulate and test various research hypotheses about relationships between the contents of different fields within the *Knowledgebase*. For example, it is possible to test the proposition that certain kinds of institutions serving certain kinds of clients are more likely than other institutions to have certain kinds of recurrent problems. Conversely, it is possible to examine a problem to see if there are particular circumstances associated with its occurrence.[4]

AskARIES as a Framework for Collaboration

Although designed with an analytical orientation, *AskARIES* can also be used as a normal annotated bibliography. Any field can be searched; terms can be linked by Boolean operators *and, or, not,* and so forth. Thus, one could search for all the entries having both *Africa* and *evaluation* in the relevant fields.

The framework itself as distinct from the data content of *AskARIES* can be used by institutions collaborating in enterprise development. Discussions with RI staff suggest that their own collections of useful documents often are not cataloged for lack of a good system to do so. Professional staff often cannot take the time to make the intellectual investment needed to develop such a system. Given a system, however, clerical staff can enter simple cataloging information.

Recognizing the usefulness of such a cataloging system, and the reality that budgetary and personnel constraints limit literature analysis only to a small selection from the literature, *AskARIES* has a companion bibliographic system, *ARIRef*. This list uses the same general structure as *AskARIES*, but contains only cataloging and indexing information on a far larger list of documents and A/V resources related to enterprise development. RIs can extend or tailor this listing to suit their particular needs, using it not only to reference the literature, but also to manage more effectively their own document collections. Entries can be merged with the ARIES entries or be kept as a separate file.

It seems likely that the sharing of a common knowledgebase will help to catalyze cooperative effort among those drawing from and adding to it. Both *AskARIES* and *ARIRef* offer potential for aggregating and for sharing information. If institutions catalog their own collections within this framework, they can easily transmit their entries to other institutions with similar interests that use the same system. Setting in place such mechanics for networking could help to coax into circulation the rich "fugitive" literature of the field. Relevant to this networking potential of *AskARIES* is the recent surge in interest in new computer tools for facilitating collaborative intellectual work. For example, computer science pioneer Douglas Engelbart and his colleague Harvey Lehtman write of a new type of "superdocument" used in the "coordinated handling of a very large and complex body of documentation and its associated external references ... a 'community handbook,' a uniform, complete, consistent, up-to-date integration of the special knowledge representing the current status of the community."[5] For the community of individuals who design and manage small enterprise development programs in the Third World, the *AskARIES Knowledgebase* represents an important step towards such a superdocument. Program managers, as they work on a relatively common set of problems in different organizations—such as CARE, Save the Children, Catholic Relief Services, and Grameen Bank—can use *AskARIES* to get focused information about many problems they typically face in program design and management.

Looking to the Future

Still at an early stage of development, *AskARIES* seeks to use the potential of personal computer not only to help manage existing information, but also to generate new insights into relationships among institutions, the context within which they operate, the clients they serve and the problems they face. The results will be only as good as the scope of the collection, the quality of the literature itself, the skill of the analysts, the imagination and discipline of the user. So far, *AskARIES* has served as a knowledgebase for this book, other publications, and several conferences. *AskARIES* has a broader potential to serve the community of institutions working with small enterprise in the developing countries, perhaps as the continually evolving community handbook described by Engelbart and Lehtman. It may help as a focal point for substantive discussion, investigation, and collaboration within this community.

As to the future, the cost of mass storage will continue to fall, particularly as the optical disk becomes a standard PC device. Desktop systems then will be able to contain full-text copies of key resource documents as well as the summary and problem-oriented information now in *AskARIES*. Massive storage also will make it possible to add such enriching materials as video vignettes illustrating the field experiences of various programs; recorded interviews with key resource people, charts, diagrams, and photographs. The concept of "hypertext" will make it easier to navigate within the knowledgebase, as related concepts can be linked in ways which will carry the user to any desired level of detail.

In organizing knowledge more usefully, expert systems seem likely to play a growing role in the technology transfer process. These are systems of rules ("if ... then ... ") operating on a knowledgebase by means of a so-called "inference engine." *AskARIES* represents a rudimentary knowledgebase. It has neither rules nor an inference engine. However, simply posing the question "Could it have rules?" has provoked useful insights. In effect, this represents simply another way of asking the familiar question: "What are the lessons learned?". The tools and techniques of expert systems allow greater sophistication in searching for such lessons. The lessons themselves can reflect a richer range of experience, can be drawn with finer variations, subtleness, and sensitivity to circumstance. The lack of tools to handle wide variations encourages the search for simple solutions, easily understood, universally applicable. With the tools to organize and make sense of a far richer knowledgebase, it should be possible to tailor programs better to fit the diversity of enterprise development institutions, objectives, clients, and contexts. Thus, rather than bringing the greater sameness and rigidity so often feared in the computer, an expert systems approach could facilitate greater and more effective diversity in program design and evaluation; could represent another important resource for seeking solutions to enterprise development problems.

Looking ahead in the context of *Seeking Solutions*, the Framework of Part I promises to remain relatively stable. The generic categories of problems seem unlikely to change profoundly, although the emphasis will shift with changing circumstances and new knowledge. The cases soon to flow from research within the PVO community, facilitated by the ARIES case workshops, promise to enrich and supplement the Cases of Part II, illuminating a broader spectrum of approaches and problems. The domain of Part III of this work will be the locus of the most profound change, as technological advances continue to expand the definition of what is desirable and feasible in an information resource. In this respect, *Seeking Solutions* with its *AskARIES* component represents only a start towards such a resource. The future holds still more powerful tools for those seeking to assist the poor through enterprise development.

Notes

1. *AskARIES* is a trademark belonging to the President and Fellows of Harvard College.

2. *VisiCalc,* developed originally by Dan Bricklin who, as a student at the Harvard Business School, wanted a "magic spreadsheet" to do "what if" analysis of financial statements. Robert Frankston, now Chief Scientist at Lotus Development Corporation, co-authored the program.

3. The program underlying *AskARIES* on first release is *Notebook II,* "the database manager for unlimited text," developed by Dean Paul Brest of the Stanford University Law School. It includes a supplemental program, *Bibliography,* for research or writing (*Notebook II* and *Bibliography* are trademarks of Pro/Tem Software Inc.). The latter program recognizes "keywords" entered into *Notebook II* files, as in *AskARIES* or *ARIRef,* its bibliographic files. When writing a paper or report, an author can include in the text these keyword references, enclosed in parentheses: (Harper: 1980). The word-processed file subsequently can be run though the *Bibliography* program, which will search *AskARIES* and/or *ARIRef* for these keywords. Triggered by these keywords, *Bibliography* will then print out at the end of the paper the full bibliographic references, in alphabetical order, in the format selected by the author. *Notebook II* also includes *Convert,* a utility program to enable the user to import information from on-line bibliographic databases, such as the one published by Commonwealth Agricultural Bureaux.

4. In exploring these new possibilities, the GIGO rule of computers must be noted carefully: garbage in, garbage out. A finding that a majority of type X institutions have type Y problems may be a function of only a few atypical type X institutions being referenced in the summarized literature; it may be that analyst M specialized in type Y recurrent problems; it may be that most type W institutions also had type X problems, but none was entered into *AskARIES*; it may be even that the literature is reflected accurately but itself contains incorrect information. While there is potential for the GIGO effect in using such a powerful computer-based tool, there also is the potential that it can generate new insights.

5. "Working Together," (*BYTE,* December 1988:245–252).

Glossary

ACCION	"action" in Spanish; a U.S.-based PVO
ACORDE	Association for Costa Rican Development Organizations
ADEMI	Association for the Development of Micro-Enterprises, Inc.; Dominican Republic
ADEPE	Asociación para el Desarrollo del Pequeño Empresario
AID	U.S. Agency for International Development
AITEC	ACCION International Technica; United States
ALOZ	Adult Literacy Organization of Zimbabwe
APTAMAI	Association of Small Industrial Maintenance Workshop Owners; Costa Rica
ARIES	Assistance to Resource Institutions for Enterprise Support
BANDEPE	Development Bank of the State Pernambuco
BB	Bangladesh Bank
BKB	Bangladesh Krishi Bank (National Agricultural Bank)
BKK	Badan Kredit Kecamatan; Indonesia
BPI	Bank of the Philippines Islands (Agribank)
BRAC	Bangladesh Rural Advancement Committee
BW	bankworker [Grameen Bank Case]
CANAMECC	Chamber of Collective Communications Media; Costa Rica
CANAPI	National Chamber of Arts and Small Industry; Costa Rica
CANARA	Chamber of Radio; Costa Rica
CARE	Cooperative American Relief Everywhere; U.S.-based PVO
CARITAS	[BRAC Case]
CBIRD	Community-Based Integrated Rural Development Strategy [Save the Children Case]
CC	Centre Chief [Grameen Bank Case]
CDC	Control Data Corporation; U.S.-based corporation
CEBRAE	Center for Assistance to Small and Medium Enterprises; Brazil
CEDP	Community and Enterprise Development Project [Senegal Case]
CEDPA	Center for Development of Population Activities
CEOSS	Coptic Evangelical Organization for Social Services; Egypt
CIDES	Cooperativa Multiactiva de Desarrollo Social; Columbia
CINDE	Costa Rican Coalition of Development Initiatives
CJEDP	Central Java Enterprise Development Project; Indonesia
CNPAR	Centre National de Perfectionnement des Artisans Rurax; Upper Volta
COSEP	Consejo Superior de la Empresa Privada; Nicaragua
CUP	University School of Puntarenas; Costa Rica

DDF   Dominican Development Foundation
DESAP   Program for Development of Small Business; Columbia
EDSA   E. de los Santos Avenue; Philippines
FEDECCREDIT   Federation of Credit Agencies; El Salvador
FES   Fundaciòn para la Educaciòn Superior; Foundation for Higher Education; Columbia
FOD   Field Operations Division [IIRR Case]
FOR   Field Operational Research [IIRR Case]
FPAC   Family Planning Association of Kenya
FPC   Field Program Committee [IIRR Case]
FSDC   Farm Systems Development Corporation; Philippines
FUCODES   Fundacion Costarricense de Desarrollo; Costa Rican Development Foundation
FUNDESIRE   regional development association in the Dominican Republic [ADEMI Case]
FY   fiscal year(s)
GBP   Grameen Bank Project; Bangladesh
GDP   gross domestic product
GFFHC   German Freedom from Hunger Campaign; West Germany
HIID   Harvard Institute for International Development
HBS   Harvard Business School
HYV   high-yielding variety
IAC   Integrated Agricultural Cooperative; Philippines
IAF   Inter-American Foundation
IDB   Inter-American Development Bank
IE   International Extension [IIRR Case]
IFAD   International Fund for Agricultural Development
IGP   income-generating project
IIRR   International Institute of Rural Reconstruction
ILO   International Labour Office
INAN   International Apprenticeship Institute; Costa Rica
INFOCOOP   National Institute of Cooperative Promotion; Costa Rica
IO   institutional officer [CARE Case]
IRBE   Indonesian Rattan Basket Exporting Company
ISA   Irrigation Systems Association; Philippines
IT   International Training [IIRR Case]
ITCR   Technology Institute of Costa Rica
LDC   less developed country
MATCH   MATCH International [Tototo Case]
MCC   Mennonite Central Committee [BRAC Case]
MDP   Management Development Program [BRAC Case]
MICROS   Microenterprise program of the Carvajal Foundation in Columbia
MOSTI   [Grameen Bank Case]
MSI   Management Systems International [Senegal Case]
MYP   multi-year plan
NCB   nationalized commercial banks [Grameen Bank Case]
NCCK   National Christian Council of Kenya
NFA   National Food Authority; Philippines
NGO   non-governmental organization
NPC   National Project Committee [Senegal Case]
NTF   New TransCentury Foundation [Senegal Case]

NTK Nabajug Tebagha Khamar; "Three Shares Farm"
       [Grameen Bank Case]
OXFAM Oxford Committee for Famine Relief; United Kingdom
PACT Private Agencies Collaborating Together; United States
PADF Pan American Development Foundation
PBSP Philippine Business for Social Progress
PIE Planning, Implementation, and Evaluation [CARE Case]
PISCES Program for Investment in the Small Capital Enterprise
       Sector
PL United States Public Law
PLANARTE Artisan Development Plan [PRODEME Case]
PLFC Production (later Project) Loan Fund Committee [IIRR Case]
PO program organizer [BRAC Case]
       program officer [CARE Case]
       people's organization(s) [IIRR Case]
POLFC People's Organization Loan Fund Committee; Philippines
PRIDECO see FEDECCREDITO
PRODEME Program for the Development of Micro-Enterprises;
       Dominican Republic
PRRM Philippine Rural Reconstruction Movement
PVC USAID Office of Private Voluntary Cooperation
PVO private voluntary organization
RCTP Rural Credit and Training Program [BRAC Case]
RDP Rural Development Program [BRAC Case]
REACH Rural Enterprise Assistance Center; Philippines
REP Kenyan Rural Enterprise Programme
ROI return on investment
RRF rural reconstruction facilitator(s) [IIRR Case]
SBA Small Business Advisory (Unit) [Senegal Case]
SCAT Strategic, Communications, Administration, Technical
       [CARE Case]
SED small enterprise development
SNP School Nutrition Program [CARE Case]
Solidarios Council of American Development Foundations
       [FUCODES Case]
SSE Small-Scale Entrepreneurs Program [Senegal Case]
TARC Training and Resource Center [BRAC Case]
TFAP Targeted Food Assistance Program [CARE Case]
TOUCH Philippine PVO [CARE Case]
UCIP Urban Community Improvement Program of the NCCK
UNESCO UN Educational, Scientific, and Cultural Organization
UNFPA-PCF UN Fund for Population Activities–Population Center
       Foundation
UNICEF UN Children Fund
UNIDO UN Industrial Development Organization
UNO Uniao Nordestina de Assistencia Pequeñas Organizacoes;
       Northeast Union of Assistance to Small Business; Brazil
USAID U.S. Agency for International Development
VO Village Organization [Senegal Case]
YWCA Young Women's Christian Organization

Bibliography

Adams, Dale W., Alfredo Antonio, and Pablo Romero. 1981. "Group Lending to the Rural Poor in the Dominican Republic: A Stunted Innovation." *Canadian Journal of Agricultural Economics* 29:217–224.

Allal, M., and E. Chuta. 1982. *Cottage Industries and Handicrafts: Some Guidelines for Employment Promotion*. Geneva, Switzerland: International Labour Office.

Alliband, Terry. 1983. *Catalysts of Development: Voluntary Agencies in India*. West Hartford, Conn.: Kumarian Press.

Almazan, Jorge Mario. 1985. "Fundacion Costarricense de Desarrollo (FUCODES): Un Esfuerzo de la Empresa Privada la Comunidad Rural." Evaluation of FUCODES by Solidarios consultant, Santo Domingo, July.

American Council of Voluntary Agencies for Foreign Service (ACVAFS). 1983. *Evaluation Sourcebook for Private and Voluntary Organizations*. Ed. Daniel Santo Pietro. New York: ACVAFS.

Anderson, Dennis. 1982. "Small Industry in Developing Countries: A Discussion of Issues." *World Development* 10(11).

———, and Mark Leiserson. 1980. "Rural Nonfarm Employment in Developing Countries." *Economic Development and Cultural Change*, vol. 28, no. 2, pp. 227–248. Chicago: University of Chicago Press.

Ardener, Shirley. 1964. "The Comparative Study of Rotating Credit Associations." *Journal of the Royal Anthropological Institute of Great Britain and Ireland* 4(2):201–229.

Ashe, Jeffrey. 1978. *Assessing Rural Needs: A Manual for Practitioners*. Cambridge, Mass.: ACCION International/AITEC.

———. 1981. *PISCES Phase One: Assisting the Smallest Scale Economic Activities of the Urban Poor: Summary and Recommendations for Donors and Practitioners*. Cambridge, Mass: ACCION International/AITEC.

———. 1985. *The PISCES II Experience: Local Efforts in Micro-Enterprise Development*. Vol. I. Washington, D.C.: U.S. Agency for International Development.

Badgley, Susanna M. 1978. "Assistance for Artisans in Senegal." Industrial Development and Finance Division, West Africa Projects Department, World Bank. Washington, D.C.: World Bank.

413

Baer, L., et al. 1985. "Le Guide des Source de Financement des Projets Locaux de Developpement au Senegal." Prepared for Africa Consultants. Dakar: ENEA Rural Management Senegal, Center for Applied International Development studies, Texas Tech University.

Bannock, G., R. E. Baxter, and R. Rees. 1978. *The Penguin Dictionary of Economics.* Harmondsworth, U.K.: Penguin.

Barrett, Stanley. 1968. "The Achievement Factor in Igbo Receptivity to Industrialization." *Canadian Review of Sociology and Anthropology* 5(2):68–83.

Belshaw, Cyril. 1965. "The Cultural Milieu of the Entrepreneur." In *Explorations in Enterprise.* Cambridge, Mass.: Harvard University Press.

Benedict, Burton. 1968. "Family Firms and Economic Development." *Southwestern Journal of Anthropology* 24(1):1–19.

———. 1979. "Family Firms and Firm Families: A Comparison of Indian, Chinese, and Creole Firms in Seychelles." In *Entrepreneurs in Cultural Context.* Eds. Greenfield, Strickon, and Aubey. Albuquerque: University of New Mexico Press.

Berry, Sara. 1985. *Fathers Work for Their Sons.* Berkeley: University of California Press.

Bieler, A., et al. 1983. *Travail, Cultures, Religions.* Geneva, Switzerland: Editions Anthropos, International Labour Office (ILO).

Biggs, Tyler. 1986. "On Measuring Relative Efficiency in a Size Distribution of Firms." Employment and Enterprise Policy Analysis Discussion Paper 2. Cambridge, Mass.: Harvard Institute for International Development, Harvard University.

Blayney, Robert, and Maria Otero. 1985. *Small and Micro-Enterprises: Contributions to Development and Future Directions for AID's Support.* Washington, D.C.: U.S. Agency for International Development (USAID).

Bonacich, Edna, and John Modell. 1980. *The Economic Basis of Ethnic Solidarity: Small Business in the Japanese American Community.* Berkeley: University of California Press.

Bonoma, Thomas V. 1981. "Questions and Answers About Case Learning." Boston: Harvard Business School, Class Discussion Note (9–582–059).

Boomgard, James, Stephen Davies, Steve Haggblade, and Donald Mead. 1986. "Subsector Analysis: Its Nature, Conduct and Potential Contribution to Small Enterprise Development." Working Paper no. 26, Department of Agricultural Economics, Michigan State University.

Boserup, Ester. 1970. *Women's Role in Economic Development.* New York: St. Martin's Press.

Bourque, Susan C., and Kay Warren. 1981. *Women of the Andes.* Ann Arbor: University of Michigan Press.

Brown, Jason. 1981a. "Case Studies: India." In *The Pisces Studies: Assisting the Smallest Economic Activities of the Urban Poor,* 337–378. Washington, D.C.: U.S. Agency for International Development.

―――. 1981b. "Case Studies: The Philippines." In *The Pisces Studies: Assisting the Smallest Economic Activities of the Urban Poor*, 253–336. Washington, D.C.: U.S. Agency for International Development.

Bruner, Jerome. 1977. *The Process of Education*. Cambridge, Mass.: Harvard University Press.

Buvinic, Mayra. 1984. "Projects for Women in the Third World: Explaining Their Misbehavior." Washington, D.C.: International Center for Research on Women, WID, U.S. Agency for International Development.

―――, and N. Youssef. 1979. *Women Headed Households: The Ignored Factor in Development*. Washington D.C.: International Center for Research on Women, WID, Bureau for Science and Technology, U.S. Agency for International Development.

Carruthers, Ian, and Robert Chambers. 1981. *Agricultural Administration* (Special Issue on Rapid Rural Appraisal) 8(6). Barking, Essex, U.K.: Applied Science Publishers.

Carvajal, Jaime. 1985. "Fundación Carvajal: A Case of Support for Micro-enterprises in Cali, Colombia." Carvajal Foundation paper presented at Regional Meeting of Donor Agencies on Small Scale Enterprise Development in Latin America, April.

Carvajal Foundation. 1983. "Recuento del Apoyo a la Microempresa en Colombia." Cali.

Cavalcanti, Clóvis. 1981. *A procura de espaço na economia urbana: o setor informal de Fortaleza*. Série População e Emprêgo, vol. 1, 10 (SUDENE); Série Estudos e Pesquisas, vol. 1, 17 (FUNDAJ). Recife, Brasília (Ministério de Trabalho).

Center for Applied International Development Studies (CAIDS). 1985. *Le Guide des Sources de Financement des Projets locaux de Developpement au Senegal*. CAIDS: Texas Tech University and ENEA Rural Management Senegal.

Chambers, Robert. 1981. "Rapid Rural Appraisal: Rationale and Repertoire." *Public Administration and Development* 1(2):95–106.

―――. 1983. *Rural Development: Putting the Last First*. New York: Longman.

Chuta, Enyinna, and Carl Liedholm. 1979. "Rural Non-Farm Employment: A Review of the State of the Art." Rural Development Paper, no. 4. East Lansing: Michigan State University.

Cifuentes Ramirez, Armando. 1973. "Concepto de Centro Parroquial." in *Revista Javeriana*, August 1973:142–145.

Clark, Noreen. 1979/81. *Education for Development and the Rural Woman*. 2 volumes. Boston: World Education, Inc.

―――, Mark Leach, Jeanne McCormack, and Candace Nelson. (n.d.) *The Tototo Home Industries Rural Development Project*. Synergos Institute Case Study. Manuscript.

Cobb, Laurel Knight. 1986. "The Relative Vulnerability of Food Aid Recipients and PVO Staff Distributors of Such Food in Famine Conditions in La Paz, Bolivia, 1982–1984." MPP paper, John F. Kennedy School of Government, Harvard University.

Cohen, Abner. 1969. *Custom and Politics in Urban Africa: A Study of Hausa Migrants in Yoruba Towns*. Berkeley: University of California Press.

————, and Norman Uphoff. 1977. "Rural Development Participation: Concepts and Measures for Project Design Implementation and Evaluation." Rural Development Monograph, no. 2. Ithaca, N.Y.: Center for International Studies, Cornell University.

Collinson, Michael. 1981. "A Low Cost Approach to Understanding Small Farmers." *Agricultural Administration* 8(6):433–450.

Control Data Corporation (CDC). 1986. "ARIES Training Evaluation Report." Prepared for U.S. Agency for International Development. Minneapolis, Minn.: CDC.

————. 1987. "Credit Management Training Needs Analysis." Prepared for U.S. Agency for International Development. Minneapolis, Minn.: CDC.

Corey, E. Raymond. 1976. "The Use of Cases in Management Education." Boston: Harvard Business School, Note (376–240).

Cotter, J. 1986. "Small Scale Enterprise Development: Project Managers Reference Guide." Prepared for USAID/PPC/CDIE.

Crandon, Libett. 1984. *Women, Enterprise and Development*. Boston: The Pathfinder Fund.

Davis, William G. 1986. "Class, Political Constraints, and Entrepreneurial Strategies: Elites and Petty Market Traders in Northern Luzon." In *Entrepreneurship and Social Change*. Eds. Sydney M. Greenfield and Arnold Strickon. Society for Economic Anthropology, Monograph 2. Lanham, Md.: University Press of America.

DeLancey, Mark. 1978. "Savings and Credit Institutions in Rural West Africa." *Rural Africana* (special issue).

Development Alternatives, Inc. (DAI). 1985. *A Case Study Analysis of the Fundación Para la Educación Superior (FES): A Developmental Perspective*. Prepared for U.S. Agency for International Development. Arlington, Va.: DAI.

de Vries, Barnard. 1981. "Public Policy and the Private Sector." *Finance and Development*. September.

DeWilde, John. (n.d.) *Development of African Enterprise*. Washington, D.C: World Bank.

Dulansey, Maryanne, and James Austin. 1985. "Small Scale Enterprise and Women." In *Gender Roles in Development Projects*. Eds. K. Overholt et al. West Hartford, Conn.: Kumarian Press.

Escobar, Weimar, and Jairo Cordoba. 1986. "Las Microempresas y la Generacion de Empleo." Masters thesis, University of the Cauca Valley, Cali, Colombia.

Esman, Paul, and Norman Uphoff. 1984. *Local Organizations: Intermediaries in Rural Development*. Ithaca, N.Y.: Cornell University Press.

Farbman, Michael, ed. 1981. *The Pisces Studies: Assisting the Smallest Economic Activities of the Urban Poor*. Washington, D.C.: U.S. Agency for International Development.

Finney, Ben R. 1971. "Would-be Entrepreneurs?" *New Guinea Research Bulletin*, no. 41. Canberra: Australian National University.

———. 1973. *Big-Men and Business: Entrepreneurship and Economic Growth in the New Guinea Highlands*. Honolulu: University Press of Hawaii.

Firth, Raymond, and Brian Yamey. 1964. *Capital, Savings and Credit in Peasant Societies*. London: George Allen and Unwin.

Fraser, Peter, and William Tucker. 1981. "Case Studies: Latin America." In *The Pisces Studies: Assisting the Smallest Economic Activities of the Urban Poor*. Washington, D.C.: U.S. Agency for International Development.

FUCODES (Fundación Costarricense de Desarrollo). Annual Report: 1983, 1984, and 1985.

———. (n.d.). "Modalidades y Requisitos de Financiamiento para la Pequeña Industria." San Jose, Costa Rica. Pamphlet.

———. 1979. "Programa de Promoción Humana y Credito para Grupos de Pescadores en Costa Rica." San Jose, Costa Rica.

———. 1983. "Metodología para Incorporar Grupos como Sujetos de Credito de FUCODES." San Jose, Costa Rica. March.

———. 1984. "Reglamento de Credito para el Programa de Credito." San Jose, Costa Rica.

———. 1986. "Programa de Desarrollo y Financiamiento de la Micro-empresa." San Jose, Costa Rica. March.

Geertz, Clifford. 1962. "The Rotating Credit Association: A 'Middle Rung' in Development." *Economic Development and Cultural Change*, vol. 1, no. 3. Chicago: University of Chicago Press.

———. 1963. *Peddlers and Princes*. Chicago: University of Chicago Press.

Geiger, T., and W. Armstrong. 1964. *The Development of Private African Entrepreneurship*. Washington D.C.: National Planning Association.

Goldmark, Susan, and Jay Rosengard. 1983. *Credit to Indonesian Entrepreneurs: An Assessment of the Badan Kredit Kecamatan Program*. Washington, D.C.: Development Alternatives, Inc.

Gordon, David L. 1978. "Employment and Development of Small Enterprises." Sector Policy Paper. Washington D.C.: World Bank.

Gorman, Robert F., ed. 1984 *Private Voluntary Organizations as Agents of Development*. Boulder, Colo.: Westview Press.

Gragg, Charles I. 1940. "Because Wisdom Can't Be Told." Reprinted from *Harvard Alumni Bulletin*, October 19, 1940. Boston: Harvard Business School (451–005).

Greaney, Francis P. 1986. "Identifying Incentives for Linkages Between: The Informal Sector in Latin America and the Formal Sector in the U.S. and Latin America." Policy Analysis Exercise (PAE), John F. Kennedy School of Government, Harvard University.

Grindle, Merilee S. 1986. Trip report to Cali and Bogota, Colombia and San Jose, Costa Rica for ARIES project. Typescript.

Gross, Stephen. 1985. "Models for Microbusiness Support in Latin America." ACCION International/AITEC paper presented at Regional Meeting of Donor Agencies on Small Scale Enterprise Development in Latin America, April.

Gupta, Shri Ranjit. 1977. "Rural Development: Problems and a Framework for Joint Action by Voluntary Agencies and Business Houses." In *Rural Development: Role of Voluntary Agencies and Business Houses.* Bombay: Indian Merchants' Chamber Economic Research and Training Foundation.

Hagen, Everett. 1962. *On the Theory of Social Change.* Homewood, Ill.: Dorsey Press.

——. 1966. "How Economic Growth Begins: A Theory of Social Change." In *Political Development and Social Change.* Eds. Jason L. Finkle and R. W. Gable, 73–83. New York: John Wiley & Sons.

——. 1980. *The Economics of Development.* Homewood, Ill.: Richard D. Irwin.

Haggblade, Steven. 1978. "Africanization from Below: The Evolution of Cameroonian Savings Societies into Western-Style Banks." *Rural Africana* (new series) 2.

——, Jacques Defay, and Bob Pitman. 1979. "Small Manufacturing and Repair Enterprises in Haiti: Survey Results." Working Paper no. 4, Michigan State University Development Series. East Lansing: Department of Agricultural Economics, Michigan State University.

——, Carl Liedholm, and Donald Mead. 1986. "The Effect of Policy and Policy Reforms on Non-Agricultural Enterprises and Employment in Developing Countries: A Review of Past Experiences." EEPA Discussion Paper no. 1. Cambridge, Mass.: Harvard Institute for International Development.

Harley, Richard. 1983. "Special Report: The Entrepreneurial Poor." Ford Foundation Letter (June): 2–3.

Harper, Malcolm. 1972. "Selection and Training for Entrepreneurship." In *Motivating Economic Achievement.* Eds. David McClelland and David Winter. New York: Free Press.

——. 1984. *Small Business in the Third World: Guidelines for Practical Assistance.* New York: John Wiley & Sons.

——, and Tan Thiam Soon. 1979. *Small Enterprise in Developing Countries: Case Studies and Conclusions.* London: Intermediate Technology Publications.

Hart, Gillian. 1972. "Some Socio-Economic Aspects of African Entrepreneurship." Occasional Paper no. 16. Grahamstown, South Africa: Institute of Social and Economic Research, Rhodes University.

Hart, Keith. 1973. "Informal Income Opportunities and Urban Employment in Ghana." *The Journal of Modern African Studies* 11(1):61–89.

Hennrich, Heidi. 1987. "Evaluation Manuals and Methods: A Guide to Guides." ARIES Working Paper no. 2, Harvard Institute for International Development (HIID). Cambridge, Mass.: HIID.

Hildebrand, Peter E. 1981. "Combining Disciplines in Rapid Appraisal: the Sondea Approach." *Agricultural Administration* 8(6):423–432.

Honadle, George, and John Hannah. 1981. "Management Performance for Rural Development: Packaged Training or Capacity Building," Washington, D.C.: Development Alternatives, Inc.

Hoselitz, Bert F. 1966. "Economic Growth and Development: Non-Economic Factors in Economic Development." In *Political Development and Social Change.* Eds. Jason L. Finkle and R.W. Gable, 183–192. New York: John Wiley & Sons.

Houghton, Mary. 1985. "The Social Impact of a Micro-Enterprise Project on the Individual and the Community." In *Proceedings of a Conference Microenterprise Development in the Third World,* April 22–24, Geneva Park, Ontario, Canada.

Hunt, Robert. 1983. "The Enterpreneurship Training Program of the Lesotho Opportunities Industrialization Center: An Evaluation of Its Impact." Washington, D.C.: Office of Private and Voluntary Cooperation, Bureau of Food for Peace and Voluntary Assistance, U.S. Agency for International Development.

———. 1984. "Voluntary Agencies and the Promotion of Enterprise." In *Private Voluntary Agents as Agents of Development.* Ed. Robert F. Gorman. Boulder, Colo.: Westview Press.

INCAE (Instituto Centroamericano de Administracion de Empresas). 1985. "Perfiles de Instituciones Privadas de Apoyo a la Micro y Pequeña Empresa en Centroamerica, Colombia, Ecuador, Panama y Republica Dominicana." November:179–200.

Indian Merchants' Chamber. 1977. *Rural Development: Role of Voluntary Agencies and Business Houses.* Bombay: Economic Research and Training Foundation.

Institute of Development Studies (IDS). 1981. "Rapid Rural Appraisal: Social Structure and Rural Economy." *IDS Bulletin* 12(4).

Inter-American Development Bank. 1984. "Ex-Post Evaluation of Two Micro-enterprise Projects." Small Projects Program, Colombia. July.

———. 1985. "Small Projects Financing Program: Support of Micro-enterprise in Colombia." Paper presented at Regional Meeting of Donor Agencies on Small Scale Enterprise Development in Latin America, April.

International Center for Research on Women (ICRW). 1980. *The Productivity of Women in Developing Countries: Measurement Issues and Recommendations.* Washington D.C.: Office of Women and Development, U.S Agency for International Development.

International Fund for Agricultural Development (IFAD). 1984. "A Bank for the Landless: The Grameen Bank." In *A Fund for the Rural Poor*, 39–40. Rome: IFAD.

International Labour Office (ILO). 1984. *Group Based Savings and Credit for the Rural Poor.* Geneva, Switzerland: ILO.

James, Estelle. 1982. "The Nonprofit Sector in International Perspective: The Case of Sri Lanka." *Journal of Comparative Economics,* pp. 99–129.

Johnston, Bruce F., and William C. Clark. 1982. *Redesigning Rural Development: A Strategic Perspective.* Baltimore and London: Johns Hopkins University Press.

Kane, Kevin, and Martin Walsh. (n.d.). *Business Training for Women's Groups: A Kenyan Study*. Prepared for PACT. Manuscript.

Kilby, Peter. 1965. *African Enterprise: Nigerian Bread Industry*. Palo Alto: Stanford University Press.

———, and David D'Zmura. 1971. *Entrepreneurship and Economic Development*. New York: Free Press.

———. 1983. "Searching for Benefits." Special study no. 28 (PN-AAL-056) U.S. Agency for International Development (USAID). Washington, D.C.: USAID.

Korten, David. 1980. "Community Organization and Rural Development: A Learning Process Approach." *Public Administration Review* 40(5):480–511.

Kozlowski, Anthony J. 1983. "International Non-Governmental Organizations as Operating Developing Agencies." In *The Role of Non-Governmental Organizations in Development Co-operation*, 12–15. Paris: OECD Development Centre.

Kramer, Ralph M. 1982. *Voluntary Agencies in the Welfare State*. Berkeley: University of California Press.

Kubr, Milan. 1983. *Successes and Failures in Meeting the Management Challenge: Strategies and Their Implementation*. Washington, D.C.: World Bank.

Lassen, Cheryl. 1980. *Reaching the Assetless Poor: Projects and Strategies for Their Self-Reliant Development*. Ithaca, N.Y.: Cornell University Rural Development Committee.

Lele, Uma. 1981. "Cooperatives and the Poor: A Comparative Perspective." *World Development* 9:55–72.

Leonard, David, and D. R. Marshall, eds. 1982. *Institutions of Rural Development for the Poor: Decentralization and Organizational Linkages*. Berkeley: Institute of International Studies, University of California.

LeVine, Robert. 1966. *Dreams and Deeds: Achievement Motivation in Nigeria*. Chicago: University of Chicago Press.

Levy, Marion Fennelly. 1988. *Each in Her Own Way: Five Women Leaders of the Developing World*. Boulder and London: Lynne Rienner Publishers.

Liedholm, Carl. 1985. "Small Scale Enterprise Credit Schemes: Administrative Costs and the Role of Inventory Norms." Working Paper no. 25, Department of Agricultural Economics, Michigan State University.

———, and Enyinna Chuta. 1976. "The Economics of Rural and Urban Small-Scale Industries in Sierra Leone." African Rural Economy Paper no. 14, Department of Agricultural Economics, Michigan State University.

———, and Donald Mead. 1985. *Small Scale Enterprises in Developing Countries: A Review of the State of the Art* (forthcoming).

Lintz, Randolph. 1981. "Third Year Evaluation of Project no. 633–0212, Partnership for Productivity: Rural Enterprise Extension Service," USAID/Botswana.

Little, I.M.D. 1987. "Small Manufacturing Enterprises in Developing Countries." *The World Bank Economic Review*, vol. 1, no. 2. Washington, D.C.: World Bank.

Long, Norman. 1979. "Multiple Enterprise in the Central Highlands of Peru." In *Entrepreneurs in Cultural Context.* Eds. Greenfield, Strickon, and Aubey. Albuquerque: University of New Mexico Press.

Longhurst, Richard. 1981. "Rapid Rural Appraisal: Social Structure and Rural Economy." *IDS Bulletin* 12(4).

Mabawonku, Adewale F. 1979. "An Economic Evaluation of Apprenticeship Training in Western Nigerian Small-Scale Industries." *African Rural Economy Paper*, no. 17, Dept. of Agricultural Economics, Michigan State University, East Lansing, Michigan.

Maldonado, Carlos. 1985. Programme d'appui au secteur non-structure urbain d'Afrique francophone: Premier Rapport d'Avancement des Activites du Programme, Fevrier 1982–Janvier 1983, Organisation Internationale du Travail.

March, Kathryn S., and Rachelle Taqqu. 1986. *Women's Informal Associations and the Organizational Capacity for Development.*. Boulder, Colo.: Westview Press.

Markey-McCabe, Linda. 1986. *The Sourcebook for Income-Generating Projects.* Washington D.C.: Robert R. Nathan Associates.

Marris, Peter, and Anthony Somerset. 1971. *African Businessmen.* London: Routledge and Kegan Paul.

Marsden, Keith. 1981. "Creating the Right Environment For Small Firms." *Finance and Development*, September.

Mazingira Institute. 1985. *A Guide to Women's Organizations and Agencies Serving Women in Kenya.* Nairobi: Mazingira Institute.

Mazumdar, Dipak. 1984. "The Issue of Small versus Large in the Indian Textile Industry: An Analytical Historical Survey." *World Bank Staff Working Paper* no. 645. Washington, D.C.: World Bank.

Mbajah, E. 1984. "Evaluation of the Partnership for Productivity Women in Development Project, Kenya." Washington, D.C.: U.S. Agency for International Development.

McClelland, David. 1961. *The Achieving Society.* Princeton, NJ: Van Nostrand.

———. 1966. "The Achievement Motive in Economic Growth." *Political Development and Social Change.* Eds. Jason L.Finkle and Richard W. Gable, 83–110. New York: John Wiley & Sons.

McCormack, Jeanne, and Candace Nelson. 1985. "Deciding for Themselves: Establishing Patterns of Leadership and Responsibility for Rural Women in Kenya" in *Reports* (World Education, Inc.), no. 24:4–6.

McCormack, Jeanne, Martin Walsh, and Candace Nelson. 1986. *Women's Group Enterprises: A Study of the Structure of Opportunity on the Kenya Coast.* Boston: World Education, Inc.

McKean, Cressida. 1982. "Helping Worker-Managed Enterprises Work." *Grassroots Development* 6(1):27–31.

McNair, Malcolm P. 1954. "Tough-mindedness and the Case Method." In *The Case Method at the Harvard Business School.* Eds. Malcolm P. McNair and Anita C. Hersum. New York: McGraw-Hill Book Co. Reprinted as (9–379–090), Boston: Harvard Business School.

Meyer, Richard. 1985. "Rural Deposit Mobilization: An Alternative Approach for Developing Rural Financial Markets." Paper prepared for AID/IFAD experts meeting on small farmer credit, Rome, Italy.

Miller, Leonard F. 1977. *Agricultural Credit and Finance in Africa.* New York: Rockefeller Foundation.

Montgomery, John D. (n.d.) Bureaucrats, Participation and Projects (forthcoming).

———. 1986. "Workshop on Intermediary Support Organizations Serving Grass-roots Institutions: Summary Report." Conference held at the Lincoln Institute of Land Policy, May 1–2, 1986, jointly sponsored with the John F. Kennedy School of Government, Harvard University.

Moock, Joyce L. 1976. "The Migration Process and Differential Economic Behavior in South Maragli, Western Kenya." Ph.D. dissertation, Columbia University.

Moore, Mike. 1981. "Beyond the Tarmac Road: A Guide for Rural Poverty Watchers." *IDS Bulletin* 12(4):47–49.

Morris, Michael. 1985. "The BAME Fleuve Cereals Marketing Study: Conclusions and Implications." Paper BAME 85–14. Dakar: Institut Senegalais de Recherches Agricoles, Bureau d'Analyses Macro-Economique.

Nafziger, Wayne. 1977. *African Capitalism: A Case Study in Nigerian Entrepreneurship.* Stanford, CA: Hoover Institution Press.

Obbo, Christine. 1980. *African Women: Their Struggle for Economic Independence.* London: Zed Press.

O'Regan, Fred, and Douglas Hellinger. 1981. "Case Studies in Africa." In *The PISCES Studies: Assisting the Smallest Economic Activities of the Urban Poor.* Washington, D.C.: U.S. Agency for International Development .

Organisation for Economic Co-operation and Development (OECD). 1981. *Directory of Non-Governmental Organizations in OECD Member Countries Active in Development Co-operation.* Paris: OECD Development Centre.

———. 1983. *The Role of Non-Governmental Organizations in Development Co-operation.* Paris: OECD Development Centre.

Page, John. 1979. "Small Enterprises in African Development: A Survey." World Bank Staff Working Paper 363. Washington, D.C.: World Bank.

———, and William Steel. 1984. "Small Enterprise Development: Economic Issues from African Experience." World Bank Technical Paper no. 26. Washington, D.C.: World Bank.

Paterson, Douglas B. 1980a. "Coping with Land Scarcity," Working Paper no. 360. Nairobi: University of Nairobi, Institute of Development Studies.

———. 1980b. "Education, Employment and Income," Working Paper no. 371. Nairobi: University of Nairobi, Institute of Development Studies.

————. 1984. *Kinship, Land, and Community: The Moral Foundations of the Abaluhya of East Bunyore (Kenya)*. Ph.D. dissertation, University of Washington. Ann Arbor: University Microfilms.

Paul, Samuel. 1982. *Managing Development Programs: The Lessons of Success*. Boulder, Colo.: Westview Press.

Pearce, David W. 1981. *The Dictionary of Modern Economics*. London: Macmillan.

Peattie, Lisa. 1982. "There's no business like shoe business. What is to be done with the informal sector: Case of the shoe business in Bogota," in *Towards a Political Economy of Urbanization*. Ed. Helen Safa. New Delhi: Oxford University Press.

Peterson, Stephen B. 1982. "Government, Cooperatives, and the Private Sector in Peasant Agriculture." In *Institutions of Rural Development for the Poor: Decentralization and Oganizational Linkages*. Eds. David K. Leonard and Dale Rogers Marshall, 73–124. Berkeley: Institute of International Studies, University of California.

Plan Nacional de Desarrollo 1982–1986. 1983. "Volvamos a la Tierra." San Jose, Costa Rica: Ministry of National Planning and Political Economy.

Popkin, Samuel L. 1979. *The Rational Peasant*. Berkeley: University of California Press.

Portes, Alejandro, and Lauren Benton. 1984. "Industrial Development and Labor Absorption: A Reinterpretation." *Population and Development*, vol. 10, no. 4, pp. 589–611.

Pratt, Brian, and Jo Boyden, eds. 1985. *The Field Directors' Handbook: An Oxfam Manual for Development Workers*. Oxford: Oxford University Press.

Quick, Stephen. 1980. "The Paradox of Popularity: Ideological Implementation in Zambia." In *Politics and Policy Implementation in the Third World*. Ed. Merilee S. Grindle, 40–63. Princeton, NJ: Princeton University Press.

Realpe Mena, Gilberto. (n.d.). "Programs MICROS-Cali: 10 Anos al Servicio del Sector Micro Empresarial." In *Impulsamos Microempresarios*. 7:12–15. Cali, Colombia.

Reichman, Rebecca L. 1984. *Women's Participation in ADEMI: The Association for the Development of Micro-Enterprises*. Cambridge, Mass.: ACCION International.

————. 1985. *Conciencia and Development: The Association of Tricicleros San Jose Obrero, a Grassroots Labor Organization in the Dominican Republic*. Cambridge, Mass.: ACCION International.

Rhoades, Robert E. 1982. "The Art of the Informal Agricultural Survey," Social Science Department Training Document. Lima, Peru: International Potato Center.

Rielly, Catherine. 1985. "Synthesis of Literature Scan on Informal, Indigenous Credit and Saving in Rural Africa." Harvard Institute for International Development (HIID). Typescript.

————. 1986. "Improving Rural Financial Markets: Appropriate Design of Savings Projects." ARIES Working Paper no. 1, Harvard Institute for International Development (HIID). Cambridge, Mass.: HIID

Sanders, Thomas G. 1983a. "Promoting Social Development: Private Sector Initiatives in Cali, Colombia." UFSI Reports (Universities Field Staff International Inc.), no. 21.

————. 1983b. "Microbusiness: Innovative Private Sector Development in Colombia," UFSI Reports (Universities Field Staff International Inc.), no. 22.

Sanyal, Bishwapriya. 1986. "Urban Informal Sector Revisited: Some Notes on the Relevance of the Concept in the 1980s." Massachusetts Institute of Technology, draft manuscript. Also printed as Inter-American Foundation Working Paper No. 1. Washington D.C.

————. 1987. "Does Development Trickle Up?" A Report to the Ford Foundation's Dhaka Office on Livelihood, Employment and Income Generation (LEIG) Program. Massachusetts Institute of Technology, draft manuscript.

Sawyer, Susan M., and Catherine Overholt. 1985. "Dominican Republic: Program for Development of Micro-Enterprises." In *Gender Roles in Development Projects*. Eds. Catherine Overholt et al., 215–243. West Hartford, Conn.: Kumarian Press.

Schumpeter, Joseph A. 1949. *The Theory of Economic Development*. Cambridge, Mass.: Harvard University Press.

Scott, James C. 1976. *The Moral Economy of the Peasant*. New Haven, Conn.: Yale University Press.

Scurrah, Martin, and Bruno Podesta. 1984. "The Experience of Worker Self-Management in Peru and Chile." *Grassroots Development* 8(1): 12–23.

Shapero, Albert, and Lisa Sokol. 1982. "The Social Dimensions of Entrepreneurship." *Encyclopedia of Entrepreneurship*. Eds. Calvin A.Kent, Donald L. Sexton, and Karl H. Vesper, 72–90. Englewood Cliffs, N.J.: Prentice Hall.

Shapiro, Benson P. 1984. "Hints for Case Teaching." Boston: Harvard Business School, Note (585–012).

Shipton, Parker M. 1989. *Bitter Money: Cultural Economy and Some African Meanings of Forbidden Commodities*. In press as Vol. 1, New Monograph Series, American Ethnological Society. Washington, D.C.

————. 1985. "Land, Credit, and Crop Transitions in Kenya." Ph.D. dissertation. Cambridge University.

Siebel, Hans Dieter. 1984. *Ansatzmöglichkeiten für die Mobilisierung von Sparkapital zur Entwicklungsfinanzierung. Genossenschaften und autochthone Spar- und Kreditvereine in Nigeria*, vol. 63. Munich, Cologne, London: Weltforum Verlag.

Siyagh, Yusuf A. 1952. *Entrepreneurs of Lebanon*. Cambridge, Mass.: Harvard University Press.

Smith, Cameron, and Bruce Tippett. 1982. *Study of Problems Related to Scaling Up Micro-Enterprise Assistance Programs, Phase I*. Needham, Mass.: Trade and Development International Corp.

Smith, David H., and F. Elkin, eds. 1981. *Volunteers, Voluntary Associations and Development*. Leiden, Netherlands: E.J. Brill.

Smith, David H., Burt R. Baldwin, and William Chittick. 1981. "U.S. National Voluntary Organizations, Transnational Orientations, and Development." In *Volunteers, Voluntary Associations and Development*. Eds. David H. Smith and Frederick Elkin. Leiden, Netherlands: E.J. Brill.

Snodgrass, Donald. 1979. "Small-Scale Manufacturing Industries: Patterns, Trends and Possible Policies." Harvard Institute for International Development (HIID) Development Discussion Paper no. 54. Cambridge, Mass.: HIID.

Sommer, John G. 1977. *Beyond Charity: U.S. Voluntary Aid for a Changing Third World*. Washington, D.C.: Overseas Development Council.

Squire, Lyn. 1981. *Employment Policy in Developing Countries: A Survey of Issues and Evidence*. New York: Oxford University Press.

Staley, Eugene, and Richard Morse. 1965. *Modern Small Scale Industry for Developing Countries*. New York: McGraw-Hill.

Steel, William F., and Yasuoki Takagi. 1983. "Small Enterprise Development and the Employment-Output Trade-Off." Oxford Economic Papers 35(3) and World Bank Reprint Series no. 305:423–446.

Strickon, Arnold. 1979. "Ethnicity and Entrepreneurship in Rural Wisconsin." In *Entrepreneurs in Cultural Context*. Eds. Greenfield, Strickon, and Aubey. Albuquerque: University of New Mexico Press.

Swift, Jeremy. 1981. "Rapid Appraisal and Cost-Effective Participatory Research in Dry Pastoral Areas of West Africa." *Agricultural Administration* 8(6):485–92.

Technical Assistance Information Clearing House (TAICH). 1983. "U.S. Non-Profit Organizations in Development Assistance Abroad." New York: TAICH.

Tendler, Judith. 1981. "Fitting the Foundation Style: The Case of Rural Credit." Written for the Inter-American Foundation (IAF).

———. 1982a. "Turning Private Voluntary Organizations Into Development Agencies: Questions for Evaluation." AID Program Evaluation Discussion Paper no. 12. Washington, D.C.: U.S. Agency for International Development (USAID).

———. 1982b. "Rural Projects Through Urban Eyes: An Interpretation of the World Bank's New-Style Rural Development Projects." World Bank Staff Working Paper no. 532. Washington, D.C.: World Bank.

———. 1983a. "Ventures in the Informal Sector and How They Worked Out in Brazil." AID Evaluation Special Study No. 12. Washington, D.C.: U.S. Agency for International Development (USAID).

——— (in collaboration with Kevin Healy and Carol O'Laughlin). 1983b. "What to Think about Cooperatives: A Guide from Bolivia." Rosslyn, Va.: The Inter-American Foundation (IAF).

———. 1984. "Captive Donors and Captivating Clients: A Nicaraguan Saga." Washington, D.C.: Inter-American Foundation (IAF).

Thomas, Barbara P. 1977. "The Role of Rural Organizations in Involving the Poor in Kenya's Development." Report prepared for the Human Resources, Institutions and Agrarian Reform Division of the Food and Agriculture Organization of the United Nations, December 1977, Nairobi, Kenya.

Timberg, Thomas. 1988. *Comparative Experiences with Micro-enterprise Projects.* Washington, D.C.: Robert R. Nathan Associates.

———, and C. V. Aiyar. 1984. *Informal Credit Markets in India.* Chicago, IL.: University of Chicago Press.

Tokman, Victor E. 1985. "The Process of Accumulation and the Weakness of the Protagonists." *CEPAL Review* 26:15–126.

Tuebner, Paul, et al. 1984. Evaluation of Project no. 633–0228, Small Enterprise Development, USAID/Botswana.

Vogel, Robert. 1982. "Savings Mobilization: The Forgotten Half of Rural Finance." Revised version of paper prepared for a colloquium on rural finance sponsored by the Economic Development Institute of the World Bank, AID, and the Ohio State University, Washington, D.C.

Von Pischke, J.D., Dale Adams, and Gordon Donald, eds. 1983. *Rural Financial Markets in Developing Countries.* Baltimore, Md.: Johns Hopkins University Press.

Wasserstrom, Robert. 1985a. *Oral Histories of Social Change.* New York: Praeger Publishers.

———. 1985b. *Grassroots Development in Latin America and the Caribbean.* New York: Praeger Publishers.

Weber, Max. 1930 [1904]. *The Protestant Ethic and the Spirit of Capitalism.* Trans. Talcott Parsons. London: George Allen and Unwin.

Weisbrod, Burton A. 1977. *The Voluntary Non-Profit Sector: An Economic Analysis.* Lexington, Mass.: D.C. Heath.

Widstrand, Carl Gosta, ed. 1970. *Cooperatives and Rural Development in East Africa.* Uppsala: The Scandinavian Institute of African Studies.

Wilson, Sir Geoffrey. 1983. "The Role of Non-Governmental Organizations in Aid to the Least-Developed Countries." In *The Role of Non-Governmental Organizations in Development Co-operation,* 16–21. Paris: OECD Development Centre.

Wines, Sarah. 1986. "Stages of Micro-Enterprise Growth in the Dominican Informal Sector." *Grassroots Development* 9(2):33–41.

World Bank. 1978. *Rural Enterprise and Nonfarm Employment.* Washington, D.C.: World Bank.

Young, Frank W., and John R. Nellis. 1985. "A Survey of Management Information Systems for Regional and Rural Development Programs," *Agricultural Administration* 19:81–99.

About the Contributors

Charles K. Mann, Harvard Institute for International Development ARIES Project Leader, is Research Associate at the Harvard Institute for International Development. Prior to joining HIID in 1985, he was Associate Director for Social and Agricultural Sciences at The Rockefeller Foundation. He is the author of numerous works relating to technology transfer and to the use of computers in developing countries. He has a special interest in case method teaching and is a graduate of the Advanced Management Program at the Harvard Business School. He holds a Ph.D. in Economics from Harvard University and a B.A. from Williams College. His recent works include *Food Policy: Frameworks for Analysis and Action* (contributor and co-editor with Barbara Huddleston) and *Microcomputers in Public Policy: Applications for Developing Countries* (contributor and co-editor with Stephen Ruth). In addition to overall design and management of the project which generated this book and the *AskARIES Knowledgebase*, he played a major role in the development of Part II and Part III.

Merilee S. Grindle is Research Associate at the Harvard Institute for International Development. A specialist in the politics of policy formulation and implementation in developing countries, she also has focused on program and project management, particularly in the field of rural development. In recent years she has been concerned with issues of employment in rural areas. She received her Ph.D. in political science from MIT and has taught at Wellesley College, Brown University, and Harvard University. She is the author of: *Bureaucrats, Politicians, and Peasants in Mexico; State and Countryside;* and *Searching for Rural Development: Labor Migration and Employment in Mexico.* She is the editor of and a contributor to *Politics and Policy Implementation in the Third World.* A forthcoming co-authored book addresses issues of policy reform in developing countries. In the ARIES project, she has contributed to developing the framework for analysis, has overseen the writing of cases and teaching notes and has played a major role in developing the *AskARIES Knowledgebase*.

Parker Shipton is Institute Associate of the Harvard Institute for International Development, and Assistant Professor of Anthropology, Harvard University. Educated at Cornell University (A.B.), Oxford University (M.Litt.), and Cambridge University (Ph.D.), he has conducted intensive field research in Kenya, The Gambia, and Colombia, and consulted for several international development agencies and African governments. His publications include various

427

articles on African social, political, and economic organization, property systems, and rural development. He is the author of two forthcoming books on rural Africa: *Bitter Money: Cultural Economy and Some African Meanings of Forbidden Commodities* and *Credit, Debt, and Culture*. Among his contributions to the ARIES project were research on small entrepreneurs and the organization of the case research on Africa.

Jeffrey Ashe was from 1978–84 Senior Associate Director of ACCION International, the Director of the PISCES Project, and the principal author of the various PISCES publications. At ACCION he introduced the PISCES group credit methodology through which the organization now reaches some 20,000 small businesses per year. Mr. Ashe has his own consulting firm and has developed and evaluated projects in Sierra Leone, Ghana, Kenya, Thailand, Bangladesh, and Costa Rica. In Boston, Arkansas, and Canada, he also assisted in adapting methodologies developed abroad to U.S. and Canadian conditions. He received his M.A. in Sociology from Boston University and his B.A. in Political Science from the University of California, Berkeley.

Ross Edgar Bigelow is an Enterprise Development Specialist in USAID's Bureau for Science and Technology. Trained as a social scientist, he received his Ph.D. in Geography at Michigan State University. Dr. Bigelow has extensive experience working in grassroots development in Africa: he is a former Peace Corps Volunteer, Ford Foundation Program Officer, Peace Corps staff member. He has taught at the college and high school levels. He has also served in AID for ten years, managing grants to private and voluntary organizations, and evaluating projects and the institution building process. In his current position, he has designed and evaluated small enterprise projects in Asia and Africa.

Margaret E. Bowman is Research Associate in the Replication and Policy Analysis Department at Technoserve, Inc. Prior to joining Technoserve, she worked as a Research Analyst with the ARIES project and Project Analyst for the Dominican Republic Association for the Development of Microenterprise (ADEMI) at ACCION International. She holds an M.P.P. from the Kennedy School of Government at Harvard University and a B.S. in Energy Policy and International Development from Stanford University.

S. Lael Brainard is completing research for her doctoral dissertation in economics at Harvard University. Prior to her research for the ARIES Senegal cases she served as a summer intern with the Ford Foundation's West Africa Office. Before attending Harvard, she was an analyst with the management consulting firm of McKinsey & Co. She received her B.A. from Wesleyan University in 1983.

Kay Calavan works with USAID/Nepal and previously worked with USAID/Bangladesh where she developed a major report on management training capacity in the country. She earned her Ph.D. in Anthropology from the University of Illinois, Urbana, an M.A. in Agronomy from the University of Maryland, and a B.A. in English/Anthropology from the University of Illinois, Urbana.

Elizabeth Campbell is the Manger of the Small Scale Enterprise and Credit Unit at Save the Children. Previously, she served as a summer intern for OEF International and served as Program Assistant with the U.S. Trade and Development Program, planning and monitoring a broad range of development projects. She received her master's degree in Social Change and Development and International Economics from Johns Hopkins University in 1986, and a B.S.F.S. from Georgetown University.

Rebecca F. Catalla is a staff member of the Research Division of the International Institute of Rural Reconstruction (IIRR) in Silang, Cavite, Philippines.

Marissa B. Espineli is a staff member of the Training Division of the International Institute of Rural Reconstruction (IIRR) in Silang, Cavite, Philippines.

H. I. Latifee is Associate Professor of Economics at the University of Chittagong, Bangladesh. He has been closely associated with the Grameen Bank since its inception as an organizer, researcher, trainer and board member. Prof. Latifee received an M.A. in Development Economics from Boston University, attended the Economics Institute at the University of Colorado, and earned his M.A. and B.A. in Economics at the University of Dhaka, Bangladesh.

Marjorie Lilly is a graduate of Skidmore College with a B.A. in Linguistics. She has written articles for the Central American Reporter, Cultural Survival Quarterly, and The Christian Science Monitor, and has reported from Guatemala. She has worked at ACCION International and collaborates in some projects with Jeffrey Ashe's micro-enterprise consultancy.

Catherine Lovell is Professor Emeritus, University of California, Riverside, Graduate School of Management. She has been a consultant to many bi-lateral and international development aid organizations as well as to NGOs in Bangladesh and Indonesia. She served as a consultant on management development to the Bangladesh Rural Advancement Committee (BRAC) from April 1985 to September 1986. She earned her Ph.D. and M.P.A. from the University of Southern California and a B.A. in Economics from the University of California, Berkeley.

Francisco Roman is completing his D.B.A at the Harvard Business School. He is on leave from the faculty of the Asian Institute of Management, where he served most recently as Program Director of the Enterprise Management Research Development Program. He is the author of over sixty management teaching cases and notes. Mr. Roman received an M.A. in Economic Development from the University of Hawaii, an M.B.A. and B.A. in Economics from Ateneo de Manila University.

Martin Walsh is a social anthropologist who has conducted extensive field research in rural areas of Kenya and Tanzania. He has published articles on political and economic systems, among other topics. He has worked with World Education, Inc. and Tototo Home Industries, investigating Women's group enterprises, and has consulted for international aid agencies and written training materials for NGOs. He holds a Ph.D., M.A. and B.A. in Social Anthropology from the University of Cambridge.

Index

Part I

430

Part II

Micro-enterprise Program Elements

Policy Themes

Recurrent Problems Categories